T0330257

WOMEN IN THE FACTORY, 1880–1930

WOMEN IN THE FACTORY, 1880–1930

CLASS AND GENDER

Beatrice Moring

THE BOYDELL PRESS

© Beatrice Moring 2024

All Rights Reserved. Except as permitted under current legislation
no part of this work may be photocopied, stored in a retrieval system,
published, performed in public, adapted, broadcast,
transmitted, recorded or reproduced in any form or by any means,
without the prior permission of the copyright owner

The right of Beatrice Moring to be identified as
the author of this work has been asserted in accordance with
sections 77 and 78 of the Copyright, Designs and Patents Act 1988

First published 2024
The Boydell Press, Woodbridge

ISBN 978 1 83765 026 2

The Boydell Press is an imprint of Boydell & Brewer Ltd
PO Box 9, Woodbridge, Suffolk IP12 3DF, UK
and of Boydell & Brewer Inc.
668 Mt Hope Avenue, Rochester, NY 14620–2731, USA
website: www.boydellandbrewer.com

A CIP catalogue record for this book is available
from the British Library

The publisher has no responsibility for the continued existence or accuracy
of URLs for external or third-party internet websites referred to in this book,
and does not guarantee that any content on such websites is, or will remain,
accurate or appropriate

CONTENTS

ILLUSTRATIONS

Figures

Tables

Appendix Tables

The author and publisher are grateful to all the institutions and individuals listed for permission to reproduce the materials in which they hold copyright. Every effort has been made to trace the copyright holders; apologies are offered for any omission, and the publisher will be pleased to add any necessary acknowledgement in subsequent editions.

Introduction
Why Women in the Factory?

What women wanted

During the first week of July, 1900, the First General Meeting of the Unions of Working Women was held in Helsinki. Representatives of 21 women's unions met in the premises of The Worker's Organisation of Helsinki, where the women's section had set up a coffee breakfast for the delegates at 8.00 in the morning. The meeting started at 9.30 in the festival hall, which was, the minutes tell us, decorated with flowers, garlands, birch leaves and banners for the occasion.

The agenda for the three day meeting had 12 points for discussion:

- How to increase unionisation among women
- The creation of central organisation of female unions
- How to achieve a working day of no more than 10 hours for women
- How to achieve a legal minimum hourly wage for women
- How to spread information about the need for female suffrage
- How to achieve unified rules about apprenticeship for women in all sectors
- The necessity of petitioning the government for a female industrial inspector
- What could be done about protecting the freedom of organisation and access to information for women in domestic service?
- How should women work to promote proletarian ideological development?
- How to get a ban on piece work
- The importance of starting a fund for economic protection during strikes and lockouts
- The possibility of starting a newspaper for working women

In the discussion, one of the delegates stated:

> It is true that we have industrial inspectors, but their time is restricted... and if you take into account that women are afraid and too shy to tell male inspectors about the conditions in the workplace. They would be less intimidated to talk to an inspector of the same sex and it is clear that a

female inspector would be able to achieve improvement in the following of workplace regulations. The ability of a female inspector to improve the moral conditions would be of even more importance ...

The meeting highlighted a number of problems, some serious, in the inspection system. It was said that, even in large factories, there seemed to be information in advance about the arrival of the inspector. In preparation for the visit, workrooms were cleaned and children, who according to the law were forbidden to work, were sent away for the day, etc. When the inspector had walked through the factory in company with the management and left, the normal disorganisation, unhygienic conditions and breakages of the law were resumed.[1]

Women and Work

Once upon a time, women had a strong presence in industry. Millions of women were engaged in industrial work: around 1900, 20–40 per cent of industrial workers were women and in certain regions and sectors like textile work their share was even higher. Despite their considerable input, there has been little focus on this aspect of industrialisation and little discussion about the economic impact of the female contribution. Many authors of economic history and the history of work active in the 1960s, 70s and 80s chose to ignore the gender aspect of the economy and only discuss class, even though the women have always been there.[2] On the contrary, it would seem that the work of women has not only been regarded as of little economic importance, but as a problem that had to be eliminated, on the lines of the work of children.

When the second wave of feminism made its mark on historical studies, groundbreaking work about the participation of working class women in the economy saw the light of day. Some studies discussed women as victims of male structures as mothers and wives; others, female input in sweated labour or factory work.[3]

---

[1]   Ensimmaisen, *yleisen työläisnaisten edustajain kokouksen pöytakirja 4, 5 ja 6 heinäkuuta 1900* (Helsinki, 1900).

[2]   Carlo Cipolla (ed.), *The Fontana Economic History of Europe*, The Emergence of Industrial Societies 1–2, The Twentieth Century 1–2 (Glasgow, 1979–82); E.J. Hobsbawm, *Industry and Empire* (Harmondsworth, 1979); E.P. Thompson, *The Making of the English Working Class* (Harmondsworth, 1968).

[3]   Judith Bennett, 'History that stands still: women's work in the European past', *Feminist Studies* 14 (1988), pp. 269–83; Louise Tilly, 'Gender, women's history and social history', *Social Science History* 13:4 (Winter 1989), pp. 439–62, on pp. 444–6; Elizabeth Roberts, *Women's Work 1840–1940* (London, 1992); Anna Clark, *Women's Silence, Men's Violence: Sexual Assault in England 1770–1845* (London, 1987); Sonya O. Rose, *Limited Livelihoods: Gender and Class in Nineteenth-Century England* (Berkeley,

These efforts have had but marginal impact on overviews of economic history. While some still maintain silence in relation to women and work, others devote a token page or two and in these a not inconsiderate part of the space is taken up by the decline of married women's work in England in the early twentieth century.[4]

The aim of this study is by focusing on working women to elevate them from obscurity and give them their rightful place as actors in history.

In this connection, it is also necessary to highlight the fact that the late nineteenth and early twentieth centuries were a time when the advancement of women into society and workplaces took place against a backdrop of resistance. This resistance was not only to be found among conservative and religious groups, but also among the working class and in unions and socialist political circles. Hiding behind the cloak of 'protection' we find activity to weaken the position of women in the workplace. In some cases this was motivated by fear of competition, in others by the desire to label women as second class citizens created for the sole purpose of procreation. Mothers and future mothers had to be protected whether they wanted it or not. Women had to serve the nation and their families and were not welcome when trying to find a public voice.[5]

The intention is to analyse issues connected with factory legislation and not uncritically accept it as a milestone on the road to greater civilisation, but as a potentially two edged sword when it comes to women. Was the legislation universally welcomed?

When we find echoes of the voices of women we also find that their attitude tended to be slightly different from that of their so-called benefactors. Women did not want to be legislated out of the workplace, they wanted better

---

1992); Ellen Ross, 'Fierce questions and taunts: married life in working class London 1870–1914', *Feminist Studies* 8 (1982), pp. 575–602; Anna Clark, *The Struggle for the Breeches. Gender and the Making of the British Working Class* (Berkeley, 1995); Pamela Sharpe (ed.), *Women's Work: The English Experience 1650–1914* (London, 1998); Harriet Bradley, *Men's Work, Women's Work* (Cambridge, 1989).

4   Ivan Berend, *An Economic History of Nineteenth Century Europe – Diversity and Industrialization* (Cambridge, 2013); Stephen Broadberry and Kevin O'Rourke (eds), *The Cambridge Economic History of Modern Europe 2, 1870 to the Present* (Cambridge, 2010).

5   June Purvis, *Hard Lessons: The Lives and Education of Working Class Women in Nineteenth-Century England* (Minneapolis, 1989), pp. 45–7; Richard Evans, 'Politics and the family: social democracy and the working class family in theory and practice', in R. Evans and W.R. Lee (eds), *The German Family: Essays on the Social History of the Family in Nineteenth and Twentieth Century Germany* (London, 2015), pp. 256–88, on pp. 271–3; Christine Thomas, 'Women and the early Labour Party: Review of Nan Sloane, "Women in the room: Labour's forgotten history"', *Socialism Today*, 19 March 2020.

conditions and pay. When representatives of 60 female unions came together in Paris in 1907, their demands included the abolishment of special regulations for women, with the exception of maternity related issues, equal pay for men and women, the inclusion of domestic service in regulated occupations, the control of their earnings by married women and the acceptance of women into male unions.[6]

A question with considerable relevance for female work was the negative attitude of the union movement. There is little doubt that the aim of the nineteenth-century unions was to promote the male breadwinner system and 'save' women from factory work. Was this aim really altruistic or was it a way of diminishing competition? The unions and the bourgeoisie both tried getting women out of the workplace using guilt and unsubstantiated claims and selective statistics about how working would hurt them and the children. They conveniently decided not to comment on female dependence and family violence.[7] Barring women from the workplace and the evils of the factory was viewed as the best solution. Because of this attitude, efforts to eliminate dangerous processes and work with poisonous substances were delayed for decades and thousands of men suffered as a consequence.[8]

The physical dangers of industrial work were not always the primary motive for efforts to exclude women. The fear of moral contamination in the workplace was raised by working class men as well as by the middle classes. Having a girl locked up in a cubbyhole behind a kitchen as a servant to a middle-class family, working 16–18 hour days, was supposedly good training for a future wife. The risks to morals could also take the shape of independent thought. When a wife went to work she became subject to influence from other women and the position of the husband could be eroded. Daughters and even wives could get ideas about controlling their own lives when they had money of their own. This was a serious threat to patriarchal society.[9]

---

6   Annie Metz, 'Marguerite Durand et l'Office du travail féminin', *Archives du Féminisme*, 13 December 2007, http://www.archivesdufeminisme.fr/ressources-en-ligne/articles-et-comptes-rendus/articles-historiques/metz-marguerite-durand-loffice-du-travail-feminin.

7   Katrina Honeyman, *Women, Gender and Industrialization in England, 1700–1870* (Basingstoke, 2000), pp. 102–6, 134–7; Clark, *The Struggle for the Breeches*; Angela John (ed.), *Unequal Opportunities: Women's Employment in England 1800–1914* (Oxford, 1986); Madeleine Guilbert, *Les femmes et l'organisation syndicale avant 1914* (Paris, 1966), pp. 401–3.

8   Barbara Harrison, 'Suffer the working day: women in the "dangerous trades", 1880–1914', *Women's Studies International Forum* 13:1/2 (1990), pp. 79–90.

9   Diana Gittins, *Fair Sex: Family Size and Structure 1900–39* (London, 1982), pp. 82–92; John Burnett, *Useful Toil, Autobiographies of Working People from the 1820s to the 1920s* (London, 1974), pp. 214–25; Joanne Meyerowitz, *Women Adrift: Independent Wage Earners in Chicago 1880–1930* (Chicago, 1988), p. 44. Examples of

The male provider ideal so beloved by the unions has gleaned considerable scepticism from scholars familiar with issues of distribution of means in the working class family.[10] Being at home and economically dependent also had other aspects and could mean isolation and misery:

> Now I had three children of whom the eldest was not even three years old. I could not leave the children and I had no one to help me. The clothes of the children as any other washing had to be done in the flat as there was no wash house ... My husband went to Worker's entertainment evenings. I could not go even once ... For the first time in my life I was unable to participate in the May Day celebrations ... I could not help that tears flowed from my eyes. I was like a prisoner, even though I was still a young girl whose peers were joyfully spending time with each other. Many of my fellow sisters, however, shared my fate, as they do still today.[11]

Possibly because of the early event of industrialisation, the discourse connected to women and industrial work has often been heavily weighted towards Britain, with some inclusion of France or Germany, even in studies with a comparative focus.[12]

When examining the past we find that, where ideological pressure and social stigmatization was not successful, it was necessary to revert to legislation.[13] We also find that the legislation or practice restricting or preventing the work of married women came to have long roots, with impact on work participation or high levels of part-time work by women in contemporary society. Therefore, viewing Britain as a model for working class family life

---

interwar attitudes to female work are vividly expressed in the book *Gaudy Night*, by Dorothy L. Sayers. She devotes considerable space to the discussion about marriage versus a career for women. Most of the female academics in the story have chosen not to marry and the option of both is not considered possible. The working class characters have a definite idea about the place of a woman: "'Wot this country wants," said Padgett, "is a 'itler." "That's right," said the foreman, "keep the girls at 'ome.'" D.L. Sayers, *Gaudy Night* (London, 1935), pp. 115, 216–22.

10   Eleanor Rathbone, *How the Casual Labourer Lives* (Liverpool, 1909); A.E. Dingle, 'Drink and working class living standards in Britain 1870–1914', *Economic History Review* 4 (1972), pp. 608–22; Margaret Pember Reeves, *Round About a Pound a Week* (London, 1913), pp. 147–9; Margery Spring Rice, *Working-Class Wives: Their Health and Conditions* (London, 1939), pp. 116–19; Carl Chinn, *They Worked All Their Lives: Women of the Urban Poor 1880–1939* (Manchester, 2006), pp. 44–6.

11   Martta Salmela-Järvinen, *Alas lyötiin vanha maailma* (Helsinki, 1966), p. 82.

12   Jordan Goodman and Katrina Honeyman, *Gainful Pursuits: The Making of Industrial Europe 1600–1914* (London, 1988), pp. 115–17.

13   Carol Dyhouse, *Feminism and the Family in England 1880–1939* (Oxford, 1989), pp. 77–81; Bradley, *Men's Work, Women's Work*, pp. 207–12.

and structures in general might not be ideal, and a wider perspective should be taken to give us better insights into the past.

One of the aims of this book is to make the voices of the women that were active in industry in other countries heard, and to show that the male bread-winner ideology was not of their making. What many women wanted was decent working conditions, not to be excluded from working life. To achieve improvements, they believed that they needed other women who were in the position to ask for and demand change.

They were ready to defend themselves and to seek support from other women. They also needed new allies. One of these potential allies was the female factory inspector.

Female inspectors

In the nineteenth century, new educational opportunities saw an increasing number of women absorbing knowledge and gaining qualifications, making them stand on an equal level (although often not recognised) with their male counterparts. In a number of European countries and beyond, the state administration opened its doors (albeit not generously) to women before they gained political rights. One of the first state or public sector appointments was that of the female factory inspector. The path into administration did not necessarily run smooth. The stories of some of these women are ones of hard work to achieve recognition and to gain the qualifications that ultimately gave them the right to take such an appointment. Reaching the status of inspector did not end the struggle: once in post they had to prove their worth and demonstrate that they could be as good, or better, than their male colleagues.

On the factory floor two groups of women met; they represented different social classes and often different values. Their story is worth telling.

The female inspector and the factory girl

Some studies of the first female factory inspectors in Britain have highlighted the dependency of these female civil servants on their protectors within the aristocracy and upper echelons of the civil service. While the activity of these women was important and made it possible for labouring women to voice their complaints against difficult working conditions, the creation of the female inspectorate had another aspect. Allowing women entry meant providing a niche for middle-class, educated women to gain recognised positions within the administration. The demand for exams and qualifications acted not only as a protective network against potentially negative male inspectors, but also against working class women venturing into the newly created extension of the female sphere. The lady inspectors were to be the actors and the factory girls the objects of inspection.[14]

It is not impossible that the pinpointing of the female inspectors as qualified specialists and the enjoyment of support from above in society was a necessity in the late nineteenth century when attacks on their integrity and capability from male colleagues did occur.[15] Where such a bastion did not exist, as for example in New Zealand, the life and activity of the women engaged in the inspectorate could be made exceedingly difficult. They became subject to personal attacks and their work was put in jeopardy.[16]

There is no doubt that the nineteenth-century British feminist movement had definite class bias. We can also, however, see that organisations like the Women's Protective and Provident League experienced a transformation in the 1880s, roughly coinciding with the name change to Women's Trade Union League. From an organisation committed to economic liberalism and dominated by middle-class ladies hostile to the unions and to state regulation it evolved into one promoting union work and state regulation of the workplace. While the leadership still had middle-class roots it increased its grassroots recruitment and leaders such as Clementina Black devoted time to collecting information about working conditions of women. By the 1890s, the extension of protective regulation for women was high on the agenda and Emelia Dilke was one of the prime movers for the employment of female inspectors to oversee such rules.[17]

It has often been pointed out that working-class women, when faced with the choice, chose class before gender, although not always willingly. It is, therefore, slightly hypocritical to pretend that their middle-class counterparts would not have reacted similarly.[18] Many of the participants in the organisa-

---

[14] Ruth Livesley, 'The politics of work: feminism, professionalisation and women inspectors of factories and workshops', *Women's History Review* 13:2 (June 2004), pp. 233–61, on pp. 236, 238–42; Helen Jones, 'Women health workers: the case of the first women factory inspectors in Britain', *Social History of Medicine* 1:2 (August 1988), pp. 165–82, on pp. 178–80; Francoise Peemans, 'Fourcaut A., Femmes a l'usine en France dans l'entre-deux guerres', *Revue belge de Philologie et d'Histoire* 64:2 (1986), pp. 441–3, on p. 442.

[15] Hilda Martindale, *Women Servants of the State 1870–1938* (London, 1938), p. 52.

[16] Barbara Harrison and Melanie Nolan, 'Reflections in colonial glass? Women factory inspectors in Britain and New Zealand 1893–1921', *Women's History Review* 13:2 (2004), pp. 275–7; Rosemary Feurer, 'The meaning of "sisterhood": the British women's movement and protective labour legislation 1870–1914', *Victorian Studies* 31 (1988), pp. 233–60, on p. 250; Philippa Levine, *Feminist Lives in Victorian England: Private Roles and Public Commitment* (Oxford, 1990), p. 165.

[17] Feurer, 'The meaning of "sisterhood"', pp. 233–60, on pp. 234–7, 255–9; Levine, *Feminist Lives in Victorian England*, pp. 163–6.

[18] Marjaliisa Hentilä, 'Maa jossa piiatkin saa äänestää', in Leena Laine and Pirjo

tions for promoting women's rights were middle class and, therefore, acted and reasoned as would be befitting to members of this group. The first female factory inspectors were no different.[19]

It is however, unfair to question the competence and integrity of a person based on their social background. Their competence has to be judged based on their actions not on the family in which they were born.

The role of female inspector was new and unchartered, a position of authority unfamiliar to many women. The female inspectors did not act in a uniform way, but each one differently and in accordance with their personality and situation.

It has been said that, in historical studies, leadership has generally been defined by traditional notions of power within hierarchical organisations and that this is not a useful model when considering women's participation in society. A definition that takes into account the opportunities available to women and the diversity of their activities is a way of finding a more flexible definition of female leadership.[20]

One of the aims of this book is to show that authority and security of position could bring forth actions showing choice between group and conscience and going with conviction instead of social group. It is true that in many cases the activity of the female inspectors was hampered by their scant numbers and rules preventing them from acting. This cannot be viewed as evidence of their desire only to promote their own careers. Undeniably they found themselves in the crossfire between different political factions and had to work quite hard to gain respect. How do we measure the effect of their work? In many cases, it is possible to demonstrate that their actions brought benefits to the women they were to represent.

Aims, inclusions and exclusions – Women and work, time and geographic aspects

More than once we have been told that Western, 'economically developed' countries experienced a withdrawal of married women from the labour market because of the pride men took in being breadwinners. The part of the story that is often ignored is the introduction of restrictive legislation on female

---

Markkola (eds), *Tuntematon työläisnainen* (Tampere, 1989), pp. 162–85, on pp. 174–5; Eva Schmitz, *Kvinnor, Kamrater ... Kvinnans roll i arbetarrörelsen* (Stockholm, 1982), pp. 53–9.

[19] Mary Drake McFeeley, *Lady Inspectors: The Campaign for a Better Workplace* (Oxford, 1988), pp. 30–1.

[20] Joy Damousi, 'Female factory inspectors and leadership in early 20th century Australia', in Joy Damousi, Kim Rubenstein and Mary Tomsic (eds), *Diversity and Leadership: Australian Women Past and Present* (Canberra, 2014), pp. 169–88.

work or the practice to fire women when they married. The countries that were the leading lights in this process are indeed the same economically developed Western countries living up to the ideal of the male breadwinner. The exclusion of women from the labour market in the twentieth century was primarily directed against educated women, but the campaign of discrimination against women in manual work started earlier and sometimes appeared in the disguise of 'protection'. One of the issues that will be discussed in this book is the nature of protective legislation and the reactions by women in different countries to the efforts of implementing rules for women only. Another question that will be discussed is how the women who had managed to get access to education and employment as government and public sector employees within the inspectorate benefited or suffered from unequal gender rules.

When we take a step into the 1870s and 1880s, the face of the economy had changed in Europe and beyond. Economic historians have a tendency of talking about 'late comers' and 'periphery' as if countries have always been engaged in a race towards more and better industrialisation and the first comers are the best ones. Today we have reached a point where we are faced with the fact that this process, which has been viewed as something very desirable and the saviour of mankind with economic misery with its coal and steel, might be the key to our destruction. In the late nineteenth century, however, many countries had had a taste of its blessings and curses. As some of the aspects became clear to decision makers, or those engaged in social and political movements, regulation and its use for mitigation of problems can widely be found on the agenda. Therefore, the timing of this study has a starting point at 1870, when large parts of Europe, the United States and countries on the other side of the globe were industrialising.

By the 1890s the industrial workforce was different from that of earlier times. Rules about the work of children had been introduced. The time period 1870 to 1920 is the time of the introduction of rules, control and inspection. It is also the time period when workplace injury was being recognised as an evil that could not be ignored. However, first and foremost it is the time of entry of the first female inspectors. It is a time of female emergence into the civil service as a result of female entry into higher and mid-level education. It is also a time of considerable presence of females in industrial work. By the 1930s, many countries had experienced a conservative backlash against women in employment. In some cases it had links to the emerging ultra-right-wing movements in Europe, in other cases it was triggered by religious or other socially conservative ideologies. As will be demonstrated, the result was closing employment opportunities to women, where they had not been closed before. These complications, as well as the large political upheavals of the 1930s, effectively draw a line in the narrative.

Because the aim of the study is to be truly far reaching, Britain will be only one of many places under discussion. Far too often one finds publications with Europe in the title but when examining the contents most of the volume is dedicated to Britain with the exception of one or two token articles. This study will discuss factory work, conditions and inspection in France, Britain, Germany, Spain, Italy, the Netherlands, Austria, Denmark, Finland, Norway, Russia, the USA, Australia, New Zealand and, where some information could be gleaned, it has been provided for other countries. Because of the geographic scope, every issue might not have been explored as widely, as those specialising in research on women and work in each of these countries would have desired.

For the same reason, some subjects familiar and central to British scholarship, like the early industrial revolution and a number of subjects connected to it, have not been included. Subjects like female work and the war economy will be absent, even though this is a book about women and work. Viewing the world from a British perspective, the entry of women into the factories of WWI and the expulsion of women after the peace is of tumultuous significance for the issue.[21] From another perspective, it might not appear to have the same impact. While many countries suffered the effects of the war, all did not necessarily have a large defence industry or exodus of men from workplaces.

The issue of female suffrage will be discussed both in relation to women's organisations and political development in many countries. Some effort will be made to penetrate the question of class division in the stance different organisations took when striving for the female vote. However, the activist campaigns in London will not be part of the narrative. The focus of the study is on working women of the working and the middle class and the politics of the workplace and beyond.

This book, despite its title, is a study of social history more than economic history and of how working women experienced their work and earnings and how they coped. While the aim has been to respect the information presented by the inspectors and workers about shortcomings and severe problems in factory work faced by women and children, it has not been the aim to delve into the details of every instance. Many excellent volumes have been written on children and early British industrialisation.[22] This book has no ambition to compete with these studies. Although children were part of the remit of female inspection, the time period in focus and the geographic spread will necessitate a slightly different approach. Where the inspectors identified problems similar to those in earlier periods, these will naturally be discussed. One should, however, remember that what will be highlighted is a time when regulation

---

[21] Gail Braybon and Penny Summerfield, *Out of the Cage: Women's Experiences in Two World Wars* (London, 1987).

[22] For example, Jane Humphries, *Childhood and Child Labour in the British Industrial Revolution* (Cambridge, 2010); Peter Kirby, *Child Labour in Britain, 1750–1870* (London, 2003).

already existed, or was being set up; on the other hand, the part played by children in the working-class family economy, or educational issues, will not be forgotten.

A female story

The story is a story of female survival. It has been said that it is ill advised to use the word strategy when discussing the working class, as the word implies long-term planning. Should this be the case, maybe one had better say that the book attempts to tackle the issues women of the working class and those of the middle classes were faced with when attempting to earn a living or contribute to the economic welfare of their families.

The specific groups of women under discussion are those who met on the factory floor. The intermingling of the two classes was not commonplace in the nineteenth century or that of pre-WWII society. However, just as the women who trained as nurses or schoolteachers might find themselves face to face with people unfamiliar to them, so did the factory inspectors. While male inspectors could distance themselves from the objects of inspection by the additional barrier of gender, the female inspectors were chosen for the particular task of approaching those that they inspected. They were expected to have conversations and to listen, not to give orders.

Despite the arrangements of making sure that the social superiority of the one group should remain clear, performing their tasks well necessitated having to give up certain privileges or codes of behaviour for some of those involved. However, the recruitment, the definitions of the tasks and the socioeconomic background was not identical in all countries. One should also not forget that the personal characteristics of the individuals were of no minor importance. Therefore, some biographical information has also been included.

While men at times tended to see women as competing with them in the marketplace, it is not necessarily absolutely clear that women viewed the issue in the same way. They just wanted to survive. Life as a woman in a world made by men is always a balancing act. How to exist without running into the restrictions that surround you, how to twist and turn to manage being a wife, a mother, a daughter, a friend and an earner?

The situation was naturally different for the working-class women on the factory floor, and the middle-class women who came in to supervise, control, advice, help and protect.

Both these groups had to make choices in how to define their roles and understand their position. While the women working on the machines were faced with pressures of society in regards to their role as mothers or future mothers, some of those sent in to inspect were denied the right to become mothers. The price they had to pay for being civil servants was a price that was never asked of their male counterparts. There is plenty of evidence that the early feminists and women of the working classes viewed issues from very different angles. Fierce attacks were sometimes launched in socialist newspapers by women on women who did not understand the particular problems of the working woman. Feminists were not uniformly positive toward female unions or women in these unions. Suspicion and aggression could manifest itself even at conferences of women. Sometimes the boundaries were clear, bourgeois women and working-class women. However, this was not always the case. When the international workers movement backed the idea of curtailing the female working day, the working women whose livelihood became endangered reacted. They preferred an income instead of protection. When the Sunday work of shop assistants was debated in the Finnish parliament, the resistance to Sunday closure came from the female socialist delegates.

Female solidarity is not self-evident and even working-class female solidarity can show cracks.

One of the reasons for employing female inspectors was that they could talk to women. Interestingly enough it would seem that this was the case. After initial suspicion and even fear, channels of communication were in many cases established. Cloak and dagger meetings after dark, involving women who were afraid of being sacked if they talked, resulted in information being transmitted to the inspectors. The story of these early years is full of interest and needs to be told. It is a story of two parties that met and what this meant for their lives.

Data and structure of the study

Gender and Class – Male Unions, Political Movements and the Female Vote

The book will commence with a discussion about working women, unions and political parties. It will describe the attitude among male-dominated unions to female workers and the tendency by women to form their own separate organisations. The chapter will also discuss female activity within socialist parties in different countries and the restrictions put on female sections both in relation to representation and issues raised. It will also comment on instances of cross-class cooperation in relation to issues like the female vote and the demands by the male party majority that the women cease communication with middle-class women.

Women in Industry – Work, Sectors, Age and Marital Status

The second chapter begins with an overview of the development of women's work from integration in the family economy towards engagement in economic activity outside the home. It will discuss the availability and accuracy of existing information about female work, for example, how the work of women was included in the system of registration and what the statistics tell us. Some comments will be devoted to the transfer from family-based production to employment outside the home for wages and how this manifests itself in statistical series. Another issue that will receive attention is the difference in regional development of industry and, therefore, the differences in opportunities for women to embark on employment in industry in different European countries and other parts of the world. This question is not unimportant, as evidence has been found of the variation of attitudes to female work depending on regional level of female employment. Some space will be devoted to the analysis of the type of industrial employment that particularly drew its workforce from the female part of society. The chapter will also discuss the age and marital status of female industrial workers.

The information has been extracted from official economic statistics and studies based on statistical surveys of the working population in the late nineteenth and early twentieth centuries. In addition, female work patterns have been explored in, for example, Lily Braun, *Die Frauenfrage: ihre geschichtliche Entwicklung und wirtschaftliche Seite* (Berlin, 1901) and R. Gonnard, *La femme dans l'industrie* (Paris, 1906). The age and marital status of female workers have also been charted in local surveys like Johan Leffler, *Zur Kenntniss von den Lebens und Lohnverhältnissen Industrieller Arbeiterinnen in Stockholm* (Stockholm, 1897) and statistics on national level like *Statistisches Jahrbuch für das Deutsche Reich* (Berlin, 1899).

Women, Earnings and the Household – Why the Factory?

One of the questions raised in this chapter is why women would embark on factory work rather than seek other employment. The discussion will include earnings in factory work, not only a comparison with male earnings but also a comparison with earnings in other fields employing women, like service. Some of the sources illuminating female earnings include surveys of industrial work in Finland, like a study of the textile sector by G.R. Snellman, *Undersökning angående textilindustrin* (Helsingfors, 1904).[23] The surveys give detailed information about male and female earnings, job descriptions and times in employment, wage levels, types of remuneration, marital status, etc. The income of female industrial workers and the economic situation of their families are also charted in surveys like: *Die Arbeits- und Lebensverhältnisse der Wiener Lohnarbeiterinnen: Ergebnisse und stenographisches Protokoll der Enquete über Frauenarbeit abgehalten in Wien vom 1. März bis 21 April 1896* and Gabriel d'Haussonville, *Salaires et misères de femmes* (Paris, 1900); Vera Hjelt, *Undersökning af yrkesarbetarnes lefnadsvillkor i Finland 1908–1909* (Helsingfors, 1911); K. Key-Åberg, *Inom textilindustrien in Norrköping sysselsatta arbetares lönevillkor och bostadsförhallanden* (Stockholm, 1896).

---

[23] The survey included 9687 workers in the textile industry.

The chapter will also discuss reasons presented by women for working and sectors that were considered preferable. It will comment on the economic aspects of working class family life and present examples of the household composition of female workers. It will analyse the economic levels of working-class families and the importance of female contributions to the family economy. Examples will be presented from various parts of Europe of female coping mechanisms where clustering with female relatives, friends or work mates was used to increase the economic stability of the household unit: Rosa Kempf, *Das Leben der Jungen Fabriksmädchen* (Leipzig, 1911); Gustaf Geijerstam, *Fabriksarbetarnes ställning i Marks härad* (Stockholm, 1894); Poul Sveistrup, 'Københavnske syerskers og smaakaarsfamiliers kostudgifter', *Nationaløkonomisk Tidsskrift*, 3:7 (1899), pp. 578–629; Board of Trade, Labour Department, *Accounts and Expenditure of Wage Earning Women and Girls* (1911) LXXXIX. PP. Cd 5963; F. Erismann, 'Die Ernährungsverhältnisse der Arbeiterbevölkerung in Centralrussland', *Archiv für Hygiene* (1889), vol. 9, pp. 23–47; Royal Commission on Labour, The Employment of Women PP 1892–4, XXIII c 6894; and Elinor Rathbone, *How the Casual Labourer Lives* (Liverpool, 1909).

In addition, oral history accounts are used to illuminate experiences and attitudes affecting female economic and family situations and the propensity for employment.

Accidents, Compensation, Laws and Inspection

Chapter Four will be devoted to a discussion about dangers in the workplace in the late nineteenth and early twentieth centuries and the debate on working conditions and insurance against the consequences of accidents. Statistics of accidental death and injury will be presented for Britain, France, Germany, Finland, Italy, Spain, USA, Russia and Denmark using both contemporary statistical series and more recent studies analysing such data. In addition, the question of dangers in the workplace apart from accidents, i.e. the raising of awareness on the existence of occupational disease, will be included.

The chapter will also be devoted to a description of the introduction of the inspection system and the nineteenth-century protective legislation in various countries.

In conjunction with the development of legislation, insurance systems and improvements in inspection, we will also discuss the special measures introduced in relation to women. Information will be presented about how women, in addition to children, came to be regarded as a group that needed special protection. The issue will be raised of how the movement for female protection instigated procedures ultimately aimed at eliminating women from the workplace and where and how such actions were met by the women themselves.

The datasets used for the chapter comprise of workplace accident statistics and studies of the same, like *Finlands Officiella Statistik, Arbetsstatistik XXVI A. Olycksfallen i arbetet* (Helsingfors, 1908); Gustav Bang, *Arbejderrisiko*

(1904); and accident reporting in the Annual reports of the Chief Inspector of Factories 1886–1915. The development of the factory inspectorate in various countries, the event of the new branch of studies on work-related disease in the nineteenth century and the nature and development of factory legislation in the late nineteenth and the early twentieth centuries are also explored.

Middle-Class Girls, Education and Entry into the Civil Service

The chapter discusses female education and changes in female educational opportunities in the nineteenth century from a comparative perspective. Primarily, the focus will be on the possibility for a woman to access degrees, which qualified her for state and other employment, but also entry into the educational sector.

The chapter will describe the entry of women into the civil service and the debate around these issues. It will also present the definitions of and the expectations on the female professional. The chapter will also comment on the backlash against female entry into the professions in the form of the introduction of formal or informal marriage bars to prevent married women from working.

The Female Factory Inspectors: How, Why and Who

Chapter Six explores the debate about the need for female inspectors from an international perspective. The question of the female sphere and morality as arguments will be analysed. The political situation and the attitudes of different groups will be commented on, as will the involvement of persons with social or political influence. It will be underlined that, in several countries, the case for choosing a woman was not only linked to the view that women are nurturing and cognisant of hygienic questions, but also that a lady inspector would be suitable to guide working-class girls and raise standards.

The definition of the relevance of competence and education for a female inspector will be discussed as well as the differences in tasks and rules in different countries. In some countries technical competence was explicitly excluded, while in other countries it was a requirement.

In addition, a description of the female inspectorate will be provided, as well as how the question of power sharing between male and female inspectors was defined.

The social and educational background of some of the early female inspectors will be presented as well as how they came to enter the profession. The level of remuneration of male and female inspectors will also be commented on. As the inspectorate tended to be part of the civil service and some countries exercised the marriage bar, the situation faced by the early female inspectors varied. Marriage could result in instant dismissal in Britain or the Netherlands while in France or Denmark it had no consequences. The chapter will also provide some examples of the type of resistance the female inspectors met in the early years, including problems and conflicts with the male inspectorate, but also support from the same.

The main datasets are biographies and autobiographies of the early female inspectors.

Factory Inspection Activity

Chapter Seven is devoted to a description of issues tackled by the female inspectors in the early years and decades of their activity. For example, the way they highlighted infringements of the rules about the working day, the work of children and the impact of this on education. The expectations were that health and hygiene would be an important part of the female remit. These questions were indeed tackled and improvements did occur. While the structure of the physical space of the workrooms might have been viewed as part of sanitation question, the danger to health and life posed by machinery was in many places not seen as belonging to the female sphere. In spite of this, such dangers were also discussed by the inspectors as were the remedies. The chapter also reveals some examples of linkages with male inspectors, social reformers and politicians for the purpose of fulfilling inspection duties, but also for the purpose of pushing for improved legislation and including new fields into factory legislation. The information has mainly been gathered from factory inspection reports, for example: the Annual Reports of the Chief Inspector of Factories in Britain 1892–1913, the reports by the female factory inspector in Finland 1903–1910, the Annual Reports of the Inspectors of Illinois 1893–1895, and *Beretning om Arbejds og Fabrikstillsynets Virksomhed Aaren* 1919 og 1920 (Copenhagen, 1922).

In addition, biographical and autobiographical publications of and by the female inspectors describing their work have been utilised.

Class, Gender and Communication

Chapter Eight describes the initial problems encountered between female inspectors and working women at the early stages of female inspection. The chapter also discusses how a system of communication was established after the early setbacks. It provides examples of how complaints were voiced by working women and the activity by the female inspectors in trying to address the issues. It will be demonstrated that a dialogue was achieved and that the dialogue resulted in action by the female inspectors. Although it would be futile to claim that the inspectors identified with the workers, there are clear indications that they did their utmost to improve the workers' conditions. The nature of their activity was on the one hand motivated by the problems they identified, but also by the problems that were presented to them by the workers. We also find a distinct desire to extend existing regulation to include more than what was in their remit rather than just oversee rules.

The information for this chapter has primarily been found in inspection reports, studies of factory inspection and biographies and autobiographies of the early female inspectors.

Conclusion

Many views have been expressed about female work participation, from a high degree of scepticism about activity beside housework, work only in wartime, to the U-shaped curve, indicating that the present levels of activity somehow represent a historical anomaly. The more information that is collected, however, demonstrates that wherever we look we find new evidence of female activity in the past.

While the early phase of industrialisation engaged large numbers of children in factory work, by the late nineteenth and early twentieth centuries, the patterns shifted towards replacing children with teenagers and adult women. While child work still existed and was gradually phased out, employing a 12-year-old was for a long time considered reasonable. Continuously, large numbers of 14-year-olds walked through the factory gates. The collection of statistics revealed, however, not only young workers but also females. This was by many viewed as an issue that should be tackled. The diminishing numbers of child workers had demonstrated that legislation could work and those desiring to erase the female presence in industry saw a solution.

Unlike the assumptions that women only worked before marriage in the past, married adult women were present in the workplace. Because of this and as a consequence of it, regulations were passed specific to married women (working hours, short Saturdays, ban on work after childbirth). In addition, other female-specific regulations were passed 'protecting' unmarried women in their role as future mothers.

Should one be ironic, one could say that the Victorian approach was unintentionally a manifestation of the view that men are of less importance for the survival of the nation.

However, it is perhaps not likely that this was the reason, but rather that conservatives wanted women back in the home and the male union activists wanted to eliminate competition. It cannot be denied that the female presence must have been viewed as a problem because of the eagerness by which the 'protection' of women was embraced.

The frontiers were not cemented-down, neither within the labour movement nor within politically conservative circles. The positions varied depending on country and the structure of the economy. The strength or weakness of the industrial sector could also result in variable outcomes for the regulation. The structure of the regulatory framework did, however, follow similar patterns both in Europe and in other continents. One of the reasons was that the political decision-makers were aware of what was going on elsewhere.

At this time in history, the rules regarding women and children were made by men, without any input from these objects of protection. Ostentatiously, the rules were for the welfare of these groups. What we find, however, is that the rules were not always to the liking of those they were supposed to benefit.

Another consequence of the development of the legislation was that nations were faced with new rules regarding the position of women and children in the workplace. It was also acknowledged that perhaps the ideal person to probe into how well the regulations were followed was not a man but a woman.

This, perhaps unintended, consequence was linked to the philosophy behind the rulings. Women were different from men; this was the reason why they had to be protected. The need for protection extended beyond working hours necessitated by their weaker constitution. They needed shorter hours and free Saturday afternoons to be able to attend to the needs of their families. They needed maternity leave so that their infant would thrive. They needed to be excluded from night work so that they would be spared moral temptation and degradation. As some of the dangers were not of a physical but a moral nature, the question that arose was: would it be suitable for a man to oversee such rules? Therefore, the patriarchal values that engendered the rulings carried within them the seed for employment of women to oversee them. Certainly there was resistance, but for anyone capable of understanding logical reasoning a case could be made for employing women. The same logic that saw the virtue in young women having female teachers supported the idea of female inspectors. What remained was to make sure that potential applicants had the right background and moral fibre to operate as mentors and role models while communicating successfully with employers in an industrial environment.

1

Gender and Class – Male Unions, Political Movements and the Female Vote

> My wife? What does she want with meetings? Let her stay at home and wash my moleskin trousers![1]

My father would in the evenings read for my mother the book by Bebel, 'The woman in Socialism'. She could not read it herself as she was busy darning socks and mending clothes.[2]

At the Conference of the amalgamated unions of France (CGT) 10–14 September 1900 the following statements were made:

- A woman's place is at home where she should occupy herself with the wellbeing of her husband and children. Female work is against nature.
- Female work is contrary to health and hygiene and causes degeneration.
- Female work is against morals and breeds promiscuity and prostitution.
- As women are paid less female work undermines men and the proletarian fight against capitalism.
- Female work is not emancipating but makes women slaves to the employer on top of family duties.
- When the proletarians have achieved the victory over the capitalists women will not need to work outside the home anymore.

And finally:

- All workers agree that the introduction of women into industry has been bad for the working class in the moral as well as the physical and economic sense. While it is not within our power, today, to change the situation, our goal is at least to ameliorate the bad effects of female industrial work.[3]

---

[1] Purvis, *Hard Lessons*, p. 46.

[2] Karin de la Roi-Frey, 'Wenn alle Stricke reissen, dann wird sie noch einmal eine Lehrerin', *Lehrerinnen in biographischen Zeugnissen* (Bochum, 2001), p. 122.

[3] Guilbert, *Les femmes et l'organisation*, pp. 189–90, 175.

When discussing the position of women in the workplace in the late nineteenth century and the ideological background against which they had to operate, it is of some importance to analyse the stance taken by the unions and the socialist movement.

In the 1970s and 1980s, the new wave of feminist research made serious challenges regarding existing views of the past. One of the debates focused on the absence of interest in the life and condition of women. The issue was raised that scholars who had challenged paradigms on political grounds and demanded the right of the working class to enter into history, themselves made unfounded claims of what women had wanted. Such claims were on the one hand linked to their own prejudices, on the other hand to those of working-class men of past centuries.[4] While this generation of female academics undertook fundamental work about working-class women and the economy, they also demonstrated the negative attitude of male unions to the working woman and the basically patriarchal ideology of the working man.[5]

Some scholars have disagreed with the idea that women were pushed out of the workplace. Instead they have claimed that the English wife preferred not to work because of the double burden. Therefore, women were supposedly in agreement with unions and working-class male ideology hostile to female work.[6]

The practical and economic consequences of housewifery in a working class context were not necessarily very advantageous, as was demonstrated by scholars familiar with issues of distribution of means in the working-class family. Such views might also not have found favour with scholars who have demonstrated that the reason for battered working-class wives staying with their abusers was the lack of an income of their own.[7]

[4]   Sally Alexander, Anna Davin and Eve Hostetler, 'Labouring women: a reply to Eric Hobsbawm', *History Workshop Journal* 8:1 (1979), pp. 174–82.

[5]   John, *Unequal Opportunities*; Rose, *Limited Livelihoods*; Ross, 'Fierce questions and taunts', pp. 575–602; Clark, *The Struggle for the Breeches*; Sharpe, *Women's Work*; Bradley, *Men's Work, Women's Work*.

[6]   Joanna Bourke, *Husbandry to Housewifery* (Oxford, 1993), pp. 18–22; Joanna Bourke, 'Housewifery in working-class England 1860–1914', in Sharpe, *Women's Work*, pp. 332–50; Catherine Hakim, *Key Issues in Women's Work* (London, 2004), pp. 18–19, 40, 70–1.

[7]   Rathbone, *How the Casual Labourer Lives*; A.E. Dingle, 'Drink and working class living standards', pp. 608–22; Margaret Llewelyn Davies (ed.), *Maternity: Letters from Working Women* (London, 1915), pp. 67–73; Pember Reeves, *Round About a Pound a Week*, pp. 147–9; Spring Rice, *Working-Class Wives*, pp. 116–19; Chinn, *They Worked All Their Lives*, pp. 44–6; James Hammerton, *Cruelty and Companionship: Conflict in Nineteenth Century Married Life* (London, 1992), pp. 42–5.

Women and the unions

The attitude of the English male unions in relation to female work is of considerable relevance for the position of women in the past. Finding examples demonstrating that male trade unions wanted pay increases for themselves and preferred their wives in their proper place at home, under their economic and physical control is not extremely difficult.[8] While female work was generally badly paid, women in textile factories managed to earn a living wage and skilled female weavers even a decent wage. These factories also sometimes had schools, which would increase the educational level of women who worked there. Literacy was not always welcomed by working-class husbands and activity outside the home frowned upon. In reality, physical abuse to underline the position of male authority was far from unusual.[9]

Patriarchal ideologies were shared not only by working men but also by the leading lights of the socialist movement. Marx himself and his sons in law, while having lofty ideas about the transformation of society, were sticklers for male authority on the domestic front and the relegation of women to household duties.[10]

The general negative attitude to female work and not allowing women to join the unions resulted in a situation where 30 per cent of the British workforce were female, but only 10 per cent were union members. On many occasions, the male members voted against female membership (just like male students and alumni voted against the right of women to receive degrees in Cambridge). This should not be understood as female lack of interest in activism. One thing that was the outcome of male hostility to female activity was the formation of female-only unions, either specialising in one factory or one sector or coming together to form unions and organisations uniting women engaged in different sectors.[11] The Women's Trade Union League (1889) unsuccessfully and without support raised the issue of equal pay. Women also came together in the Co-operative Women's Guild (1883) and the National Federation of Women Workers (1906). The strike action of the female match workers in 1888 has often been held up as an example of women being willing to strike and unite, to promote their interests if given a chance.[12]

8   Lynn Abrams, *The Making of Modern Woman* (London, 2002), pp. 196–7.

9   Purvis, *Hard Lessons*, pp. 34–6, 45–6; Deirdre Beddoe, *Discovering Women's History* (London, 1998), p. 95.

10   Francis Wheen, *Karl Marx* (London, 1999), pp. 350–3.

11   Beddoe, *Discovering*, pp. 94–7.

12   Nicole Busby and Rebecca Zahn, *A Dangerous Combination?*, https://dangerouswomenproject.org/2016/06/20/womens-trade-unionism; Patricia Branca, *Women in Europe since 1750* (London, 1978), p. 159; M.C. Bradbrook, *That Infidel Place: A Short History of Girton College 1869–1969* (Cambridge, 1969).

In the United States, female activism channelled itself into the forming of specialist female unions and by the 1880s women started to join the national federation, the Knights of Labor. When the Knights lost its importance and was replaced by The American Federation of Labor, the interest in the amalgamation of female organisations evaporated. A look at female activism, when it was possible, shows that women could display considerable tenacity in strike situations and persist against all odds until they gained their goal. One interesting feature is that female activism and union work seems to have been in focus particularly among widows and married women, rather than the young and single, even though these tended to form the majority among female workers.[13] Another interesting feature is that later assessments of strike success have demonstrated that the more balance between the sexes a union had, the more likely it was to gain its goals in a strike.[14]

The level of female unionisation was, however, low and the labour movement reoriented itself towards supporting legislation for shorter hours and restriction of jobs for women. In this move for protection of women, reformers and trade unionists could join forces. While regulations about workplace safety were welcome, the legislation specific to women weakened their position in the labour market. The female rules reduced their desirability as workers and weakened their competition with men. Employers would not adjust working hours but rather let the women go. This outcome was satisfactory to the male-dominated unions and would have been catastrophic for women, had the development not coincided with increasing demand for women in new sectors of clerical and shop work.[15]

Although there was considerable union activity in late nineteenth-century Russia, the efforts to activate women were variable. The Moscow Worker's Union published leaflets aimed at women in the 1890s, and some of the leaders urged the workers to join forces. On the grassroots level, however, the male workers viewed the women with suspicion and sometimes antagonism. Female literacy was very low, they were badly organised and their level of knowledge in political matters was often defective. They had also been coerced by employers to act contrary to the interest of men eager for organisation in several instances. As political agitation was illegal, female activists tried

---

[13] Carole Turbin, 'Beyond conventional wisdom: women, wage work, household economic contribution, and labour activism in a mid-nineteenth century working class community', in Carol Groneman and Mary Beth Norton (eds), 'To Toil the Livelong Day': America's Women at Work, 1780–1980 (Ithaca, 1987), pp. 47–67, on pp. 59–63.

[14] Anna Jacobs and Larry Isaac, 'Gender composition in contentious collective action: "girl strikers" in gilded age America – harmful, helpful or both?', Social Science History 43:4 (2019), pp. 733–64.

[15] Alice Kessler-Harris, Women Have Always Worked: A Concise History (Chicago, 2018), pp. 97–100.

to approach women workers through organisations like the Sunday school movement to raise their awareness. The situation was not improved by the fact that political activity often was in the hands of skilled male workers who had created unions for the purpose of protecting their craft and income against unskilled males and women. This did not prevent women from actively taking part in strikes, however. As union work and political activism was illegal there were continuous arrests of leaders, particularly among the intellectuals, which made contact with the workers difficult. On the other hand, in tricky situations it was not unknown for female social democrats to take on the spreading of clandestine material on behalf of their male comrades. The activist Vera Karelina expressed her situation as that the mass of male workers felt that public activity was not a woman's affair, that her sphere for action was the machine in the factory and the stove at home, and that her task was to bring up the children.[16] Such views were not far from Clara Zetkin's statement about the ideal working class couple: 'When the proletarian then says "my wife", he adds to this in his mind: "the comrade of my ideals, the companion of my exertions, the educator of my children for the future struggle".'[17]

From the 1880s, women in France were engaged in many strikes of their own. The issues were efforts by employers to reduce wages, unjust fines or actions against sexual harassment from foremen. In many cases, these strikes could be well organised and fierce in spite of lack of support from male unions, male family members and society, particularly the Church. Women were not eager to join trade unions; in 1900 women encompassed only 5.5 per cent of the union membership although by 1911 it had risen to 9.8 per cent. One of the main reasons was the negative attitude of the Syndicalists to women and work. The unions had, throughout the 1860s and 1870s, had a firm doctrine of male breadwinner ideology and women as wives and homemakers. As late as 1898, in the congress of the CGT (Confederation General du Travail) a motion was carried about the male provider and that only in cases of widowhood or being single without a provider could women be accepted as workers with the right to equal pay. In its activity in the early decades of the twentieth century, the CGT campaigned for the free Sunday and Saturday half day to make it possible for working mothers to attend to their family duties. Some unions, specifically the printers, were absolutely hostile to women's work because of the difference in pay scale. Until 1912, they refused to admit women into the union and even went on strike when women were employed. One of the examples of the stance of the unions was when Emma Couriau, a female printer married to a male printer, was refused entry into the printers union in Lyon. In addition to baring her, the husband was excluded because of the

---

[16] Jane McDermid and Anna Hillyar, *Women and Work in Russia 1880–1930* (London, 1998), pp. 109–17.

[17] Evans, 'Politics and the family', p. 272.

local union having taken the decision that union members were not to allow their wives to engage in printing. The matter was widely debated by feminist organisations as well as in journals published by the unions and working-class organisations. When the female printers received support from bourgeois feminists it caused an uproar. Although part of the leadership turned against the printers union, generally speaking, particularly at local level, women had little acceptance within the movement. When the female printers formed their own union and it became necessary for them to turn to the central government to gain official recognition, the women who had participated actively in the campaign, like Marguerite Durand, the editor of the journal *La Fronde*, were lambasted in the union press as wanting to destroy the unions and turning working men and women against each other.[18]

In the 1880s and 1890s there was repeated strike activity among female textile workers in different parts of Sweden. Even though the women were generally not union members and the unions not always positive to the activity, they did take action to limit working hours and raise wages. Unpleasant behaviour by foremen could also be the reason for action with demands of dismissal. Some factories tended to employ foreign foremen, because of their technical knowledge. In some cases, the lack of respect for the women resulted in direct action by the female workers. In rare cases, like that of the bookbinders in Stockholm, the union accepted female membership and men and women worked together, achieving a successful outcome of the strike in 1899. At this point the strike action could also specifically target the right to form a union and of unionised members to retain the right to keep their jobs.[19]

While activism increased among women in the 1890s, the women tended to form female sections or subsections of the male unions, as it was far from unusual for the men to oppose female participation in unions and political life. While the tobacco workers union accepted female membership, several other unions, like the bakery workers, building workers and tailors, rejected female membership or encouraged women to form their own organisations. Despite attempts by the female unions to gain support in their efforts to promote equality in wage levels, the male unions, apart from the tobacco workers, did not consider the issue important enough to pursue. Therefore, at union congresses, the female delegates repeatedly raised the questions of equal pay and female suffrage without receiving much support.[20] In 1902, the Women's

---

[18] James F. McMillan, *France and Women 1789–1914: Gender, Society and Politics* (London, 2000), pp. 182–7; Guilbert, *Les femmes et l'organisation*, pp. 400–3; Madeleine Guilbert, 'Femmes et syndicats en France', *Sociologie et Sociétés* 6:1 (1974), pp. 157–69, on pp. 158–9.

[19] Schmitz, *Kvinnor, Kamrater*, pp. 31–5.

[20] Schmitz, *Kvinnor, Kamrater*, pp. 39–41.

Union was formed to operate as a facilitator for the female unions and raise their issues at the Labour Union congresses.[21]

In Finland, the early female unionisation proceeded through the establishing of female specialist unions, like one for the seamstresses in 1890, the washerwomen in 1898 and the servants and outdoor workers in 1899. Around this time there still existed some cross-class communication among female activists for the purpose of encouraging female unionisation. Union participation among women remained, however, low and by 1906 only 12 per cent of all workers belonging to unions were women. The Union of Female Workers was founded in 1900. Although the focus in the early days was on improvement of working conditions, the parliamentary reform establishing the universal vote pushed activity in the direction of party politics rather than union work. After the formation of the umbrella organisation (the Finnish Union) in 1907, the female social democrats wanted to focus their energy on political activity instead of union matters and canvass for joining the Worker's Party. At the first meeting of the union, 19 out of the 365 delegates were female. In practice, the union did not focus greatly on female issues and, therefore, a lot of the work fell on the Social Democratic women's section. The Social Democratic party continued to be male dominated, with a 77 per cent male membership in 1910 and 66 per cent in 1921. The leadership was not exclusively male but the women were few and the same goes for delegates at party conferences. However, the unions came to see a point in female recruitment and the female share of unionised workers increased to 18 per cent in 1922, 22 per cent in 1928 and 23 per cent in 1938. The movement did incorporate issues related to women in the 1930s when motions were passed for 3.5 months of maternity payments in connection with childbirth, a ban on work in unhealthy conditions and equal pay for women to improve their economic situation. When the International Union Congress in Amsterdam 1930 proposed the introduction of a ban for married women's work and the delegates from Belgium insisted on the need for raising male wages to make them the sole breadwinners it generated a discussion among unions and political parties. In Sweden, parliament introduced a ban on the night work of women in 1911. In Finland, however, the unions did not go along with the central European line. In 1930, the Finnish Union presented their social policy manifest and it stated unequivocally that the work of women represented a bonus for the family and for society and restricting it had no benefits.[22]

---

21 Schmitz, *Kvinnor, Kamrater,* pp. 43–7.

22 Maria Lähteenmäki, *Mahdollisuuksien aika, Työläisnaiset ja yhteiskunnan muutos 1910–30 luvun Suomessa* (Helsinki, 1995), pp. 149–51, 163–7. The Swedish night work ban for women was introduced in 1911 and lasted until 1962, Schmitz, *Kvinnor, Kamrater*, pp. 66–9.

Socialist party politics and the position of women

In addition to female work, the issue of the vote demonstrated where priorities were to be found among male socialists in many countries. The Labour Representation Committee in England was formed in 1900 and became The Labour Party in 1906, having strong support among female textile workers in Lancashire. The stance of the party on the vote question was a demand for a universal adult male vote. Working-class women in the northwest collected names on petitions and arranged protests in favour of the female vote. They also linked the question to problems with low pay and working conditions. However, at Labour congresses and Trades Union congresses, women's suffrage was voted down and many women turned to the Women's Suffrage and Political Union formed in 1903. As their middle-class leaders became frustrated with their lack of progress they distanced themselves from these organisations and some adopted a more radical policy of direct action, which attracted publicity. This alienated the working-class women who aimed for a democratically organised mass campaign. Finally, in 1912, the Labour Party conference voted for a reform of the voting system including votes for women.[23]

When activists among the left-wing parties in France, Germany and Austria commented on their path to political activism there were distinct differences in the patterns described by men and women. Men often found their way to unions and parties through workmates and discussions in the workplace. Women, on the other hand, came into contact with socialist ideas through fathers and brothers in the home. Male family member brought them pamphlets and newspapers to read and in many cases also took them along to political meetings. Although the labour movement was not over-fond of female speakers at important conferences, women could have the platform and demonstrate that they had absorbed the ideology. On the other hand, some fathers only allowed their daughters to come to meetings when they could accompany them.[24]

The stance of the Social Democratic movement and Party in Germany was decidedly patriarchal. The need for women to work was seen as resulting in the ruin of family life. The ideal was raising the earning potential of men so that their wives could stay at home. These views were expressed both by men and by women within the party.[25] An analysis on the family circumstances of a large number of women joining the party shows, however, that only a

---

[23] Thomas, 'Women and the early Labour Party'.

[24] Mary Jo Maynes, *Taking the Hard Road: Life Course in French and German Workers' Autobiographies in the Era of Industrialization* (Chapel Hill, 1995), pp. 156–7, 161–3.

[25] Evans, 'Politics and the family', pp. 256–88, 271–3.

small minority were engaged in paid employment. The vast majority were housewives with husbands active in the party. What is of some interest is that, even though female engagement in the party was restricted to female sections engaging in issues related to house and home and female and child welfare, even this was seen as a threat to male authority. As women's sections within the party gained more independence, the activity was banned, and after 1911 the holding of national conferences for women was also banned.[26] The struggle for the vote came to be left primarily to middle class feminist organisations like *Deutscher Verband für Frauenstimmrecht*, most prominently engaging in the journal *Zeitschrift für Frauenstimmrecht*, published from 1907 under the editorship of Anita Augsburg and later Minna Cauer.[27]

Right-wing newspapers deplored the lure of the socialists to entice young women away from domestic work within a morally healthy environment in favour of the ruin awaiting them in factories and making them socialists. The stated aim of the German factory laws was to protect the family, to curtail the working day for married women so that they could perform their family duties. The laws did nothing for domestic workers, shop workers or those in agriculture.[28]

In France, the situation within party politics varied from that of the unions. The *Partie Ouvrier Francais* had its base in textile areas with large numbers of female workers. The party never set as its aim to ban female work but incorporated male and female workers as part of the exploited proletariat in its discourse. On the other hand, in their propaganda, the strong male was at the forefront, flanked by his companion, the female in need of protection. The male worker and provider not only provided, but also set out to protect the women against the sexual exploitation of the bourgeois male.[29]

In the late nineteenth century, the feminist movement in Austria promoted their activity through several publications discussing education, female work and suffrage. While some of the working women had been close to one or another of the feminist organisations, the 1890s brought about specific organisations for working women and a parallel system of publications. Women in factory work stood close to the Social Democratic movement even though no female delegates were accepted at the founding meeting of the Party. One of the leaders was Adelheid Popp, a keen activist for protection of workers in factories. In *die Arbeterinnenzeitung*, the 8 hour day for women was often raised, as was the right for women to come together and join organisations and political parties like men. The Austrian situation was additionally complicated

26 Evans, 'Politics and the family', pp. 266, 276.

27 *Zeitschrift für Frauenstimmrecht* (Journal for the right of women to vote) (Berlin, 1907–18).

28 Evans, 'Politics and the family', pp. 259–60.

29 McMillan, *France and Women*, pp. 182–7.

by the existence of Catholic institutions for women, some recruiting among the working class some among the middle class. These organisations tended to emphasise the need for women to appreciate their position as wives, mothers and homemakers and receive protection to fulfil such a position. The idea of the home as a haven was, however, not universally accepted. For example, a contribution to the *Arbeiterinnezeitung* in 1902 highlighted the legal oppression of married women and the wide acceptance of violence by husbands.[30]

The question of the female vote took a meandering route in the late nineteenth century. The older, property-based franchise system did not exclude female property owners, although their numbers were limited. The late nineteenth century saw activity among women's movement like the 'Frauenvereine' and Social Democratic women, to extend the franchise to ordinary women. Demonstrations were arranged and petitions written in the 1890s. However, when a reform of the voting system was approved in 1896, women were excluded from the extension. By 1906 a split had developed between the middle-class and Social Democratic women. Adelheid Popp and others aligned themselves with the Party leadership in giving priority to a universal male vote, to promote the class struggle. Universal male suffrage was introduced in 1906 with the stated exclusion of all women, including the female property owners that previously had had the vote. Women were to be excluded because of their place being in the home and because they were not 'true citizens' who could be conscripted to the army. Not until the passing of the new constitution in 1918 did women gain the right to vote alongside men.[31]

In the parts of Poland that were incorporated in the Austro-Hungarian Empire, women were excluded from political parties and organisations by an act from 1867. This did not stop professional women like school teachers from forming associations and demanding to be heard. The multiple-tier voting system was similar to that in the rest of the empire, with female property owners having the vote in local elections, while professional women did not. Women could not stand for election, only men, and the husbands of married women used the votes of their wives. To be able to vote in national elections one needed to be the owner of substantial landed property if female. In the 1890s, the Social Democratic Party supported an electoral reform that would include votes for women in Galicia. Although the franchise was extended in

---

[30] Irmgard Helperstorfer, 'Die Frauenrechsbewegung und ihre Ziele', in Reingard Witzmann (ed.), *Die Frau im Korsett, Wiener Frauenalltag zwischen Klischee und Wirklichkeit 1848–1920* (Wien, 1985), pp. 21–9, on pp. 24–7; Josef Ehmer, 'Frauenarbeit und Arbeiterfamilie in Wien', in Hans-Ulrich Wehler (ed.), *Frauen in der Geschichte des 19. und 20. Jahrhunderts* (Göttingen, 1981), pp. 438–73, on p. 463; *Arbeiterinnezeitung* 22 (1902), pp. 4–5.

[31] Elisabeth Freismuth, 'Die Frau im öffentlichen Recht', in Witzmann, *Die Frau im Korsett*, pp. 30–40, on pp. 32–7.

1896, women were still excluded. This situation persisted until WWI. The Galician women's movement continued its activity in the suffrage question but also incorporated ideas about patriotism and independence.[32]

Similarly, in Hungary, women were subject to Austrian legislation and prohibited from joining political organisations. Here the efforts were concentrated on gaining access to higher education and entry into the professions. These goals were reached in the 1890s. However, when women were allowed to go to the polls after the end of WWI in 1920, they did not support the progressive and social democratic groups that had worked for an extension of female rights, but instead gave their votes to the conservative Christian National Party.[33]

In 1889, the Social Democratic Worker's Party of Sweden was formed, with a program of socialism and class struggle. A statement at the first party conference firmly established a hierarchical system of women recruited into the party to support the men in their struggle. The lack of interest in the issues of female workers resulted in women running a parallel organisation, starting as the General Club of Women in Stockholm 1892, consisting of female unions and working women but also female intellectuals and activists, with the aim to promote their interests.[34]

One of the early decisions taken by the Worker's Party was to work for universal suffrage for men and women. From 1862, unmarried women and widows had the right to vote in local elections, although not married women. The voting was also linked to the size of local tax paid by individuals, which resulted in women having fever votes. Female organisations and unions saw the vote question as central but this view was not shared by the leaders of the Worker's Party. In 1902, a Liberal member of parliament proposed an extension of the vote to include women, but when the Liberals formed a government in 1905, the prime minister stated that including women in the voting reform would delay the work. Therefore, the Worker's Party decided at their conference that gaining universal male suffrage was to have priority and the issue of the female vote was not to be allowed to delay the process. Despite great dissatisfaction at the grassroots level and demands for a new conference, the line of the party was accepted. At the International Socialist Women's Conference in Copenhagen, 1910, a motion was passed of not cooperating with bourgeois women in the suffrage question, but only with others within the socialist movement. Thereby, the suffrage issue became more or

---

[32] Rudolf Jaworski, 'Galicia: initiatives for the emancipation of Polish women', in Rudolf Jaworski and Bianka Pietrow-Ennker, *Women in Polish Society* (Boulder, 1992), pp. 71–90, on pp. 84–7.

[33] Maria Kovacs, 'The politics of emancipation in Hungary', History Department Working Paper, Series 1, Central European University (Budapest, 1994), pp. 81–8.

[34] Schmitz, *Kvinnor, Kamrater*, pp. 43–7.

less completely handled by the feminist movement, even though the socialist women arranged a yearly 'Woman's Day' when the need for the female vote was raised. Not until 1921 did women in Sweden gain the right to vote.[35]

Early vote success stories

When we analyse the developments that led to women acquiring the vote before WWI, we find that although feminist organisations existed and the need to extend the vote was discussed, it would seem that local conditions and conceptions about citizenship were of a greater importance than radical feminism. It would appear that a combination of internal political struggles and the view of women as companions, coworkers and mothers concerned about the welfare of the nation made it more likely for men to see them as entitled to political power.

The activity for the extension of the vote to women in Australia and New Zealand did not experience the split on class lines we can detect in many European countries. The discourse progressed differently and was closely linked to the debate on alcohol. One of the prime campaigners for the female vote in New Zealand, Kate Sheppard, was a founding member of the Women's Christian Temperance Union, which combined efforts to gain the franchise with social justice and reform. Another active member of the Temperance Union was Harriet Morison, trade unionist, lay preacher for the Bible Christian church, factory inspector from 1906 and founding member of Women's Franchise Legion in 1892.[36]

One might perhaps say that the franchise process had links to the process of establishing a new national identity, better and more enlightened than that of the old motherland. In the debate, the desire to be first and demonstrate a high level of civilization, unity and frontier spirit was voiced.[37]

In New Zealand a movement for women's suffrage commenced its activity in the late 1870s within the parameters of the newly established Liberal Party.

---

[35] Schmitz, *Kvinnor, Kamrater*, pp. 53–9.

[36] Tessa K. Malcolm, 'Sheppard, Katherine Wilson', Dictionary of New Zealand Biography, Te Ara – the Encyclopedia of New Zealand, https://teara.govt.nz/en/biographies/2s20/sheppard-katherine-wilson; Melanie Nolan and Penelope Harper, 'Morison, Harriet', *Dictionary of New Zealand Biography* Te Ara, https://teara.govt.nz/en/biographies (accessed 10 November 2020).

[37] Raewyn Dalziel, 'An experiment in the social laboratory', in Ian Fletcher, Philippa Levine and Laura Mayhall (eds), *Women's Suffrage in the British Empire: Citizenship, Nation and Race* (London, 2012), pp. 87–102; Judith Smart, 'Modernity and mother-heartedness – spirituality and religious meaning in Australian women's suffrage and citizenship movements 1890s–1920s', in Fletcher et al., *Women's Suffrage in the British Empire*, pp. 51–67.

An internal political struggle between conservative large landowners and other groups saw a contribution of the female vote as a potential for a political shift. Although women gained the right to sit on school boards, an inclusion of female taxpayers in the electorate was voted down in 1878. However, by 1883, even the conservatives allowed women to be included in liquor licensing boards. The new Liberal government of 1891 raised the female vote question again and gained the support from the Labour Party, but the proposal was voted down with a small margin by the Conservatives. As women had been active in the prohibition movement for a long time, the Conservative opposition, believing that strong anti-alcohol legislation would strike a blow against the Liberals, decided to back female suffrage in 1893. Therefore, in September 1893 all women in New Zealand were given the right to vote, although not to stand as candidates for the national parliament. The right to stand came after WWI.[38]

In South Australia, the population structure varied from that of some other regions: the population was stable, family oriented and men did not outnumber women to any great extent. The Women's Suffrage League had been active since the 1880s and the temperance movement had strong support among their many female members. Women had found a voice in the new Christian movements linked to Methodists, Baptists and Presbyterians. In this environment the ideology of female charity, compassion and social reform was fostered and women were seen as crucial for the building of the new nation. The Liberal Party as well as the radical liberals and Labour, together with the temperance activists, were in favour of the female vote and after some drawbacks it was achieved in 1895. In Western Australia the conservative farmers resolved to align themselves with other groups in the interest of social stability, and women were awarded the vote in 1899. The project of uniting the Australian colonies into a federation had been on the cards for a long time. By the late 1890s, some progress had been made and work started on a new constitution and, by 1901, the union with a federal parliament was established. In 1902, when the decision had to be taken whether women in the parts of Australia who did not have the vote were to receive it, or whether those who had should be deprived of it, the vote was extended to all Australian women. While women did have the right to vote, it took four decades until the first women entered the federal parliament. In the areas where there had

[38] Ross Evans Paulson, *Women's Suffrage and Prohibition: A Comparative Study of Equality and Social Control* (Glenview, Illinois, 1973), pp. 125–9; https://web.archive.org/web/20130512153424/http://www.abs.gov.au/AU; Megan Cook, 'Women's movement', Te Ara – The Encyclopedia of New Zealand http:// www.TeAra.govt.nz/en/womens-movement/print (accessed 18 November 2021) (published May 2011).

been strong opposition against the female vote, delays of up to 20 years can also be observed until women could become candidates in regional elections.[39]

Furthermore, in Finland, the road to female suffrage had connections to the prohibition movement. The negative aspects of the drink problem were highlighted among working-class women's organisations, religious groups and social reformers. For this reason the movement came to activate people across social and gender barriers. The aims were to create a sober, hard-working nation and in this process the participation of women was vital. This attitude was embodied in Hedvig Gebhard, elected to parliament in 1907 with the slogan 'Unity is Power' and encouraging women as wives and mothers to vote for a woman defending the home and the nation against alcohol[40] The middle-class feminist movement had started its activity in the 1880s but by the end of the century it had split into two. The Finnish Women's Association visualised the female vote as primarily an issue for educated women, while the Union of Women's Rights (1892) dedicated its efforts towards gender equality in education and social reform. In the meantime, the Finnish Worker's Party (founded in 1899) adopted a manifesto of equality between men and women. The party program stated the need for universal suffrage for over-21 year-olds. The rural nature of the country as a whole and the importance of female participation in the agrarian economy created the interesting contradiction of conservative farmers being willing to award women, irrespective of marital status, the vote. On the other hand, hesitance and division could be discerned among the other groups in the estate assembly, although the female efforts within the resistance movement to the Russification efforts of the 1890s were recognised. The general strike of 1905, however, speeded up the process and a reform of the voting system was hammered through. To the surprise of many, a consensus was reached between conservative and radical groups and a proposal for constitutional reform containing universal adult suffrage (men and women) and a parliament with one house or chamber was voted through in 1906. What might seem even more surprising is that the Russian Emperor, in the aftermath of the 1905 uprising, gave this reform his seal of approval. Thereby Finland, although at this time an autonomous part of the Russian Empire and not a sovereign state, became the first country in Europe where all women had the vote.[41]

[39] Evans Paulson, *Women's Suffrage and Prohibition*, pp. 125, 130–1; Marian Sawer, Women and Government in Australia, The Wayback machine https://web.archive.org/web/20130512153424/http://www.abs.gov.au/AU; Smart, 'Modernity and mother-heartedness', pp. 52–6.

[40] Irma Sulkunen, *Raittius kansalais uskontona* (Helsinki, 1986), pp. 270–8.

[41] Irma Sulkunen, 'The General Strike and women's suffrage', http://www.helsinki.fi/sukupuolentutkimus/aanioikeus/en/articles/strike.htm; Irma Sulkunen, 'Paradoksien aanioikeus', in Knapas, Smeds and Stromberg (eds), *Boken on vart land*

In the first election in 1907, out of 200 members of parliament, 19 women were elected. Overall, the Social Democrats got about 40 per cent of the seats, 10 per cent of these were held by women. Of the 60 per cent held by bourgeois parties, 6 per cent were female. In 1926, the first female government minister, Miina Sillanpaa, a founding member of the Servant's Union in the 1890s and a staunch worker for the welfare of illegitimate children, took on the duties of running social affairs.[42]

Conclusion

There is no doubt that the conditions in late nineteenth-century factories were bad, the women and men could see this with their own eyes, and said so. However, what many of the male unions wanted was to eliminate the competition from the female workers and relegate their wives to the home. On the other hand, it would be unfair to claim that all working men had this attitude, just as it would be to say that all working women were dreaming of being housewives without an income of their own.

What women wanted was improvement of their working conditions, humane treatment and better pay. Because of this, they formed their own unions when the men did not welcome them. Activity within the political parties also proved to be a challenge. For a woman to progress she had to adopt the male view, like Clara Zetkin. Male-dominated organisations did not see the need to push for childcare or the female vote. The Social Democratic movement before WWI found a majority to work for male suffrage only, and female suffrage 'later'. This did not mean that the women's organisations within the movement were in agreement, but they were in a minority. Many efforts were made to get their voice heard. The anti-suffragists were not to be found among working women of whatever class, but among men and housewives.

The disinclination of the socialists to listen to female delegates or the female sections in most European countries is also well exemplified in the hostility to family planning, by some viewed as a capitalist plot to diminish the working class. Female moral standards were not only regarded as important by conservative groups but also among working-class males. It cannot be denied that the early activity of the New Malthusians had a tendency to see the need for family limitation as necessary for a working class, rather than their own social group. In some cases the arguments were linked to the need to 'improve the race', which by the working class was seen as criticism of their lifestyle and mores. The socialists hit back by blaming the middle classes for

---

1996 (Helsinki, 1996), pp. 331–9; Evans Paulson, *Women's Suffrage and Prohibition,* pp. 146–51; Beatrice Moring, 'Production without labour market participation', *Historicka demografie* 43/2 (2019), pp. 233–56.

[42] Lähteenmäki, *Mahdollisuuksien aika*, pp. 166–7, 192.

undermining their economy and using and corrupting their women. As contraception tended to be identified by both groups with extra marital sexuality, it suffered from official condemnation and in many countries not only the devices but information about contraception was illegal in the late nineteenth and early twentieth centuries. Surreptitiously, the middle classes embarked on family planning and an underground movement for the spreading of information existed in many countries. However, the working-class housewife, with a large family, tended to be one of the last parties to gain access to contraception, and in desperation, some reverted to the use of illegal abortions.[43] To find the views of women on the issue of work and family matters we have to explore the organisations, sub-organisations and publications run by the women themselves. Likewise, working-class newspapers will not always be the best sources of information as editorial policies could result in censorship in relation to certain subjects.[44]

When women did receive the vote and could be represented by women, we do get an inkling of what women wanted. It is perhaps not surprising to find that one of the things the Social Democrat women worked for in the Finnish Parliament was the abolishment of male legal and economic authority in marriage and support for unmarried mothers. Equally, the plight of single mothers was highlighted by female delegates in countries like Austria when they entered the political arena in the 1920s.

---

[43] Susie Steinbach, *Women in England 1760–1914* (London, 2004), pp. 122–5; Reay Tannahill, *Sex in History* (London, 1981), pp. 398–401; Branca, *Women in Europe since 1750*, pp. 166–7; Abrams, *The Making of Modern Woman*, pp. 164–7; Ingrid Primander, *Elise Ottesen-Jensen-Arbetarrorelsen-Mannens eller Mansklighetens Rorelse?* (Stockholm, 1980), pp. 72–7; Pat Quiggin, *No Rising Generation: Women and Fertility in Late Nineteenth Century Australia* (Canberra, 1988), pp. 104–9; Gittins, *Fair Sex*, pp. 62–5; Schmitz, *Kvinnor, Kamrater*, p. 61. In 1910, a law was passed by the Swedish parliament criminalising all information about contraception. The law was not repealed until 1938.

[44] Primander, *Elise Ottesen-Jensen*, pp. 24–30.

2

Women in Industry: Work, Sectors, Age and Marital Status

In preindustrial Europe, the family was the production unit in crafts and agriculture, particularly while production was on a small scale and the producers were the owners of the means of production. Even in sectors like mining where families hired themselves out to others, the tasks were divided between family members and together one earned a 'family wage'. The capitalisation of agriculture in southern and eastern England and the gradual change of textile production into protoindustrial activity, where those who did the work only owned their skill and ability to work, went hand in hand with the disintegration of the family as a work unit. Over the nineteenth century, the mechanisation not only affected the opportunities of women but an increasing share of women and men became paid workers learning to tend machines rather than skilled craftsmen/women. An issue voiced with considerable concern by William Morris and the members of the Arts and Crafts movement. In Britain, the lack of statistical series registering economic activity before the mid-nineteenth century prevents us from pronouncing anything about the number of women who worked side by side with their husbands in craft shops or even mining. Considering the tendency of statisticians in other countries to only register the occupation of the household head, it is unlikely that we would have been provided with information about the activity of the wife and children even if there were data.

The advent of the mechanisation process and the opportunities to employ women and children only, and not together with a male household head, resulted in the rise of new problems and eventually the decision that the state needed to intervene and create protective legislation. Why? Because when these groups were no longer supervised by a father/husband, his replacement, the factory overseer, became the person with the right to disciplinary action. In addition, the factory owners introduced such a multitude of economic sanctions that only the lack of other feasible options could make such work attractive. With a population short of land or capital, a factory system of an unpleasant nature could be the only option for survival for members of the proletariat. The fact that GDP in countries on the European continent indicate a lower standard of living than England is linked to the fact that an agricultural sector with a high level of in-house production remained present in these countries.

By the end of the nineteenth century, urbanisation and industrialisation was firmly established in most European countries. Despite the difference in population size of European countries, with capitals like Berlin having a population of more than 2 million in 1900, London 6 million and Paris 3 million, while Stockholm boasted only 250,000 inhabitants and Helsinki 100,000, the problems of industrialisation had reached every one of these countries. The industrial areas increased at an explosive rate: in 1880, Barcelona had more than 300,000 inhabitants and by 1910 more than 500,000; Manchester, 340,000 in 1880 and 714,000 in 1910. Even the Nordic countries, where towns of a couple of thousand inhabitants were common, sported industrial centres such as Tampere, with almost 40,000 people in 1901. The employment opportunities in textile factories, metalwork, machine industry and sectors furnishing urban centres with the necessary services and goods provided new options for young people. Moving to find work became the norm, and industrial populations were often migrants.[1]

Unlike the urban craftsman, the industrial worker was no longer a specialist, although employment could often be secured. Low-paid shift work, seasonal unemployment and a segregated labour market were the downside of urban life. While the poor families in rural areas of Northern and Central Europe in many cases had been able to keep some animals or engage in household production, this was not the case in most towns and wage work outside the home was often necessary. Industrial work was increasingly available for women, but married women and widows with young children could encounter problems in working full time, and some suffered the unwelcome consequences of protective legislation.[2]

---

[1]   Paul Bairoch, 'Villes et développement économique dans une perspective historique', in Anne-Lise Head-König, Luigi Lorenzetti and Beatrice Veyrassat (eds), *Famille, parenté et réseaux en Occident* (Genève, 2001), pp. 263–83, on p. 268; Sten Carlsson and Jerker Rosen, *Svensk Historia 2* (Stockholm, 1970), pp. 466–7; *Statistisk årsbok for Helsingfors 1908* (Helsingfors, 1910), pp. 95, 101; Johan Leffler, *Zur Kenntniss von den Lebens und Lohnverhältnissen Industrieller Arbeiterinnen in Stockholm* (Stockholm, 1897), pp. 15–19, 25, 137; Christina Borderias, 'Women's work and household economic strategies in industrializing Catalonia', *Social History* 29:3 (August 2004), pp. 373–83, on p. 378; Pertti Haapala, *Tehtaan valossa* (Tampere, 1986), pp. 364–5.

[2]   Sakari Heikkinen, *Labour and the Market* (Helsinki, 1997), pp. 85, 160; Pirjo Markkola, *Työläiskodin synty* (Helsinki, 1994), pp. 107, 110; Beatrice Moring, 'Widows, children and assistance from society in urban Northern Europe 1890–1910', *The History of the Family* 13:1 (2008), pp. 105–17, on pp. 106–7; Beatrice Moring, 'Strategies and networks: family earnings and institutional contributions to women's households in urban Sweden and Finland 1890–1910', in Tindara Addabo, Marie-Pierre Arrizabalaga,

From family to factory

In preindustrial times, the family was generally viewed as a production unit, with the male household head as the representative in society, but with the expectation that all household members participated in the activity. Therefore, locating economic statistics revealing information about female economic engagement can be difficult. While task sharing on a family farm can be reasonably comprehensible, the same organisational model has not necessarily been accepted as existing within other fields of activity. However, at a community level, some calculations have been made capturing considerable female activity levels for the eighteenth and early nineteenth centuries.[3] Before the 1840s, the participation of whole families in British mining was far from unusual. The middle classes, however, objected to women working in mines and the Children's Employment Commission (1840) highlighted the physical and moral problem of women in the mines. By 1842, The Mines Act banned female and child underground work, and family activity had to be restricted to the surface. New heavy industries, such as the railroads, electricity and iron and steel production tended to engage males exclusively.[4]

Textile production has traditionally been seen as part of the female domain but historically, particularly in areas of guild regulation, the family could collaborate and practice task division, although the male household head was the crafts master. For example, women, children and the old were washing wool, carding and spinning whereas men engaged in weaving and dyeing cloth. Spinning could be combined with household duties and was therefore seen as a suitable activity for women. Before mechanisation a lot of spinners

---

Christina Borderias and Alastair Owens (eds), *Gender Inequalities, Households and the Production of Well-Being in Modern Europe* (London, 2010), pp. 77–94, on pp. 82–5.

3   Ivy Pinchbeck, *Women Workers and the Industrial Revolution 1750–1850* (London, 1930), pp. 1–2; Bridget Hill, *Women, Work and Sexual Policy in Eighteenth Century England* (London, 1994), pp. 28–9, 48; Pamela Sharpe, 'The female labour market in English agriculture during the industrial revolution: expansion or contraction?', in Nigel Goose (ed.), *Women's Work in Industrial England* (Hertfordshire, 2007), pp. 51–75, on pp. 52–4; Robert B. Shoemaker, *Gender in English Society 1650–1850* (Harlow, 1998), pp. 151–3; Richard Wall 'Some implications of the earnings and expenditure patterns of married women in populations of the past', in John Henderson and Richard Wall (eds), *Poor Women and Children in the European Past* (London, 1994), pp. 312–35, on pp. 326–8.

4   Ellen Jordan, 'The exclusion of women from industry in 19th century Britain', *Comparative Studies in Society and History* 31 (1989), pp. 273–96, on pp. 276, 287, 295; Angela John, *By the Sweat of Their Brow: Women Workers in Victorian Coal Mines* (London, 1980), pp. 21–5, 55–7, 78; Jane Mark-Lawson and Anne Witz, 'From family labour to "family wage"? The case of women's labour in 19th century coalmining', *Social History* 13 (1988), pp. 151–74, on p. 167.

were needed and this did provide extra income for women. In England, the linen industry employed fewer men than the woollen industry, where men were combing, dressing, shearing and dyeing. After the introduction of broad silk weaving in late seventeenth-century London, men had a virtual monopoly on weaving, assisted by women and children. The decline in apprenticeship regulation and the introduction of smaller looms provided opportunities for women to weave wool, linen, silk and cotton. Framework knitting was usually practiced by men, while the wife was winding the yarn, filling the shuttles and finishing the stockings. However, by the eighteenth century, framework knitting was increasingly also practised by women and children.[5]

The introduction of machines in the textile sector from the 1760s reduced the demand for hand spinning. The spinning mule created factory work for men as did the Jacquard loom and the Dutch engine loom. As technology improved, employers started to use women to cut production costs. Men were employed on different processes or as supervisors and mechanics, receiving higher wages. The early decades of the nineteenth century saw the workforce in England dominated by young persons and women. The woollen mills of the West Riding of Yorkshire had more than 50 per cent of workers who were under 21 years old. In the 1830s, the cotton industry employed 65,000 women and 60,000 men. In 1844, the Factory commissioner stated that 'a vast majority of the persons employed at night and for long hours during the day are females. Their labour is cheaper, and they are more easily induced to undergo severe bodily fatigue than men'. After 1850, more females were employed, but many married women often performed textile work at home within the 'putting-out' sector, making lace or gloves, knitting stockings and practicing handloom weaving.[6]

Continental Europe

On the European continent the family collaborated in agricultural work but the crafts were also family enterprises. In urban areas like Vienna the production of luxury goods had an important position within the local economy. By the late eighteenth century, one-fifth of all occupational activity was linked to protoindustrial silk manufacture, mostly based on household production. While

---

5   Peter Earle, *A City Full of People* (London, 1994), pp. 116, 118; Maxine Berg, 'Women's work, mechanisation and the early phases of industrialisation in England', in P. Joyce (ed.), *Historical Meanings of Work* (Cambridge, 1987), pp. 64–98, on pp. 71, 74, 80; Pamela Sharpe, *Adapting to Capitalism: Working Women in the English Economy 1700–1850* (New York, 1996), p. 33; Amy Ericson, 'Married women's occupations in 18th century London', *Continuity and Change* 23:2 (2008), pp. 267–308.

6   Eric Richards, 'Women in the English economy since 1700', *History* 59 (1974), pp. 337–57, on p. 346; Pat Hudson, 'Proto-industrialisation: the case of West Riding', *History Workshop Journal* 12 (1981), pp. 34–61, on pp. 60–1.

a large part of the female work was concentrated to winding, spooling and other aiding activities, it was not unheard of for women to engage in actual silk weaving. In 1807, the sources even document an active independent female master silk weaver. Little is known about exactly which tasks were handled by wives of masters and journeymen, but there is ample documentation about the necessity of their contributions.[7]

In high-skill occupations, like French silk weaving and silk ribbon manufacture, the wife had a particularly important position for successful enterprise and economic survival. The silk weavers in early nineteenth-century Saint Chamond married the daughters of silk weavers. These women had trained from their early years both in assisting with the work and running the business. Many French lace makers were the wives and daughters of farmers and their activity was viewed by economists, not as an occupation, but as supplementary activity undertaken during the slack period of the agricultural year. In actual fact, all work in the French lace making industry, except the trade in lace and the making of patterns, was executed by females.[8]

Where the family economy was based both on agriculture and protoindustrial activity finding information about the female input is often difficult. In nineteenth-century Saxony, smallholders engaged in hand loom weaving. Although originally a male occupation, the tasks were increasingly handled by women, while men sought occasional work around the region. In the latter part of the century the weaver could officially be the husband but the work was undertaken by the wife, as was peddling the finished product.[9] The share cropping families of northern Italy combined agriculture with protoindustry. Not only did the farmers engage in silk worm production but the wives worked in silk reeling and winding silk onto spindles, originally in their own homes, or later, when manufacturing was concentrated, on premises owned by the employer.[10]

In northern Spain, women were an important part of the protoindustrial textile activity within the boundary of the family. As in Germany, we also

---

7   Josef Ehmer, 'Frauenarbeit und Arbeiterfamilie in Wien', in Hans-Ulrich Wehler (ed.), *Frauen in der Geschichte des 19. und 20. Jahrhunderts* (Göttingen, 1981), pp. 438–73, on pp. 443–4.

8   Elinor Accampo, *Industrialization, Family Life and Class Relations: Saint Chamond, 1815–1914* (Berkeley, 1989), pp. 21–7; Olwen Hufton, *The Prospect Before Her* (New York, 1996), pp. 168–9; John F. Sweets, 'The lacemakers of Le Puy in the nineteenth century', in Daryl M. Hafter (ed.), *European Women and Pre-Industrial Craft* (Bloomington, 1995), pp. 67–86, on pp. 71–4.

9   Jean H. Quataert, 'Survival strategies in a Saxon textile district during the early phases of industrialization', in Daryl M. Hafter (ed.), *European Women and Pre-Industrial Craft* (Bloomington, 1995), pp. 153–78, on pp. 164–9.

10   Patrizia Sione, 'From home to factory: women in the nineteenth-century Italian silk industry', in Daryl M. Hafter (ed.), *European Women and Pre-Industrial Craft* (Bloomington, 1995), pp. 137–52.

find examples of a division of labour, with male agricultural work and female textile work in the vicinity of urban and semi-urban centres. However, what seems particularly interesting is that, with the change to industrial textile enterprises during the nineteenth century, female participation seemed to intensify, and marriage did not necessarily terminate the occupational careers of women. In some locations the increase in family size and the attainment of working age by several children had an impact on factory work by married women. On the other hand examples are also available of the use of the extended family as a solution to childcare problems. This was particularly common when the earnings of the wife were central to the wellbeing of the family.[11]

Registration of the work of women

The nineteenth century is a time of paradoxes in relation to women and work. On the one hand, trade regulations were eased, and women allowed access to fields previously closed to them. Changes in legislation also made it possible for women to participate in economic life, and during the second part of the century, the right of married women to control their assets and earnings gained legal backing. The expansion of industrial work, at the expense of family based traditional handicrafts, also opened up employment opportunities for women and children, as registered nonskilled workers. In parallel with this development we find, however, an ideological onslaught against female work. The process was linked to the increasing political importance of the bourgeoisie, and a continuing discourse promoting an idealised image of women as homemakers and existing within a separate sphere. The view that the separate sphere ideology was not only a theoretical ideal but depicted reality has been accepted by many historians.[12]

There are many conflicting views on whether the Industrial Revolution increased the female employment opportunities in Britain, or if the result was

[11] Borderias, 'Women's work and household economic strategies', pp. 373–83, on p. 379; Enriqueta Camps, 'Transitions in women's and children's work patterns and implications for the study of family income and household structure: a case study from the Catalan textile sector (1850–1925)', *The History of the Family* III:2 (1998), pp. 137–53; Alós Llorenç Ferrer, 'Notas sobre la familia y el trabajo de la mujer en la Catalunya Central (siglos XVIII–XX)', *Boletin de la Asociación de Demografia Histórica* XII:2–3 (1994), pp. 199–232; Nicolau Roser, 'Trabajo asalariado, formación y constitución de la familia. La demanda de trabajo en la colonia textil Sedó y los comportamientos demograficos de la población, 1850–1930', dissertation, Autonomous University of Barcelona (Barcelona, 1983); Montserrat Llonch Casanovas, 'Insercion laboral de la immigracion y sistema de reclutamiento de la fabrica textil: Vilassar de Dalt, 1910–1945', *Boletin de la Asociación de Demografia Histórica* XII:2–3 (1994), pp. 149–61.

[12] Leonore Davidoff and Catherine Hall, *Family Fortunes: Men and Women of the English Middle Class 1780–1850* (London, 1987), pp. 279–80, 312–13; Shoemaker, *Gender in English Society 1650–1850*, pp. 113–15.

a shrinking female labour market. The censuses seem to indicate that there was little change in the registered part of women in employment between 1870 and 1930, what happened between 1750 and 1870 is less clear. It has been argued that growing intensification and capitalism tends to lead to exclusion of women. It would also seem that the south east of England, in particular, experienced a constricting labour market for women. On the other hand, it has been suggested that the nineteenth century brought universally negative attitudes to married women's work and as a consequence women worked on the sly in their homes in the sweated trades, invisible and unrecorded.[13]

Censuses have received serious critique as sources of information about female productivity. The exploration of alternative sources, like wage lists, family budgets, trade directories and licenses as well as tax lists paint a different picture. A considerable amount of female work would not have been registered by census takers, but it still had an important impact on the family economy.[14]

If we look at the censuses and the series of economic statistics we find a number of differences between females in registered employment in Europe. One reason is the variation in registration and age barriers; another, changes introduced for the definition of work and occupation. The definition of occupation was, in most cases, permanent work outside the home. Therefore, women in England who made a vital contribution to the rural economy, particularly in places like Kent, in the form of hop picking and fruit picking, were never registered as in occupation, i.e. tons of fruit apparently picked itself and magically appeared on the market. Such rules naturally also contributed to the low percentages of women registered as engaged in agriculture.[15]

While the importance of the agricultural sector as an employer had been radically reduced in England already by the time of the first reliable censuses, it remained important in the rest of Europe. The nature of the agricultural enterprises also varied considerably. While certain regions had moved towards

[13] Roberts, *Women's Work*, pp. 14–22; Rachel Fuchs and Victoria Thompson, *Women in 19th Century Europe* (London/New York, 2005), pp. 61, 75–7; Shoemaker, *Gender in English Society*, pp. 306–10.

[14] Edward Higgs, 'Women's occupations and work in the nineteenth century censuses', *History Workshop Journal* 23 (1987), pp. 59–82; Roberts, *Women's Work*, pp. 18–21; Nicola Verdon, *Rural Women Workers in 19th Century England* (London, 2002), pp. 117–19.

[15] Ehmer, 'Frauenarbeit und Arbeiterfamilie', p. 440; Gilda O'Neill, *Lost Voices: Memories of a Vanished Way of Life* (London, 2006), pp. 16–20, 23–4; Nicola Verdon, 'Hay, hops and harvest: women's work in agriculture in nineteenth century Sussex', in Nigel Goose (ed.), *Women's Work in Industrial England* (Hertfordshire, 2007), pp. 76–96; Pinchbeck, *Women Workers*, pp. 58–63; Jane Humphries and Jacob Weisdorf, 'The wages of women in England 1260–1850', *Oxford Economic and Social History Working Papers* 33 (Oxford, 2014); Jane Humphries and Benjamin Schneider, 'Spinning the Industrial Revolution', *Discussion Paper in Economic and Social History* 145 (University of Oxford, June 2016).

ever larger arable units, others still remained firmly part of a system of family farms with mixed economic activities. Where the family still retained its position as a productive unit, women were indeed working, but the view that the male household head and agricultural servants were the only productive persons resulted in the statistics not recognising them as economically active.[16] Therefore, an improvement in registration or a change in the definition of 'active' could have a radical impact on the proportion of females in the labouring population. In Finland, the change in the economic statistics from 1880 to include daughters over 15 working on the parental farm, as assisting household members, improved information about female work. The wives of farmers were accepted by the statisticians as assisting in 1920, but were not registered as in full time work until 1950. Even so, these improvements make it possible to correct existing figures, showing an increase of the female share of the active population from 30 to 41 per cent and in the activity of females over 15 from 48 to 56 per cent. In France, the wives of farmers were not registered as working in 1901 but were included among the occupationally active in 1906, which increased the figures of numbers of working women by nearly a million (Table 2.1).[17]

Table 2.1   Registered active female population in France (in millions) and percentages.

	All sectors	% of active females	Non-agriculture	% of active females
1866	4.643	30	2.768	33.8
1881	5.362	32.5	2.970	34.4
1896	6.419	33.8	3.651	34.8
1901	6.804	34.5	4.142	36
1906	7.693	37	4.356	36.6
1911	7.719	37	4.491	36

Source: James F. McMillan, *France and Women 1789–1914, Gender, Society and Politics* (London, 2000).

[16] Christina Borderias, *Entre líneas: trabajo e identidad femenina en la España contemporánea la Compañía Telefónica, 1924–1980* (Barcelona, 1993), p. 19.

[17] Kaarina Vattula, 'Kvinnors förvärvsarbete i Norden under 100 år 1870–1970', *Studia Historica Jyväskyläensia* 27 (Jyvaskyla, 1983), pp. 35–51, on pp. 38–9; Kaarina Vattula, 'Lähtöviivallako? Naisten ammatissatoimivuudesta, tilastoista ja kotitaloudesta', in Leena Laine and Pirjo Markkola (eds), *Tuntematon työläisnainen* (Tampere, 1989), pp. 13–38, on pp. 21–2; McMillan, *France and Women*, pp. 160–1.

Generally, the registration of industrial work is more reliable, partly because of the interest by the authorities in this economic sector. Even here, however, there have been examples of defective collection of information.[18]

Although there was a tendency to work until you dropped in the nineteenth century, it has still been demonstrated that, even using the self-reporting in censuses, older men in Britain retired, or were forced out of the labour force at older ages. There is also evidence that in late nineteenth- and early twentieth-century England and Germany the earning capacity of the male manual and industrial worker was to a large extent linked to age and dropped radically between the ages of 40 and 60. Therefore, economic input from wives and children was necessary for family survival.[19] Despite the tendency to push women into hidden fields like home work, the registered share of adult females in employment in many European countries remained around 30 per cent and increased in France as well as Germany from the 1890s to the early 1900s.[20]

Female work in figures

Whichever way one wants to look at the development, industrialisation was a fact and every year the industrial populations increased. In England, with a head start, 1895 saw 3.5 million people working in factories, and 1907, 5.1 million. In 1891, the female textile workers numbered 500,000, and in 1911, 530,000 in England and Wales.[21]

[18] Roberts, *Women's Work*, p. 19; Borderias, 'Women's work and household economic strategies', p. 381.

[19] Matthew Woollard, 'The employment and retirement of older men 1851–1881', *Continuity and Change* 17:3 (2002), pp. 437–64; Paul Johnson, 'Age, gender and the wage in Britain 1830–1930', in Peter Scholliers and Leonard Schwartz, *Experiencing Wages: Social and Cultural Aspects of Wage Forms in Europe since 1500* (New York, 2003), pp. 229–50, on pp. 238–41; Heilwig Schomerus, 'The family life-cycle: a study of factory workers in 19th century Württenberg', in Evans and Lee, *The German Family*, pp. 175–93, on pp. 186–8.

[20] McMillan, *France and Women,* pp. 160–2; Robyn Dasey, 'Women's work and the family: women garment workers in Berlin and Hamburg before the First World War', in Evans and Lee, *The German Family*, pp. 221–55, on pp. 228–31; R. Gonnard, *La femme dans l'industrie* (Paris, 1906), pp. 32, 35–6, 52; Enriqueta Camps, *La Formación del Mercado de Trabajo Industrial en la Cataluña del Siglo XIX* (Madrid, 1995), pp. 165–6, 192, 214–15; Lily Braun, *Die Frauenfrage: ihre geschichtliche Entwicklung und wirtschaftliche Seite* (Berlin, 1901).

[21] Dora L. Costa, 'From mill town to board room: the rise of women's paid labor', *Journal of Economic Perspectives* 14:4 (2000), pp. 101–22, on p. 106; Roberts, *Women's Work*, p. 34.

A look at the official figures for the female participation rates in late nineteenth- and early twentieth-century Europe reveals a general tendency of increase among female registered workers. In France we find an increase in the female share of the active population from 30 to 37 per cent between 1866 and 1911. In Germany and Austria there was a considerable increase in both male and female industrial workers from the 1880s to the 1890s and continuing up to WWI, although the agrarian sector was still important. Even in Russia, industrialisation was making its mark as an employer of women, and in 1911, 28 per cent of industrial workers in Australia were women. The fairly low registered female participation rates in the USA raises the question of whether we are dealing with the problem of hidden work within the household and family enterprise or actual numbers.[22]

It is, however, interesting to find that by the late nineteenth century the numbers of women in employment in France and Germany were as high as or higher than in England. In addition, the numbers of women in industry and in some cases the proportion of female workers in general was as high or higher on the continent as in the cradle of the industrial revolution (Table 2.2).

Table 2.2   Number of women registered as occupationally active and their share of the working population in Britain, France, Germany, New Zealand, Russia and the USA.

	Women active	% of working population	Women in industry	% of workers in industry
France 1896	6.4 million	33.8		36
Germany 1895	6.5 million	29.8	1.5 million	18.4
Britain 1891	4.4 million	31	1.5 million	35
USA 1890				18.4
New Zealand 1896				25
France 1906	7.6 million	37	1.8 million	35
Germany 1907	9.4 million	33.8	2.1 million	18.7
Britain 1901	4.7 million	29		
Russia 1910			0.6 million	32
USA 1910	7.0 million	20		

[22]   Braun, *Die Frauenfrage*; Margarete Grandner, 'Special labor protection for women in Austria 1860–1918', in Ulla Wikander, Alice Kessler-Harris and Jane Lewis (eds), *Protecting Women: Labour Legislation in Europe, the United States and Australia 1880–1920* (Urbana, 1995), pp. 150–81, on p. 169; Renate Howe, 'A paradise for working men but not working women: women's wagework and protective legislation in Australia 1890–1914', in Wikander et al., *Protecting Women*, pp. 318–35, on p. 319.

Sources: James F. McMillan, *France and Women 1789–1914, Gender, Society and Politics* (London, 2000), pp. 160–1; Eilidh Garrett, 'The dawning of a new era? Women's work in England and Wales at the turn of the twentieth century', in Nigel Goose (ed.), *Women's Work in Industrial England* (Hertfordshire, 2007), pp. 314–62, on pp. 322, 325; *German History in Documents and Images, Forging an Empire: Bismarckian Germany 1866–1890*, Table: Gainfully employed persons and their dependents by economic sector, pp. 1–2; Statistisches Jahrbuch für das Deutsche Reich (Berlin, 1895), Statistisches Amt; Statistisches Jahrbuch für das Deutsche Reich (Berlin, 1907), Statistisches Amt; Deborah Simonton, *A History of European Women's Work* (London, 1998), p. 223; R. Gonnard, *La femme dans l'industrie* (Paris, 1906), pp. 52–3, 160–2; Rose Glickman, *Russian Factory Women: Workplace and Society 1880–1914* (Berkeley, 1984), p. 83; Lynn Weiner, *From Working Girl to Working Mother* (Chapel Hill, 1985), p. 4; Annie McLean, 'Factory Legislation for Women in the United States', The American Journal of Sociology (1897–8), pp. 183–205, on p. 186; Melanie Nolan, 'Hawthorne, Margaret, Jane Scott', Dictionary of New Zealand, Biography-Te Ara.

On the continent, the agricultural sector still remained a major source of employment for women, but their presence was being felt in trade and industry. Even in countries with a heavy reliance on agriculture, like Denmark, there was an increase of the industrial workforce both male and female between 1897 and 1906, resulting in about 50,000 women being engaged in industrial work in the early twentieth century. However, the share of females in industry shows considerable variation in the Nordic countries, with Denmark and Finland having a comparatively large share of female industrial workers in relation to Sweden (Table 2.3).

Table 2.3   The female share of the registered occupationally active population in the Nordic countries, percentages.

	1880	1890	1900	1910	1920	Industry
Denmark	28	30	35	34	30	30 (1906)
Norway	33	35	35	35	28	23 (1912)
Sweden	28	28	33	27	30	17 (1913)
Finland	38	37		38	41	30 (1913)

Source: Kaarina Vattula, 'Kvinnors forvärvsarbete i Norden under 100 år 1870–1970', *Studia Historica Jyväskyläensia* 27 (Jyvaskyla, 1983), pp. 35–51, tables 1–3.

A closer examination of the sectors where we find large percentages of women reveals unsurprising gender-specific lines of division. Women often sought employment in the textile industry, garment production and the food and drinks industry, as well as retail and hospitality. In Germany the textile, garments and food and drink industries gave work to 4 million women in 1905. By the first years of the twentieth century, we find a high level of female engagement in French industry although agriculture still remained a sizable sector. Unsurprisingly, also here the textile and garment industries accounted for a large proportion of the female workers (Table 2.4). Even in fairly different corners of Europe, the images of female industrial and commercial activity retain similar traits (Austria, Finland, Britain and Russia, Table 2.5).[23]

Table 2.4   The female share of workers in specific sectors in Germany and France in millions and percentages.

Sector	Germany Women 1895	%	France Women 1905	%
Agriculture	2.7	33.2	2.7	32.6
Industry	1.5	18.4	1.8	34.4
Trade	0.58	24.8	0.57	35.6
Domestic service	1.5	87.4	0.7	77.2
Civil service, etc.	0.17	12.4	0.10	15.1
Total	6.5	29.8	6.3	34.6

Sources: *German History in Documents and Images, Forging an Empire: Bismarckian Germany 1866–1890*, Table: Gainfully employed persons and their dependents by economic sector, pp. 1–2; Statistisches Jahrbuch für das Deutsche Reich (Berlin, 1895), Statistisches Amt; R. Gonnard, *La femme dans l'industrie* (Paris, 1906), pp. 32–8, 44; Statistisches Jahrbuch für das Deutsche Reich (Berlin, 1899), Statistisches Amt; Statistisches Jahrbuch für das Deutsche Reich (Berlin, 1907), Statistisches Amt.

With 1.5 million women in manufacture in Britain in the 1890s, the remarkable thing was that an even larger number was engaged in domestic service. While Germany had 2 million more women in registered employment in the last decade of the nineteenth century, the number of female domestic servants was no higher and in France the levels were radically lower.[24] Certainly some of this could be explained by the presence of agricultural work, but there is also the possibility of regional differences. For example, in Spain a look at the regional distribution of female participation in the official labour market demonstrates that where the opportunities for industrial work

[23] Gonnard, *La femme dans l'industrie*, pp. 52–3, 160–2' Riitta Hjerppe and Per Schybergson, *Kvinnoarbetare i industrins genombrottsskede 1850–1913*, Institute of Economic and Social History, University of Helsinki (Helsinki, 1977), pp. 5–8; Grandner, 'Special labor protection', pp. 150–81, on p. 169; Eilidh Garrett, 'The dawning of a new era? Women's work in England and Wales at the turn of the twentieth century', in Nigel Goose (ed.), *Women's Work in Industrial England* (Hertfordshire, 2007), pp. 314–62, on p. 325.

[24] Nigel Goose, 'Working women in industrial England', in Goose, *Women's Work*, pp. 1–28, on p. 9; Roberts, *Women's Work*, p. 31; *German History in Documents and Images, Forging an Empire: Bismarckian Germany 1866–1890*, Table: Gainfully employed persons and their dependents by economic sector, pp. 1–2; Gonnard, *La femme dans l'industrie*, pp. 32–8, 44.

were more limited, as in the south, working as a servant tended to be one of the few options. We can also see that in such areas overall female participation rates seem to have been much lower.[25] The situation was not totally unlike that in Britain, where the employment opportunities for women show considerable regional variation. The textile areas of Lancashire had a very different profile, particularly in relation to the eastern and south-eastern areas, where going into service was the main alternative for women wanting to work.[26]

Table 2.5   The female share of the workforce in certain sectors in Finland, Austria, Britain and Russia, early twentieth century, percentages.

Sectors	Finland 1913	Austria 1910	Britain 1911	Russia 1910
Tobacco	86			
Textile	70	53	58	52
Garment	50		66	
Chemical	45	27	23	33
Paper	30	28	36*	26
Printing	25			
Drinks	30			
Food	30	26	28	20

Note: *Britain 1911: Paper and printing.
Sources: Riitta Hjerppe and Per Schybergson, *Kvinnoarbetare i industrins genombrottsskede 1850–1913* (Helsinki, 1977), pp. 5–8; Margarete Grandner, 'Special labor protection for women in Austria 1860–1918', in Ulla Wikander, Alice Kessler-Harris and Jane Lewis (eds), *Protecting Women: Labour Legislation in Europe, the United States and Australia 1880–1920* (Urbana, 1995), pp. 150–81, on p. 169; Eilidh Garrett, 'The dawning of a new era? Women's work in England and Wales at the turn of the twentieth century', in Nigel Goose (ed.), *Women's Work in Industrial England* (Hertfordshire, 2007), pp. 314–62, on p. 325; Rose Glickman, *Russian Factory Women* (Berkeley, 1984), p. 80.

As everywhere, industrial development required certain prerequisites to thrive. Industrialisation tended not to develop in a geographically uniform way, on the contrary, regional concentration was more common. Not everybody is acquainted with the fact that both Spanish and Italian industrial development, particularly in textiles, had a highly regional basis. In the nineteenth century, the main industrial centres were located in the north in both countries.[27]

---

[25]   Rosa Maria Capel Martinez, 'Mujer y trabajo en España de Alfonso XIII', in R.M. Capel Martinez (ed.), *Mujer y Sociedad en España 1700–1775* (Madrid, 1982), pp. 207–40, on p. 216.

[26]   Gittins, *Fair Sex*, pp. 95–8.

[27]   Antonio Parejo, 'De la región a la ciudad. Un nuevo enfoque de la historia

The textile industry, with considerable opportunities for women, was particularly well represented in Catalonia, in actual fact we find that of 50,000 women working in textiles within Spain, no less than 40,000 were active in Catalonia (Table 2.6). However, small towns elsewhere in the north also made it possible for women to find factory work. In the late nineteenth century, northwest small towns operated industrial establishments with a workforce of 40 per cent women and in San Sebastian the tobacco factory gave permanent work to hundreds of women. Finding factory work for the women of the family usually saved the household from economic hardship.[28] The textile industry has a history, not only as an employer of women, but also one that saw many children in its ranks, particularly in the mid-nineteenth century.[29] A look at the female employment situation in Spain in general shows radically different patterns between the north and south, with low levels of female employment in the south and such employment primarily in the service sector, i.e. work as a domestic servant. This can be seen as part of the nineteenth-century trend of feminisation of the servant profession in England, France and Spain.[30]

Table 2.6   Male and female industrial work in Spain 1910.

Industrial work					
Spain	**Men**	**Women**	**Catalonia**	**Men**	**Women**
1910	561,700	177,500	1910	138,118	62,860
	76%	24%		69%	31%
Textile industry					
1910	75,413	50,290	1910	51,592	40,104
	60%	40%		56.3%	43.7%
Percentage of all workers working in the textile sector	13.4	28.3		37.3	63.8

industrial Española contemporànea', *Historia Industrial* 30:1 (2006), pp. 52–102, on pp. 66–70; Montserrat Llonch Casanovas, *Tejiendo en red. La industria del género de punto en Cataluña 1891–1936* (Barcelona, 2007), p. 141.

[28] Llonch Casanovas, *Tejiendo en red*, pp. 140–1; Lola Valverde Lamfus, 'Survival strategies of poor women in two localities in Guipuzcoa in the nineteenth and twentieth centuries', in Beatrice Moring (ed.), *Female Strategies in the Modern World* (London, 2012), pp. 33–44, on p. 39.

[29] Ferrer Alós, 'Notas sobre la familia', pp. 199–232, on pp. 206–11.

[30] Capel Martinez, 'Mujer y trabajo en España de Alfonso XIII', pp. 213–16; Carmen Sarasua, *Criados, nodrizas y amos, el servicio doméstico en la formación del mercado de trabajo madrileño 1758–1868* (Madrid, 1994), pp. 42–3.

Source: Montserrat Llonch Casanovas, *Tejiendo en red. La industria del género de punto en Cataluña 1891–1936* (Barcelona, 2007), p. 141.

Interestingly enough, there are similarities in the industrial location patterns of Italy: a high concentration of activity in the north, particularly for textile industries, and consequently regionally diverging patterns in female employment structure. In the late nineteenth and early twentieth centuries, female labour force participation varied from 56 per cent in the northern industrial region to 17 per cent in Sicily in the south.[31] Three out of four women in Italian industry worked in textiles and the heartland of textiles was to be found in Lombardy and surrounding areas. The notion of disciplined factory work seems to have penetrated the region in the sense that the working year was registered as longer in the north than the south.[32]

Table 2.7   Women and industrial work in Italy.

Italy 1905	Female Workers		Female Workers
Industrial work	414,236	Textile industry	321,022
Of industry workers	50%	Garment	21,709
Lombardy	219,665	Other industry	77,505
Piemont	83,496		
Venice	50,412		

Source: R. Gonnard, *La femme dans l'industrie* (Paris, 1906), pp. 54–5.

The phenomenon of the attraction of the textile industry to female workers can also be detected in other parts of Europe. Certain regions had little to offer but agricultural or service work, with meagre earnings. However, where available, the more stable earnings in industry and the chances of getting employment in the textile sector made its mark in employment statistics. In Hungary, for example, although only 21 per cent of the industrial workers were women, more than half of those in the textile industry were female. Similarly in Poland the difference between women in employment and women working in textiles is clear to be seen (Table 2.8).

[31] Giulia Manchini, *Women's Labour Force Participation in Italy 1861–2016* (Rome, 2017), HB Working Paper Series, n. 8, pp. 20–2, 66–7.
[32] Gonnard, *La femme dans l'industrie*, pp. 54–5 (working days per year: Liguria and Piedmont 282, Lombardy 265, Veneto-Emilia 259, central Italy 252, in the south 245).

Table 2.8   The female share of the employed in Poland and Hungary, late nineteenth and early twentieth centuries.

Females	1904–8	1904–8	1904–8	1901
	Galicia	Bialystok	Congress Kingdom	Hungary
Textile industry	35%	42%	49%	57%
All industry			33%	21%
Of all employed 1897			23.7%	

Note: The numbers from Hungary only relate to inspected factories and workplaces.
Sources: Anna Zarnowska and Elzbeieta Kaczynska, 'Market related work and household work: proletarian women in Poland in the 19th century', in Erik Aerts, Paul Klep, Jurgen Kocka and Marina Thornborg (eds), *Women in the Labour Force* (Leuven, 1990), pp. 80–9, on p. 81; Rosita Schwimmer, 'Berichte der ungarischen Gewerbeinspektion', *Arbeiterinnenzeitung* 22 (1902), pp. 5–6.

Women and work, marital status, age and occupation

While the early phases of industrialisation saw the engagement of large numbers of children in industrial work, the introduction of legislation about age of work, working hours, conditions, etc. resulted in changes in the composition of the work force. One should also remember that the first sector subject to regulations was industry. However, not only children were seen as in need of protection, but also women. The shift from agrarian pursuits to industry and work outside the home among women fuelled a growing concern about the effect on the family and future generations. According to many nineteenth-century social reformers, the outcome of women working in factories could be nothing but neglect of children and disintegration of the social fabric. This discussion continued in some countries for some considerable time and affected political decision-making as late as after WWII. The so called 'marriage bar', which stopped women from working in sectors like teaching or the civil service, was clearly politically and ideologically motivated and had no links whatsoever to concerns about the health or wellbeing of women. In the late nineteenth and the early twentieth centuries, legislation was passed closing certain types of work to women and children. The result of such legislation could be that women were barred from work that might have been combined with family duties. It also meant that some economic sectors became totally male dominated. Being a working-class woman could, therefore, be extremely problematic. It is also ironic that a scrutiny of labour statistics shows that, while the concern about children, industry and welfare was well founded, the fear of a threat to motherhood was based on reality to a much slighter degree. A study of the female industrial workforce reveals that the unmarried represented the largest category in all European countries. For example in early twentieth-century Denmark, 26 per cent of the women in industry were married, while 66 per cent unmarried. By 1899, 25 per cent of all women registered as working in German industry were married and in Italy in 1903, 24 per cent. Of these, a very large proportion were active in the textile sector. In the town of Barcelona with good employment opportunities for women 58 per cent of the active females were single in 1900 while 28 per cent married and 15 per cent were widows.[33]

Communities dominated by industries embracing female activity, particularly in the textile sector, like for example the jute industry in Dundee, could present occupational levels of 40–50 per cent among married women.[34]

Table 2.9   Women, marital state and employment in Germany, France, Britain and the USA 1895–1925.

	Single	Married	Widowed
Germany 1895	52%	12%	40%
Germany 1907	60%	26%	40%
Germany 1925	80%	30%	35%
France 1896	50%	40%	40%
France 1911	60%	50%	40%
France 1921	65%	50%	42%
Britain 1911	70%	10%	30%
Britain 1921	60%	10%	25%
USA 1910	61%	11%	15%
USA 1920	77%	9%	*

Note: In the USA, women who had ever been married were included in the singles group in the 1920s.
Sources: Deborah Simonton, *A History of European Women's Work* (London, 1998), p. 192; William Hubbard, *Familiengeschichte, Materialen zur deutschen Familie seit dem Ende des 18. Jahrhunderts* (Munchen, 1983); *Statistisches Jahrbuch für das Deutsche Reich* (Berlin, 1895), *Statistisches Amt; Statistisches Jahrbuch für das Deutsche Reich* (Berlin, 1907), Statistisches Amt; Dora L. Costa, 'From mill town to board room: the rise of women's paid labor', *Journal of Economic Perspectives* 14:4 (2000), pp. 101–22, on p. 10; Lynn Y. Weiner, *From Working Girl to Working Mother* (Chapel Hill, 1985), p. 6.

[33] Fuchs and Thompson, *Women in 19th Century Europe*, p. 71; Leffler, *Zur Kenntniss*, pp. 15–17; Anna-Birte Ravn, '"Lagging far behind all civilized nations": the debate over protective labor legislation for women in Denmark 1899–1913', in Wikander et al., *Protecting Women*, pp. 210–33, on p. 211; Gonnard, *La femme dans l'industrie*, pp. 53–4; Francesca Beltio, *The Sexual Division of Labour: The Italian Case* (Oxford, 1988), pp. 59–61; Borderias, *Entre líneas*, p. 70.

[34] Dundee Social Union, *Report on Housing and Industrial Conditions in Dundee* (Dundee, 1905), pp. 25, 45.

Although a large proportion of the female workers were unmarried there are cases of the group being artificially inflated because of choices at the data gathering stage. In a recent publication, DeValt analysed the occupational figures in the US census of the early twentieth century, there she detected a systematic mislabelling of women who had ever been married but were not now (e.g. widows) as single (Table 2.9). A look at females in work life and in industrial work revealed a higher percentage of married, separated and widowed women than what has previously been assumed.[35] Studies of local US communities have also demonstrated that, on the one hand, widows show considerable activity rates, and in areas with textile employment, like Fall River, married women also demonstrate fairly high levels of activity in comparison with urban areas with different economic patterns (Table 2.10).

Table 2.10   Occupational activity of widows and married women in US local communities 1880–1920.

Employed			
	Pittsburgh	**Fall River**	**Baltimore**
Widows 1880	15%	23%	36%
Widows 1900	29%	29%	36%
Widows 1920	33%	34%	38%
Wives 1880	3%	16%	5%
Wives 1900	3%	20%	10%
Wives 1920	6%	25%	14%

Source: S.J. Kleinberg, 'Children's and Mother's Wage Labor in Three US Cities 1880–1920', *Social Science History* 29:1 (2005), pp. 45–76, on p. 66.

In addition, if we look at women in industry we find that, far from the popular notion of 'factory girls', the women in industry of whatever marital status tended to be adults, not teenagers. We should also note that, while the percentage of single female industrial workers in late nineteenth-century Stockholm was fairly high, cohabitation without marriage was reasonably common among the urban working class. There is also evidence from towns

---

[35] Ileen DeValt, '"Everybody works but father": why the census misdirected historians of women's employment', *Social Science History* 40:3 (2016), pp. 369–83, on pp. 370–7; Christina Borderias Mondejar, Roser Gonzalez-Bagaria and Conchi Villar Garruta, 'El trabajo femenino en la Cataluña industriál (1919–1930): una propuesta de reconstrucción', *Revista de Demografía Historica* XXIX:1 (2011), pp. 55–88, on pp. 72–6.

like Vienna and Helsinki that being single was not necessarily the same as not having a partner and/or children. Such partnerships (in Finland called 'wolf couples') were formed sometimes for economic reasons, sometimes because of anti-clerical political ideology.[36]

The Stockholm survey recorded information about women in a number of different activities besides factory work, anything that could be called 'industry', including manual work on building sites. It is clear from this that age seems to have affected the type of work women were engaged in. The girls in their early teens were doing gardening, textile work and carrying milk, only a handful worked in the cotton factory. The eldest women included in the survey held down qualified occupations at the silk factory. Scrutiny of the age breakdown demonstrates that, while the largest group of women were in their 20s, nearly 40 per cent of the women in industrial work were over 30 and a not insignificant share more than 40 years old (Table 2.11).[37] A study of industrial working conditions in 1890s western Sweden also demonstrated that women working in the textile factories were mostly adult. Young women between 20 and 29 were easy to find, but teenagers were few and far between. While the textile factories in Catalonia employed large numbers of young girls, we find that the bulk of the women in the industrial work force were between 20 and 45 years old.[38] Equally, the numerous girls between 15 and 25 in the New England textile works in 1900 did not represent the majority of the female workers, even though the labour force participation of the 30- to 45-year-olds was around 35 per cent.[39]

[36] Margareta Matovic, 'The Stockholm marriage: extra legal family formation in Stockholm 1860–1890', *Continuity and Change* 1:3 (1986), pp. 385–414; Salmela-Järvinen, *Alas lyötiin vanha maailma*, pp. 64–6, 77–8; John Fout, 'The Viennese Enquête of 1896 on working women', in Ruth Ellen Joeres and Mary Jo Maynes (eds), *German Women in the 18th and 19th Centuries* (Bloomington, 1986), pp. 42–60, on pp. 51–2. In the Nordic countries, the issue was also linked to medieval legislation about marriage and legitimacy of children affecting attitudes to pre-marital cohabitation through to the nineteenth century; Beatrice Moring, 'Female migrants, partner choice and socio-economic destiny – Finnish women in Stockholm in the 17th and 18th century', *Revista de Demografia Historica* XXXIX:1 (2021), pp. 53–75, on pp. 61–2.

[37] Leffler, *Zur Kenntniss*, pp. 34–7.

[38] Gustaf Geijerstam, *Fabriksarbetarnes ställning i Marks härad* (Stockholm, 1894), pp. 28–35; Borderias Mondejar et al., 'El trabajo femenino', pp. 72–6.

[39] Tamara Hareven, *Family Time and Industrial Time* (Cambridge/New York, 1982), p. 191.

Table 2.11   Women, industrial work and age in Sweden and Finland.

Stockholm 1896	12–13	14–19	20–9	30–9	40–9	50–77	
	0.7%	20.1%	40.57%	21.3%	10.69%	6.54%	
Finland, textile 1904	**12–14**	**15–19**	**20–4**	**25–9**	**30–9**	**40–9**	**50–79**
	2.1%	23.4%	24.6%	15.9%	15.8%	9.8%	8.4%

Sources: Leffler, *Zur Kenntniss*, pp. 33–6; G.R. Snellman, *Undersökning av textilindustrin* (Helsinki, 1904).

In late nineteenth-century Russia, despite efforts by factory owners to delay the introduction of protective legislation for children, the implementation of such measures ultimately resulted in a trend where children in factory work were replaced by adult women. In the 1880s, 14 per cent of the females working in Moscow province were under 15 years, by 1908 only 2 per cent can be found in this age category. During the same time period the percentage of married women in registered work increased from 40 to 53 per cent.[40] The situation in Russia indicates that the trend, as elsewhere, to elevate the ages of factory workers through legal restrictions had affected the presence of young girls in favour of adult women (Table 2.12).

Table 2.12   Employment of married females in Russia, percentages.

Married females	In factory work	In Russia
15–19	13.3	15.4
20–9	59.7	76
30–9	60	88
40–9	50	81
50–9	33	66

Source: Robert E. Johnson, 'Family relations and the urban-rural nexus', in David Ransel (ed.), *The Family in Imperial Russia* (Urbana, 1978), pp. 263–79, on p. 268.

Seeking employment could be vital for a woman of the working class. In France and Germany 40 per cent of widows were registered as working for a living in the late nineteenth and early twentieth centuries. In Britain the percentage was somewhat lower (Table 2.9). The reasons for this can be linked to

---

[40] G.R. Snellman, *Undersökning angående textilindustrin* (Helsingfors, 1904), pp. 40–3; Rose Glickman, *Russian Factory Women: Workplace and Society 1880–1914* (Berkeley, 1984), pp. 94–6.

Figure 1 Being in a factory photograph could be a special occasion when best clothes were worn and children were brought in to participate. Workers outside Tolkis paper mill 1898. SLS 1053 65, Archive for Popular Culture, Helsinki.

the defective registration of casual work, but also to the declining opportunities for females on the British labour market in the nineteenth century.[41]

While generally speaking industrial work was gender segregated, it also seems that certain industries had a greater attraction for women with a family. We find that, for example, in the Nordic countries, the type of work that attracted married women shows some variation. The Swedish census of 1910 revealed that married women seemed to favour tobacco and textiles, and widows, glass works and breweries. Tobacco was different from some other types of factory work in having more flexible working hours, and the piece work remuneration gave access to reasonable earnings. Although the general trends were similar in Sweden and Finland, the female participation was higher in some sectors in the Finnish case. Surveys conducted in the period 1902–11 revealed that, in addition to tobacco and textiles, married women and widows gravitated towards the saw mills and the paper mills, and even machine works, while married women had a reasonable presence in the bakeries.[42]

Newly expanded textile towns with more than 50 per cent female workers generally employed young unmarried women. However, among the women in paper mills and particularly those working night shifts, widows and married women were present. One-third of the female workers in the paper mills had children. One reason for the popularity of this sector was that it also included rag sorting and picking. The wages in this fairly disgusting task were based on piece work rates and the hours were flexible. In addition to factory work per se, widows and married women could be found engaged in ceramics, washing, hand knitting and even working as bricklayer's assistants. Whatever the activity, the greatest problem was the low wages. Even when in full-time employment, women could earn no more than 2/3 of the male wage. However, industrial wages were far superior to those in casual work like washing and cleaning, where the remuneration was not proportional to the labour input.[43]

The decrease in the figures of overall female occupational engagement in early twentieth-century Italy seems to be connected to the restrictions on the work of children. Between 1901 and 1911, the participation rates of girls between the ages of 10 and 14 decreased to 20 per cent. As the overall female activity rate only dropped from 30 to 29 per cent, it would seem that the recruitment among teenagers and youg women experienced some increase.[44]

[41] Humphries and Weisdorf, 'The wages of women'; Deborah Simonton, *A History of European Women's Work: 1700 to the Present* (London, 1998), p. 192.

[42] Lynn Karlsson, *Mothers as Breadwinners: Myth or Reality in Early Swedish Industry?* (Uppsala, 1995), pp. 19–20; G.R. Snellman, *Undersökning angående textilindustrin*, pp. 40–3; Markkola, *Työläiskodin*, p. 263.

[43] G.R. Snellman, *Undersökning angående pappersindustrin* (Helsingfors, 1912), p. 29; Leffler, *Zur Kenntniss*, pp. 15–17; Markkola, *Työläiskodin*, pp. 107, 110, 263; Haapala, *Tehtaan valossa*, pp. 38, 41, 370; Heikkinen, *Labour and the Market*, pp. 85, 160.

[44] Beltio, *The Sexual Division of Labour*, pp. 50–1, 58. Female activity in 1911: 29.0 per cent all ages, 15–20-year-olds 52.6 per cent, 10–14-year-olds 31.5 per cent. Male activity: 66.2 per cent, 15–20-year-olds 89.9 per cent, 10–14-year-olds 53.0 per cent, female activity rate 1901 37.5 per cent, 1911 35.1 per cent, decrease over time

By the late nineteenth century, we also find very few girls under the age of 14 in German industry, but a considerable number of 14- to 16-year-olds. The vast majority belonged to the over 21-year-olds (1895). In Britain in 1896, 25 per cent of all female workers in industries subject to inspection were 13–18 years old and 2 per cent were 11–14 years old.

A look at the ages of women in industrial work in northern Spain reveals that while the early decades of industrialisation had an extreme dominance of young women we will find that by the turn of the century female activity among adult and middle-aged women was far from unusual. As to the activity rates of married women in the early years of the twentieth century, there seems to be a clear correlation between family size and activity. Women with one child show a much higher propensity to be engaged in the factories than those with larger families, particularly if they had several working sons.[45] Similarly, studies on family level in the USA have pointed towards the withdrawal of women from the labour market in older ages if they had working adult children.[46]

On the other hand, there is evidence of fairly similar occupational levels of married women irrespective of age, for example, in Germany, however, with some increase after the age of 40, indicating an increase in activity when children grew up (see Table 2.13).

Table 2.13   Occupational activity of married women in Germany, percentages.

Age	1895	1907
15–19	15.7	22.5
20–5		21.6
25–9	11.9 (20–9)	21.9
30–9	11.8	25.4
40–9	12.7	28.6
50–9	12.7	29.5
60+	10	23.3
Total	12.0	25.8

Source: Hubbard, William, *Familiengeschichte, materialen zur deutschen Familie seit dem Ende des 18. Jahrhunderts* (Munchen, 1983), p. 156.

---

because of fewer child workers and also work among the elderly, 1905 in textile industry 10,927 girls less than 10 years old, 59,543 12–15 years, 119,738 15–21 years and 130,815 women older than 21.

45   Llonch Casanovas, *Tejiendo en red*, pp. 143–4; Fuchs and Thompson, *Women in 19th Century Europe*, p. 71; Humphries, *Childhood and Child Labour*, p. 110; Enriqueta Camps, 'Mercados de trabajo modernos sin estado del bienestar: el sector textil catalan durante la dictadura de Primo de Rivera', in *Homaje al Doctor Jordi Nadal: La industrialización y el desarollo económico de España* (Barcelona, 2002), pp. 1206–18.

46   S.J. Kleinberg, 'Children's and mothers' wage labor in three US cities 1880–1920', *Social Science History* 29:1 (2005), pp. 45–76, on pp. 67–8.

Conclusion

It is difficult to determine the level of female occupational activity in the eighteenth century and earlier. Women were often engaged in family enterprises like farming in the countryside and trade and crafts in urban areas. The manner of registration and the rules for gathering information has varied over time and place. In agriculture, the view was often that the head of the household was active and the family members in best case assisting. Census registration of economic activity of wives and children in the nineteenth century could also be hampered by how work was defined. By the end of the nineteenth century, registration of female work in urban areas generally improved, but information in censuses tends to be inferior in relation to industrial statistics and company wage lists. As the industrial work force tended to be relatively well documented, we have undisputable evidence that there was a considerable input of female work in industry, particularly in sectors related to textiles, food and drink.

In many countries, great regional differences can be detected, with specific industrial areas like North West England, Northern Italy or Catalonia in Spain. In such areas, industrialisation and high rates of female employment went hand in hand. From the 1880s and 90s an increasing interest in implementing compulsory education, in connection with regulatory measures related to factory work of children, boosted the employment opportunities of women in industry. The early years of the twentieth century saw record levels of women entering factories. While there was a general consensus that it was good for young people to work, there were variable opinions of when one ceased to be a child and became a young person. With more women opting for industrial work, the issue was also raised of whether it was a good thing for married women and mothers to be in factory employment.

3

Women, Earnings and the Household – Why the Factory?

A shilling of your own is worth two that he gives you.[1]

Research on the subject of women and work has for decades underlined that women were underpaid in relation to men, and that women not only had tasks with less respect but were also forced to labour under inhuman conditions, particularly in factories. This might inspire the question, if factory work was so horrible for women (unlike for men?) why did women enter the factories?

In retrospect there is never a shortage of good ideas and suggestions about what would have been a sensible choice, and the late nineteenth and early twentieth centuries supplied their fair share of social reformers and people with views about how the working classes should live and the need to get women out of the factories.

Working-class women and families of the past were painfully aware of their need to eat, and the differences in male and female earnings were not restricted to factory employment. Whatever work a woman chose to do, she would earn less than a man. Today we talk about equal pay, which even though guaranteed by law, is not actually a reality in Western countries. In the past, women had to take reality into consideration and deal with whatever choices were available. In such a situation the factory might not have been the worst option.[2]

Middle-class social reformers considered domestic service as a suitable job for young women: it was safe and in a family, under control of 'respectable people' and girls would acquire domestic skills that would be useful when they married and became wives and mothers. In actual fact, the work was badly paid, had terrible hours, no freedom and privacy, no job security and in case of pregnancy, resulted in loss both of employment and home. While farm work was also badly paid, the social distance between employer and employee could be a lot closer. In addition, in many parts of Europe, rural society handled the question of pregnancy more smoothly; there were even

---

1   Clementina Black, *Married Women's Work* (London, 1915), p. 4.
2   Rosa Kempf, *Das Leben der jungen Fabrikmädchen* (Leipzig, 1911), p. 156.

regions, most prominently in German-speaking parts of Europe and Iceland, where mothers could keep their children with them when employed as live-in farm workers. Factories regularly employed unmarried mothers, as well as widows and deserted women. As long as the work was performed promptly, private life could remain private.[3]

As it was necessary to make choices and weigh the pros and cons of different occupations, we must not expect that a woman in 1900 would automatically go for a job that was indoors, clean and in a 'secure environment'. In a working-class autobiography describing life as a widow's daughter in 1890s Finland, a girl relates how her mother and the other female mortar carriers in Helsinki silenced the jibes of the boys from the building sites. While working on a building site was low status work, those of the tobacco factory did not receive a huge amount of respect either. Domestic servants received the least respect and were generally looked upon with disdain, while seamstresses were seen almost as ladies. The mother, however, preferred the hard work of mortar carrying to 'starving with needle and thread' even though she owned a sewing machine.[4]

The social reformers of the turn of the century did not only cry out against female factory work, but particularly against working mothers and the detrimental effect they had on family life and the health of their children.[5] As we have seen above, more than half the women in the working population were not mothers but single. On the other hand, there is evidence of a general tendency to minimize the proportion of female industrial workers, for example, in northern Spain, and recently, serious flaws in the documentation of marital state in the USA census of the early twentieth century have been detected.[6] Therefore, when we talk about women in the factory, we are talking about women of all ages and of different marital statuses.

In rural societies, the idea of pooling family resources and everybody doing their bit was seen as perfectly normal. While Britain has had a longer history of

---

[3] Georg Nørregaard, *Arbejdsforhold indenfor dansk Haandværk og Industri 1857–1899* (Copenhagen, 1943), p. 158; Elisabeth Mantl, *Heirat als Privileg* (Wien, 1997), pp. 124–5, 210–13; Erhard Chvojka, *Grossmutter, Enkelkindern erinnern sich* (Wien, 1992), pp. 47–50, 83–5; Gisli Gunnlaugsson, *Family and Household in Iceland 1801–1930* (Uppsala, 1988), pp. 109, 115–16; G.R. Snellman, *Undersökning av textilindustrin (Helsingfors, 1904)*, pp. 34–5.

[4] Martta Salmela-Järvinen, *Kun se parasta on ollut* (Helsinki, 1965), pp. 148–9.

[5] The Annual Report for 1910 of the Chief Medical Officer of the Board of Education revealed that assumptions were made about a direct connection between the employment of mothers and malnutrition in children. However, this assumption was not based on evidence of any kind (Cd 5925, pp. 29–30).

[6] Ilena DeValt, '"Everybody works but father"', pp. 369–84, on pp. 370–7; Borderias Mondejar et al., 'El trabajo femenino', pp. 55–88, on pp. 72–6.

urbanisation and industrialisation than many other countries, on the European continent, working in industry in the late nineteenth century meant for many families the first step out of the agrarian economy. The notion of the family working within a complimentary system was not necessarily an alien concept. Even in places like England, it would seem that fathers had no hesitation in sending their children out to work at an early age, whatever ideas they might have had about the place of the wife. Others disliked the idea of their wives working outside the home but found no problem in sweated work in the home or in keeping lodgers.[7] It would seem that attitudes tended to vary with the availability of work for women. Just like the difference in attitude to female work in agriculture, with a positive attitude in the north of England and in Scotland and a negative in the southeast,[8] textile factory areas often had less restrictive and more practical attitudes to female work. Many men realised that their own earnings were insufficient for the family.

> Well she wanted to work to advance herself. First of all, if she hadn't worked, we'd never have been able to build a house. She worked many years weaving. When she had babies she went a while not working ... Then one of her sisters built a house and she wanted to do as much as her. It was her mother who saw to our baby and I was in the house as much as my wife. We washed dishes together. We worked together.[9]

> My husband never stopped me going to work when we needed the money. I also had to make all the clothes, even the pants for the little boys. I used to sell sandwiches to the girls in the mill it they didn't bring their lunch. My husband was just across the street ... and he used to whistle from the mill yard and tell me how many sandwiches he wanted.[10]

Because of the social reformers' relentless campaigns for the need of married women to stay at home (despite surveys showing that the working mother could make the difference between children being sufficiently fed and not)[11] a number of women saw themselves accused of being bad mothers and,

---

7   Regina Kopl and Leopold Redl, *Das Totale Ensemble, Ein Führer duch die Industriekultur In südlicher Wiener Becken* (Wien, 1989), pp. 85, 140; Jane Humphries, *Childhood and Child Labour* (Cambridge, 2010), pp. 110–14; Chinn, *They Worked All Their Lives*, pp. 46, 60–1.

8   Royal Commission of Labour 1892–4, XXIII, c.6894; Reports from commissioners, inspectors and others, p. 20, General Report 1892–4. I–V.XXXV. PP. C 6894, Section B, pp. 81–2, 127–8, Section D, pp. 27–30.

9   Hareven, *Family Time*, p. 204.

10   Tamara Hareven and Randolph Langenbach, *Amoskeag: Life and Work in an American Factory City in New England* (London, 1979), p. 261.

11   Medical Officers Report to the Committee of the Privy Council, Conditions of

therefore, in need of defending their position. Hence, when asked, only a few women would actually say that they wanted to work, while the majority stated that they were obliged to work, for the welfare of the family (Table 3.1).

The following reasons were listed when women answered the inquiry by the Women's Industrial Council on Married Women's work 1907–14:

- To support self and child(ren), family.
- To support self.
- To add to or supplement husband's income.
- To supplement husband's income (drinks).
- Husband wastes money on gambling.
- Husband worthless, gives no money, lives off wife.
- Husband out of work.
- Husband invalid.
- To have a little saved for husband's slack time.
- To keep things going.
- Started working when husband ill and continued working.
- Worked before married, gave it up, started again and likes it.
- To add to income and because she likes it.[12]

Table 3.1　Married women's work, Britain 1907.

| **Reasons for working** | | | | | | | |
Widow	Deserted	Husband out of work	Husband ill	To supplement earnings	Other reasons	Not stated	Total
139	22	43	36	356	11	9	616
22.5	3.6	7.0	5.8	57.8	1.8	1.5	100

Source: Clementina Black, *Married Women's Work* (London, 1915), Appendix III, p. 283.

Likewise, the reasons given by married women in Germany in 1899 for factory work underlined the economic necessity of work in most cases. Both the Black inquiry and studies from Austria and Germany highlighted the fact of the continuous problem of male temporary or seasonal unemployment and unreliability (Table 3.2). Other studies have also demonstrated an intensification of female activity when the earnings of the husband were absent.[13]

Nourishment, Smith 1864, PP XXVII; The Annual Report for 1910 of the Chief Medical Officer of the Board of Education.

[12] Black, *Married Women's Work*, Appendix I.

[13] Carolyn M. Moehling, 'Women's work and men's unemployment', *Journal of*

Table 3.2   Reasons for factory work by married women in Germany 1899.

	Ever married women	Husband's wages too small	To support family members	To make savings or pay debts	To live better	Husband gives no money	No specific reason
Liegnitz	2102	1051	21	84	357	588	
Magdeburg	2629	1006	26	152	472	957	19
Luneburg	2030	1084				745	201
Hildesheim	1081	533				417	131
Wiesbaden	902	435		47	141	279	
Oberbayern	1253	496	95	120	219	317	6
Zittau	4449	2502		1736		211	

Source: William Hubbard, *Familiengeschichte, materialen zur deutschen Familie seit dem Ende des 18. Jahrhunderts* (Munchen, 1983), p. 157.

In the late nineteenth century, French industry cyclical male unemployment created problems for the family economy, and the work of married women acted as an important security buffer. It was often the key ingredient protecting the family.[14] Similarly, in Spain, the earnings of the urban male breadwinner were insecure and often insufficient. Only families with multiple earners, particularly if they included adult women, could create a situation of relative economic prosperity.[15] Surveys from textile communities in the United States have also demonstrated that the situation when the family had to rely on income from the father was vastly inferior to when the family contained working children, a working wife or the contribution to the household economy of lodgers.[16] The situation in Northern Europe was not much different, urban life was plagued by periods of decreased demand due to international market conditions and

---

Economic History 61:4 (2001), pp. 926–49, on pp. 926–31, 935–7, 947; Black, *Married Women's Work*, pp. 4–5, 22–3, 29, 272; Richard Wall, 'Work, welfare and the family: an illustration of the adaptive family economy', in Lloyd Bonfield, Richard Smith and Keith Wrightson (eds), *The World We Have Gained* (Oxford, 1986), pp. 279–80; Fout, 'The Viennese Enquête', pp. 42–60.

14   Accampo, *Industrialization, Family Life and Class Relations*, pp. 90–2.

15   Christina Borderias and Pilar Lopez, 'A gendered view of family budgets in mid-nineteenth century Barcelona', *Histoire et Mesure* XVIII:1–2 (2003), pp. 113–46.

16   John Modell, 'Patterns of consumption, acculturation and family income strategies in late nineteen-century America', in Tamara Hareven and Maris Vinovskis (eds), *Family and Population in Nineteenth Century America* (Princeton, 1978), pp. 206–40, on pp. 233–5.

seasonal standstill of some sectors, like building and seafaring, because of winter weather. Therefore, relying on the income of one person could prove problematic for the family.[17]

Female work, sectors and earnings

While it is fairly clear that the economic input of women was welcome to balance the family budget in working class households, why did they enter the factory? The answer might not have been the attraction of the factory per se as much as in the unattractiveness of other alternatives. For example, in late nineteenth-century Poland, the work of women was so badly paid in most sectors that finding a job in a textile factory could be the one opportunity for a woman to support herself and possibly even a child.[18] Although domestic work in the USA was much better remunerated than in Europe, it was seen as degrading. By the early twentieth century, any work was considered superior to domestic service and only immigrant women were willing to enter this sphere. In France, as in Britain and many other European countries, the unreasonable working day, which could easily be 16 hours or more, might have made a 12-hour day in a factory seem like a more attractive proposal.[19]

The factories varied considerably depending on location. In Austria it was not unusual that factories provided housing, sometimes of good, sometimes of variable quality. In addition perks like firewood could be provided. The factory communities could be self-contained social entities with all life oriented towards the workplace and workmates. Sometimes, factory accommodation could be retained after the death of a father if family members worked for the same employer, however, if not, eviction was possible. Some factories had halls where widows and their children were housed. Factory schools were relatively common and in some areas a kindergarten was provided to enable married women to work.[20] The factory accommodation was not always free, but in some cases subsidized, and the availability of firewood and access to gardens could make life for married and unmarried workers reasonable.[21]

---

[17] Vera Hjelt, *Undersökning af yrkesarbetarnes lefnadsvillkor i Finland 1908–1909* (Helsingfors, 1911), pp. 20–31; Heikkinen, *Labour and the Market*; Geijerstam, *Fabriksarbetarnes*, pp. 74–5.

[18] Anna Zarnovska, 'Women in working class families', in Rudolf Jaworski and Bianka Pietrow-Ennker (eds), *Women in Polish Society* (New York, 1992), pp. 163–76, on p. 173.

[19] Kessler-Harris, *Women Have Always Worked*, pp. 82–3, 86; McMillan, *France and Women*, pp. 174–5; Liz Stanley (ed.), *The Diaries of Hannah Culwick, Victorian Maidservant* (London, 1985), pp. 152–60, 174–7; Burnett, *Useful Toil*, pp. 216–17.

[20] Kopl and Redl, *Das Totale Ensemble*, pp. 66, 78–9, 82–4, 152.

[21] Geijerstam, *Fabriksarbetarnes*, pp. 70–4.

The issue of earnings was, however, for many people of paramount importance. When a woman entered working life, the prime question might not necessarily have been what she could earn in relation to a man, but what she might earn in another sector. In France, the female wages in industry varied between 1.60 and 4.10 francs in the 1890s. In printing, it was possible to earn 3.55 francs and in manufacture slightly less. It is not unreasonable to assume that the direction a woman took was affected by wages in the textile industry varying from 400 to 700 francs per year, while those in service varied between 240 and 480 francs.[22] Similarly, in Germany and Britain, the wages to which a servant could aspire were much more meagre than those in industry (see Table 3.3).

Table 3.3 Examples of female earnings, late nineteenth and early twentieth centuries.

Earnings	France frs	Germany mk	Spain pts	USA $	Britain £
Textile industry	400–700/ year	288–624/year	2.25/day	8–9/week	35–7/year
Domestic service	240–480/ year	240/year	0.50–0.75/ day	3–3.20/ week	16–18/ year
Agriculture			1/day		

Sources: R. Gonnard, *La femme dans la industrie* (Paris, 1906), pp. 103–5; James McMillan, *France and Women* (London, 2000), pp. 174–5; Lily Braun *Die Frauenfrage: ihre geschichtliche Entwicklung und wirtschaftliche Seite* (Berlin, 1901); Rosa Capel Martinez, 'Mujer y trabajo en España de Alfonso XIII', in R.M. Capel Martinez (ed.), *Mujer y Sociedad en España 1700–1775* (Madrid, 1982), pp. 220–2; Alice Kessler-Harris, *Women Have Always Worked* (Chicago, 2018), p. 86; Tamara Hareven, *Family Time and Industrial Time* (Cambridge/New York, 1982), p. 428; Snellman, *Undersökning av textilindustrin* (Helsingfors, 1904), p. 121;Edward Higgs, 'Domestic Service and Household Production', in Angela John (ed.), *Unequal Opportunities* (London, 1986), pp. 125–52, on p. 138.

During the first decade of the twentieth century, engaging in domestic work in Spain would bring in only half of the earnings in agriculture, and while the starting wage in the northern Spanish textile industry was similar to that in agriculture, the average earnings were twice as high.[23]

Even in Russia the textile industry provided better opportunities for earnings in comparison with almost all other types of work. In this sector a woman

[22] McMillan, *France and Women*, pp. 174–5, Gonnard, *La femme dans l'industrie*, pp. 103–5; Braun, *Die Frauenfrage*.

[23] Capel Martinez, 'Mujer y trabajo en España de Alfonso XIII', pp. 207–40, on pp. 220–2.

could reach 70 per cent of male wages. Although the work was hard and the days long it was seen as preferable to the 'slavery' of domestic service with no freedom, no life and no respect.[24]

At the eve of WWI, certain factory areas in Lancashire with high levels of unionisation had achieved serious improvement in female wage levels. The Nelson factory reoriented towards high-quality cloth from 1900, produced both for the domestic market and for exports. As the work required skill it was well paid. By 1913, the Nelson weavers were the highest paid in Lancashire. Wages for men and women were 29 shillings per week, well above the 20 shillings, earned by up to 40 per cent of the Edwardian working class. The fact that women received the same wage as men, making them the highest paid women workers in the country, was extraordinary. In such an environment women continued working after marriage until one or two children could become half-timers. Families with working mothers and children could have a weekly income of up to £3 during the most intensive period of the family life cycle.[25]

The information that could be gathered about female earnings from a survey in early twentieth-century Finland unsurprisingly revealed that those engaged in factory work demonstrated reasonable earnings and in many cases more than the mean earnings recorded in factory wage statistics. The women in the survey were adult and household heads, and could therefore present a longer work career that those included in the factory statistics. A study of women in needlework confirmed the images that had been presented by studies for England and France and explained the statement about 'starving with needle and thread'. More than 60 per cent of the women in needlework barely earned enough to support themselves.[26] While earnings in textile factories could not be considered generous, it would seem that earning enough to support oneself, or even oneself and a child, was not out of the question when the teenage years were left behind.[27]

---

[24] Glickman, *Russian Factory Women*, pp. 60–1; Snellman, *Undersökning angående textilindustrin*, pp. 34–5.

[25] Alan Fowler and Lesley Fowler, *The History of the Nelson Weavers Association* (Manchester, 1985), pp. 22–4.

[26] Vera Hjelt, *Undersökning af nålarbeterskornas yrkesförhållanden i Finland* (Helsingfors, 1908), p. 92; Vera Hjelt, *Undersökning af yrkesarbetarnes*, pp. 2–42; Thomas Oliver, 'The diet of toil', *The Lancet*, June (1895), pp. 1630, 1634–5; Gabriel Paul Othenin de Cleron d'Haussonville, *Salaires et misères de femmes* (Paris, 1900), pp. 4–11.

[27] Beatrice Moring, 'Women, work and survival strategies in urban Northern Europe before the First World War', in Beatrice Moring (ed.), *Female Economic Strategies in the Modern World* (London, 2012), pp. 45–72, on pp. 54–6.

Gender, factory earnings and skill

Scholars of the 1980s and 90s engaged in the studies of women's work and wages were generally in agreement about the causes for the lower wages of women in industrial work being linked to concepts of gender, and the result of discrimination. This view has more recently been disputed, and the explanation put forward that the lesser physical strength of women in combination with lack of permanency in employment and, therefore, different skill levels were the root causes of the difference in wages in the past.[28] The discussion has to some extent suffered from the problem that one part of the argument was linked to what reasons an employer would have (or give) to pay women less (an economic or profit argument), while others have seen it as an issue of actual female physical capacity and have also discussed the reasons for female absence because of child bearing (a fairness or moral argument).[29]

In the early years of the twentieth century, the Industrial Board of Finland took the initiative to survey the working conditions in a series of industrial sectors. The issues that were chartered were wage levels, types of remuneration, working hours, times in employment of workers, their marital and family status, etc. One of the first industrial sectors to be studied was the textile industry (1904); the survey included no less than 9687 workers.

Table 3.4   Gender and time in employment, Finnish textile industry 1904.

	Males, textile nr	Textile %	Females textile nr	Textile %
1 year or less	294	10.2	898	13.2
1–2	203	7.0	748	11.0
2–5	723	24.9	2208	32.5
5–10	608	21.0	1569	23.1
10–20	464	16.1	676	10.0
20–30	267	9.2	320	4.7
30+	336	11.6	372	5.5
Total	2895		6792	

Source: G.R. Snellman, *Undersökning av textilindustrin* (Helsingfors, 1904), pp. 136–7.

---

28 Joyce Burnette, *Gender, Work and Wages in Industrial Revolution Britain* (Cambridge, 2008); Deborah Valenze, *The First Industrial Woman* (New York, 1995); Louise A. Tilly and Joan W. Scott, *Women, Work and the Family* (New York, 1978); Rose, *Limited Livelihoods*.

29 Amy Froide, 'Disciplinary differences: a historian's take on why wages differed by gender in eighteenth and nineteenth century Britain', *Social Science History* 33:4 (2009), pp. 465–72.

As the study recorded information about how long different individuals had been working, it has been possible to scrutinise the validity of the assumption that length of male and female work careers was of decisive importance for earnings. The work career argument was substantiated by the findings. A larger proportion of women than men had entered employment relatively recently. Therefore, the mean earnings of women would be affected by the number of new recruits. More than 20 per cent had been less than two years in employment. On the other hand, the study also revealed that actually more women than men had been employed in the textile factories for more than 20 years (Table 3.4).

The correlation between earnings and time in employment is fairly clear. A long work career had a positive impact on the level of income both for men and women. However, it would seem that they operated with different scales. Of the women who had been in employment for two years or less, 15 per cent were in the lowest income bracket (under 300 marks per year) while 20 per cent of the males were paid such wages. Of the other new female arrivals 61 per cent earned between 300 and 500 marks and 23 per cent 500–1000 marks. Of the males employed 2 years or less none earned 300–500 marks, 55 per cent 500–1000 and 25 per cent +1000 marks. If we analyse the situation of persons who had been working between 10 and 20 years we find that 34 per cent of the males had reached the highest income bracket (+1000) and 65 per cent the next highest, while none of the women with similar employment history had reached an income over 1000 marks and 76 per cent earned 750–1000 marks. Among those working for more than 20 years, we find similar discrepancies in male and female wages (Table 3.5).

The conclusion that can be drawn for the textile industry is that it would seem that a similar employment history would not give women the chance of earning the same as men.

Table 3.5   Gender, earnings and time at work, Finnish textile industry, percentages.

	M	F	M	F	M	F	M	F
Marks	-300		300–500		500–1000		1000+	
2 y or less	20.0	15.4		61.5	55.0	23.1	25.0	
2–10 y	11.1	5.9	11.9	47.8	61.6	47.2	15.4	0.01
10–20 y		0.2	0.7	23.9	64.9	75.9	34.4	
20 + y			0.4	36.9	62.5	62.9	37.1	0.2

Source: G.R. Snellman, *Undersökning av textilindustrin* (Helsingfors, 1904), pp. 226–7.

It would also seem that the female textile workers in early twentieth-century Finland operated in an environment with a considerable degree of task segregation – all winders were women (Table 3.6). This result is in agreement with earlier findings and discussion. Task segregation by gender did and does create a situation where differences in wage levels appear to be supported by logical reasoning. The industries do, however, reveal some task duplication, as in weaving, carding and spooling. In all these cases, there are indications of a difference in payment between men and women to the advantage of men. For example, while 36 per cent of male weavers had reached wages of over 1000 marks, no females could aspire to this (Table 3.6).

Table 3.6   Wages by gender and task, Finnish cotton industry, percentages.

	M	F	M	F	M	F	M	F
Task	-300 mark		300–500		500–1000		1000 +	
Foremen					25.0	31.3	75.0	68.7
Loom construction			0.8		33.1		66.1	
Pickers, mixers			5.9	87.5	94.1	12.5		
Carders	12.7		8.4	76.5	77.5	23.5	1.4	
Pre-weavers	33.3			42.1	66.7	57.9		
Weavers		4.7		65.1	63.2	30.2	36.8	
Repairers	74.1		1.8	100	24.1			
Changers	64.7	53.0	29.4	47.0	5.9			
Winders				48.1		51.9		
Spoolers		0.6		39.1	100	60.3		
Designers				10.0	100	90.0		
Joiners			2.3		63.6		34.1	
Fabric weavers		0.1	9.1	18.4	84.1	81.3	6.8	0.2
Office	9.1	13.8	25.5	27.6	38.1	58.6	27.3	

Source: G.R. Snellman *Undersökning av textilindustrin* (Helsingfors, 1904), pp. 226–7.

It would therefore appear that the reasons for divergence in wages of men and women in this type of industrial work were linked to segregation of work tasks rather than lack of skill or stability of employment. Work careers of 20 years or more indicate a fair amount of stability. It also creates some question marks around the idea that all women ceased working at marriage. As 10 per cent of the women in the survey were married and an additional 9 per cent were mothers, these figures tend to support the idea of textile communities living by their own rules and providing a chance for women to be breadwinners.[30]

Average earnings by men and women as a group were obviously affected by the fact that many young women in the textile factories had only worked for a year or two. Some tasks were clearly gender specific, which simplified the skewed wage structure and, irrespective of length of time in employment, men were generally paid more. Remuneration for the same task was also gender differentiated with men having higher wages (3.6).

As women in all sectors of the economy were paid less, it is hardly surprising that this was replicated in industrial work. If the employer could cut costs by employing women, why would he not do so? It is of course possible that the employer saw women as less effective workers than men but it is more likely that costs in general was the decisive factor. There was fairly general agreement about the defective unionisation of women in the late nineteenth and early twentieth centuries, and in such a position they were less likely to be listened to. Male unions, while deploring their low wages and therefore competition, did certainly not champion their cause.[31] On the other hand, progressing career-wise was not out of the question for a woman. While Minoletti has presented evidence of women being barred from reaching positions of authority in the English textile industry,[32] this does not seem to have been the case in Finland. Although the wool industry displayed no female foremen, both the cotton and tricot industries engaged female foremen and female career advancement was possible.[33] There is also evidence from New England that women were able to advance in their careers and get jobs demanding a higher skill level. Their situation might not have been as good at that of men but in an industry like textiles such options were not closed

---

[30] In Dundee, with a jute industry and a large female workforce in the early twentieth century, the work of married women was common and female occupational levels were considerably higher than in other Scottish urban areas: Dundee 54.6 per cent versus Glasgow 39.3 per cent and Edinburgh 40.7 per cent. Dundee Social Union, *Report on Housing and Industrial Conditions in Dundee*, pp. 18–22, 65.

[31] Gonnard, *La femme dans l'industrie*; Burnette, *Gender, Work and Wages*; Ensimmäinen, *yleisen työläisnaisten*.

[32] Paul Minoletti, 'The importance of ideology: the shift to factory production and its effect on women's employment opportunities in the English textile industries 1760–1850', *Continuity and Change* 28:1 (2013), pp. 121–46.

[33] Snellman, *Undersökning angående textilindustrin*, pp. 226–7; G.R. Snellman, *Undersökning av tobaksindustrin* (Helsingfors, 1903), pp. 86–7.

to females (Table 3.7). As the factories were predominantly populated by women, employing women to oversee other women resulted in further savings in salary costs.[34]

Table 3.7   Career mobility by gender and age at starting work, New England cotton industry.

Job mobility	Starting at 12–15	16–25	26–35	36–45	46–73	Total
Males	N=48	N=238	N=80	N=50	N=56	N=472
Down	16.7	16.0	20.0	24.0	12.5	17.2
No change	43.8	58.0	70.0	68.0	73.2	61.4
Up	39.6	26.1	10.0	8.0	14.3	21.4
Females	N=42	N=212	N=75	N=36	N=13	N=378
Down	11.9	14.2	14.7	22.2	7.7	14.6
No change	59.5	68.4	70.7	69.4	84.6	68.5
Up	28.6	17.5	14.7	8.3	7.7	16.9

Source: Tamara Hareven, *Family Time and Industrial time* (Cambridge, 1982), p. 277.

The issue of increasing earnings or advancement was not a universal option. As a comparison, it is interesting to reflect on the wage structure in the second half of the nineteenth century in the textile industry of northern Spain. There, the starting salary of females was roughly 50 per cent of that of males. For men, it increased with the number of years in employment, from 10 reales to 20 per day after twenty years of service. In the case of women, however, the starting salary was slightly more than 5 reales and increased over a 20-year period to 7.5 reales. In the Spanish case, staying in the factory opened opportunities for promotion among men, while women were basically engaged in the same tasks, irrespective of time at work. However, by the 1920s, the situation had changed and there was considerable improvement in female salary levels.[35] It would therefore seem that chances for advancement in industrial work varied with location and possibly industrial sector, as it has been demonstrated that, for example, in the Spanish tobacco industry, female earnings could rise to levels that made the wife the main breadwinner. Likewise, the possibility of a woman achieving a male income seems not to have been out of the question among Swedish tobacco workers.[36]

[34] Hareven, *Family Time*, pp. 272–7.
[35] Camps, *La Formacion del Mercado*, pp. 198–9.
[36] Lina Galvez, 'Breadwinning patterns and family exogenous factors', in A.

There are scant chances of finding reliable evidence for or against the idea that the employers assumed lower female productivity or strength, however, we do find that there was some task overlap and a continuing discrepancy in wage levels. While women suffered from the gender gap in wages, a long working career had a positive effect on earnings. The majority of women were able to earn a reasonable wage. The question of considerable importance is, were the earnings sufficient to support the woman and possibly a child or even a small family. Was it possible to be a female textile worker and the family breadwinner?

Earnings and survival

By the late nineteenth century, many countries in Europe and beyond were facing the fact that society had undergone change, that urbanisation and industrialisation had touched large groups of people and that these groups could not be ignored politically and economically. Although the living conditions of the poor had been the focus of interest for philanthropists earlier in the century, the years around 1900 saw a multiplicity of calculations related to input of nutrition, capacity to work and spending on food in working-class households. The Nordic countries were no exceptions to these trends. In Finland, the economists were more or less in agreement that earnings of about 800 marks per year were necessary for a family of two adults and two children, with an additional 100 marks for each extra child. 400 marks per year was seen as sufficient for a single adult.[37] When we examine the average earnings of women in the textile industry we find that, apart from girls under 18, all the females earned enough to support themselves, but few enough for a family. In a budget study of 1908, none of the women in factory work earned less than the minimum of 400 marks and the majority considerably more (Table 3.8).[38]

Janssens (ed.), *The Rise and Decline of the Male Breadwinner Family? International Review of Social History, Supplements* 5 (1998), pp. 87–128; Maria Stanfors, Tim Leunig, Bjorn Eriksson and Tobias Karlsson, 'Gender productivity and the nature of work and pay: evidence from the late 19th century tobacco industry', *Economic History Review* 67:1 (2014), pp. 48–65.

[37] Oscar Groundstroem, *Helsingin työväen taloudellisista oloista* (Porvoo, 1897), pp. 107–8, 114–15.

[38] Vera Hjelt, *Undersökning af yrkesarbetarnes*, pp. 2–42; Snellman, *Undersökning angående textilindustrin*, pp. 226–7.

Table 3.8   Male and female earnings in the Finnish textile industry 1904.

Males	Yearly earnings, mean in Fmk	Number of persons	Females	Yearly earnings, mean in Fmk	Number of persons
Under 18	295	134	under 18	340	207
18–30	764	464	18–30	519	1750
30–45	1009	634	30–45	556	590
45–60	977	389	45–60	523	255
60+	890	119	60+	468	41

Source: G.R. Snellman, *Undersökning av textilindustrin* (Helsingfors, 1904), pp. 226–7.

Similar estimates about minimum needs were also calculated by Swedish economists and statisticians. A study on female industrial workers in Stockholm indicated that one-third (30.1 per cent) of the women had a yearly income of 470 crowns or more, and supported themselves with ease. The most substantial earnings were generated in breweries and in building work. Another third (32.2 per cent) earned between 365 to 470 crowns, which enabled them to support themselves, although with some difficulty. The group with the lowest income (37 per cent), of less than 365 crowns, was not able to supply their own basic needs. The study included all types and ages of women in industrial work and revealed that those with the smallest earnings were usually teenagers or young unmarried women living with their parents. Some were also mothers who relied on working children for support or augmented their income with assistance from the poor-relief authorities. The mean age of girls earning 260 crown or less was 14.4 years. An analysis of the patterns of earnings revealed, unsurprisingly, that the longer time a woman had spent in employment the better her chances were to acquire a better standard of earnings. Women with less than a year, or one to five years in employment, could not aspire to the income of one with 5–10 years in the workplace.[39] Another survey from the 1890s, this time about women in textile factories, demonstrated that 32 per cent earned more than 470 crowns, 58 per cent between 375 and 470 crowns and 10 per cent less than 375 crowns. In the textile areas no less than 48 per cent of the women had at least one other earning person in the household, in most cases a daughter. Some received rent support and some kept lodgers who contributed towards the rent. Women in cotton weaving had earnings of between 457 and 630 crowns per year, in the wool factory the earnings varied between 380 and 635 crowns. In 1894, the number of work days for female weavers in the cotton factory remained steadily 280 and the earnings

[39] Leffler, *Zur Kenntniss*, pp. 68–70, 80–2, 131.

between 412 and 579 per year. On the other hand, female spinners could only demonstrate earnings of 258 crowns. While the gender segregation of work tasks sometimes makes it difficult to estimate the differences between male and female earnings we find that, when comparison can be made, female earnings were around half of those of males. One-third of the widows and unmarried mothers included in the study could demonstrate a decent household income, and only 10 per cent fell into the lowest income bracket.[40]

In the early years of the twentieth century, the daily wage for working men in France was superficially high enough to support a family. The problem for males, as for females, was the issue of seasonal unemployment. Women in the needle trades could have reasonable earnings when at work, but would suffer hardship during the dead season. Therefore, although the daily earnings for a woman in a factory might be lower, the level of permanency could create better possibilities for survival, as the yearly income brought the person above subsistence level.[41]

The story repeated itself in the northern Italian industrial areas of Piedmont and Liguria. With 282 full working days a year, which was normal in the region around 1900, men earned 390 lira or more, enough to support themselves, but seldom a family. 9 per cent of women in the textile factories earned more than 2 lira per day, 20 per cent 1.5–2 lira and 43 per cent 1–1.5 lira. 28 per cent earned less than a lira per day and fell definitely under subsistence level. The average earnings for female industrial workers over 15 were around 1.20 lira per day. While supporting a family or even oneself could be a problem, for most women the earnings in industry were still superior to those in agricultural work.[42]

We therefore find that when discussing female earnings the mean is not necessarily the most illuminating number. It can be useful when comparing male and female wages, but not as useful when discussing the possibilities for female household heads to support a family, or survive as a single person. In such cases what we want is information about adult women, not teenage girls. We must also not forget that the male breadwinner idea was in many cases just a dream and the female contribution to the household economy vital. In the second half of the nineteenth century, in Barcelona, the daily cost for supporting a family was c.a. 8.5 pesetas, for a single man 6.3 and for a single woman, 3.8 pesetas. The wages in the textile industry for a man varied between 8 and 12 pesetas per day and those of a female spinner were 8–9 pesetas.[43]

[40] K. Key-Åberg, *Inom textilindustrin i Norrköping sysselsatta arbetares lönev-illkor och bostadsförhallanden* (Stockholm, 1896), pp. 36–81, 92–6.

[41] Gonnard, *La femme dans l'industrie*, pp. 106–9, 125–6, 251–3.

[42] Beltio, *The Sexual Division of Labour*, pp. 104–5; H. Lichtenfelt, 'Ueber die Ernahrung der Italiener', *Archiv für die Physiologie* 99 (1903), pp. 1–29, on p. 14.

[43] Borderias and Lopez, 'A gendered view', pp. 113–46, on pp. 138–9.

In Germany, a survey from 1907 revealed a considerable difference in earnings between men and women in the textile industry, with male earnings of 28 marks per week and female of 15 marks per week. Despite such discrepancies, the earnings of a husband and father in industrial work was insufficient for a family in the majority of cases and the work input of wife and children necessary.[44]

From a wider perspective, industrial areas have by no means been uniform. In the St Petersburg area, as in Poland, the factories operated about 290 days per year, in central Russia 285, while in the eastern Russian areas, only 270 days. When in operation the machines were running continuously and shift followed shift. In some places whole families, fathers, mothers and children were working together. During the intensive agricultural season, however, many factories in the east closed their doors, because all the workers had left to participate in the harvest.[45] Therefore, the family economy was not based on industrial earnings all year round but supplemented with income from agriculture.

If we analyse budget studies of working men's families from the early years of the 1900s, they tend to point in the direction that the economic input by the wife was very small. One reason for this was that the families usually included in such studies were so called 'normal families'. Such families were defined to include families with young children only; they also often excluded extended families or even families with lodgers.[46] As, in addition, income from boarders and lodgers was sometimes registered as income by the husband and sometimes separately, but seldom viewed as earned by the wife, the share of the female input tended to be very small. Particularly in British studies the input of the wife tends to hover between 5 and 10 per cent of the household income. While much has been said about the wages of women in industry and how poor they were in comparison with those of men, we are talking about differences of up to 50 per cent, not 90 per cent. Likewise, the insertion of age restrictions on family members for inclusion in surveys would affect what the children could bring into the household as earnings. Studies approaching the issue from another angle, i.e. that of young females in industry, have unearthed family economies where the income of the mother was between 50 and 70 per cent of that of the father and, in addition, teenage children brought

[44] Ingeborg Weber Kellerman, *Die Deutsche Familie* (Frankfurt am Main, 1974), pp. 135–6; *German History in Documents and Images, Volume 4, Forging an Empire: Bismarckian Germany 1866–1890*, Nominal wages.

[45] Snellman, *Undersökning angående textilindustrin*, pp. 36–7; Glickman, *Russian Factory Women*, p. 103.

[46] Beatrice Moring, 'Women, family, work and welfare in Europe in the long 19th century. Budget studies, the nuclear family and the male breadwinner', *Revista de Demografía Historica* XXXIII:II (2015), pp. 119–52.

in a contribution.[47] Studies of working-class families without any clauses for 'normality' have revealed that the nuclear, male-headed 'normal' household represented less than half of male-headed households.[48]

As has been pointed out above, there is reason to remember that budget studies might not be the ideal tool for looking into earnings of women, or even their contributions to the household economy, unless such exercises are undertaken with extreme caution. If we want to know what women were earning and how they survived on these earnings, we might be better served by looking to industrial wage statistics or accounts.

Table 3.9 Gender and wages in the textile industry in Denmark, Italy, Russia, Britain and Germany, late nineteenth and early twentieth centuries.

Year	Textile industry	Female wages as percentage of male
1888	Denmark	55
1903	Italy	46–57
1904	Russia, Moscow region	65
1906	Britain	58.5
1913	Germany	84

Sources: G.R. Snellman *Undersökning av textilindustrin* (Helsingfors, 1904), pp. 34–5 (Moscow region: adult male 14–15 roubles/month, adult female 10 roubles, 15–17 year old male 7.5, female 6.5 and child 4–5 roubles); Josef Mooser, *Arbeiterleben in Deutschland 1900–1970* (Frankfurt, 1984), p. 91; Elizabeth Roberts, *Women's Work 1840–1940* (London, 1988), p. 26; Francesca Beltio, *The Sexual Division of Labour: The Italian Case* (Oxford, 1988), pp. 104–6; Georg Norregaard, *Arbejdsforhold indenfor Dansk Hanndverk og Industri 1857–1899* (Copenhagen, 1943).

Family and household

Papa said: 'Well now, my little girl, we'll no longer be around the house. We'll have to look out so we can work'. I told him, 'I'm going today with my cousin to the mills.' My father was never able to support a family of eight children on 1.10 $ per day ... We had to help our father; I was the oldest one. Four dollars and twenty cents per week – I couldn't go far with that.[49]

---

[47] Kempf, *Das Leben der jungen Fabrikmädchen*, pp. 215–17.

[48] Moring, 'Women, family, work and welfare', pp. 128–9; A.L. Bowley and A. Burnett-Hurst, *Livelihood and Poverty: A Study of Economic Conditions of Working Class Households in Northampton, Warrington, Stanley and Reading* (London, 1915), p. 63; Hareven, *Family Time*, pp. 160–1.

[49] Hareven and Langenbach, *Amoskeag*, pp. 67–8.

There is no doubt that the children of the working class were encouraged to enter working life at an early age and the hope of entering higher education was usually not an option. This was, however, not only the case in female-headed households: working men could also be eager to send their children out to work.[50] While children could be a burden at young ages and co-earners in their teens and later, the child-rich families were not to be found in the female-headed households but those of working men. Single mothers or widows, in surveys and family studies, tended to have one or two children, sometimes three (Table 3.10). The lack of contraception and the presence of a father could result in frequent pregnancies and a continuous presence of infants, making female work difficult or impossible.[51]

> My mother said she always had 'one in the crib and one in the oven', so it was pretty rough on her.[52]

3.10 Textile and tobacco workers in Finland: number of children.

Textile	1 child	2	3	4	5+	Total children	Total workers
Male workers	335	356	296	173	285	4258	1445
Female workers	246	153	78	40	26	1090	543
Tobacco							
Male workers	62	38	41	18	32	514	191
Female workers	176	79	51	21	21	684	348

Sources: G.R. Snellman, *Undersökning av textilindustrin* (Helsingfors, 1904), pp. 32–5: G.R. Snellman, *Undersökning av tobaksindustrin* (Helsingfors, 1903), pp. 26–7.

Although some parents were eager for the children to start earning and some saw any work as good, others tried to find jobs for their family members in the same factory that they were working in. While, for example, in Russia, whole families could be hired for factory work, it was also not out of the question to find parents and their children or siblings working in the same factory in

---

50 Humphries, *Childhood and Child Labour*, p. 110; Hareven, *Family Time*, p. 209; Geijerstam, *Fabriksarbetarnes*, pp. 70–1.
51 Hareven and Langenbach, *Amoskeag*, pp. 255–7; Hareven, *Family Time*, pp. 182–3, 200; Tekla Hultin, *Yötyöntekijättäret Suomen teollisuudessa* (Helsinki, 1911), pp. 44–7; Leffler, *Zur Kenntnis*, pp. 16–20.
52 Hareven and Langenbach, *Amoskeag*, p. 197.

the USA or Scandinavia.[53] There are also examples of mothers trying to find
an entry point into fields where proper training would be available and higher
salary levels or status could ultimately be within reach of the child.

> I myself have never worked in the factory. I was in the post office. My
> mother and later my husband, said, don't go there. They did not want me
> to go into the factory. How should I put it, the young girls in the factory
> they do not have refined speech. My mother said, I have worked there so
> many years, I don't want you to go there, and therefore I found myself a
> job in the post office.[54]

> Mrs. Gronlund would have taken me as a servant but I wanted to be appren-
> ticed to a trade. In those days there were not many choices for a girl. I
> could have started a trainee seamstress or an errand girl in a shop ... but
> I had a hankering for books. My mother objected to bookbinders because
> of the danger of tuberculosis but a printing works seemed a good choice.[55]

Even though industrialisation is often seen as connected to the hegemony of
the nuclear male breadwinner family, areas with abundant female work opportunities present a more varied image of household composition. Women in
Swedish textile mills of the 1890s, like those in industrial work in Stockholm,
often co-resided with widowed mothers, unmarried sisters or workmates.[56]
The solution to the problem of small incomes among female factory workers
seems to have been female kinship connections and female clustering. Lodging
or renting together with female workmates was also usual, and sometimes a
combination of kinship clustering and lodging was practised (Table 3.11). In
factories operating in a rural setting, it was fairly common for the workers to
augment their household budget with a potato patch.[57] Widows and unmarried
mothers with young children also seem to have sought the company of kin
or taken in lodgers for the purpose of assistance with childcare. An example
of such a household would be one consisting of a 15-year-old factory worker,
her parents, a widowed grandmother, her unmarried sister and an illegitimate
baby. Many daughters tended to stay with their mothers. In the textile town of
Norrkoping, one out of three young industrial workers lived with their parent

[53] Hareven, *Family Time*, p. 92; Geijerstam, *Fabriksarbetarnes*, pp. 28–36;
Snellman, *Undersökning angående textilindustrin*, p. 36; Glickman, *Russian Factory
Women*, p. 103.

[54] Kopl and Redl, *Das Totale Ensemble*, p. 69.

[55] Salmela-Järvinen, *Alas lyötiin vanha maailma*, pp. 9–10.

[56] Birgitta Plymoth, *Fattigvård och filantropi i Norrköping 1872–1914* (Stockholm,
1999), p. 65; Key-Åberg, *Inom textilindustrin*, pp. 48–9; Leffler, *Zur Kenntnis*, pp.
15–19, 25, 137.

[57] Geijerstam, *Fabriksarbetarnes*, pp. 28–35.

or parents, of which the vast majority were young women, and the households of widows in industrial work contained children of different ages.[58]

Table 3.11   Residence patterns of female industrial workers in Sweden, Germany and Britain, late nineteenth and early twentieth centuries.

	Widowed female textile workers, Sweden 1894	Unmarried female textile workers Sweden 1894	Unmarried female factory workers, Germany 1911	Women in industrial work, Britain 1911
Residence with parent(s) or kin			79	28.6
With mother		14	18.4	46.4
With father			0.7	7.2
With siblings (sisters)	18.2	14		7.1
With working child	54.5			
Rent independently		4		7.1
Rent with workmates	18	52		
Residence as lodger		5	1.8	3.6
Minor child in the household	9	4		

Sources: Rosa Kempf, *Das Leben der Jungen Fabriksmädchen* (Leipzig, 1911), pp. 13, 161, 178–9; Geijerstam, *Fabriksarbetarnes*, pp. 28–35; Board of Trade, Labour Department, *Accounts and Expenditure of Wage Earning Women and Girls* (1911), LXXXIX. PP. Cd 5963, pp. 11, 17, 20, 31, 41, 44, 46, 52, 55, 57, 60, 63, 73–5, 85; Leffler, *Zur Kenntniss*, pp. 16–17, 110–13.

Textile towns and urban areas of late nineteenth- and early twentieth-century Finland, Germany and Austria replicated the patterns of unmarried women living with family and widows sharing households with children, kin or lodgers. In old age, many women were found in the household of a married daughter. A

[58] Geijerstam, *Fabriksarbetarnes*, pp. 55, 57, 63; Leffler, *Zur Kenntnis*, pp. 15, 103, 110–15, 125, 137.

survey of the Finnish textile industry revealed that the female workers lived with mothers or siblings twice as often as their male counterparts.[59]

The issue of combining family duties with employment also came to the forefront in a survey in 1920s Finland. A large proportion of women could be found among those engaging in night shift work and 63 per cent of the widows in the group were supplying the needs of young children, while the rest had children with some earnings. The majority were residing with a family member, like mother, sister, grandmother or other kin, who did the childminding where young children were present.[60] It would seem that French industrial workers also saw the advantages of kinship collaboration. No less than 70 per cent of industrial workers born in Saint Chamond, in the Lyon region, lived with a parent or relative in the mid-nineteenth century. The collaborative strategies could include both housing and other monetary issues and presented the native workers with advantages not available for migrants. Studies of the living conditions among industrial workers in Austria and Germany have also indicated the clustering of females and adaptive kinship strategies involving female relatives and friends.[61]

> Bis zum vierten Kind hab' ich bei der Mutter gewohnt – und der Mann auch. Da waren wir bei den Eltern in Kost. Ich hab' gearbeitet, und der Mann hat gearbeitet, und die Mutter hat mir auf die Kinder aufpasst. (Until the birth of my fourth child I and my husband lived with my mother. We had a communal household with my parents. I worked and my husband worked and my mother looked after the children.)[62]

In the textile communities of Catalonia we also find plenty of examples of the extended family collaborating for childcare purposes. The family facilitated the work of married women after compulsory schooling brought children out of the work force. While certain families engaged in continuous cohabitation strategies, we find an increasing number of extended families during the

---

[59] G.R. Snellman, *Undersökning angående pappersindustrin*, p. 29; Snellman, *Undersökning angående textilindustrin*, p. 132; Moring, 'Widows, children and assistance', pp. 105–17, on pp. 111–12; Moring, 'Strategies and networks', pp. 77–94, on pp. 86–7; Hjelt, *Undersökning af yrkesarbetarnes*, pp. 2–42; Salmela-Järvinen, *Kun se parasta*, pp. 76–7.

[60] Markkola, *Työläiskodin*, p. 111; OSF XXXII, 1, Sosiaalisia Erkoistutkimuksia 12 (Special social studies), Yötyöntekijättäret (Helsinki, 1935), pp. 8, 10–11, 14, 98–9.

[61] Accampo, *Industrialization, Family Life and Class Relations*, pp. 102–3, 228–30; Chvojka, *Grossmutter*, pp. 84–5, 106–7; Kempf, *Das Leben der jungen Fabrikmädchen*, pp. 162, 183; Sylvia Hahn, 'Women in older ages', *The History of the Family* 7:1 (2002), pp. 33–58, on pp. 48–52.

[62] Kopl and Redl, *Das Totale Ensemble*, p. 63.

childbearing decades in female life.[63] Working-class biographies from early twentieth-century Britain have also evidenced strong economic ties between mothers and children. A survey by the Board of Trade from 1911 demonstrated that no less than 53 per cent of the young working women co-resided either with mothers or sisters or both. Close knit families with adult children, pooling their resources with widowed mothers to support siblings and maintain the family have also been documented from early twentieth-century Irish textile areas. The variable systems of female collaboration in industrial Lancashire, including women of different marital status, have also been highlighted by Michael Anderson.[64]

The family permutations of female factory workers who did not marry, but rarely lived alone, can be exemplified by the story of Louise Larsen, a Danish textile worker. She went into the factory at 14 in the late nineteenth century. After she changed jobs to one with higher wages some years later, her sister left her place as a servant and joined her, closely followed by a younger sister. Four years later, when the elder sister had married and left and the father died, the two girls kept the family. The mother died when Louise was in her early 20s. At this point, she took over the household duties and care of two young brothers while the sister was joined by a brother in the factory. With the aid of a knitting machine she contributed to the family economy from home, which was particularly welcome during the lockout in 1897 when the sister was unable to work. When Louise reached the age of 25, the brothers had been launched into the world and the two sisters resumed work in the factory and residence together. When in her late 30s, the sister died, and for a couple of years Louise lived with an old lady, mostly for the company. In the end, however, she returned to the flat where she had spent most of her life. For another 20 years she worked at the factory, kept a flat of her own, but shared meals with the old lady every day after work.[65]

63 Llonch Casanovas, *Teijendo en red*, pp. 143–6; Fuchs and Thompson, *Women in 19th Century Europe*, p. 71; Camps, 'Mercados de trabajo modernos', pp. 1206–18; Borderias and Lopez, 'A gendered view', pp. 144–6.

64 Ellen Ross, 'Rediscovering London's working class mothers, 1870–1918', in Jane Lewis (ed.), *Labour and Love: Women's Experience of Home and the Family* (London, 1986), pp. 73–98, on pp. 85–7; Marilyn Cohen, 'Survival strategies in female-headed households: linen workers in Tullyish, County Down 1901', *Journal of Family History* XVII (1992), pp. 303–18, on p. 308; Michael Anderson, *Family Structure in Nineteenth Century Lancashire* (Cambridge, 1971), pp. 139–44; Michael Anderson, 'The social position of spinsters in mid-Victorian Britain', *Journal of Family History* 9:4 (1984), pp. 377–93, on pp. 390–1; Board of Trade, Labour Department, *Accounts and Expenditure of Wage Earning Women and Girls* (1911), LXXXIX. PP. Cd 5963, pp. 11, 17, 20, 31, 41, 44, 46, 52, 55, 57, 60, 63, 73–5, 85.

65 Gunhild Agger and Hans Nielsen, *Hverdagsliv og klasserfaring i Danmark 1870–1920* (Aalborg, 1980), pp. 95–100.

Table 3.12 Adult female employment and number of working family members, Manchester, New England 1900.

Other employed family members	0	1	2	3+
Wife, N	275	77	32	60
Working	14.5	11.7		
Not working	85.5	88.3		
Female head N	33	30	16	21
Working	48.5	40.0	43.8	14.3
Not working	51.5	60.0	56.2	85.7

Source: Tamara Hareven, *Family Time and Industrial Time* (1982), p. 209.

Lodgers and living conditions, factory accommodation

The late nineteenth-century towns in the Nordic countries, as in the rest of Europe, suffered from a considerable shortage of housing. The wages of workers were sorely stretched and the cost of housing could form a critical stumbling block. As a result, instead of struggling with the rent the young and unmarried tended to lodge with married couples or widows; sometimes they rented rooms together.[66] Such solutions were, however, not unheard of even among the higher social strata. Kin, friends and men or women with no suitable relations in town or schoolchildren boarded out populated the extra rooms of the middle-class families and beds or floors of the working class.[67] In turn of the century St Petersburg, 26 per cent of the population lived as lodgers. The most likely homes where lodgers could be found were those of labourers and craftsmen. The situation was similar in Moscow:

> We rented three rooms but lived only in the small room and if things got rough we even rented out our room and lived in the kitchen. We cooked and

[66] Gustaf Geijerstam, *Anteckningar om arbetarförhållanden i Stockholm* (Stockholm, 1894), pp. 55, 57, 63; Leffler, *Zur Kenntniss*, pp. 103, 110, 125; Key-Åberg, *Inom textilindustrin*, pp. 36–81; *Census of Norway*, the town of Moss, 1801, 1901; Sidsel Ericksen, Per Ingesman, Mogens Melchiorsen and John Pedersen (eds), *Socialhistorie og samfundsforandring* (Arhus, 1984), pp. 225–60, on pp. 244–5; Alf Nordström, *Om arbetarbostäder i Stockholm under 1800-talets senare del* (Stockholm, 1948).

[67] Heikki Waris, *Työläisyhteiskunnan syntyminen Helsingin Pitkänsillan pohjoispuolelle II* (Helsinki, 1934), pp. 253–60; A. Gauffin, *Bostadsbehof och barnantal med afseende sarskildt a inneboendesystemet i arbetarfamiljerna i Helsingfors* (Helsingfors, 1915), pp. 24–7; Anna Maria Astrom and Maud Sundman (eds), *Hemma bäst: Minnen fran barndomshem i Helsingfors* (Helsingfors, 1990), pp. 33, 89, 92, 135, 179.

washed for the boarders and cleaned up, for which they paid extra money. Our boarders were workers.[68]

In nineteenth-century Vienna, the proportion of households with lodgers varied between 15 and 19 per cent depending on the part of town, with a decrease at the end of the century. The lodgers were of several different kinds: some rented a whole room while others only a bed or a place for a bed. Certain occupational groups were particularly prone to lodging, for example, women engaged in textile work or factory work. In general, the lodgers tended to be young rather than middle aged or old, reflecting the fact that lodging was connected to the first face of migration into urban areas.[69] Although the nineteenth-century German middle class viewed lodging as a sign of moral inferiority, for the working class it was an economic necessity while the children were young. In spite of the fact that the housing situation improved in German towns in the early twentieth century, we find that still in the 1920s, 18 per cent of families with an unemployed head and 5 per cent of those headed by a labourer had a lodger or boarder.[70] Similarly, the presence of boarders was common in US working-class households in the early twentieth century, both when women were working outside the home and in even higher degree when they were not.[71]

We moved to a large house with tens of rooms and a lot of inhabitants. We got a room facing the street on the second floor and now we had to take many lodgers. Maija Salin and her son Bruno moved in with us and soon came the sisters Alina and Selma. There were six of us in a room that would not have been large for two.[72]

The oral history accounts telling about sharing with work-mates is certainly substantiated by an analysis of female landlords and lodgers. Finding several women sharing an occupation is a commonplace in female-headed households at the turn of the century.[73] In some situations, the cohabitation lasted for decades with a gradual merging of life and economy:

[68] Timur Valetov, 'Migration and the household: urban living arrangements in late 19th and early 20th century Russia', *The History of the Family* 13:2 (2008), pp. 163–77, on p. 175.

[69] Josef Ehmer, 'The making of the "modern family" in Vienna 1780–1930', *History and Society in Central Europe* 1:1 (1991), pp. 7–28, on p. 13; Josef Ehmer, *Familienstruktur und Arbeitsorganisation im frühindustriellen Wien* (Wien, 1980), pp. 150–61.

[70] Josef Mooser, *Arbeiterleben in Deutschland* (Frankfurt, 1984), pp. 142–3.

[71] Hareven, *Family Time*, p. 210.

[72] Salmela-Järvinen, *Kun se parasta*, pp. 112–13.

[73] Census of Helsinki, 1900, National Archive, Helsinki: female-headed households, Kallio, Harju.

To start with, we had mostly separate meals, but if one made soup on a Sunday, the other one was given a plateful. Coffee was bought together from the start. Sugar we bought separately. Then we decided to buy everything together, except sugar. When Tilda's teeth got bad, I ate the hard bits of bread and she got the soft ones. We didn't have any problems. Thirty eight years we lived together. When people wondered how we could get on I said: "Sometimes we argue and then we make up". All the cooking and cleaning we did together.[74]

Table 3.13　Widows engaged in industrial work and their co-resident children, 1890s Sweden, urban communities.

Norrkoping	%	Stockholm	%	Norrkoping	%
0 child	28	0 child	25	0 child	28
1 child	34	1 child	32.9	0 child with income	22
2 children	14	2 children	21.5	1 child with income	26
3 children	10	3 children	8.9	2 children with income	18
4+ children	14	4+ children	11.4	3+ children with income	4

Sources: K. Key-Aberg *Inom textilindustrien in Norrkoping sysselsatta arbetares lonevillkor och bostadsforhallanden* (Stockholm, 1896), pp. 48–50; Leffler, *Zur Kenntniss*, pp. 16–19, 25.

Money, gender, contribution and consumption

There are some studies that indicate that, despite the fact that men in industry had the higher earnings, their ability to keep a family together after the loss of a partner was inferior to that of women. Widows, on the other hand, held their families together through united efforts with children and kin.[75]

While the question of co-residence can be established in many cases, we do not always know what the contribution of the child was to the economy of the family. The surveys that did tackle this issue, like the one from 1890s Stockholm, reveal that where there was common residence, there was usually pooling of resources – 52 per cent of the widows had a child or children with earnings contributing to the family economy (Table 3.13). Only those with

[74] Markkola, *Työläiskodin*, p. 81.
[75] Plymoth, *Fattigvard*, p. 65; Anita Goransson, *Fran familj till fabrik* (Lund, 1988), pp. 249–451, 259.

children who were not in employment (20 per cent) did not receive a contribution. Sometimes a daughter handed over all her earnings to the mother. Married sons with a stable income would also occasionally assist mothers.[76]

In Finnish working-class households headed by women, more than a third had another adult, generally a child over the age of 18, contributing. Even though two-thirds had only minor children, some of these still managed to generate some income. Most of children's earnings were absorbed into a communal economy in these families. Pocket money was handed out or small sums kept for lunches and other expenses, but whenever the economic situation became difficult, the children contributed everything. In one out of five families, the children earned about 30 per cent of the family income. In one out of three, the children provided between a third and a tenth of the family budget. It was common for children to take on jobs running errands, or selling newspapers, from the ages of 10 or 12. In the early twentieth century, compulsory schooling ended at the age of 14 and that was when the full-time work started for the children of the working classes.[77]

Gender and family

Once the children reached older ages, a gender difference can be detected. Adult daughters stayed on longer and contributed to the family economy (see, for example, the Louise Larsen biography). We also found that, when widows reached old age, the carer was a daughter more often than a son. Even married daughters took their mothers into their homes and tended to them when faced with illness and disability. It was not unknown for sons to provide for old mothers, some giving both money and care. Of widows in a Finnish industrial community in 1900, 25 per cent lived with adult or married daughters and only 7 per cent with adult sons. However, whenever there were children, there was assistance. The widows who were childless co-resided in some instances with siblings. Others shared household and rent with lodgers or lived as lodgers themselves. The female units exchanging services as well as providing economic input in the form of rent was not exclusive to Finland. Similar stories are available from Swedish towns and industrial areas where women could find work.[78] Women's budgets and industrial surveys reveal

---

[76] Key-Åberg, *Inom textilindustrin*, p. 48; Geijerstam, *Anteckningar*, pp. 55, 57, 63; Leffler, *Zur Kenntniss*, pp. 103, 110, 125.

[77] Hjelt, *Undersökning af yrkesarbetarnes*, pp. 24–9; Salmela-Järvinen, *Kun se parasta*, pp. 25 89; Salmela-Järvinen, *Alas lyötiin vanha maailma*, pp. 5–6, 10; Astrom and Sundman, *Hemma bäst*, pp. 96–8; Markkola, *Työläiskodin*, p. 111; G.R. Snellman, *Tutkimus Helsingin, Turun, Tampereen ja Viipurin kansakoululaisten tyoskenteysta koulun ulkopuolella* (Helsinki, 1908).

[78] Geijerstam, *Anteckningar*, pp. 539–44; Geijerstam, *Fabriksarbetarnes*, pp.

cohabitation between adult women and their mothers and siblings at different stages in life. They also reveal a tendency among daughters to contribute economically to a greater extent than sons. The 1911 survey from Britain also revealed numerous cases of daughters handing their wages to their mother and receiving pocket money in return.[79]

The gender differences in attitude to family obligations seem to have commenced in puberty. Male and female children surrendered their money to their mother, but when becoming part of the adult or semi-adult group, things changed. In the textile towns of the USA, daughters delivered 95 per cent of their earnings to their parents while sons only contributed 83 per cent. German studies show daughters often giving all or most of their wages to their mothers and helping around the house. Sons expected service in the shape of cooking and washing and kept the larger part of their money to themselves. In addition, like their fathers, they expected a larger share of expensive food items like meat. Also, like fathers, the outtake of the family food budget was not adjusted when the contribution ceased, in unemployment.[80]

The assumption has often been made that a household with more income was a household where the family members had a higher standard of living. However, while males had higher earnings, they were perennial consumers of pricey items like meat, tobacco and alcohol.[81] British surveys repeatedly contain the information that to eat meat was an adult masculine privilege. In an urbanised male bread-winner system, it might seem rational to maintain an unequal distribution to guarantee the working potential of the breadwinner. The husband 'needed' meat to be able to work; therefore, the wife deprived herself and her children of nourishment, not only in Britain but also in urban areas in other parts of Europe. Studies from the 1930s have, however, shown that the 'need' of the husband to have the meat was there even when he was unemployed. In some situations, the males of the household were a drain on the resources. Smith drew the conclusion that the English worker was

---

28–36, 56–7; Leffler, *Zur Kenntniss*, pp. 103, 110, 125; Key-Åberg, *Inom textilindustrin*, pp. 36–81; Moring, 'Widows, children and assistance', pp. 105–17.

[79] Moring, 'Widows, children and assistance', pp. 111–12; Moring, 'Strategies and networks', p. 87; Hultin, *Yötyöntekijättäret*, pp. 36–7; Census of Helsinki, 1900; OSF XXXII, 1, Yötyöntekijättäret (Helsinki, 1935), pp. 112–15; Board of Trade, Labour Department, *Accounts and Expenditure of Wage Earning Women and Girls* (1911).

[80] Hareven, *Family Time*, p. 189; Kempf, *Das Leben der jungen Fabrikmädchen*, contributions and distribution, pp. 150–4, 162, 222–3.

[81] Poul Sveistrup, 'Københavnske syerskers og smaakaarsfamiliers kostudgifter', *Nationaløkonomisk Tidsskrift* 3:7 (1899), pp. 578–629, on pp. 578–82, 627; Pember Reeves, *Round About a Pound a Week*, pp. 16–17; Astrom and Sundman, *Hemma bäst*, p. 181; Spring Rice, *Working-Class Wives*, pp. 173–4, 177–9.

reasonably well fed. As he was aware of the unequal distribution, he raised, however, some questions about the situation of their wives and children.[82]

The late nineteenth-century temperance movement and social reformers highlighted the fact that a considerable part of working class income was spent on drink, and a British survey of the 1890s revealed that in no less than 23 per cent of the families 5 shillings a week went directly to the pub and in another 30 per cent 2–5 shillings was spent on alcohol. In the 1870s, no less than 14 per cent of consumer expenditure went on drink, and beer consumption hovered around 30 gallons per person. While there was a slight decrease in spending levels towards the turn of the century the actual consumption per person did not decrease until after 1910.[83] Working-class budgets do not always reveal the costs to the family. Drink taken outside the home was often not included in the budgets or it could be hidden under miscellaneous expenses. At times, however, the wife was ignorant about her husband's earnings and expenditure on alcohol.[84] Oral history collections reveal that in some parts of Europe it was commonplace for men to send out for beer from work, particularly on Saturdays, but even at other times, drinking at work or after was not unheard of. When men went out drinking, the wife had to manage on what was left. In turn-of-the-century Stockholm, an estimated 12 per cent of the working-class budget was used for alcohol.[85] It is, therefore, not surprising that the temperance movement seems to have had specific attraction for women. Not only do we find that married women joined the movement and participated in the activity, but also unmarried women seem to have joined the ranks.[86]

82 Medical Officers Report to the Committee of the Privy Council, Conditions of Nourishment (Smith, 1864); Mary Chamberlain, *Fenwomen: A Portrait of Women in an English Village, History Workshop Series* (Oxford, 1975), pp. 35–6; The Royal Commission of Labour 1893, pp. 136–7, 158–9; Pember Reeves, *Round About a Pound a Week*, pp. 57–8, 113–14; Spring Rice, *Working-Class Wives*, pp. 173–4; Kempf, *Das Leben der jungen Fabrikmädchen*, pp. 152–4.

83 Lady Bell, *At the Works* (London, 1907), p. 247; J. Rowntree and A. Sherwell, *The Temperance Problem and Social Reform* (London, 1900); A.E. Dingle, 'Drink and working-class living standards', pp. 608–22, on pp. 609–14.

84 Rathbone, *How the Casual Labourer Lives*, pp. 13–14, 73; D. Noël Paton, J. Crauford Dunlop and Elsie Maud Inglis, *Study of the Diet of the Labouring Class in Edinburgh* (Edinburgh, 1902), pp. 17, 22; Seebohm Rowntree, *A Study of Town Life* (London, 1903), pp. 363–4, 372–9.

85 Waris, *Työläisyhteiskunnan*, pp. 62–4; Yvonne Hirdman, *Magfrågan: Stockholm 1870–1920* (Stockholm, 1983), p. 23; Kopl and Redl, *Das Totale Ensemble*, p. 65.

86 Sulkunen, *Raittius kansalais uskontona*, pp. 33–4, 156, 188, 166, 202–3; Board of Trade, Labour Department, *Accounts and Expenditure of Wage Earning Women and Girls* (1911), pp. 54, 56, 59, 72; Ruth Bordin, *Women and Temperance: The Quest for Power and Liberty 1873–1900* (Philadelphia, 1981).

In the 1890s, the 6th and 7th Commission of Labor conducted extensive studies into the economic conditions of factory populations both in the United States and in Europe. The reports revealed the fact that industrial populations were by no means uniform. The share of income of different family members varied radically between sectors. While the families from heavy industries like steel and coal demonstrated a predominance of male breadwinning and limited female economic activity outside the household, the textile sector was very different. Unsurprisingly, in wool and cotton, the male share of the family income was lower and the female activity rate higher. Where fathers in heavy industries brought in between 71 and 85 per cent of the household income, their share was between 55 and 74 per cent in textiles. What is perhaps of even greater interest is that the distribution of expenditure also varied. Where the wife and children brought in a larger share of the income, the expenditure on alcohol and tobacco was lower. In addition, the money put aside for necessities for young children was also of a more substantial nature.[87]

The question that then arises is, was it possible for women to manage on their lower earnings and how? A study of the economic and family circumstances of girls in factory work in early twentieth-century Germany has revealed that girls living with working mothers were in a better position than those in male breadwinner families. Where the mother was working, the family income was no worse, on the other hand, the distribution of the assets was different. While vegetable soup had a prominent position in the working-class diet, the women did not spend on alcohol and tobacco and the sharing of available meat was conducted in a more equal manner.[88]

A comparison of expenditure in all female households with those of male-headed ones in turn of the century Britain indicate that the share of food in total expenditure was not radically higher. With an average of 51 per cent in male-headed labourers' households and that in female households varying between 34 and 52 per cent, it is questionable to label working women as in a state of deprivation.[89]

Likewise, a comparison of male- and female-headed households included in a Finnish budget study found that households without adult males had no expenditure on alcohol and tobacco. The amount spent on food per person and day was 47 pennies in women's households and 50 pennies in male-headed units. The structure of the spending was, however, different. Where women did not have to please a male, less meat was bought and a larger

[87] The 6th and 7th Annual Reports of the US Commissioner of Labor 1890 and 1891.

[88] Kempf, *Das Leben der jungen Fabrikmädchen*, pp. 145–7, 150–1.

[89] Beatrice Moring and Richard Wall, *Widows in European Economy and Society 1600–1920* (Woodbridge, 2017), p. 55; Board of Trade, Labour Department, *Accounts and Expenditure of Wage Earning Women and Girls* (1911), pp. 93–5.

share of the food budget was spent on bread and milk. Women bought less butter but slightly more cheese and considerably more vegetables. While the Nordic porridge and rye bread consumption made its mark in both male and female diets, women satisfied their families with a higher proportion of these commodities. On the other hand, the presence of larger quantities of milk gave the children some decent sustenance. A calculation of available calories per person and day in 34 female-headed households gives a result of 2050 calories per person. Converted to consumption units the result would be 3200 calories. The figures for male-headed households would be 1830 per person and 3700 per consumption unit.[90] The basis for the consumption unit is always problematic in the case of older children, the assumption that children and teenagers, even when working, need radically less food than adult males can be debatable. That children did get less in the working-class areas of Helsinki is evidenced by the health surveys in primary schools of the early twentieth century.[91] The redistributed spending of women had, however, the consequence that by replacing expensive meat calories with cheap milk calories the protein intake could be kept at a reasonable level. The higher intake of vegetables also provided some assistance to health and development. Feeding a family on a lower income was of course a balancing act. The women in Helsinki, like those in Stockholm, bought old bread from the bakery or reduced items from rural traders.[92]

Even in the case of Russian women in textile factories, we can detect specific female survival strategies. The unmarried workers formed food collectives called 'Artel', with joint food purchases and cooking. The female 'Artels' had less means than their male equivalents and spent no money on alcohol and much less on meat. The share of rye bread, buckwheat, cabbage, mushrooms, onions, etc. was high. The meals tended to consist of soups, pottage, porridge and similar dishes. The menu was monotonous but the calorie intake was about 2800 per day, which was actually slightly higher or similar to that of women in agricultural work in central Russia[93] (Table 3.14).

The budgets of women in textile work in late nineteenth-century Copenhagen reflects these findings. The mean expenditure on food per day per person was less for widows than for the male-headed households. The structure of the expenditure was, however, different, depending on gender structure. Widows and unmarried mothers, with children and relatives in the household, structured

[90] Hjelt, *Undersökning*, pp. 44–5, 70, 78–80, 190–201; Moring and Wall, *Widows*, p. 61, Table 12.

[91] Waris, *Työläisyhteiskunnan*, pp. 57–9.

[92] Hirdman, *Magfrågan*, pp. 79–81; Salmela-Järvinen, *Kun se parasta*, p. 111; Waris, *Työläisyhteiskunnan*, pp. 33, 38, 44; Moring and Wall, *Widows*, pp. 60–3.

[93] F. Erismann, 'Die Ernährungsverhältnisse der Arbeiterbevölkerung in Centralrussland', *Archiv für Hygiene* 9 (1889), pp. 23–47.

their expenditure towards bread, oats and milk. The women with husbands bought more meat, fish, butter, beer and spirits. The only items that the women indulged in were coffee and sugar.[94] A comparison of the budgets of widows in Stockholm in the 1890s with those of male working-class households reflects the observations above. Widows and single working-class women spent more on bread, cereal and milk and less on meat than did male-headed households. Single women, like men with small families, had more available for themselves. The distribution of foodstuffs was, however, not equal and a widow consuming 2000 calories or less was not likely to be in a worse situation as to her share of the food or indeed the meat that was available than she had been as a wife of a poor labourer.[95]

Table 3.14   The diet of factory workers in the Moscow area, Russia.

	Female workers/day	Male workers/day	Families
Rye bread	780.3 grams	862	638
Buckwheat	210.6	257	149
Sauerkraut	123	203	77
Meat	30.5	84	50
Potatoes	0	36	50
Oil	17	34	18
Fat (lard)	25.3	26	3.7
Wheat flour	5	19.7	81
Peas	0	12.6	2.2
Pork	0	12	10.2
White bread	10	8.5	13.5
Pickled fish	1.8	8	44.2
Fresh fish	0	6	2.8
Butter	0	3.4	5.6
Mushrooms	1	1	0
Pasta	0.2	0.19	0
Eggs	0	0.03	0.17
Sausage	0	0.01	1.3

Source: F. Erismann, 'Die Ernährungsverhältnisse der Arbeiterbevölkerung in Centralrussland', *Archiv für Hygiene* (1889), vol. 9 pp. 23–47.

[94] Sveistrup, 'Københavnske syerskers', pp. 612–15, 619, 627.
[95] Hirdman, *Magfrågan*, pp. 50–3, 290; Leffler, *Zur Kenntniss*, pp. 130–5.

Conclusion

So why did women go to the factory? It would seem that the most important reason was money. Unmarried women and widows had to work, but so did many who had a husband, because the earnings of one person, even if that person was a man, were not sufficient. Unlike what the proponents of 'male pride' want us to believe, not all husbands objected to a wife in employment. As married women were well aware of the negative views the middle classes had of working mothers, the necessity of working was stressed whenever they were asked for the reasons. Some, however, dared to express their desire for money of their own, which they could control. But why the factory, why not other types of work? The choices were not endless for a woman with barely any education. Apart from agricultural work in rural areas there was mainly service or textile work in the home and the factory. Any work of the putting-out type was extremely badly paid until the changes in labour legislation at and after the turn of the century. Domestic service was badly paid, had particularly long hours and no freedom. It was also low-status work and servants were not only seen as inferiors by their employers but also by surrounding society. Therefore, factory work with all its baggage of long days, heat, dust and exhausting conditions, paid better than most other options and could give some chances of employment security and a living, or almost a living, wage. Certainly it was no secret that women were paid less than men, but that was the case in all sectors. While the entry level in factory earnings for women was low, the earnings did not necessarily remain low in all places. Women in factory work could earn enough to keep themselves and in some cases even dependants. Where young women barely earned enough to survive, various strategies came into play. It is of some interest to note that, in many countries, single female factory workers sought security in collaboration and co-residence with female relatives, if they could not remain in the parental home. The co-resident sisters, mothers and daughters, with or without children, were a recurring urban industrial phenomenon. While one female income might be difficult to live on, two made it easier and three even more so. In some cases, very interesting systems were set up, like the food collectives run by female workers in Russian factories, whereby sufficient nourishment could be attained even on a female income.

Therefore, we have to accept that women in the past assessed their options and chose what could be the best of two, or three, bad ones. The goal was, however, to manage, survive and bring up their families.

4

Accidents, Compensation, Laws and Inspection

The rules of this law are to be applied to every machine that can pose a danger for the life or health of a person using them. This applies to machines powered by steam, gas, water, wind etc. or by animals. It applies both to machines used for the work and those generating power and all connecting wheels, axels, power cords or belts, electrical cords etc. used for connecting the power to work machines.

... Working machines should be constructed and placed and connecting moving parts be fenced or covered so that the workers engaged with them could only in case of extreme carelessness come into connection with moving parts when pursuing their normal duties.

(First and second paragraphs of the Law about Preventing Accidents
When Using Machines etc. of 12 April 1889, by royal declaration,
Christian IX of Denmark)

Table 4.1 Reported accidents, Germany 1898, per sector.

Industry	Deaths	Incapacity less than 13 weeks	Industry	Deaths	Incapacity less than 13 weeks
Mining	1262	41,881	Sugar	44	2241
Building	937	30,733	Leather	29	963
Transport	369	13,688	Fine mechanic	22	3724
Machine works	293	36,699	Gas	18	2069
Stonework	252	5142	Glass	13	1076
Shipping	249	3958	Ceramics	13	770
Iron and steel	215	30,900	Food	11	997

Drink	150	9741	Garment industry	9	1072
Ship building	134	4916	Book printing	8	1305
Brickworks	134	3393	Musical instruments	4	443
Wood	119	10,368	Chimney sweep	5	93
Flour mills	92	1928	Tobacco	4	421
Textile	90	7416	Abattoirs	3	1,005
Chemical	77	6165	Industry altogether	4613	226,026
Paper	57	3459	Rural, agrarian	2598	55,476

Source: *Statistisches Jahrbuch für das Deutsche Reich* (Berlin, 1899).

A factory could be a dangerous place. The textile mills at Lowell, Massachusetts, praised by Charles Dickens in 1842 as something miles away from the horrors of similar places in Britain, deteriorated over time under economic pressure. In 1860, Pemberton Mill in Lawrence was the scene of a horrendous catastrophe. All five floors of the factory collapsed while in operation and then a fire broke out. 88 people died and 116 were injured. The defects in columns in the building had been discovered in 1854 but nothing had been done.[1] Most accidents were naturally not of this magnitude, but could have a devastating effect on the people involved and their families.

Before the development of the welfare state and legislation protecting wages and loss of earnings through illness and accidents, the section of society depending on their ability to work had minimal ability to secure their old age. Therefore, those regularly turning to society for permanent assistance were the poor workers and their widows. The introduction of mandatory accident insurance in the early twentieth century protected workers and their families against loss of earnings and was in the end viewed in a positive light by society, as it reduced the need for poor relief.[2]

[1]   Robert F. Dalzell, *The Good Rich and What They Cost Us* (New Haven, 2013), pp. 58, 66, 179.
[2]   The first laws about old age pensions were introduced in Scandinavia before WWI. The size of the pension was proportional to contributions in line with systems in Germany, Britain and other North European countries. Carlsson and Rosen, *Svensk Historia 2*, pp. 470, 557–8; Kai Häggman, 'Fran åldring till glad pensioner,

In Germany, industrial accident insurance was introduced through the Accident Insurance Act of 1884. The act was part of social insurance legislation commencing in 1883 with the Health Insurance Bill. A health service was established on a local basis and the cost divided between employers one-third and workers two-thirds. Contributions were made to sickness funds for employees when in need of medical care. Minimum payments for medical treatment and sick pay (up to 13 weeks) were fixed. The accident insurance paid for medical treatment and a pension of up to two-thirds of earned wages, if the worker was fully disabled. The program was expanded to include agricultural workers in 1886. The entire expense rested on the employers, who formed corporations representing particular trades for the purpose. Similar rules were introduced in Austria in 1888 and Hungary in 1891. The 1889 Old Age and Disability Insurance Bill stipulated a pension at the age of 70 and for persons permanently disabled. This system was financed by contributions from workers, employers and the state.[3]

The British Workmen's Compensation Act of 1897 introduced the rule that the employer was to compensate a workman injured at work, or if killed, his dependants. The compensation was to be paid irrespective of any negligence of the employee. Compulsory sickness insurance was brought in in 1911, incidentally, the same year as in Russia. In France, the workman's compensation in case of accidents became regulated in 1898 and in New Zealand in 1900. President Theodore Roosevelt was eager to bring the United States in line with Germany and Britain and, in 1908, Congress passed a compensation act covering government employees. In New York, two years later, legislation about compensation in connection with industrial accidents was brought in. However, one of the statutes was later declared unconstitutional by the local Supreme Court. Although 10 states passed workmen's compensation laws in 1911 and were followed by others, the last one (Mississippi) did not join the trend until 1948.[4] The American Federation of Labor was initially negative to the compensation system as taking employers to court had in some cases resulted in generous compensation payments. By 1909, however, Samuel Gompers, president of the AFL, gave his backing and that of the organisation to the new compensation system.[5]

National accident insurance schemes with payments to widows and orphans were introduced in Finland and Norway in the 1890s. In Sweden, the accident

---

pensionssystem och pensionstagare i Finland på 1900-talet', *Historisk Tidskrift för Finland* 2 (1998), pp. 337–55.

[3]   Hajo Holborn, *A History of Modern Germany – 1840–1945* (Princeton, 1969), pp. 291–3.

[4]   Stefan A. Riesenfeld, 'Contemporary trends in compensation for industrial accidents here and abroad', *California Law Review* 42:4 (October 1954), pp. 532–3.

[5]   U.S. Department of Labor, *Progressive Era Investigations*, http://www.dol.gov/programs/history.

cover of 1901 was based on voluntary contributions (like in Denmark), with the result that many men opted out. By 1916, however, anybody employed in industrial or comparative work was obliged to participate in the accident insurance system.[6]

The Finnish Economic Act of 1879 had obligated employers to pay attention to the health and capacity of their workers and take 'necessary action' for protection of the workers against bodily harm when performing their duties. The legislation of protection of workers 1889 introduced clearer definitions of 'necessary'. The Industrial Accident Law of 1895, however, transformed the situation. Before 1895, the worker had to prove that the employer was guilty of negligence, thereby creating a situation where accidents could happen. The actual name of the 1895 law, 'A law about the responsibility of employers for the bodily harm of an employee', accurately describes the shift in attitude by the legislative body. The legislation did not, however, cover all types of economic activity. Agricultural work, logging and log transport, crafts or even work on the construction of buildings of one floor were not included in the accident insurance law. The nature of the legislation was also clearly related to the assessment of danger posed by machinery and the responsibilities of the owners of such machinery to maintain their functionality and protect the workers from dangerous contact. As statistics was already available demonstrating links between tiredness at the end of long shifts and accidents, the rulings were very clear that only in cases of aggravated carelessness by the worker could he/she be deemed responsible and not the proprietor.[7] The introduction of the law had been preceded by lengthy discussions about the desirable structure of it. Opinions were expressed as to whether the introduction of an insurance system would result in a greater disinclination among employers to increase safety in the workplace. Was diligence more likely if they were directly held responsible and obliged to pay compensation in case of an accident? Others voiced the opinion that an insurance system would be a better guarantee for the worker to receive economic support in a time of need. While the 1895 law introduced a system of obligatory accident insurance, this did only cover cases of death and accidents resulting in permanent incapacity or inability to work for more than 120 days. The great majority of accidents that had to be reported were not covered by the compulsory insurance.[8] In 1898–1900, the insured workers numbered about 60,000 in Finland and,

---

6 Statistiska centralbyrån, *Historisk Statistik för Sverige* (Stockholm, 1960), p. 164; Jouko Jaakkola, 'Sosiaalisen kysymyksen yhteiskunta', in Jouko Jaakkola, Panu Pulma, Mirja Satka and Kyösti Urponen (eds), *Armeliaisuus, yhtesöapu, sosiaaliturva* (Helsinki, 1994), pp. 71–162, on p. 197; Carlsson and Rosen, *Svensk Historia 2*, pp. 466–7; Hazel Armstrong, 'Workplace safety and accident compensation', *Te Ara The Encyclopedia of New Zealand*, http://TeAra.govt.nz/workplace-safety-and-accident-compensation.

7 Pauli Kettunen, *Suojelu, Suoritus, Subjekti* (Helsinki, 1994), pp. 44, 46–7.

8 Kettunen, *Suojelu, Suoritus*, pp. 49–50.

by 1913, this had increased to 115,000. During the same period the insured companies multiplied from 1700 to 4700.[9]

Table 4.2　Accidents in Finland reported to the industrial inspectors 1890–1914.

Type of injury	Number	%
Fatal	775	2.6
Total invalidity	314	1.0
Partial invalidity	4705	14.3
Non-permanent injury	26,011	79.3
Unknown	986	3.0
Total	32,791	100

Source: OSF XXVI, *Suomen Virallinen Tilasto*, Työtilastoa, A. Työssä kohdanneet tapaturmat (Helsinki, 1915).

In Spain, parliament started discussing the issue of industrial accidents from the 1880s. In 1900, the Labour Accidents Law came into being and, in 1906, the Labour Inspection Service was created to oversee adherence to the existing laws. In the period 1908–23, the factory inspectors repeatedly complained about the implementation of the law. The problems were lack of a sufficient number of inspectors, problems with coordination between the local and central administration and the influence of employers in local communities. They also pointed out that the system of fines was inadequate. The 1900 law introduced a system of compensation to workers in case of accidents. The legislation followed Britain in that the firms could choose between using insurance companies or setting up their own accident funds. When the accident resulted in death, compensation was paid to the family for seven months and up to two years, depending on the number of dependants. The compensation in other accidents was related to the type of injury: permanent total disability, two year's wages; inability to continue doing the same work, one and a half year's wages; partial disability, loss of arm or leg, one year's wages. Temporary disability like broken limbs gave 50 per cent of the wage before 1922. In 1933, the system underwent a reform with the introduction of obligatory insurance, life annuities and increase of premiums.[10]

According to the industrial inspectors, even serious accidents were sometimes not reported because of the ignorance of the workers of the law

---

[9]　OSF XXVI Tyotilasoa. A. Tyossa kohdanneet tapaturmat 1890–1914 (Helsinki, 1915).

[10]　Javier Silvestre Rodrigues, *Workplace Accidents and Early Safety Policies: Spain 1900–1934*, Working Paper, Department of Economics – TARGET, University of British Columbia (Vancouver, 2005), pp. 6–7.

and their rights or fear of sacking. Illiteracy was fairly wide spread and small sums handed out by employers could be accepted as settlement. As a consequence, the hope that the employers would invest in safety measures rather than pay compensation to injured workers did not become a reality. The important unions also seemed to have less interest in workplace safety than in wage issues and the length of the working day, and did not actively encourage workers to push for improvements. When examining the statistics of Spanish workplace accidents it would seem that an increase in the number of work days in contrast to a period of prolonged strike action had a serious impact on the number of accidents, both fatal and nonfatal. This would indicate that intensification of work, i.e. participation in work activity, was one of the decisive factors in whether workers were prone to accidents. The statistics from the period from 1910 also show that certain sectors – construction, metal, mining, chemicals and transport – had the highest levels of accidents, but overall, the accident level in Spain was fairly similar to other European countries.[11]

The Italian state introduced the first workplace accident insurance legislation in 1898. The law made it obligatory for employers to insure their workers against accidents and to make technical improvements to prevent the occurrence of such accidents. The first piece of legislation excluded small workplaces, mines and manufacture of explosives. During 1899, however, special accident insurance regulations were passed for mines, explosives factories and, in 1900, for the construction industry. Over the following years, more sectors were brought into the system of insurance, culminating in 1903 with the inclusion of the transport sector. To the extent that a difference with Spain can be detected, it would be linked to the greater emphasis placed on accident prevention and improvement of the work environment in the Italian case.[12]

While the introduction of the insurance schemes brought about the collection of information about accidents, a comparison between countries might not be as informative as one would desire. The distribution between sectors is, to a considerable degree, connected to the economic structure of individual countries and the prevalence of certain occupations. For example, for geographic reasons, some countries had more mines and, therefore, more mining accidents. While the German insurance system would make it less likely that accidents would stay unreported, other countries might not have displayed the same level of diligence. When viewed from a gender perspective, however, we find that areas of exclusive or majority male participation by and

11 Silvestre Rodrigues, *Workplace Accidents*, pp. 8–11; Maria Jesús Espuny Tomás, 'Los accidentes de trabajo: perspectiva histórica', *IUS Labor* 3 (2005), pp. 1–10.

12 Roland Dubini, *L'unita d'Italia e la tutela da infortuni*, https://www.punto-sicuro.it/sicurezza-sul-lavoro-C-1, pp. 2–4; Camera Dei Deputati, *Relazioni della Commissione Parlamentare di Inchiesta sulle Condizioni dei Lavoratori in Italia* (Rome, 1963), pp. 39–41.

Figure 2   While the welfare of workers had become a topic of interest
by the 1890s, the workers did not always have the same trust in experts
as the experts themselves. *Der neue Postillion, Humoristisch-satirisches
Halbmonatsblatt der schweitzerischen Arbeiterschaft*, nr 126, October 1897.

large appear to have been of a more dangerous nature than those populated by women (see Table 4.3).

Table 4.3   Reported accidents, France 1904, per sector.

Professions	Deaths	Incapacity permanent	Incapacity temporary	Not clear	Total
Agriculture	88	262	2574	108	2932
Industry					
Mining	2	3	327	14	340
Garment	7	22	1659	33	1721
Book printing	5	53	1975	21	2054
Paper etc.	13	116	3430	49	3608
Chemical	52	122	10,120	172	10,466
Food and drink	100	200	12,309	256	13,374
Textile	33	414	13,921	113	14,481
Wood	31	616	14,564	279	15,540
Metal	55	100	17,174	137	17,466
Construction	307	638	27,465	619	29,030
Transport	374	513	32,788	655	34,330

Source: *Bulletin de l'inspection du travail* (Paris, 1905).

In parallel with the first steps towards a social security system, other consequences of industrial activity had come into focus. While accidents had increased because of the use of machines, working conditions also saw the interest of the medical profession and social reformers. Between 1860 and 1890, the question of threats to human health in the workplace, i.e. occupational disease, was the subject of a plethora of studies. Among other professions, the working environment and contact with toxic substances of glassworkers, workers engaged in lacquering furniture, ceramics, enamelwork, electric batteries, artificial pearls, etc. were examined. The results were published, among others, by Adrien Proust, *Nouvelle maladie professionelle chez les polisseurs de camees* 1878, Henri Napias, *Inspection hygiénique des fabriques et ateliers* 1883. These studies draw a clear line from workrooms saturated with poisonous dust to illness in workers. The solution was seen by Poincaré in his *Traité d'hygiène industriel à l'usage des médecins et des membres de conseils d'hygiène,* from 1886, where he underlined the need for specialists in medicine and hygiene to be engaged in the process of creating a healthier workplace.[13]

The factory and the workshop as a place in the need of regulating was an issue that had arisen already earlier in the century. Britain, with its early industrial development, saw a need to act when the situation of children in factories and workplaces had come to the attention of the general public and political decision-makers. The first factory inspectors were appointed under the provisions of the Factories Act of 1833. Initially, their main duty was to prevent injury and overworking in child textile workers. The conditions facing them were dire, with children kept at work for days with only food breaks.[14] The four inspectors were responsible for approximately 3000 textile mills and had powers to enter mills and question workers. They were also able to formulate new regulations and laws to ensure the Factories Act could be suitably enforced. Despite serious opposition from contemporary politicians and employers, the factory inspectors were able to influence subsequent legislation relating to machinery guarding and accident reporting. By 1868 there were 35 inspectors and sub-inspectors, each responsible for a distinct geographical area. Changes to legislation during the period 1860 to 1871 extended the Factories Act to practically all workplaces and the inspectors took on the role of technical advisers in addition to their enforcement duties. The 1878 Factory and Workshops Act stipulated that all factories and workshops employing more than 50 people were to be inspected regularly by government inspectors, not local authorities as before.

As in Britain, the early regulations in France and Germany regarding working life were specifically targeting the work of children in factories. Already, before unification, the State of Prussia had introduced a regulation for child protection in 1839, and the 1850s saw the establishment of a factory inspectorate in Aachen, Arnsberg and Dusseldorf. The common denominator of the nineteenth-century factory legislation in Europe was that the state legislative bodies passed rules that were never viewed as unconstitutional, even though they created restrictions for free enterprise. The parliament of the newly unified Germany went through lengthy debates, but once legislation had been passed, the regulations about the work of children applied to all

---

13 Caroline Moriceau, 'Les perceptions des risques au travail dans la seconde moitié du XIX siècle', *Revue d'histoire moderne et contemporaine* 56:1 (2009), pp. 11–27. Napias, Henri, 'Inspection hygiénique des fabriques et ateliers', *Annales d'hygiène publique et de médecine légale* 10 (1883), pp. 412–25; Poincaré, Emile Leon, *Traité d'hygiène industriel à l'usage des medecins et des membres de conseils d'hygiène* (Paris, 1886); Proust, Adrien, 'Nouvelle maladie professionelle chez les polisseuses de camées', *Annales d'hygiène publique et de médecine légale* 50 (1878), pp. 193–206

14 Extract from British Parliamentary Papers (1836) No 353, Factory Inspectors report.

states. The protection of the life and health of workers was in principle part already of older legislation, but by 1869, these rules were firmed down and covered not only factories but also other workplaces. The two important exceptions were farm work and work in the home. The need for protection of workers were raised by the unions in the 1870s and in this case 'protection' included curtailing of working time for men, women and children but also protection from accidents and poisonous substances and control of rules by factory inspectors.[15]

For a large part of the nineteenth century, the adherence to factory laws was to be supervised on a local level by the local police force. While the issue of authority did of course not arise, the ability of this body to attend to the question of minors working instead of attending school, or later, when regulations multiplied, to oversee the factory laws, was limited. Therefore, by the 1870s, several states saw the necessity to create a special group of inspectors, primarily for control of the work of children and young people, for example, Baden 1870 and Sachsen 1872. In addition, the issue of protection of the life and health of workers was added to the tasks. In 1878, the inspection of factories became mandatory in Germany as a whole. Because of the dangers posed by machinery, particularly in Prussia, the definition of necessary skills for the inspectors leaned in the direction of knowledge of chemistry, engineering and technology. However, some of the inspectors also represented the pharmacological sector. Doctors, on the other hand, were not particularly favoured for the posts until the early years of the twentieth century. Although Prussia employed as many as 18 inspectors in 1881, the other states counted the numbers in single figures. The increase in the 1890s was, however, rapid: Prussia employed 216 inspectors in 1900 and, by 1913, 565 inspectors were to be found in Germany.[16]

In Russia, factory inspection was established in 1882. As elsewhere, the inspectorate was created for the purpose of making sure that the labour laws would not remain empty words. The institution was originally called 'factory inspection for underage workers', underlining the fact that the labour laws were in the first instance created to prevent factory work of young children. One chief inspector and four district factory inspectors were employed.[17] The need for additional rules and a larger body to oversee the adherence to these rules resulted in labour laws in 1884, 1891, 1894, 1897 and 1899. Simultaneously, the inspectorate grew, first to 20, later 36 and, by 1900, no

---

15 Wolfgang Ayass, *Arbeiterschutz* (Stuttgart-Jena, 1996), pp. ix–xxii.

16 Ayass, *Arbeiterschutz*, pp. xxvii–xxx.

17 Andrei Volodin, *Russian Factory Inspection (1882–1918): Cui Bono?* (Paris, 2008), pp. 3–4.

fewer than 203 persons. However, in a country the size of Russia, even 200 inspectors had problems in keeping on top of things.[18]

It did not escape the notice of administrators and social reformers in the United States that factory legislation was being passed in Europe and particularly in Britain. The focus on such issues varied, however, considerably between different states. While a minimum age for employment became law as early as 1832, protective labour legislation came into the forefront of discussion primarily in the industrialised areas of the northeast and particularly regions with a strong union movement. In 1852, the state of Ohio passed a law limiting women's hours in industry and some other states introduced similar regulations. There were, on the other hand, limited ways of overseeing that such rules were followed. In 1874, Massachusetts set a 10 hour limit for female workers, but it was not until 1908 that such rules could be unequivocally seen as constitutional. The first factory safety and health law in America was passed in Massachusetts in 1877 and two years later a factory inspection force was established to make sure the law would not become a dead letter. Within the next 20 years, 14 states introduced factory legislation and 10 gave inspectors the right to order guarding of machinery. Many also authorized them to ban cleaning of moving machinery, guarding elevator shafts, request installation of ventilation and fans, and request improvement of sanitary conditions. In addition, some inspectors could enforce child labour laws. The dominant labour organisation in the 1870s and 1880s, The Knights of Labor, was actively pursuing the establishing of labour statistics bureaus, to chart workplace conditions and gather accident statistics, to demonstrate the need for improvement. From 1881, the American Federation of Labor consolidated the union sector and came to play a major role in political issues related to working conditions and regulations. These unions supported the idea of factory and workplace inspections as a means to tackle the question of workplace accidents as well as unhealthy working environments. On the other hand, one must not forget that while regulations as to working ages and working hours of children were linked to the wellbeing of the young generation, special regulations for women were not always viewed identically by women and male-dominated unions.[19]

The safety of the workplace was, on the other hand, a question that had wide consensus among all workers. The removal of health hazards were however not always unproblematic. Even though the statements from inspectors in Massachusetts indicated that factory owners generally responded positively to the installation of safety guards on machinery and actively requested preinstalled guards when replacing and modernising, some safety devices were

---

[18] Volodin, *Russian Factory Inspection*, p. 13.

[19] U.S. Department of Labor: Office of the Assistant Secretary for Administration and Management, *Factory Inspection Legislation*, http://www.dol.gov/programs/history.

removed by workers when they considered that their output was affected. While there were employers who obstructed the work of factory inspectors, others had no objection to installing fans and improving ventilation. Positive advice and information about improved technology and safety devices was often even received with gratitude. Regulations, although viewed negatively when under review, once passed were accepted, particularly if all competitors had to make the same updates or modifications.[20]

In the early years of the twentieth century, a new field of medicine in the USA came into being with the studies of Alice Hamilton on work-related diseases. Hamilton lived in Chicago and was linked to Hull House where she had observed working class people and noted that people of particular occupations were suffering from the same kind of health problems. Although occupational disease was a known phenomenon among the medical profession in Europe, little or no research existed in the USA. In 1907, the first occupational disease commission was established in Illinois and, in 1909, Hamilton was asked to join. She, however, chose to become chief researcher for the commission rather than an ordinary member. With the assistance of scientists, physicians and others, lists were drawn up of toxic substances and a selection of hazards and ailments were brought into focus. Hamilton concentrated her efforts on lead, mercury and arsenic. She studied the trades of lead smelting and refining, the making of white lead pigment, printing, painting and the making of storage batteries. She demonstrated the connection between lead poisoning and sanitary-ware enamelling and the ingestion of lead-contaminated food through handling when making lead paste, plus the inhalation of airborne lead particles in emptying pans of the powder. In an enamel-ware plant, she found that 92 out of 148 workers suffered from lead poisoning, in some cases the onset being as short as after 10 days' work. On a national level, one of the members of the research group the American Association for Labor Legislation, John B. Andrews, took it upon himself to demonstrate the connection between white phosphorous and phosphorous necrosis in match making, the so called 'Prossy jaw'. The disease was sometimes fatal, but it always caused severe pain and disfigurement, as the cure involved the amputation of the jaw bone or part of it. Andrews investigated 15 match factories and with research results including photographs he proceeded (1910) to lobby Congress for the banning of white phosphorous on the lines of European countries. While the USA had refused to sign an international treaty banning the substance, a prohibitive tax on phosphorous matches was introduced through the so called Esch act in 1912.[21]

[20] U.S. Department of Labor, *Inspection, Enforcement, Compliance*, http://www. dol.gov/programs/history.

[21] U.S. Department of Labor, *Progressive Era Investigations*, http://www.dol.gov/ programs/history.

Table 4.4   Workplace accidents, Denmark 1900–1903.

Age	Male	Female	Accidents within compensation rules	
10–20	392	55	Fatal	52
20–30	885	74	Disability 25% or more	119
30–40	829	38	Disability less than 25%	420
40–50	676	33	No permanent disability	233
50–60	453	20		
60+	206	4		
Total	3441	224	Total	824

Source: Gustav Bang, *Arbejderrisiko* (1904) Arbejdernes livsforhold under kapitalismen http://perbenny.dk/1912.html.

Table 4.5   Reported accidents, Finland 1906, gender and age.

Industry	Men	Women	Children under 15	Children 15–17	Deaths	Incapacity permanent
Sawmills	690	75	3	53	21	205
Mechanical workshops	316	3	1	23	1	63
Paper mills	184	11	1	7	9	68
Iron and steel	170			9		21
Railway	87	2		2	12	2
Construction	62		1			29
Textile	75	114	2	35	3	33
Stone	58			1		32
Glass	25	2	8	8		1
Alcohol	43	7		2	1	4
Brickworks	23	2		2		6
Food	42	7	1	2		5
Sea transport	16				3	25
Printing	15	6	1	6		8
Leather etc.	16	2		3		7
Ceramics	10					3
Chemical industry	9	4		2	1	2

Mining	7			1	4
Other	32	6	1	1	15
Total	1.883	241	19	156	53	535

Source: OSF, *Finlands Officiella Statistik, Arbetsstatistik XXVI A. Olycksfallen i arbetet* (Helsingfors, 1908), pp. 15, 18, 22.

Table 4.6   Reported factory and workshop accidents in Britan 1855–1914, gender and age.

Year	Men	Women	Boys 13–18	Girls 13–18	Boys 11–14	Girls 11–14
1885–6	3487	687	1612	570	223	77
1886–7	3610	648	1715	597	171	86
1887–8	3759	732	1973	646	226	101
1888–9	4035	812	2152	658	212	98
1889–90	4102	799	2360	660	212	78
1890–1	4236	787	2399	742	272	91
1891–2	4491	834	2352	671	214	81
1892–3	4181	696	2343	675	211	80
1895	5618	910	2845	821	199	73
1896	7946	1229	3913	1102	183	60
1897	9325	1256	4146	1030	154	70
1898	11,611	1498	4786	1114	161	54
1899	14,154	1732	5284	1355	170	67
1900	18,020	1852	6205	1387	169	40
1903	20,809	2297	5802	1444	124	33
1904	20,712	2200	5535	1369	108	37
1905	22,611	2377	5468	1414	99	33
1906	25,688	2636	5679	1541	112	40
1908	29,161	3490	6909	2153	132	57
1910	30,289	3974	7039	2252	187	53
1911	33,035	4354	8650	2796	113	50
1914	34,521	4390	10,413	3025	159	55

Notes: Total accidents: 1900 79,020, 1901 83,760, 1902 90,355. Fatal accidents: 1896 597, 1906 1116, 1911 1182.
Sources: *Annual reports of the Chief Inspector of factories 1886–1915* 1896 PP 1897 XVII Reports, commissions 3, Factories and Workshops, Appendix 7, Zz 2.

A study of the development of accidents in Britain between 1885 and 1914 reveals that, while accidents among the youngest age groups had decreased, accidents among the older teenagers and adults had increased considerably. It is of course not possible to determine to what extent lack of reporting in the 1885 impacted on the numbers. By 1914, however, it is evident that engagement in the war industry had an effect on the workplace dangers for young people.

Protective legislation for women and children – protection or discrimination

> We don't have our wives and daughters to be the factory owners' slaves. Our women belong to us.[22]

By the nineteenth century, the misuse of child labour in factory production and the negative effects of this activity on the health and education prospects of such children was being repeatedly highlighted and criticised. After the instigation of public enquiries and studies by social reformers, the first pieces of legislation regulating the working hours of children were brought in. In the face of considerable opposition and claims that the economy was going to be ruined, Britain introduced the first regulations in 1833 and 1844, followed by France in 1841.[23] The second half of the nineteenth century brought out the fact that the workplace was no longer only controlled by the owner but also a matter for society. The workers formed unions that pressed for statistics to reveal the reality of working conditions. Society introduced inspections to reveal the situation and to control that laws were followed. The new factory laws mandated the reporting of accidents and accident statistics became a part of many inspection reports.

The factory and workplace legislation itself experienced a change. The early rules had focused on the work of children and eliminating the youngest generations from factory work or restricting the time they spent there. The updated legislation began to internalise the idea of making the workplace safer. However it also had another side, restricting the work of women. The arguments were multifarious: factories were bad for (female) morals and for health, particularly the health of mothers or mothers to be, and, therefore, they posed a threat to the nation. As in discussions about infant mortality or child health and wellbeing, the mother was always targeted and blamed if she shirked her duty in providing the nation with healthy sons that could be sent out to war. In the late nineteenth century, country after country in Europe introduced a ban on night work for women. 'Night' tended to be a fairly loose concept in that it could be defined in many ways as to time. The ban was

---

[22] Grandner, 'Special labor protection', pp. 150–81, on p. 165.
[23] Ursula Henriques, *Before the Welfare State: Social Administration in Early Industrial Britain* (London, 1979), pp. 93–8.

introduced 1883 in Austria, 1888 in the Netherlands, 1891 in Germany, 1892 in France and 1902 in Italy, to name some countries.

In restricting the right of women to work, social and political conservatives saw eye to eye with male unions and the socialist movement. Here, the different ideologies could be united, female competition in the workplace eliminated for the loftiest reasons and the male breadwinner ideology boosted. Through rules that specifically targeted women – different hours, different working week, a ban on night work – the position of women in the workplace was eroded. In the worst cases, married women were excluded from regular work and had to scrape an income from casual service work and underpaid work in the home. In other cases, they soldiered on. The many rules regarding women, however, created a situation where the overseeing of the restrictions could be carried out better by a woman and a new female field saw the daylight.[24]

The employment statistics of the late nineteenth century revealed that women and children tended to be found in certain types of industry, often related to textile and food production, i.e. the sectors where women had been found even in a pre-mechanised society. A comparison between industrial sectors also demonstrate that the most accident prone were those primarily populated by males. Britain, with a large industrial population, registered a number of accidents involving women and young people, particularly teenage boys. Over time, however, the youngest categories displayed a decrease among the under-14 year olds (Table 4.6).

It is not unlikely that the positive trend was linked to increased regulation. The use of children for work in textile factories and the evils of child labour outside the home with uncontrolled working hours and an unregulated workplace had set reformers and philanthropists in motion, not just in Britain where the problem was extensive, but also in other countries. In many countries, restrictions were put on industry while little or no rules existed for agriculture and related pursuits. Small businesses were also widely excluded. Although the early regulations primarily targeted factory work and not agriculture, such an approach was not totally devoid of logic. A comparison between accidents in industry and agriculture in France in the early 1900s is a good example of the potential dangers to life and health in the one sector in comparison with the other (Table 4.3). When special rules about the working day for children and young people was discussed, an argument was made for the effect of fatigue on concentration and, therefore, introducing elements of danger for the young when working in conjunction with machinery. Age limits for factory work were being introduced in a number of countries (see Table 4.7); the nineteenth century also saw the introduction of rules about the working day

---

[24] Howe, 'A paradise for working men', pp. 318–35; Alice Kessler-Harris, 'The paradox of motherhood: night work restrictions in the United States', in Wikander et al., *Protecting Women*, pp. 337–56.

for children and curtailing of the working day for children still of school age (see Appendix 4).

Table 4.7   Minimum age for children's factory work in selected countries.

Country	Year	Min. age	Year	Min. age	Year	Min. Age
Switzerland	1815	9	1867	14		
Britain	1819	9	1874	10	1891	11
Prussia/ Germany	1839	9	1866	14	1875 (G)	14
France	1841	8	1874	12	1885	13
Russia	1882	11				
Italy	1886	9	1902	12		
Finland	1889	12	1903	14		
Netherlands	1889	12				
Spain	1900	10				

Source: Adelaide Anderson and Carroll D. Wright, 'Labour legislation', *Encyclopaedia Britannica* (11th ed.) (Cambridge, 1911).

It is of some interest that the earliest rules about factory work of children were introduced in Switzerland, a country usually more identified with agriculture. The other interesting phenomenon is that, with the exception of maternity leave and the overtime rule, many of the Swiss regulations applied equally to men and women, unlike in most other countries. In 1815, children under the age of nine were forbidden to work in factories. The regulations also introduced maximum working time for teenagers. Other rules about the working day followed and by 1864 all Swiss factories were restricted to operating 12 hours per day only. By 1873, all cantons had a mandatory maternity leave of six weeks. A federal law of 1877 banned night work for women and men, raised working age in factories to 14 years, fixed the working day to 11 hours, banned overtime for married women and added an extra two weeks before confinement to female working restrictions. The rules about working hours were extended to millinery production in 1884 and all workplaces with more than three people. In 1904, shop work was also included, leaving only domestic servants and farm workers outside regulation.[25]

The approach to the welfare of workers was, however, different in most of the rest of Europe. While any suggestion of restrictions was often met by

---

[25] Regina Wecker, 'Equality for men? Factory laws, protective legislation for women in Switzerland and the Swiss effort for international protection', in Wikander et al., *Protecting Women*, pp. 63–90, on pp. 65–73.

protests by conservatives and lobbying from the manufacturers claiming that the business would go under, the arguments for female protection tended to have support from religious conservatives and the socialist movement. Because of the orientation of women in industry, there is little evidence of women embarking en masse into male workplaces and depriving men of their jobs. Despite this, there seems to have been a lingering fear of female competition. The lowering of wages because of women did covertly or overtly figure both in attitudes of male unions and the socialist movement of the late nineteenth century. It was not until the twentieth century that the union movement in some countries figured out that by demanding equal pay this issue could be resolved. Despite practical evidence showing that the male breadwinner idea was an illusion, it remained an ideal within not only bourgeois but also working-class male ideology. It is of course not difficult to understand that patriarchal attitudes were by no means the exclusive property of the middle classes. It is, however, interesting how the need to protect women, and against which dangers, was integrated into socialist and union proclamations and into legislation related to workplace protection. While the idea of protection for men from accidents could be included in manifestos, on a practical level, inspectors saw men removing guards to machinery and refusing to wear protective equipment; the weaker vessel, however, had to be protected by cutting her work day or week.

Table 4.8   Special regulations about work of adult women in selected countries.

Country	Year	Working day	Year	'Maternity leave'
Britain	1847	10 hrs/day	1891	4 weeks
Textile	1850	10.5 hrs/day		
	1878	56 hrs/week		
Austria	1883	60 hrs/week	1885	4 weeks
			1888	With benefits
France	1900	11 hrs/day		
	1905	10.5 hrs/day		
Germany	1887	10 hrs/day	1878	3 weeks
			1887	4 weeks
			1891	6 weeks
Netherlands	1888	11 hrs/day	1888	4 weeks
Italy			1902	4 weeks
Spain			1900	3 weeks
Norway			1892	6 weeks

Sources: Sabine Schmitt, '"All these forms of women's work which endanger public health and public welfare": protective labour legislation for women in Germany 1878–1914', in U. Wikander, A. Kessler-Harris and Jane Lewis (eds), *Protecting Women:*

Labour Legislation in Europe, the United States and Australia 1880–1920 (Urbana, 1995), pp. 125–49, on pp. 136–8, 141–2; Rosa Maria Capel Martinez, 'Mujer y Trabajo en la España de Alfonso XIII', in *Mujer y Sociedad en España 1700–1975*, pp. 226–8; Adelaide Anderson and Carroll D. Wright, 'Labour legislation', *Encyclopaedia Britannica* (11th ed.) (Cambridge, 1911).

Work time and workplace

Already, by the 1830s and 1840s, attempts to regulate the working hours in British textile factories saw women grouped together with children and teenagers as categories in the need of special rules. When we analyse workplace regulation we find that all the early rules concerned children and women only. Whenever a rule was introduced for boys under 18, it was also applied to women of all ages. Therefore, the working day for women varied considerably from that of men. Once the domestic workshops were brought under workplace regulations in 1878, ever increasing categories of women were subject to special rules. The 1890s factory regulations brought in another set of changes. Although women were in focus in the rule about women being prohibited from working for four weeks after giving birth, a set of rules about the general working conditions now saw the light. Machinery was to be fenced and trapdoors closed, the Home Secretary was given the power to limit the time of employment of any class of person (including adult males) when handling poisonous material. The sanitary authority was to be involved in inspecting workrooms for health hazards. In 1895, regulations were introduced about the temperature in workrooms, the provision of lavatories if poisonous substances were handled, mandatory reporting of industrial poisoning and penalties for allowing clothes to be made in localities with infectious disease present. Accidents had to be investigated and reported, standards were set for overcrowding and the inspectors were given the power to order fans. Safeguards against fire were stipulated and children were prohibited from cleaning machinery. In 1901, fire escapes became mandatory and the regulation of overtime for adults was tightened. There was again a focus on dangerous processes and reporting accidents. Laundries were now brought under inspection and ventilation, drainage of floors and examination of steam boilers brought under the rules.[26]

Already, by 1850, it had become clear that rules without control had little impact. Therefore, a system of factory inspection had to be set up. However, the early inspection system had inadequate manpower in relation to the herculean task. In addition, the fact that some of the inspectors had strong

---

[26] Adelaide Anderson, *Women in the Factory: An Administrative Adventure, 1893 to 1921* (London, 1922), pp. 30–1, 39–45; Adelaide Anderson and Carroll D. Wright, 'Labour legislation', *Encyclopaedia Britannica* (11th ed.) (Cambridge, 1911).

local connections did not necessarily aid in objectivity and the ideal priorities. In 1878, some radical changes were introduced. Not only were all factories and workshops employing more than 50 people to be inspected regularly but the inspecting body was to consist of government inspectors, not ones employed by the local authority. In combination with the civil service reforms of 1871, this opened the new positions to persons capable of passing examinations instead of attaining them through privilege and connections. The qualification was now crucial. As the bulk of the regulations tended to aim at the protection of women and children, the 1870s also saw the beginning of the discussion of whether women should be employed as inspectors.[27]

The second part of the nineteenth century saw a plethora of rules regarding women in Germany. The Socialist movement was all for protection of women, and conservative women's organisations also highlighted the particularly importance of the protection of mothers.[28] In 1878, a prohibition on women working for three weeks after childbirth was introduced. The same ruling also banned the work of women underground in mines and in dangerous industries at night. Saturday and Sunday female work was to cease at 6 pm, and married women were to work no more than 10 hours per day.

The Workers Protection Act of 1891 set up strict regulations to ensure workplace safety, banned work on Sundays, introduced a maximum 11 hour day for women and 10 hours for children under 16 and prohibited night work for these groups. Maternity leave was also extended to 6 weeks after childbirth. After the end of WWI, in 1918, an 8 hour day was brought in for all workers. Bourgeois women's groups in Germany started to demand the installation of female factory inspectors from the 1890s. They even set up special training courses for future female inspectors.[29]

The early workplace regulations in France, as elsewhere, targeted the age at which children were allowed to work and their working day. A ban on night work by children and teens was passed in 1841. Although the working day for adults was fixed at 12 hours in the 1840s, exceptions were allowed by local authorities in, for example, printing, engineering works, work at furnaces, manufacture of projectiles for war and government work related to defence or national security. When the minimum age of work in factories was raised to 12 years in 1874, 16 divisional industrial inspectors were appointed by the state to control the legality of working hours. By the 1880s, workplaces using

[27] Henriques, *Before the Welfare State*, pp. 93–8; Anderson, *Women in the Factory*, pp. 27–8.

[28] Sabine Schmitt, '"All these forms of women's work which endanger public health and public welfare": protective labour legislation for women in Germany 1878–1914', in Wikander et al., *Protecting Women*, pp. 125–49, on pp. 136–8, 141–2.

[29] Schmitt, '"All these forms of women's work"', pp. 126–7, 131–8, 140–2; Ayass, *Arbeiterschutz*, pp. xxv–xxvi.

engines or employing more than 20 workers became subject to inspections even if no children or teenagers were employed. However, in 1892, regulations specifically targeting women came into force prohibiting night work, curtailing the working week and banning work in mines. In 1900, the working day for women and young workers was reduced to 11 hours and the working age was raised to 13, followed by additional rules about hours. Finally, in 1906, the 6 day week for women and teens was extended to include men and from 1910 the inspection process was reoriented towards hygiene, accident prevention and amelioration of conflicts.[30]

The labour legislation in Austria had strong support from Catholic social reformers. The protection of small artisans and tradesmen against free competition was combined with making Sunday a holiday free from work. The concerns about women and the young were expressed in reduced working hours for teenagers (16–18 year olds and for young women between 16 and 21) including no night work for boys under 18 and for women. The overseeing of these rules from 1883 was to be the task of factory inspectors. Two years later, an 11 hour day and a ban on women working within 4 weeks after childbirth was introduced. The economic consequences of this unpaid maternity leave were ameliorated in 1888 through moderate benefits under the Workers Sickness Insurance Act. However, small workshops were not subject to the rules and, therefore, it was possible to make adjustments to the ban on night work for textile manufacturing. Rules about work time were also elastic in that breaks were not included in the 11 hours.[31]

The line of the Christian Social Party was not to improve the working conditions but ban female work altogether. Some male socialists agreed with this ideology. 'We don't have our wives and daughters to be the factory owners' slaves. Our women belong to us' (weaver and factory worker, 1893). Women's sections of unions were not popular among men, and after their introduction in 1903 they were subject to strict control by the male unions. However, the fear of female competition prevalent in the 1870s had abated by the end of the century and the Austrian social democrats demanded an 8 hour day for men and women, no Sunday work, no night work and no special categories. In 1896, the demands for equal pay were also seen as a way of solving the problem of unfair competition.[32]

In 1896, Social Democratic leaders together with liberal reformers and middle-class women's organisations conducted a survey on the working and

[30] Sylvie Schweitzer, *Les inspectrices du travail 1878–1974* (Rennes, 2016), pp. 15, 59–61. In France in 1892, the working day for adults was 12 hours, in 1900 it was 11 hours, and in 1902 in mixed workplaces, including women and young people, it was 10.5 hours. By 1936, with a new government (Front Populaire), the working week was adjusted from 48 to 40 hours for all workers (Schweitzer, *Les inspectrices*, p. 85).

[31] Grandner, 'Special labor protection', pp. 157–60.

[32] Grandner, 'Special labor protection', pp. 161–2, 165.

living conditions of female workers in Vienna, in which 6 women and 36 men questioned 178 women about their working conditions. Women's clubs issued a petition about the exploitation of female apprentices and limited training, small wages, exaggerated fines for small mistakes, long hours, unsanitary conditions and sexual harassment. There was unity in petitioning for legal measures, increased control and female factory inspectors who could better examine sanitary conditions. The female inspectors were to make sure that current law about hours and night work were followed.[33]

In the first years of the twentieth century, a sharp dividing line was established between the politics of the Christian Party with its program of banning female work and the Social Democrats petitioning for the protection of life, health and morals of women workers. It was acknowledged that not all married women were young mothers, some were the family breadwinner and that many families depended on the female economic contribution. As women were not allowed to join political organisations before 1918 in Austria, and unions could, but did not, accept female members until 1893, there was little or no discussion of female working conditions in the late nineteenth century. While the union leaders made a U-turn, like in Germany, and started to agitate for special protection of women only, shorter hours, free Saturday afternoons, etc., the grassroots Social Democratic women pushed for better regulation of the workplace, particularly through engaging of female factory inspectors. By 1898, the Social Democrats had come to back the proposal and called in parliament for the appointment of female factory inspectors. By the turn of the century the Ministry of Commerce had hired women to support the male inspectors and in 1906 the female assistants gained official status. It was, however, impossible for a woman to become a state official, i.e. inspector, and they had to rely on their ability to persuade their male superiors to take action in case of problems, although it was well known that young people were subjected to abuse in the workplace.[34]

Regulation could have both a positive and a negative impact, as the presence of the rules could be used to eliminate women from the workforce or maintain an unequal wage structure. In the Netherlands, the rules of the 1880s about the 11 hour day and restrictions to female work applied to factories and workshops and did not include agriculture or domestic work. On the other hand, an increasingly negative attitude to the work of married women outside the home resulted in covert or overt exclusion in some sectors. In addition, the restricted working hours and the ban on Sunday work, with the addition of curtailed Saturdays, had serious consequences for female employment, particularly in the dairy industry. As the late nineteenth century also saw the shift from hand to machine manufacture being linked to an increasing male takeover in

---

[33] Fout, 'The Viennese Enquête', pp. 42–60; Grandner, 'Special labor protection', pp. 165, 170.

[34] Grandner, 'Special labor protection', pp. 157, 163–7, 171–3.

textiles, as well as food and drinks manufacture, the female presence in the labour force decreased.[35]

In Australia, the introduction of state rules in the 1890s about time limits and a ban on female night work were readily accepted. The resistance found in some European countries and particularly in the USA cannot be detected. On the other hand, the unified tariffs had some unexpected consequences. They created a more secure employment situation and a wage structure without sudden loss of income for women. However, they also fixed an income gap of about 50 per cent between men and women and firmed down skilled and well paid jobs in the textile industry as a male domain. In addition, the early twentieth century saw a state policy geared towards male family wages and the elimination of married females from industrial work. While certain feminists still pleaded for equal pay and equal treatment, not only male unions but also women in the labour movement drifted towards the position of defining women as mothers or mothers to be and, therefore, persons to be supported by male breadwinners.[36]

Women at a primitive stage in the periphery – The debate on night work, class and gender in the Nordic countries

Industrial development in the Nordic countries mostly did not start until after 1850 and in the 1890s agriculture still retained its position as an important economic sector. By the end of the century the number of industrial workers in Denmark was about 170,000 and 21 per cent of these were women. In Norway, the majority of women in the labour market worked as servants, seamstresses or in cleaning and service; of the women in registered employment in the capital only 12 per cent were factory workers.[37] The debate on women and night work took place more or less simultaneously in Denmark, Finland and Norway. The need to protect women was strongly supported by male unions and socialists

---

[35] Ulla Jansz, 'Women workers? The labour law and the debate on protective legislation in the Netherlands', in Wikander et al., *Protecting Women*, pp. 188–209, on pp. 195–9; Marlou Schrover, 'Cooling up women's work: women workers in the Dutch food industries 1889–1960', in G. de Groot and M. Schrover (eds), *Women Workers and Technological Change in Europe in the 19th and the 20th Century* (London, 1995), pp. 170–92, on pp. 173–6; Gertjen de Groot, 'Foreign technology and the gender division of labour in a Dutch cotton spinning mill', in G. de Groot and M. Schrover (eds), *Women Workers and Technological Change*, pp. 52–66, on pp. 60–2; Martina Kramers, 'Fra Holland', *Kvinden og samfundet* 35 (1919), p. 56.

[36] Howe, 'A paradise for working men', pp. 318–35.

[37] Ravn, '"Lagging far behind"', p. 211; Gro Hageman, 'Protection or equality? Debates on protective legislation in Norway', in Wikander et al., *Protecting Women*, pp. 267–90, on p. 272.

as well as a number of conservatives, while the feminist movement took a different view. In Finland, the entry of women into parliament in 1907 made it possible for female delegates to voice their opinions on the matter. One of the active participants was the first female industrial inspector, who expressed some scepticism about the issue in her reports and in parliament. As a result of her activity, a survey was conducted before any decisions were to be taken. The outcome of this survey was also followed in the neighbouring countries.[38] The survey, published in 1911, revealed that the percentages of married and widowed women in night work was not dissimilar to those in daytime work in some industrial sectors. One of the things the survey illuminated was that a considerable proportion of the women were breadwinners or providing a necessary contribution to the family economy. In the paper mills, no less than 30 per cent of women on the night shifts were widows. While sawmills were not a large female employer, the night shifts had a considerable female presence. The surveyed women were vocal in their condemnation of plans to restrict their right to work nights, unless similar restrictions would be introduced for men. They were aware of operating in a niche giving opportunity for employment and a slightly better wage. They also stated that the options were night work or unemployment. In spite of strain caused by lack of sleep they expressed worries about possible restrictions to night work, as they did not believe that work during the day would be available. The main reason given for working nights was that the income of other family members was insufficient and that night shift work could be combined with family duties. The majority of these women had young children in the household although some had at least one child with earnings. After consulting the results of the survey the parliament in Finland did not go along with the large number of other European countries in passing legislation against female night work.[39]

In Denmark, the Liberal Party increased its support among middle-class farmers in the nineteenth century, while the Conservatives mainly represented the old elite. The farmers disliked any kind of regulation and particularly anything touching the farming sector. As a consequence, the factory laws were politically problematic. Although a law about the protection of children had been accepted in 1873, restrictions on female night work in line with those on the European continent became heavily contested from several quarters. In Norway the politically strong groups also had their backing in middle-class freeholders and small farmers among whom women had a relatively free and independent position. The feminist organisations, on the other hand, were close to the Liberal Party. As Norway was going through a battle for independence

---

[38] '*Forkempere for Kvinders Arbejdfrihed I Finland*', *Kvinden og samfundet* 6:26 (30.3 1910), pp. 59–60.

[39] Hultin, *Yötyöntekijättäret*, pp. 44–7; *Kvinden og samfundet* 6:26 (30.3 1910), pp. 59–60.

from Sweden at the turn of the century, nationalism and democracy were seen as part of the same ideology. Feminism, education and good working conditions found fairly general support and less resistance than in many countries and the female activity among the nationalist movement was rewarded with the vote in national elections (1907) two years after independence.[40]

In Denmark and in Norway both conservative and Social Democratic politicians used the argument about regulation abroad or international agreements of 'civilised nations' as a reason for introducing a ban on female night work and shorter working hours for women. From 1890, the Norwegian Labour Party lobbied for a shorter working day for married women and a ban on female night work. When the Factory Protection Act of Norway was brought in in 1892, in addition to regulating the work of children, it introduced a ban on women working in mines, cleaning and oiling machines in motion and no work six weeks after childbirth. In 1901, the Liberal Party introduced a proposal for national labour insurance and an 8 hour day, as well as improvements to the factory legislation.[41]

As Danish women did not have the vote until 1915, the debate in parliament had no female participants. The debate outside, on the other hand, attracted the attention of many groups of women. Already, in 1900, female unions (Printers, Unskilled Female Workers, the Female Tailors' Union and the Dressmakers Union) held meetings to debate the proposal for a factory bill. About one-third of the female workers in Copenhagen were union members. The support for maternity leave was general but the participants asked how women would support themselves when out of work. In 1911, the women's branch of the in Danish Printers' Union and the Union of Women Workers in Denmark held protest meetings in Copenhagen against plans for a ban on night work, which attracted 1200 women. A resolution was sent to parliament from the meeting rejecting the proposal. As the farmers in the Liberal Party were against state intervention in general, they did not push for the night work ban. Therefore, while the 1901 and 1913 factory acts stipulated a four week maternity leave, they did not include night work restrictions for women.[42]

When it became clear that the Danish Parliament had rejected the ban on female night work the Norwegian feminists held a meeting in Kristiania. The delegates adopted a resolution in opposition to any night work prohibition

[40] Ravn, '"Lagging far behind"', p. 213; Hageman, 'Protection or equality?', pp. 272, 274–5.

[41] Ravn, '"Lagging far behind"', p. 214; Hageman, 'Protection or equality?', pp. 269–70; Ragna Schou, 'Arbejderbeskyttelse – kvindebeskyttelse', Kvinden og samfundet 7:24 (15.3 1908), pp. 81–2.

[42] Ravn, '"Lagging far behind"', pp. 216, 222–4; Louise Neergaard, 'Fabrikloven vedtaget i Folketinget', Kvinden og samfundet 8:29 (30.4 1913), pp. 114–15; Louise Neergaard, 'Fabriklovens Revision', Kvinden og samfundet 3:27 (15.2 1911), pp. 24–5.

for women. This placed the feminists on a collision course with the Labour movement. After the demand for a ban on women's night work was passed at the Bern Convention in 1906, the feminists in Norway started a campaign which gained support from many women's groups. The socialist women, however, followed the party line and that of the Socialist International, which caused a split between female socialists and Liberal and bourgeois feminists. The female printing workers joined the debate and argued that such a ban, and shorter hours for women, would have a negative effect on their employment situation. The cost of female protection was losing your job to men. Women from the mining industry also joined the debate as they had been told that a ban on female night work would mean no more employment for women. While the debate for bourgeois women was one regarding the principle of equality, for working women it was a question of jobs.[43]

In 1909, the Norwegian parliament introduced a ban on work by children under the age of 10, and reduced hours for children under 18. The ban on night work for women was voted down in parliament as was the ratification of the Bern Convention of 1906.[44]

From 1901, an increasing amount of protective legislation for women was introduced in Sweden. It generally took the form of preventing women from performing specific tasks or working in specific fields. The early twentieth century also brought a proposal for banning female night work. The proposal did not include the sweated home workers but only fields where women competed with men, like printing, bookbinding, bakeries, sugar refineries and textile work. The female unions launched a campaign against the proposal and were joined by the feminist movement. At the Social Democratic Party conference in 1908, the women were accused of class betrayal as they collaborated with feminists and opposed the decision of the Socialist International agreement about curtailing night work for women. The umbrella organisation for the unions declined to discuss the matter altogether and in 1908 parliament voted down the proposal. However, when the matter was raised in 1909, the proposal was accepted and from 1911, all night work by women was banned. As a result, women lost their jobs in the printing industry, bakeries and sugar factories. The law was not amended until 1962 when a general ban on night work was introduced.[45]

At the Congress of the Second International in 1910, the Danish and Swedish associations of Social Democratic Women wanted to push for a resolution about banning night work not only for women but also for men. This suggestion was voted down by the 14 other countries. Clara Zetkin described the episode as an indicator that the Danish and Swedish Social Democratic women were

43 Hageman, 'Protection or equality?', pp. 273–5.
44 Hageman, 'Protection or equality?', pp. 271, 275–6.
45 Schmitz, *Kvinnor, Kamrater* (Stockholm, 1982), pp. 62–9.

still enmeshed in an earlier more primitive stage of development, only to be expected from women at the periphery.[46]

In 1914, the Second Nordic Meeting on the Woman Question (including both feminist organisations and female social democrats), held in Copenhagen, rejected special legislation for women except maternity leave. Interestingly enough, one of the few supporters of the night work ban was one of the first industrial inspectors, Ragna Schou, while one of the most vocal supporters of the rejection of night work ban was the other factory inspector, Julie Arenholt. However, the president of the women's branch of the Danish Printers' Union argued that 'men of all classes and political convictions have united to strike a blow against women', therefore, women of all classes had to unite and fight it. Night work was well paid and a way for women to earn more money, the working hours and conditions well regulated. These women were also union members, unlike the hordes of home workers, the female ranks of whom women would have to join when banned from their present activities. Regulating women out of some workplaces would also increase gender segregation and being stuck with low earnings.[47]

The dispute was and remained more about principles than economy on the national level as in Denmark only about 300 women worked in factories at night around 1900. These were women engaged in printing industries, textiles and paper works. In Norway the printing industry employed a couple of hundred women in night work and in addition to mining the only other industry potentially affected by night work restrictions would have been the canning industry.[48]

Conclusion

A look at nineteenth-century labour legislation reveals that the early protective measures were directed at excluding certain groups from work in a dangerous environment or cutting down on the time spent in such an environment. These groups were primarily children and young people, but also women. The reasons varied depended on ideological orientation but caused an interesting proximity between conservatives, clerical groups and radical union members and socialists. Women, who had no voice, were to be protected by the men who had one.

Only the second phase of legislation tried to get to grips with the actual environment. When these measures came they were directed at obvious and visible dangers such as open hatches, lift shafts, blocked or absent fire escapes and, after that, working conditions, in the sense of temperature, air quality,

---

46 Ravn, '"Lagging far behind"', p. 220.
47 Ravn, '"Lagging far behind"', pp. 220–2.
48 Hageman, 'Protection or equality?', p. 272; Ravn, '"Lagging far behind"', p. 211.

dampness, light, etc., that could be easily measured. More invisible threats took some time to be addressed, although the work of doctors and scientists did a lot to illuminate the connection between the health of workers and the handling of certain substances. Even in this case there was a tendency to separate women and young people from poisonous substances rather than banning dangerous processes and protecting all workers.[49]

The introduction of legislation, however, had the consequence that assurance was needed that the legislation was implemented. Therefore, it became necessary to employ inspectors. The fact that a lot of the legislation tended to focus on women and children raised the issue of the need to employ women to inspect these groups.

[49] Harrison, 'Suffer the working day', pp. 79–90.

5

Middle Class Girls, Education and Entry into the Civil Service

> I was the only girl in the college. It caused a terrible stir. The priest in my home town who used to play cards with my father said to him: 'Mr Einstein, I am sorry to say that I cannot play cards with you any longer as you have sent Herta to a boys' school and by doing so you are supporting the destruction of morals'.[1]

In the late nineteenth century, women had made considerable progress into the educational system. From societies with little or no formal education for women in the early 1800s, schools, exams and even universities had opened their doors for girls. In some cases, the origins of the development can be found in the Enlightenment, in other cases, political, economic or other local issues contributed to the increased inclusion of women in educational efforts. In large parts of Europe, however, the activity of the nineteenth-century women's movements focused on female access to education and the right to use accrued knowledge by taking office within wider society. The education system, healthcare and social care were logical extensions of the female sphere. The civil service, however, a logical enough route for educated women, was for a long time closed, until new innovations created activities deemed suitable for women. Female entry into social welfare activities related to women and children also found support in many quarters.[2]

While the increase in access to education followed similar patterns of development, one should not ignore the influence of the higher degree of involvement by the state or local administration in continental and Northern Europe in comparison with the private nature of education in Britain and the USA.

The early steps for including girls into the education system in post-revolutionary France had their roots in the 1830s and the first teacher training school, the Normal School for Girls, was founded in 1838. For a long time the Catholic Church had a strong grip on the female educational sector and from 1867 this virtual monopoly was contested by the state. The private sector had

---

[1] de la Roi-Frey, 'Wenn alle Stricke reissen', p. 122.
[2] Fuchs and Thompson, *Women in 19th Century Europe*, pp. 173–4.

been offering women teacher training from the 1850s but not until the 1880s was a state secondary schools system created for women. The system was based on the ideology of equal but different, catering for the political circles viewing women's role as primarily domestic. While the teachers recruited for the female colleges were well educated, the curriculum embodied parallel, not identical, exams to those of boys, with the result that to gain entry into university a dispensation had to be obtained. However, although the option of taking the baccalaureate with a dispensation had been available since the 1860s and gaining admittance to the universities in Paris was possible from the 1870s, equality in education was still some time away. After the educational reform of 1902, many of the state colleges for girls started to prepare their students for the new version of the baccalaureate. This option resulted in an increasing popularity of secondary study and ever more girls recruited into the system. The complete amalgamation of curricula and exam systems between male and female colleges did not, however, occur until 1924.[3]

In Bavaria, the first private teacher training institute had opened as early as 1814; in Prussia, the state started training female teachers in 1832. The nineteenth century saw a steady increase of state-run gymnasiums in most parts of Germany. By the 1890s, women gained admittance to university studies and from 1895 it became possible for women to take the regular entrance examination, the *Abitur*. The year before WWI, 1913, 6 per cent of all university students were women.[4] The attitudes to female education varied considerably in the middle classes. Female ambitions were sometimes countered with economic arguments, 'the money has to be used for your brothers' education', sometimes by traditionalist arguments, 'nothing is more repulsive or more useless than a learned unpractical woman'. On the other hand, not all parents saw female education in a negative light. When Lina Kreusler was embarking on a position within the higher education system of women in Hamburg, her father was told by a prominent local politician: 'No daughter on our social level has ever worked for her living'. The answer of her father was: 'Well then my daughter will be the first'.[5]

From the 1860s there was a growing movement for the acceptance of women into institutions of higher education in Austria. In the last decades of

3   Fuchs and Thompson, *Women in 19th Century Europe*, pp. 92–3; Jo Burr Margadant, *Madame le Professeur: Women Educators in the Third Republic* (Princeton, 1990), pp. 17–20, 23–4, 34, 55–6, 100–1, 217–18, 249.

4   de la Roi-Frey, 'Wenn alle Stricke reissen', pp. 15–17; James Albisetti, 'Female education in German speaking Austria, Germany and Switzerland 1866–1914', in D. F. Good, M. Grandner and M. Maynes (eds), *Austrian Women in the 19th and 20th Centuries* (Providence, 1996), pp. 43, 48–9; Fuchs and Thompson, *Women in 19th Century Europe*, p. 92.

5   de la Roi-Frey, 'Wenn alle Stricke reissen', pp. 105, 109, 121.

the nineteenth century, colleges for girls were set up with the aim of preparing young women for entry to the universities. By 1910, the goal was achieved. Simultaneously, women entered the teaching sector and employment in the post and telegraph system. Women were not, however, employed with full time contracts like men, and feminist organisations like *Allgemeine Österreichische Frauenverein* launched campaigns for women to haven equal status in the civil service. Improvement was gained in 1914 but not until 1921 was an equal position achieved.[6]

After the consolidation of Protestantism embodied by the Lutheran Church in the sixteenth century, rules were gradually introduced in the Nordic countries making it obligatory for all adults to be able to read the Bible. In the seventeenth and eighteenth centuries, yearly reading tests became the norm in Sweden and Finland. A ban on marriage for those unable to comprehend the essence of the Christian faith was used as a lever to increase interest in biblical knowledge. As a result, rudimentary reading ability was not unusual and economic advice literature could be found in the households of ordinary people, in addition to Bibles, hymnbooks and religious tracts. The basics were taught at home and the Church ran confirmation classes with reading tests in all parishes. The primary school with free education for girls and boys was introduced in Sweden in the 1840s and Finland in the 1860s. The first publicly funded teacher training colleges for women were founded in Denmark in 1859, in Sweden in 1861 and in Finland in 1863.[7]

The graduates of the teacher training colleges were assumed to aim their efforts towards teaching girls and young children. Although the municipality of Copenhagen ruled that female teachers could be employed in primary schools, some time passed before posts opened up in secondary education. However, the entry of girls into the state-run secondary schools prompted the employment of female teachers and specific legislation was passed to this effect in 1903. The female salaries were fixed to slightly less than those of males and an explicit rule was passed that women were excluded from holding the post of head teacher in the state secondary system. The share of female teachers in Copenhagen increased to 60 per cent by the end of the century and in 1894 women were also given the right to be appointed as school inspectors. In 1903, the female inspectors of schools gained equal salaries and rights with their male counterparts. In rural areas, females were

---

6   Helperstorfer, 'Die Frauenrechsbewegung und ihre Ziele', pp. 21–9, on pp. 24–7.

7   Loftur Guttormsson, 'The development of popular religious literacy in the seventeenth and eighteenth centuries', *Scandinavian Journal of History* 15:1 (1990), pp. 7–33; Ingrid Markussen, 'The development of writing ability in the Nordic countries in the eighteenth and nineteenth centuries', *Scandinavian Journal of History* 15:1 (1990), pp. 37–63, on p. 60; Margit Astrom, *Emma Irene Astrom* (Helsingfors, 1967), pp. 58–9; Mervi, Kaarninen, *Nykyajan tytöt* (Helsinki, 1995), pp. 22–4.

widely employed. While there was a certain amount of equality in salary levels, overall they were very low and provided a livelihood only because they included free housing and firewood.[8]

In Sweden, women were given access to the baccalaureate in 1870 and to university study and degrees in 1873. Danish women were allowed university degrees from 1875 and the first two university engineers received their degree in 1897. Even though women in Finland could be awarded the baccalaureate from 1870 and embark on university studies and be awarded university degrees, in each case a dispensation had to be applied for. In 1901, when the dispensation rule was abolished, 14 per cent of the university students were female. However, the notion that women should engage with other women in issues of health and education had resulted in rulings about the right to practice medicine in 1897 and to become teachers in secondary schools for girls in 1898. Even though academic studies had opened up for women, professorships did not become available to women in the old universities of Sweden until 1911 and even then the posts were restricted to departments where women would not be superior to male colleagues. The department of mathematics of the newly established independent University of Stockholm, however, opened teaching posts to women and employed the Russian mathematician Sofia Kovalevskaia as professor in 1883. In Finland, women became entitled to university teaching posts in 1916.[9]

In Russia, female education was not rated highly in rural areas: still in the late nineteenth century the literacy rate was around 20 per cent, with females scoring more poorly than men. In urban and industrial areas the situation was slightly better, with about 30 per cent of women and 50 per cent of men able to read. Among the nobility and the urban middle class, female literacy was not viewed in a negative light and the first girls' schools were introduced at the time of Catherine the Great. State secondary education became available to women in the 1850s, teacher training in the 1870s and university (medical) studies in the 1860s. Degrees in many subjects were, however, not available. The first woman to earn a university degree, Nadezhda Suslova, did so at the University of Zurich in 1867, an institution that had admitted women since 1865 and therefore catered for women from many different countries. On the other hand, by 1914, Russian universities had produced 1500 female doctors, three times as many as could be found in England or Germany, and another

---

[8]   Astrid Paludan-Muller and Louise Neeregaard, 'Arbejdskaar for Kvinder I Samarbejde med Maend III, Stats og Kommune Skoler', *Kvinden og samfundet* 23 (30.9, 1907), pp. 127–8.

[9]   Sinja Sveinsdottir, 'Agnes Nielsen', *Nationaltidende* (25.1 1937); Carlsson and Rosen, *Svensk Historia 2*, p. 335. In 1881, the first female student gained a master's degree at the University of Helsinki; Astrom, *Emma Irene Astrom*, pp. 105–6, 117–18; Natalia Pushkareva, *Women in Russian History* (Abingdon, 1997), p. 210.

1000 were graduating annually. Unlike in Europe and the USA, medicine did not have the high status of, for example law, a subject where female students were not accepted.[10]

As in other countries, the profession of female teacher was one of the first acceptable professions, particularly as teacher of young children or girls. Also, like elsewhere, the female salaries were lower than those of men and professional respect in limited supply. However, by 1906, women were found in the secondary sector, as headmistresses in girls' schools and even teaching in boys' grammar schools. In urban areas like St Petersburg we find women holding the post of deputy headmistress and school inspector.[11]

Primary education in Spain was for a long time to a considerable degree in the hands of the Church. Literacy levels in rural and urban areas varied considerably, and still in 1940 more than 20 per cent of the population was unable to read. Female education was not seen as a priority, but by the 1880s, professional schools like the one for post and telegraph work had started their activity. The same decade also saw the first teacher training colleges. Secondary education was for a long time separate for girls and boys, but in the early years of the twentieth century institutes of higher study for women began operating, like schools of nursing and library work. Where women could access education aiming for administrative work, it was understood that superior posts were exclusively for men. In the 1920s, feminist organisations began producing publications highlighting the need for political reform to improve the position of women.[12]

Overseas areas where Europeans had settled over time were not always very preoccupied with education. In 1850s New Zealand around 25 per cent of the settlers (Pakeha) were illiterate and another 14 per cent, although able to read, had not learned to write. The Maori population was mainly served by missionary schools. In 1877, however, an education act was passed that introduced universal, compulsory and free education for children between the ages of 7 and 13. While to start with attendance varied considerably,

---

[10] Fuchs and Thompson, *Women in 19th Century Europe*, pp. 82, 98; Pushkareva, *Women in Russian History*, p. 143; McDermid and Hillyar, *Women and Work*, pp. 68–72.

[11] McDermid and Hillyar, *Women and Work*, pp. 74–5.

[12] Borderias, *Entre líneas*, pp. 60–3; Rosa Capel Martinez, 'La apertura del horizonte cultural', in Rosa Capel Martinez (ed.), *Mujer y Sociedad en España 1700–1775* (Madrid, 1982), pp. 120–6; Gloria Angeles and Franco Rubio, 'La contribución de la mujer española a la política contemporánea: de la restauración a la guerra civil (1876–1939)', in Capel Martinez (ed.), *Mujer y Sociedad*, pp. 241–66, on pp. 245–6; María Encarna Nicolás Marín and Basilisa López García, 'La situación de la mujer a través de los movimientos de apostolado seglar: la contribución a la legitimación del franquismo (1939–1956)', in Capel Martinez (ed.), *Mujer y Sociedad*, p. 370.

particularly in rural areas, education became accessible and with it the presence of the female primary school teacher. Secondary private schools for boys started appearing in towns from the 1860s and in 1871 the first secondary school for girls saw the light. The introduction of female secondary education had met with some resistance but once it became a possibility it also included the chance of sitting exams. Thereby, when the first university was founded in 1871, it catered not only for male but also female students. One cannot claim that the attitude to women of learning was universally positive, however, their attendance in arts subjects was accepted and only law and medicine remained difficult for women to access.[13]

In Australia, there was still considerable variation in literacy levels in the 1860s and 70s. Even after free compulsory education was introduced in most regions between 1868 and 1880, the levels of school attendance cannot always be determined. In the countryside, the expectation of children's participation in work tasks remained unchanged and the school inspector's reports could state: '...at such crises as cherry picking, potato planting etc. the dearness of outside labour makes the value of children's services too considerable to be foregone'. Girls were also generally expected to assist with child minding and housework. In urban areas there was less tolerance of slippage in school attendance. The expansion of primary education did, however, boost the need for trained teachers and this became a popular niche for women. By 1879, all teachers were expected to have obtained a Licence to Teach to hold office. Although the remuneration was generally less generous for female teachers, the system run by public funds guaranteed a steady income. An interesting feature of the Australian system was the engagement of wives of male teachers to supervise subjects for girls, like textile work, in schools with all male staff. The private schools for girls received some critique for their limited curriculum with too much emphasis on ladylike subjects such as music, drawing and deportment. The fact that higher education was becoming available was heralded as hopefully having the effect of a general raising of standards in women's education. The 1880 education act ruled that high schools for girls and boys could be established. Ancient and modern languages, history, literature, mathematics and sciences were to be compulsory subjects for boys and modern languages, history, music and some mathematics and science for girls. The international discussion about female entry to universities was followed with interest in the newspapers. When a woman gained her bachelors' degree in New Zealand in 1877, the *Australasian* asked why

---

13 Nancy Swarbrick, 'Primary and secondary education – education from 1840 to 1918', Te Ara – the *Encyclopedia of New Zealand*, http://www.TeAra.govt. nz/en/primary-and-secondary-education; Dorothy Page, 'Dalrymple, Learmoth White', *Dictionary of New Zealand*, http://www.TeAra.govt.nz/en/biographies/1d2/dalrymple-learmoth-white.

this could not be the case in Australia. When Melbourne University started accepting women in 1880, the news were greeted with approval. In 1883, the first women in Melbourne gained their BA degrees and in the meantime the University of Adelaide had opened their doors to women. Sydney University followed suit in 1882. In parallel with this development, the clerical sector became interested in the recruitment of women trained in vocational schools specialising in telegraph work and typing.[14]

Even though the notion that women as well as men should be able to read the Bible was a feature of many communities in the USA from the earliest time, higher education of women was deemed less important. By the early nineteenth century, families with aspirations might send their daughters to finishing schools, but the educational goals of such institutions could be very variable. By the mid-nineteenth century a number of academies for young women, or seminaries, were in operation. While the curriculum could be fairly extensive, their philosophy tended to be the training of good wives and mothers who did learn enough music to be able to support themselves in case of widowhood or other economic calamities. The teaching profession did, however, attract young women as a respectable way of earning one's living. The early twentieth century did generally bring about a change in the distribution of female work: manual work and domestic service decreased while the clerical sector evidenced a massive influx. Female white-collar workers increased from 1.8 million in 1910 to 3.2 million in 1920.[15] During the 1860s and 1870s, elite educational establishments for women like Vassar, Smith and Wellesley opened their doors for white middle-class girls. The creation of a state system included mandatory acceptance of females and by 1880 one third of the registered college students were female.[16] It should, however, be clarified that undergraduate college education in the USA, both in the sense of curricula and the age at entry, had more similarities with higher secondary education in Europe, i.e. the years leading up to the baccalaureate, than with actual university studies.[17]

---

[14] Quiggin, *No Rising Generation*, pp. 80–5, 90–1, 94.

[15] Jewel Smith, *Transforming Women's Education: Liberal Arts and Music in Female Seminaries* (Urbana, 2019), pp. 12–13, 24, 74–85; Kessler-Harris, *Women Have Always Worked*, p. 82; Claudia Goldin, *Marriage Bars: Discrimination against Women Workers 1920s to 1950s* (Cambridge, MA, 1988), Working Paper 2747, p. 4; Winifred Wandersee, *Women's Work and Family Values 1920–1940* (Cambridge, MA, 1981), p. 89.

[16] Kathryn Kish Sklar, *Florence Kelley and the Nation's Work: The Rise of Women's Political Culture 1830–1900* (Yale, 1995), pp. 50–3.

[17] Margadant, *Madame le Professeur*, pp. 216–18, 249. Baccalaureate A comprised the Latin-Greek programme, B the Latin-modern languages programme, C the Latin-sciences programme and D the sciences-modern languages programme. The second

In nineteenth-century Britain, and before, middle-class women established and ran schools on their own. The expectation was generally that young children and girls should be taught by women. Little formal training was needed and as the governess became a popular institution, this was a career option, badly paid but respectable. The nineteenth century brought an increased demand for formal education and degrees. British women's higher education received little state sponsorship until fairly late in the century. However, private ladies colleges and teacher training colleges were set up from the 1840s and from 1869 these establishments could apply for state support. The ladies colleges of Cambridge University (Newnham and Girton) ran informal courses for women without examinations. By the 1880s, the young ladies could sit University examinations separately, but were awarded no degrees. Elsewhere, in London and Edinburgh, women were accepted for university studies from the 1870s. Oxford and Cambridge, however, blocked women from graduating until after WWI: the 1920s for Oxford and 1947 for Cambridge.[18]

One should not, however, ignore the fact that higher education was reserved for a privileged few. Emily Davies, the founder of Girton College, marketed her institution as a place where the daughters of the well-to-do would prepare themselves for the role of wife and mother. In her 'Questions Relating to Women' from 1868 she states:

> ... if neither governess nor mother know, how can they teach? So long as education is not provided for them how can it be provided by them? ... the two thousand sisters of the two thousand undergraduates in Oxford and Cambridge are scattered up and down *country houses and parsonages. The Hall and the Rectory* are centres of light for a whole parish. If their light be darkness how great is that darkness.

The fees of 100 guineas per year, two rooms at the disposal of students and the multitude of servants guaranteed that the daughters of gentlemen would not

---

stage of the exam included philosophy and mathematics. Florence Kelley studied Latin, Greek, modern languages (French and German), history, literature, social and political science and geometry as part of her undergraduate Arts course at Cornell; Sklar, *Florence Kelley*, p. 341.

18 Margaret Hunt, *The Middling Sort: Commerce, Gender and the Family in England 1680–1780* (Berkeley, 1996), pp. 168–9; Penelope Corfield, *Power and the Professions in Britain 1700–1850* (London, 1995), p. 187; Davidoff and Hall, *Family Fortunes*, pp. 265–6, 293–6; Rosemary O'Day, *Education and Society 1500–1800* (London, 1982), p. 27. Early women's colleges include establishments such as: Queens College (1848), The Bedford College (1849), the North London Collegiate School (1850), the Hitchin College (1863), Hitchin and Girton College (1869); Bradbrook, *That Infidel Place*, pp. 11–13, 158–9; Fuchs and Thompson, *Women in 19th Century Europe*, pp. 92–3, 97, 99.

have to experience life that was not fitted to their station. On the other hand, Davies also saw the career of teacher as an option for the young women.[19]

While some of the American seminaries for women included doing part of the domestic tasks in the school,[20] this was not the case in England. The female colleges were most certainly not the environment for 'sisterhood' but one where upper-class women were served hand and foot by working-class women. Still, in 1919, the working day of the college servant in Girton started at 5 o'clock in the morning with cleaning fireplaces and lighting fires by candle light, stumbling over crockery left by the female students, while making sure that the rooms were nice and warm when the students stated to move for breakfast at 8 o'clock. After breakfast, the beds were made and the rooms cleaned and then followed a day of cleaning intersected with dining room or kitchen duties. The working day did not end until 10 o'clock at night, when the lucky ones bedded down in rooms of four while the less fortunate in rooms of eight girls. Table service was provided at meals and the servants where loaded with trays of up to twenty plates filled with food. During the early years of the college, in the 1870s, the servants did not retain employment for more than 10 weeks, after which they were dismissed for the holidays with the possibility of re-engagement when term started if their work had been deemed satisfactory.[21]

This was the environment in which suffragists and the leading lights for female emancipation spent their formative years. This was also where some of the women later engaged in factory inspection gained their academic credentials.

Women, salaries and the civil service

The emergence of the middle classes into administration had brought the ideas of competence, knowledge and qualifications as important for a new group of civil servants. While connections and membership of the nobility could be a decided advantage, a pedigree without qualifications was no longer viewed as an ideal for recruitment in many European countries. Gaining access to the right qualifications had previously been out of the question for women, but by the late nineteenth century, this was no longer the case. While clerical work became gradually more feminised both in Europe and the United States, breaking into the civil service was not easy. The early appointments had to be linked to issues making being a woman an advantage rather than a

[19] Emily Davies, 'Some account of a proposed new college for women', in *Thoughts on Some Questions Relating to Women 1860–1908* (London, 1910), p. 97; Girton College archive; Bradbrook, *That Infidel Place*, pp. 17–18, 57–9.

[20] Smith, *Transforming Women's Education*, p. 69.

[21] Girton College library and archive; *Memories of a Servant (1919–48)*; Emily Davies correspondence.

disadvantage, as in the use of innovations like the typewriter or in telephone or telegraph operation.[22]

In Britain, the number of female clerks increased from 150,000 in 1911 to more than a million in 1931. At the beginning, there was segregation of work on gender lines for moral reasons. Employers hesitated at the extra costs to find suitable space for women, including building female toilets. It was also viewed that work was to be separated to make interaction between men and women unnecessary.[23]

Despite the practical problems, it soon became clear that there were economic advantages for the administration to augment the share of female clerical workers. The Telegraph Act of 1869 granted the Postmaster-General a monopoly on inland telegraph business and he became obliged to buy any existing telegraph companies. He thereby also acquired the female telegraph operators working in these companies. Mr. Scudamore realised that the women could be useful and he not only retained the women who had worked as telegraph operators but also started engaging women clerks. In 1871 he reported:

> In the first place they have an eminent degree of quickness of eye and ear and a delicacy of touch which are essential qualifications for a good operator. In the second place they take more kindly than men and boys to do sedentary employment, and are more patient during long confinement to one place. In the third place, the wages, which will draw male operators from but an inferior class of the community, will draw female operators from a superior class. Female operators thus drawn from a superior class will, as a rule, write better than the male clerks, and spell more correctly; and, where the staff is mixed, the female clerks will raise the tone of the whole staff.[24]

> They are less disposed than men to combine for the purpose of extorting higher wages, and this is by no means an unimportant matter. On one ground it is especially desirable that we should extend the employment of women. Permanently established civil servants invariably expect their remuneration to increase with their years of service, and they look for this increased remuneration even in cases, necessarily very numerous in which far from the very nature of their employment they can be of no more use or value in the twentieth than in the fifth year of their service ... Women however, will solve these difficulties for the department by retiring for the

[22] Lynn Y. Weiner, *From Working Girl to Working Mother: The Female Labor Force in the United States 1820–1980* (Chapel Hill, 1985), pp. 28–9; Meyerowitz, *Women Adrift*, pp. 30–1; Deborah Simonton, *A History of European Women's Work*, pp. 238–40; Kessler-Harris, *Women Have Always Worked*, pp. 82–3.

[23] Roberts, *Women's Work*, p. 38; Lee Holcombe, *Victorian Ladies at Work: Middle Class Working Women in England and Wales 1850–1914* (Hamden, CT, 1973), p. 186; Martindale, *Women Servants*.

[24] Martindale, *Women Servants*, p. 17.

purpose of getting married as soon as they get the chance. It is true that we do not, as the companies did, punish marriage by dismissal. It is also true that we encourage married women to return to service: but as a rule those who marry will retire, and those only will return whose married life is less fortunate and prosperous than they had hoped.

On the whole it may be stated without fear of contradiction that, if we place an equal number of females and males on the same ascending scale of pay, the aggregate pay to the females will always be less than the aggregate pay to males; that within a certain range of duty, the work will be better done by the females than by the males, because the females will be drawn from a somewhat superior class; and further, that there will always be fewer females than males on the pension list.[25]

Table 5.1   Civil Service salaries in Britain and Denmark.

Britain	Male/year	Female/ year	Denmark	Male/ year	Female/ year
II division clerks 1881	£80–350	£65–150	Trainee clerk	720 crowns	480 crowns
Typists 1914	£156–208/ year	£52–68/ year	7 years in office	800 crowns	960 crowns
Shorthand typists/writers	£104–300/ year	£72–8/ year	Top salary	2400 crowns	1860 crowns
Superintendents of typists	£250–350/ year	£91/year			
Chief super- intendents of typists		£104/year			

Sources: Royal Commission on Civil Service, Appendix to 2 Report, P.P. 1912–13 XV, 61–2, 247, First Appendix to Fourth Report, PP 1914 XVI, 23; Select Committee on Post Office Servants PP 1906, XII, 964–7; Select Committee on Post Office Servants, P.P. 1913, X, 155–6; Lee Holcombe, *Victorian Ladies at Work* (London, 1973), p. 174; Louise Neergaard, 'Arbejdskaar for Kvinder I Samarbejde med Maend, Kvinner I Jernbane, Telegraf og Post Etaterne', *Kvinden og samfundet* 23 (15.4, 1907), pp. 51–2.

The Inland Revenue was one of the early government offices that started employing women for typing work. In 1888, Sir Algernon West informed the Ridley Commission that 'these typewriting women' were particularly useful for all important letters, wrote twice as fast as a quick writer, could replace

---

[25] 'Report on the re-organisation of the telegraph system in the United Kingdon 1871', in Martindale, *Women Servants*, pp. 18–19.

male copyists, were accurate and very intelligent and cheap with no super-annuation. Another department announced in 1889, 'we have two women typewriters who earn 23 and 21 shillings per week and they turn out as much work as four male copyists would do'. The salaries of male copyists was £100 per year. By 1914, the GPO and the Inland Revenue held open competitive examinations for recruitment. Other departments nominated typists who were submitted to the Civil Service Commission for examination in a few subjects.[26] However, even when women were employed to do the same work as men and performed the same tasks, they could not be promoted in the same way. Women supervised women, had fewer supervisory posts and received lower salaries. In 1906, there were four supervisory classes for male telegraph workers in London, with salaries from 170 to 500 pounds. For women there were three supervisory classes with salaries from 100 to 300 pounds.[27]

When a government committee had discovered that women were doing identical work for less pay in the Post Office Savings Bank, the department rearranged the work to justify the inequality. When another commission was set to investigate, the Secretary to the Post Office admitted that the reason was to make it possible for officials to say that men and women were not doing equal work.[28]

The argument went that women needed less money because they did not support families. To this, the counter argument was made that women do support families and relatives (for example widows). Such an argument actually raised the question: if the point was to help supporting dependants then why were unmarried men paid the same as married men? Women were said to take more sick leave and could therefore be considered more costly (13 days per year, men 8 days per year). To this the counter argument was that if women were paid more, they would be healthier because they could buy more food, live in good premises and have good clothes. Women were also said to cause problems because they left employment at marriage and new clerks had to be trained. This was countered with the statement that women did not leave of their own choice but they wer dismissed because of the marriage bar. Women were also considered less valuable as they performed no night duty in the telegraph office. The reply to this was naturally that women did not choose these working hours, but were barred from night work by law. A closer look would reveal that men who did night duty actually had a shorter working week and lighter work because at night time there was less work in a telegraph office.[29]

26 Martindale, *Women Servants*, pp. 65–8.
27 Select Committee on Post Office Servants PP 1906, XII, 775.
28 Royal Commission on Civil Service, Appendix to Second Report, PP 1912–13, XV, 23, 28–9, 247, 268; Appendix to Fourth Report, PP 1914, XVI, 353.
29 Royal Commission on Civil Service, First Appendix to Fourth Report, PP 1914, XVI, 17–18; Holcombe, *Victorian Ladies*, pp. 186–8.

Figure 3   Although gaining access to education and the professions was viewed as a step forward by feminist organizations, these views were not always shared by contemporary caricaturists. Postcard c. 1900, private collection.

In France, clerical work, the post office, telegraph and phone sectors were major employers of women from the 1830s, and in the early twentieth century even maternity leave was introduced. The Dutch postal service opened for women in the 1870s. The administration sector soon came within the reach of women and in 1892 the state appointed the first female industrial inspectors.[30]

In Germany, after an initial increase of female employment in the postal service in the 1870s a decision was taken to phase out the female presence. This trend was, however, turned from 1889, when the female intake to telephone and telegraph work expanded. Women were also engaged in the administrative sector and, by 1913, the German civil service employed around 30,000 women. More than 20,000 had passed the civil service examinations; posts at higher levels were, however, only within the reach of the few women who had managed to acquire a university degree. The first female industrial inspector with a university education had engaged in studies in Switzerland.[31]

Women were accepted for certain tasks in the Finnish civil service in the second half of the nineteenth century. In the 1860s women could be employed in the postal service although with a different salary scale than men: by 1888, a female post office keeper could earn as much as 600 marks per year, while male post office clerks earned up to 2200 marks per year already in the 1860s.[32] In Spain, the clerical sector saw an increase of women and particularly technological innovations like the telephone, typewriter and telegraph had a major impact. The modernisation of the telephone service in the 1920s radically increased the opportunities for female employment.[33]

Denmark opened the doors for women into the state and municipal sector in the 1860s and 70s. As elsewhere, the postal service and the telegraph service were fairly early on the scene; however, the state-run railways also began to employ women for office work and ticket printing in the 1890s. A fairly interesting trait was the purely female job of station guard, awarded only to women married to men working for the railways as track repairers. The job carried very little remuneration but came with free housing in the station building and a percentage on the ticket sales. By the first years of the twentieth century, some of the administrative work was amalgamated and women gained access to the same training programs as men. The telegraph service even introduced an equal pay system, the marriage bar was abolished in 1905 and two months maternity leave introduced, where the new mother could supply a replacement to do the work during this period. The Bureau of Statistics and the National Archives were also early employers of women. The first held in its ranks in

[30] Fuchs and Thompson, *Women in 19th Century Europe*, pp. 81, 93.

[31] Helen Boak, 'The state as an employer of women in the Weimar Republic', in W.R. Lee and Eve Rosenhaft (eds), *State, Social Policy and Social Change in Germany 1880–1994* (Oxford, 1997), pp. 64–101, on pp. 66–8.

[32] Anne Ollila, *Jalo velvollisuus, virkanaisena 1800-luvun lopun Suomessa* (Tampere, 2000), pp. 75–6.

[33] Borderias, *Entre líneas*, pp. 93–7.

the 1890s both the future factory inspector Anette Vedel and one of the leading lights of the feminist movement, Meta Hansen. The ministries, on the other hand, showed some variation in their employment policies.[34]

Swedish women gained partial access to state employment after 1909. In the 1920s, most of this sector became free for women in all the Nordic countries apart from the Church and the defence sector. Parts of the Swedish state administration applied a marriage bar, which was lifted in the late 20s or 30s.[35]

Table 5.2   Wage scales of male and female Post Office sorting clerks and telegraphers in Britain 1914.

Age+ years in service	Wage in Shillings			
	Male Class I pre-1908	Male 1914	Female Class I pre-1908	Female 1914
18 years		18		15
19 years	19	20	16	18
20 years	21	22	17	20
21 years	23	24	19	22
+ years	25	26	20	24
	27	28	22	26
	29	31	23	28
	33	33	25	29
	35	35	26	30
Max	56	62	35	36
Provinces	16–56	18–62	16–35	15–36
London	20–62		18–38	

Sources: Reports of the Select Committee on Post Office Servants 1907 and 1913, Cd 7355, 1914, pp. 12–16; The Hobhouse revision 1906, supervisory positions below assistant postmasters, five classes, salaries £100–500, for women two classes with salaries of £85–170, Select Committee on Post Office Servants pp 1906, XII, 775.

[34] Louise Neergaard, 'Arbejdskaar for Kvinder I Samarbejde med Maend, Kvinner I Jernbane, Telegraf og Post Etaterne', *Kvinden og samfundet* 23 (15.4, 1907), pp. 51–2; Astrid Paludan-Muller, 'Arbejdskaar for Kvinder I Samarbejde med Maend II, Kvinderne I Ministerierne og Magtsaten', *Kvinden og samfundet* 23 (30.6, 1907), pp. 91–2; *Kvinden og samfundet* 7 (1941).

[35] Ida Blom, 'Veien til juridisk likestellning', *Historica IV, Foredrag vid det XVIII nordiska historikermotet 1981* (Jyvaskyla, 1983), pp. 68–9; Vattula, 'Kvinnors förvärvsarbete', pp. 48–9; Carlsson and Rosen, *Svensk Historia 2*, p. 494.

Table 5.3   Estimates of weekly wages of clerks in Britain 1910–14.

	Men	**Women**	**Conditions of women clerks 1910**	
Insurance	53s 6d	23s	Good education, shorthand, typing, foreign languages	£2–4/week
Commerce and industry	40s	15s 6d	Intelligent girls, typing, copying	£1–30s/week
Banks	53 s		Some training in commercial school, 2 rate typewriting	10–15s/week
Transport service	36s	20–28s min. 11s 6d		
Average earnings of clerks 1914	55–85s/week £143–221/year	15–25s/week £39–65/year		

Sources: Annual report of the chief inspector of factories and workshops 1910, special report on the hours and conditions of work in type writing offices pp 1911 xxii 197–8; Royal commission of the civil service, appendix to the fourth report, pp 1914 xvi, 21; Lee Holcombe, *Victorian Ladies at Work* (London, 1973), pp. 150–1; Royal commission on poor laws and relief of distress, vol. iv pp 1909 xli, 86.

The Empire strikes back – the marriage bar

There is no doubt that the issue of middle-class values – the female sphere being equated with the domestic sphere – created social pressures on women once they were allowed access to education and entry into the professions. However, we also find another backlash, the marriage bar. In many countries the price a woman had to pay for being a professional was enforced celibacy. This was the case particularly in the English-speaking part of the world: Britain, the USA, Ireland and the British Commonwealth, for example Australia.[36]

In Britain the male teaching unions had steadfastly refused to take an interest in the wellbeing of women teachers and actively supported discriminatory

---

[36] Beddoe, *Discovering*, p. 97; Martin Stanley, 'Women in the Civil Service', https://civilservant.org.uk/women-history.html; Lynelle Briggs, 'Celebration of the 40th anniversary of the lifting of the Marriage Bar', http://www.apsc.gov.au/media/briggs201106.htm; Rachel Patterson, 'Women of Ireland: change toward social and political equality in the 21st century Irish Republic', https://web.archive.org/web/20151008154655/https://martindale.cc.lehigh.edu/files/Patterson.pdf; Dyhouse, *Feminism and the Family*, pp. 77–80.

policies. The women formed their own separate union in 1909, but they were unable to resist actions taken by the state and local authorities to weaken their position on the labour market. While legislation introduced in 1919 (the Sex Disqualification Removal Bill) was supposed to abolish discrimination against women in the civil service and increase equality in salary levels, it confirmed the legality of the marriage bar. From 1922, one region after another started not only dismissing female schoolteachers at marriage but also weeding out those already married.[37]

Fields not traditionally feminine did not welcome women; in 1928, a country with the population of Britain had only 82 female dentists, 21 female architects and 10 chartered accountants. Although female professions like nursing and teaching were open to women (154,000 nurses and 134,000 female teachers in the late 1930s), these professions came with strings attached. The post-WWI negative attitudes to female work resulted in even unmarried female office workers being abused for 'taking the jobs of men'. The marriage bar was in effect in most parts of Britain until made illegal in 1944; however, some regions would not employ married teachers as late as the 1950s. The Civil Service had introduced the marriage bar in 1894, although the Post Office would not appoint married women from the 1870s on. Not until 1946 was the marriage bar lifted in the British Civil Service, and the Foreign Service did not accept married women until 1973.[38] In New Zealand, the public services were closed to married clerical workers from the early twentieth century to 1947.[39]

The education sector in the United States exercised marriage bars and many women in Canada and parts of the USA of the late nineteenth and early twentieth centuries went into business as they were unable to stay in employment in the public sector, and often also the private, if they were married.[40]

Such attitudes and rules were not the monopoly of the English-speaking world. In Austria, female teachers were expected to leave if married but were given the right to apply for staying in the profession after marriage from 1918.[41] Although Sweden did not introduce a universal marriage bar covering all sectors, it did de facto exist through the 1920s and 30s. In 1936, new

[37] Bradley, *Men's Work, Women's Work*, pp. 211–12, 47; Holcombe, *Victorian Ladies*, p. 45; Martindale, *Women Servants*, p. 159.

[38] Braybon and Summerfield, *Out of the Cage*, pp. 138–40; Stanley, 'Women in the Civil Service'; Martindale, *Women Servants*, pp. 146–50.

[39] Harrison and Nolan, 'Reflections in colonial glass?', p. 280.

[40] Beatrice Craig, *Women and Business since 1500* (London, 2016), pp. 106–7; Goldin, *Marriage Bars*, pp. 3–4, 36.

[41] Reingard Witzmann, 'Zwischen anpassung und Fortschritt – Der Berufsalltag der Frau', in Witzmann, *Die Frau im Korsett*, pp. 11–20, on p. 18; Fuchs and Thompson, *Women in 19th Century Europe*, p. 78.

regulations were brought in abolishing the right to sack female civil servants upon marriage, pregnancy or engagement.[42]

In the Netherlands, married women were excluded from the right to work in the civil service from 1924 until 1957. The attitude to the work of mothers was generally negative and included private employers. Legislation restricting hours of female work also affected the attractiveness of women in the labour market and the share of married women in the labour force shrank from 25 per cent in 1899 to 2 per cent in 1930, the lowest in Western Europe.[43]

During WWI, offices and workplaces in Germany filled with women replacing men at the front. The post-war era, however, brought a number of changes. In 1919, a law enacted by the central government made it illegal to sack women in state employment when they married. Although some states found little problem in following the rule, some regions, like Bavaria, absolutely refused. They mitigated the blow by instating severance packages but would not allow married school teachers on the grounds that seeing a pregnant teacher could have a negative effect on the children. Some offices, like the postal service, also feared to be drowned in women and offered female clerks money if they agreed to leave when they married. As a result of this development, the German Postal Service saw a decrease of female employees from 51,000 in 1923 to 32,000 in 1934.[44] While attitudes in Germany had continuously been negative in some circles to working mothers, the rise of the Nazi party to political power resulted in an absolute moratorium on the work of married women from 1933.[45] In Spain, restrictions against married women working in trade and commerce had existed since the 1880s and attitudes to the work of married women became more negative in the 1920s and 30s. A marriage bar was introduced from 1938 and a number of economic sectors became closed to women.[46]

While the expectation among the middle classes in many countries was that married women should cease working if they could afford it, forcing women out of employment with the aid of laws and statutes was not universal, and in some countries unheard of. For example, in France, a husband had the right to object to his wife being in employment, but the state placed no

[42] However, the two female inspectors employed before the ban did not marry, and even those active in the 1940s resigned when they married or became mothers. Annika Akerblom, *Arbetarskydd för kvinnor: kvinnlig yrkesinspektion i Sverige 1913–1948* (Uppsala, 1998), pp. 46–50.

[43] Marianne Bousardt, *Onder Vrouwelijke Hoede, Vrouwen bij de Arbeidsinspectie* (s-Gravenhage, 1990), pp. 49, 54.

[44] Boak, 'The state as an employer', pp. 64–101, on pp. 70–7.

[45] Eleanor Riemer and John Fout (eds), *European Women: A Documentary History, 1789–1945* (Brighton, 1980), p. 112.

[46] Borderias, *Entre líneas*, pp. 33, 36–7, 70.

barriers in her way. Society could disapprove or a specific employer could apply a rule of not engaging married women, but state organisations had no rule of systematic discrimination against married women. On the other hand, in France, like elsewhere, the practice of engaging women for less-important posts or teaching young children or girls only was common. In the 1930s, a period not known for extensive liberalism in Finnish history, 24 per cent of primary school teachers, 16 per cent of council civil servants, 19 per cent of office workers and 16 per cent of midwives were married women. When in the 1930s female teachers in England were sacked at marriage, Finnish local councils employed married couples to teach in primary schools. Similar examples of husband and wife in the same district in education or the civil service can be found from early twentieth-century France and Denmark.[47]

Table 5.4   Salaries of teachers in Britain and Denmark.

1914 Britain	Male	Female	1907 Denmark	Male	Female
Teachers with certificates, heads	£176	£122	Copenhagen finish	3000 crowns	2000 crowns
Assistant teachers	£127	£92	Copenhagen start	1500 crowns	1400 crowns
Un-certificated Heads	£94	£68	Urban finish	2400 crowns	1500 crowns
Assistant teachers	£65	£54	Urban start	1000 crowns	800 crowns

Sources: L. Holcombe, *Victorian Ladies at Work*, p. 43; E. Morley, *Women Workers in Seven professions, A Survey of their Economic Conditions and Prospects,* p. 45; Astrid Paludan Muller, 'Arbejdskaar for kvinder i Samarbejde med Maend', *Kvinden og samfundet* 16:23 (30.9 1907).

[47] Schweitzer, *Les inspectrices*, pp. 21–2, 42–5; Beatrice Craig, *Female Enterprise behind the Discursive Veil in Nineteenth Century Northern France* (London, 2016), pp. 150–1; Lähteenmäki, *Mahdollisuuksien aika*, p. 31; Maria Lähteenmäki, 'Ansioäidit arvossaan', in Raimo Parikka (ed.), *Työ ja Työttömyys* (Helsinki, 1994), pp. 66–83, on pp. 69–73.

Table 5.5   Marriage and career of French college teachers who graduated in the 1880s and 1890s.

Husband	Wife left teaching	Wife remained in teaching	Total	Number
Teacher	14.5%	84.5%	47.1%	33
Other	48.6%	51.4%	52.9%	37
Total	32.9%	67.1%	100%	70
Number	23	47		

Source: Jo Burr Margadant, *Madame le Professeur: Women Educators in the Third Republic* (Princeton, 1990), p. 143.

Conclusion

In the nineteenth century, higher education was coming into the reach of middle-class women. While teacher training colleges in many countries saw the inclusion of young women with different backgrounds, university studies were only within the reach of the economically well situated. The approach to education and the preparation for life after studies also varied in different countries. While some female colleges in the USA saw a virtue in the learning and performing of domestic tasks, Oxford and Cambridge surrounded their students with servants, making sure that they never had to soil their hands or forget that they were ladies.

The increase in educational opportunities created an increasing group of women with the desire to use their attainments. While the educational sector absorbed some of these women, some pressure also arose to allow women entry into administration. The innovations of the typewriter, the telegraph and the telephone service opened new niches for women. The growing need for secretarial assistance in a field with an ever increasing need for paperwork also saw the advantages of admitting women with skills and education, who demanded smaller salaries than men. This development was a balancing act: on the one hand, saving money, on the other hand, making sure that the hierarchical structure was maintained. Where women were employed in operating new machines they were less of a threat than in performing more traditional administrative duties. The problem was, however, solved in Britain and some other countries by the introduction of the marriage bar. Sacking women at marriage made their work careers shorter and the chances of advancement less likely. Retaining a certain number of spinsters was possible, particularly by keeping male and female tasks separate.

The separate sphere ideology had, however, the consequence that women could insist that women should handle issues related to female education, health and life. This ultimately led to demands for female inspection of female workplaces.

6

The Female Factory Inspectors –
How, Why and Who

> I doubt very much whether the office of factory inspector is suitable for women.
>
> (UK Chief Inspector of Factories, 1879)

In face of considerable opposition and claims that the economy was going to be ruined, Britain introduced the first workplace regulations in 1833 and 1844, followed by France in 1841. It soon became apparent, however, that legislation without control had little impact on the work of children and a system of factory inspection was set up in these countries within a year of the new legislation. The early inspection system left much to be desired: initially, four factory inspectors were deemed sufficient for the whole of Britain. Furthermore, some of the early inspectors were not particularly active, some had tendencies to bond with the factory owners because of recruitment, salaries or ideology.[1]

In 1874, a state-funded system with 15 inspectors overseeing a regional inspectorate was introduced in France and by 1891 no less than 73 departmental inspectors had been engaged. The department of Seine saw the engagement of women in the inspections of schools and welfare institutions already in 1878 and from 1892 the state also appointed women for inspecting factories employing women and children.[2]

Safety and hygiene problems were also raised outside Britain and France during the second half of the nineteenth century by doctors, philanthropists and factory workers. Regulations about accident funds financed not only by workers but also factory owners raised more awareness in relation to dangerous machinery. The state and local governments, which had little desire

---

[1] Henriques, *Before the Welfare State*, pp. 93–8; Beatrice Moring, 'Bourgeois and international networks as strategies for female civil servants in the late 19th and the early 20th century Europe', in Marie-Pierre Arrizabalaga, Diana Burgos-Vigna and Mercedes Yusta (eds), *Femmes sans Frontières* (Berne, 2011), pp. 271–90, on pp. 273–4.

[2] Schweitzer, *Les inspectrices*, pp. 26–7, 151–7.

to take on the economic responsibility for individuals loosing health and limbs in the factories, saw the benefits of an inspection system eliminating obvious dangers. As a result, many countries in Europe and members of the British Commonwealth introduced workplace legislation and inspection by the 1880s.[3]

Feminism, social reform and the discussion about female factory inspectors

The late nineteenth century was the time of the rising specialist. Traditional notions were looked down upon; the urban landscape was transformed not only by the tramway and streetlights but also by piped water, the water closet and the creation of milk and meat inspection offices. Old superstition was to be replaced by new rationality, embodied in the knowledge of technology, chemistry and medicine. A new society needed new officials with the ability to analyse, understand and present rational arguments. The middle classes had nothing to lose and everything to win from such a development. The increasing interest in collection of data and social progress was manifested in publications such as *Zeitschrift für Wohnungswesen, Le Musée, The Progress* and *Industria*, as well as in international organisations and conferences.[4] The sons and daughters of this emerging group were eager to embrace the knowledge and the challenges.

Although the administration sector was partially closed to women in nineteenth-century Europe, it was considered that they could be incorporated to handle tasks related to social matters, women and children. Therefore, inspecting schools or the workplaces of women was in several countries the first properly qualified post for women within the state administration.[5]

The process of the employment of women in the factory inspectorate started in 1870s Britain with a resolution by the Trades Union Congress 1878 urging the government to appoint female inspectors. The prime mover was Emma

---

3   Harrison and Nolan, 'Reflections in colonial glass?', pp. 266–7; Sabine Schmitt, *Der Arbeiterinnenschutz in deutschen Kaiserreich* (Stuttgart, 1995); Jussi Kuusanmäki, *Sosiaalipolitiikkaa ja kaupunkisuunnittelua, Tietoa, taitoa asiantuntemusta Helsinki eurooppalaisessa kehityksessä 1875–1917* (Helsinki, 1992), p. 134; Volodin, *Russian Factory Inspection*, pp. 4–5; U.S. Department of Labor, *Factory Inspection Legislation*, 1–2.

4   Werner Coze and Jürgen Kocka, *Bildungsbürgetum in 19. Jahrhundert, I. Bildungssystem und Professionalisierung im internationalen Vergleich* (Stuttgart, 1988), pp. 9–16; E.P. Hennock, *British Social Reform and German Precedents, the Case of Social insurance 1880–1914* (Oxford, 1987), p. 29; Kuusanmäki, *Sosiaalipolitiikkaa*, pp. 38–41.

5   Schmitt, *Der Arbeiterinnenschutz*, p. 141.

Ann Paterson, a woman of working-class origin who had risen through organisational work. The positive although careful response to the initiative resulted in a violent outburst from the Chief Inspector of Factories in 1879:

> I doubt very much whether the office of factory inspector is suitable for women ... In my last report I gave some outline sketches of a day's work of an inspector. A perusal of these would force a conviction that it was the work for a man and not a woman, the general and multifarious duties of an inspector of factories would really be incompatible with the gentle and home-loving character of a woman ... Factory inspecting requires activity and acumen and the stern authority of a man to enforce obedience to his interrogatories. It is not an agreeable duty for a man, but I cannot conceive that such functions would commend themselves to a woman, or that she could successfully discharge them. I question the success of a female inspector in appearing at a metropolitan police court, conducting her case and having to submit herself in the witness-box to the cross-examination of an astute attorney ... it has been urged that where women are employed some enquiries could be more appropriately made by women ... but it is seldom necessary to put a single question to a female, and I do not see how the services of ladies could be made available to render the administration of the law more effective. Possibly some details here and there might be superintended by a female inspector, but looking at what is required I fail to see the advantages likely to arise from her ministrations at a factory or workshop, so opposite to the sphere of her good work in the hospital, the school or the home.[6]

In Germany, similar negative voices were heard from the male factory inspectorate in the 1890s. The views were here that unpaid ladies from the charity sector could if necessary be used.[7] When the issue was raised in Sweden, the male inspectors made clear that if such a proposal was to become reality it should be clear that the women should be subject to the authority of male inspectors and their duties restricted to health and hygiene questions.[8]

An undisputable fact was, however, that surveys by state commissions and collections of economic statistics had demonstrated that a considerable part of the labour force consisted of women and children and that their situation was far from ideal.[9] While those eager for regulation represented groups with considerable variation in attitude, from proponents of regulating women

---

6   Martindale, *Women Servants*, pp. 51–2.
7   Schmitt, *Der Arbeiterinnenschutz*, pp. 142–3.
8   Akerblom, *Arbetarskydd*, pp. 26–7.
9   Anderson, *Women in the Factory*, pp. 15–16; Vattula, 'Kvinnors förvärvsarbete', pp. 38–41; Vattula, 'Lähtöviivallako?', pp. 14–15.

out of the workplace, to those desiring protection from dangerous tasks, to defenders of morality, the issue had to be addressed. In the 1880s stricter rules on work with poisonous substances were introduced in Britain. The 1891 Factory Act put the minimum employment age at 11 years and in addition a moratorium on women working 4 weeks after giving birth was brought in. The necessity of having female inspectors was again raised by persons with links to philanthropic work, child welfare and feminism.[10]

Many of the early arguments for the need for female inspectors presented the engagement of women in social issues as a primary reason. As the nineteenth century hosted a continuing debate about the moral corruption of factory work, it was easy to make a case for the need for women inspecting women and children. Female inspectors could enter dormitories, changing rooms and the homes of other women, which was not the case for male inspectors.[11] In Britain as well as Germany and Scandinavia, it was underlined that women could probe into bullying and sexual harassment by superiors and male colleagues, and were assumed to get more honest answers. There was also agreement about the need for female inspectors between working-class women and the middle-class women's movement.[12]

The issue of recruitment was not, however, uncomplicated. By the 1890s, working women had already started forming unions and organisations promoting health, welfare and education, organisations that operated separately from those of their middle-class feminist counterparts. Feminist organisations engaged in the debate about the right to education and the vote, like the Society for Promoting the Employment of Women (SPEW) in Britain or *Bund Deutscher Frauevereine* in Germany, often assumed to speak for all women. Their eagerness to highlight the interests of all women sometimes also brought them into conflict with female unions and social democratic organisations.[13]

---

[10] Akerblom, *Arbetarskydd*, p. 9; Celia Davies, 'The health visitor as mother's friend: a woman's place in public health 1900–14', *Social History of Medicine* 1:1 (April 1988), pp. 52–3; Jones, 'Women health workers', pp. 165–7; Martindale, *Women Servants*, pp. 46–7; Gertrude Tuckwell, Constance Smith, May Tennant, Nellie Adler and Adelaide Anderson, *Woman in Industry from Seven Points of View* (London, 1908), pp. 146–52; McFeeley, *Lady Inspectors*, pp. 7–8.

[11] Schmitt, *Der Arbeiterinnenschutz*, p. 70; Harrison and Nolan, 'Reflections', p. 170; Anderson, *Women in the Factory*, pp. 143–5.

[12] Ensimmainen, *yleisen työläisnaisten*; Schmitt, *Der Arbeiterinnenschutz*, pp. 64–7, 143; Anderson, *Women in the Factory*, pp. 6–8; Kerstin Hesselgren, 'Den kvinnliga yrkes och sundhetsinspektionen i England', *Dagny* 15 (1904), pp. 313–33, on pp. 313–18; Ester Hjelt-Cajanus, *Vera Hjelt, en banbryterska* (Helsingfors, 1946), pp. 143–5.

[13] McFeeley, *Lady Inspectors*, pp. 14–15; Schmitt, *Der Arbeiterinnenschutz*, pp.

In Britain, the employment of the first female industrial inspectors was run on class lines. The Royal Commission on Labour 1891–3 became the recruitment ground, and the coterie around prominent members of the Liberal Party promoted their protégées in this process.[14] The intrusion of people who were not 'ladies' was effectively blocked and the distance between the 'lady inspector' and 'the factory girl' was firmly established.

Two things made the development in the United States different from that of Europe. First, the issue of inspections was a matter for the individual member states, not the central government, and second, the process was not primarily driven by middle class reformists but to a large extent through local labour movements. The backlash also tended to be, for the United States, specific argumentation about whether factory laws were constitutional or not, rather than about whether women were able to act as inspectors. In several instances, factory legislation developed, as elsewhere, in conjunction with, or as a result of, the collection of statistics on labour conditions and accidents. The propensity for introducing labour legislation and a system of inspection, however, tended to depend on local political structures and the power of unions. Therefore, the industrialised east, with Massachusetts and Connecticut, New York and Pennsylvania, were the pioneers in introducing protective labour legislation.[15] On the other hand, while Illinois, although industrialised was far from being in the vanguard, one of the first female inspectors, Florence Kelley, was active in the efforts of the Working Women's Societies for employing female inspectors, which brought successes in Pennsylvania (1889), New York (1890) and Massachusetts (1891), before she herself was appointed factory inspector in Chicago in 1893.[16]

The definition of the post – qualifications, rights and duties of the female inspector

The first female state-employed inspector in France started her activity in 1892; in Britain, the female inspectorate was introduced in 1893. Denmark and Norway appointed inspectors in 1901 and 1910, respectively. By 1908, the first female inspector started her work as controller of the working conditions of women in the Belgian textile industries. The female factory and work place inspectorate was separated from that of their male counterparts in Britain,

---

68–71; Hentilä, 'Maa jossa piiatkin', pp. 162–85, on p. 180; Heintz Niggemann, *Emanzipation zwischen Sozialismus und Feminismus* (Wuppertal, 1981), pp. 154–5.

[14] Elaine Harrison, *Officials of Royal Commissions of Inquiry 1870–1939* (London, 1995), Introduction; McFeeley, *Lady Inspectors*, pp. 13–15.

[15] U.S. Department of Labor, *Factory Inspection Legislation*.

[16] Sklar, *Florence Kelley*, pp. 141–3.

France, Belgium, Demark and Norway. While male inspectors were usually tied to a specific region, the female inspectors inspected workplaces with only or mainly female workers in different parts of the country. At the reorganisation of the British inspection system in 1908, the definition of the duties of the female inspectors was expressed in the following manner:

> Exclusively or primarily of investigation of accidents to women and girls in laundries and clothing factories, supervision of industries, investigation of industrial poisoning among women and girls, routine inspection of all factories and workshops that employ women and girls wherever special regulations apply. They were also to administer the provisions of the law governing sanitary accommodations, child labour and the employment of women after childbirth.[17]

The task of female inspectors was to see to the protection of women and children in the workplace and that current legislation was followed. They were often responsible for inspecting workplaces occupied with handicrafts. In Denmark, the focus was set on the sanitary conditions in workplaces employing women and adherence to protective legislation in relation to children. However, the inspectors were also expected to negotiate with owners about improvements to the workplace. In Norway, the female inspector was primarily engaged with sanitation and moral issues. The condition of and potential danger posed by machinery was part of the remit of the male inspectorate and outside the scope of women.[18] In Germany, Austria and the Netherlands, the women were defined as assistant inspectors working under male superiors. Their work focused on the living and social conditions of workers and philanthropic activity aimed at the labouring population. The Prussian female inspectors were expected to have training in hygiene and welfare. In Austria, however, they were authorised to mediate in conflicts between workers and employers.[19]

When the female inspectorate was set up in Finland in 1903, the qualifications included a requirement to demonstrate knowledge of technical matters and a degree from an institution of higher education – an institute of polytechnics, university, baccalaureate – and/or experience of working in the industrial sector. Even though the title was assistant inspector, the tasks

---

17 Anderson, *Women in the Factory*, pp. 12–13, 141–2.

18 Vera Hjelt, *Berättelse afgifven af kvinnliga yrkesinspektören i Helsingfors, Tammerfors och Uleaborgs distrikt för 1909 jamte reseberättelse* (Helsingfors, 1910), p. 89; Elna Dahlberg, 'Om kvindelig Fabriksinspection', *Kvinden og samfundet* 24:20 (1.12 1904), pp. 197–8; Akerblom, *Arbetarskydd*, pp. 24–6.

19 Schmitt, *Der Arbeiterinnenschutz*, pp. 143–4; Vera Hjelt, *Berättelse afgifven af kvinnliga yrkesinspektören i Finland för år 1908* (Helsingfors, 1909), pp. 91–2; Akerblom, *Arbetarskydd*, p. 25.

were even more extensive than those of their male colleagues. They were to oversee the adherence to existing labour legislation in factories and other workplaces and see to the welfare of women and children. They were to examine the working conditions of young people, their health and see that they were allowed access to education. They were to look into the nutritional and housing situation of women, to promote factory canteens and the establishment of healthcare and pension funds. They were to promote hygiene and moral standards in the workplace and mediate in conflicts between workers and employers. In 1905, when the female inspector was still responsible for the whole country, she inspected more than 400 factories and workshops in a year.[20]

Education versus position, contacts and networks

Britain, Germany, France and the Netherlands

When examining the appointments of the first female inspectors it is futile to deny the importance of the social network for opening up of opportunities and furthering access to positions. Recommendations and proposals came from influential people (friends) engaged in the same organisations (women's organisations, philanthropic organisations) or who were connected by blood or though marriage. Over time, such processes might have weakened, but in the late nineteenth century and the first decade of the twentieth century, this was often the case. It is, however, of some interest that in the attainment of positions that have been viewed as a female victory over patriarchal structures, male protectors or mentors were often crucial for success. Livesley has analysed the networking and use of old power (the aristocracy) and new power (male civil servants) in the process that resulted in the appointment of the first female industrial inspectors in Britain and their successful activity.[21]

The background for female entry into the inspectorate in Britain was a political change favouring the Liberal Party. It was also facilitated through the work of The Royal Commission on Labour (1891–3). This was the first commission to employ female assistant commissioners, thanks to the chairman, the Duke of Devonshire. The lady assistant commissioners were recruited to collect information about women's work and working conditions. Among the ladies chosen for the task were May Abraham, who had worked as secretary to Lady Emilia Dilke, a prominent Liberal and leader of the

---

[20] Hjelt, *Berättelse afgifven af kvinnliga yrkesinspektören i Finland för år 1903* (Helsingfors, 1904); Vera Hjelt, *Berättelse afgifven af kvinnliga yrkesinspektören i Finland för år 1905* (Helsingfors, 1906).

[21] Livesley, 'The politics of work', pp. 233–61, on pp. 245, 252; Harrison and Nolan, 'Reflections', p. 272.

Women's Trade Union Association, and Clara Collett, a coworker of Charles Booth with experience of survey activity. The commission secretaries Geoffrey Drage and John Burnett recruited numerous female clerks, no fewer than 21 out of 27 were women and no fewer than 13 were Oxbridge graduates. In one of Drage's submissions for appointment of two lady clerks, he noted that he had 'names of several ladies of high scholastic distinction at the Universities. It would be impossible to obtain men possessing such qualifications at the salary of 150 per annum, the lowest sum for which they will undertake such work'.[22]

When the efforts to create the post of Lady Inspector of Factories and Workplaces in Britain were successful in 1893, the experience of the commission work was seen as a major reason for appointing May Abraham (Tennant). She had a solid middle-class background and the close connection to Lady Dilke and the Liberal Party should not be forgotten. Unlike her Scottish colleague, Mary Paterson, who had a university degree, Abraham lacked any formal qualifications. These first two inspectors, Abraham and Paterson, were appointed on recommendation, based on activity and personal characteristics. However, when the female inspectorate was expanded with Adelaide Anderson and Lucy Deane in 1894, a rule was brought in that all female inspectors had to sit the Civil Service examination. The inspectors' examination included spelling, English composition, arithmetic, handwriting and knowledge and understanding of factory legislation. The candidates had to sit written and oral tests.[23] While a suitable social background was seen as relevant for a lady inspector, actual qualifications also mattered. Adelaide Anderson (Prinicipal Lady Inspector 1897–1921), had worked as a clerk for the Commission of Labour and she combined a degree from Cambridge with considerable language skills.[24] Lucy Deane and Rose Squire (1895), early recruits like Anderson, had diplomas in hygiene and experience of work as sanitary inspectors. Deane also managed to become the protégé of Abraham and, therefore, enjoyed the support of Lady Dilke. Squire was an old colleague of Deane and also managed to establish some contacts to the influential group within the Liberal Party.[25]

22 Harrison, *Officials of Royal Commissions*, Introduction.

23 McFeeley, *Lady Inspectors*, pp. 15, 24–5; Livesley, 'The politics of work', pp. 245–6; Harrison and Nolan, 'Reflections', p. 270.

24 Martindale, *Women Servants*, pp. 46–9.

25 McFeeley, *Lady Inspectors*, pp. 13–16.

Table 6.1   Previous occupations of factory inspectors in Britain 1907.

Male inspectors		Female inspectors	
University degree	11		
School master	9	Clerk with Royal commission	2
Engineering degree	10	Sanitary inspector	3
Engineer no degree	30	Sanitary inspector, BSc.	1
Army	3	Bacteriologist	1
Lawyer	1	Inspector of children's institutions	1
Manufacturer or manager	15	Lecturer in hygiene	1
Master or foreman	5	Social work	1
Sanitary inspector	3	Secretary to principal lady inspector	1
Clerk in government office	4	Private secretary	1
Clerk for factory or union	3		
Analyst	2		
Total	96		12

Note: Of the female inspectors, five had a university degree.
Source: Royal Commission on Civil Service, Appendix to 2 Report, P.P. 1912–13 XV, 125–6.

By 1907, the inspectorate had grown considerably, with 96 male inspectors, of whom 44 were assistant inspectors, and 12 female inspectors. The system of competitive examinations was not brought in for the male inspectors until 1890 and for male assistant inspectors until 1900. A scrutiny of where the parties had gained their experience reveals a very different image for men and women (see Table 6.1). The females tended to have a background in health, hygiene or clerical work (and five had university degrees). The male inspectors, on the other hand, demonstrated a considerable share of men with experience of manufacture or engineering, mostly practical. One should also not forget the former soldiers and the masters and foremen.[26] Such an occupational profile might well explain why talking to female factory workers had been seen as unnecessary and that 'the stern authority of a man to enforce obedience to his interrogatories'[27] had, in the 1870s and 1880s, been envisaged as more important than probing into the health and welfare of the workers.

[26] Royal Commission on Civil Service, Appendix to Second Report, PP 1912–13, XV, 125.
[27] Martindale, *Female servants*, 1938, pp. 51–2.

In Germany, male industrial inspectors were generally expected to demonstrate competence in engineering or other technical matters. The recruitment of the female assistant inspectors, however, was firmly oriented towards the middle-class lady and moral worth.[28] Apart from in Baden, where Elisabeth von Richthofen held a degree with a specialisation in protective legislation for workers, followed by Marie Baum with a degree in chemistry,[29] academic degrees or technical knowledge was deemed less important than a ladylike disposition. Defining the female inspectors as assisting inspectors had the double advantage of paying them less and keeping them firmly under the authority of their male counterparts. While Anna Reichert in Berlin had some connection to industry by being a former head of a shirt factory, it was more common to have a past in social reform or philanthropy, like Cecilie Dose, in Dresden. Working-class organisations and newspapers expressed dismay at the appointment of Miss Hauser in Offenbach, deeming it typical for the attitude of the upper classes to appoint a former supervisor of a lunatic asylum to protect, or rather supervise, working women. The fact that Marie Gruner in Würtenberg was the widow of a factory owner did not escape notice either.[30]

In the Netherlands, like in Germany, the female inspectors were defined as assistants, even though a female section was later created. The need for professional exams and diplomas was originally seen as less important than a pleasing ladylike personality and capacity to provide guidance for young women in addition to seeing to the welfare of children. The early female appointees, A.A. Nuysink (1899) and E. Kleerenkoper (1900), were pharmacists, E.J. Tilanus (1900) had a past in social work, while E. Breitchat had run a handicrafts school; only Arends-Slingerlandt had had any connection to factories and factory work. By the time of the recruitment of a second generation of inspectors, around WWI, the expectations had increased and we find that academic or commercial diplomas or degrees had become the norm. In the early days of the twentieth century, it was also ruled that women with certificates or diplomas were to receive similar salaries to those of males with the same examinations working in the Civil Service.[31]

The first generation of French female inspectors (recruited from 1878 onwards), generally had a middle-class background with education in the liberal arts. Their fathers were doctors, lawyers, merchants, industrialists or civil servants. Many entered inspection work from social work, philanthropy

---

[28] Ayass, *Arbeiterschutz*, pp. xxxii–xxxiii; Michael Karl, *Fabriksinspektoren in Preussen: Das Personal de Geverbeaufsicht 1845–1945* (Opladen, 1993), pp. 174, 255, 336–7.

[29] Elisabeth von Richthofen, *Über die historischen Wandlungen in der Stellung der autoritären Parteien zur Arbeiterschutzgesetzgebung und die Motive dieser Wandlungen*, thesis (Heidelberg, 1901).

[30] Schmitt, *Der Arbeiterinnenschutz*, pp. 144–9; Karl, *Fabriksinspektoren in Preussen*, pp. 242–4.

[31] Bousardt, *Onder Vrouwelijke*, pp. 34–40, 51–2.

or education. In the years before the 1890s, sometimes female inspectors worked on a part-time basis.

From 1893, the women who wanted to embark on a career as inspector had to pass an entrance examination (concours), similar, but not identical, to that of the male inspectors. While a number of the recruits had qualifications from female colleges, we also find early examples of women with university degrees. For instance Alice de la Ruell-Geubel, who had studied law, received her university degree in 1901 and entered the profession the same year. The demand for a relatively high educational level guaranteed that recruitment was usually from middle-class families. By the early twentieth century, however, the candidates for the 'concours' also included primary school teachers, office workers and even women engaged in textile work, which illuminates the increased female access to secondary education.[32]

Scandinavia

In the late nineteenth century, the intellectual elite in the Nordic countries was still quite small and contacts or recommendations within the group readily attainable. This group was generally well educated and embraced internationalism, particularly in the fields of technology and natural sciences. Studies in other countries, or at least travel with the purpose of learning, was viewed as normal. Doctors, engineers and urban officials spent shorter or longer times at institutions in Germany or the other Nordic countries. Contacts were established and maintained.[33] In the case of the Nordic inspectors, the impact of networking varied slightly depending on time and place, but many of them had contacts to the early feminist movement. As far as gaining qualifications, the implications are clear. Only middle-class women could have found the contacts and funds that opened the doors to study abroad when suitable qualifications could not be gained at home. Annette Vedel, the first female inspector in Denmark, had a university degree in mathematics from the University of Stockholm, where women could be admitted before it became possible in Denmark. From 1896, she held a post at the National Statistical Bureau in Copenhagen, where she collected statistics on the standard of living of the working classes. Such a career made her eminently suitable for the work as factory inspector with the writing of reports and collecting statistics being a necessary part of the tasks.[34] Her colleague Julie Arenholt studied at the

[32] Schweitzer, *Les inspectrices*, pp. 28–30.

[33] Kuusanmäki, *Sosiaalipolitiikkaa*, pp. 121–4, 177, 185; Marjatta Hietala, *Tietoa, taitoa, asiantuntemusta: Helsinki Eurooppalaisessa kehityksessä 1875–1917* (Helsinki, 1992).

[34] Carl Lundin, *Nya Stockholm* (Stockholm, 1890), pp. 384, 391–2; Tim Knudsen, 'Vedel, Fanny Annette', *Dansk Kvindebiografisk Leksikon*, http://www.kvinfo.dk/

Polytechnic Institute, later the University of Technology, in Copenhagen and was the first woman to attain a degree in factory engineering in 1901. The third inspector, Ragna Schou, had a bachelors' degree from the University of Copenhagen (1906) and, in addition to having had four years employment at the Bureau of Statistics, she had also passed the Civil Service exam.[35]

Vera Hjelt, in Finland, was the daughter of a headmaster and part of a network that made it possible for her first to train as a teacher, and later attain a special diploma in woodwork in Sweden. After her return home she ran a small furniture factory and a school of woodwork. The second female inspector in Finland, Jenny Markelin-Svensson, was a farmer's daughter who, after studies at the School of Polytechnics, became the first woman to attain a degree in civil engineering.[36]

Betzy Kjelsberg came from a family of skippers and merchants, and was married to a lawyer. She had a secondary education exam but her studies for the baccalaureate were interrupted by her marriage. However, she had experience of organising health insurance schemes for shop workers, running a school for home economics and a milk hygiene project. She also participated in feminist organisations and left-wing party politics.[37] Assistant inspector Marie Aslaksrud was a teacher with experience of school boards and in local politics; she was also nominated to stand for parliament as a candidate for the Workers' Party. She died at the age of 45 in 1911 and was succeeded in the inspectorate by Ragna Bugge the following year. Bugge combined the training of a hospital nurse with a finished apprenticeship in carpentry. She left the inspectorate in 1916 to become the first female head of the National Poor Relief Service. From 1914, the female inspectorate was extended with another assistance post with a regional location in western Norway. Johanne Steen had a background in household economics and, after three years as inspector, she went into teaching household economics and running the Union of Teachers. The then newly employed Sophie Ronnevig and Marie Sundby had both trained in hospital nursing. The turnover among the assistant

---

side/597/bio/1389; Anna Thestrup, 'Kvinder i offentlige institutioner', *Fortid og Nutid* 3 (1991), pp. 175–96.

35 Anna-Birte Ravn, 'Ragna Schou', *Dansk Kvindebiografisk Leksikon*, http:// kvinfo.dk/side/597/bio1211/origin/170; Anna-Birte Ravn, 'Julie Arenholt', *Dansk Kvindebiografisk Leksikon*, http://www.kvinfo.dk/side/597/bio1062; 'Fabriksinspektor cand.polit. Julie Arenholt', *Kvinden og samfundet* 21:26 (1910), pp. 239–40; 'Danmarks forste fabriksinspectrice', *Kvinden og Samfundet* (23.11 1901), p. 181.

36 Hjelt-Cajanus, *Vera Hjelt*, pp. 32–3; Jussi Kuusanmäki, 'Markelin-Svensson, Jenny (1882–1929)', *Suomen Kansallisbibliografia* (Helsinki, 2005), pp. 556–7.

37 Magnhild Folkvord, *Betzy Kjelsberg: feminist og brubyggjar* (Oslo, 2016), pp. 11, 24–6, 30–1, 42–6, 56–60, 82–3; Gunhild Ramm Reistad, 'Betzy Kjelsberg (1866–1950)', http://kvinnesak.no/info.

inspectors was high, partly because they had no opportunity to advance into higher ranks and become full inspectors earning better salaries like their male counterparts. Ronnevig and Sundby, however, remained in their posts until retirement in 1948.[38]

New Zealand, Australia and the USA

As in Europe, the collection of statistics about the state of the working classes became the gateway for women into the inspectorate. Grace Neill, the first female factory inspector in New Zealand, worked as a member of the Queensland Royal Commission in 1891, making enquiries into the conditions of workers in shops and factories. Neill had originally trained in nursing and midwifery, but the introduction by a mutual friend to the minister of Labour, Reeves, led to an appointment as editor for The Journal of Labour. Soon after (1894), she was appointed inspector of factories and workshops.[39] The other three female factory inspectors, appointed before 1919, Margaret Scott (Hawthorne), Harriet Morison and Selina Hale had connections to the trade union movement, with backgrounds in crafts or textile work. Harriet Morison was engaged as secretary in the Tailoresses' Union and carried out unofficial workplace inspections before her appointment to inspector in 1906. She was demoted from factory inspector to head the Auckland Women's Employment Bureau in 1908. As the shortage of inspectors for female workplaces was considerable, her services were later retained on a part-time basis and continued until 1921.[40]

Although only 11,104 women were registered as working in factories in Australia, the first woman inspector was appointed as early as in 1894. Margaret Gardiner Cuthbertson had started her career as a telephone switchboard attendant in the Postmaster Generals department. At the age of 30, she found herself in the position of supervising the general accommodation, ventilation and sanitary conditions in factories. She was also charged with probing pay rates, hours of work and conditions of apprenticeship of female factory workers.[41] The connections between trade unions and the early woman inspectors were often more prominent in Australia than in Europe. Augusta Zadow, appointed inspector in 1895, had established the Working Women's Trade Union in 1890. After the introduction of the 1894 factories inspection act she was a logical candidate for the post of inspector.[42] Agnes Anderson

---

[38] Folkvord, *Betzy Kjelsberg*, pp. 102–3.

[39] Harrison and Nolan, 'Reflections', p. 271.

[40] Harrison and Nolan, 'Reflections', pp. 271–7, 280.

[41] Anthea Hyslop, 'Cuthbertson, Margaret Gardiner (1864–1944)', *Australian Dictionary of Biography*, adb.anu.edu.au/biography/cuthbertson-margaret-gardiner-5858.

[42] Helen Jones, 'Augusta Zadow', Australian Dictionary of Biography, adb.anu.

Milne became the second female factory inspector in Australia after death of Augusta Zadow in 1896. Her background was working class with a history of working in the trade unions and the Christian and temperance organisations for social reform.[43] Annie Duncan, appointed in 1897, had a middle-class background. Her interests were focused on sanitary issues. She travelled to England and attended courses with the National Health Institute and with the Royal Sanitary Institute in London. In 1894, she passed her examination for Inspector of Nuisances and was appointed to the South Kensington district in London. There she was befriended by Lucy Deane, and became acquainted with some of the other the English female factory inspectors. After three years, she returned to Australia and was appointed factory inspector for New South Wales.[44] The fifth Australian female inspector, Isabella Golding, entered the profession via education, as did some of the female inspectors in France. She commenced her professional career as a teacher, became inspector of schools in 1900, and in 1913, she entered the world of factory inspection.[45]

The most prominent female inspector in the United States was Florence Kelley. She was active within the movement that achieved female appointments to the inspectorates in Pennsylvania and New York before she herself took on the post as inspector in Chicago, Illinois. Her father was the congressman William D Kelley, from Pennsylvania, an abolitionist, labour reform advocate and a supporter of women's rights. She had graduated from Cornell in 1882 and studied Law and Government at the University of Zurich, one of the few higher education establishments that accepted women students. She married a fellow student and had three children, the family settled in New York. In the 1880s, she was active in the union movement and in women's societies in Philadelphia and New York. By 1891, she had begun working at Hull House in Chicago and, in 1892, she became Special Agent of the Illinois State Bureau of Labor Statistics. As an investigator into sweatshops for the Illinois General Assembly Joint Special Commission, she demonstrated her competence for collecting information about labour and social conditions and was appointed factory inspector for four years in 1893.[46] Alzina Parsons Stevens was appointed chief assistant to Florence Kelley. Parsons had been engaged in union organising within the Knights of Labor. She had also been

---

edu.au/biography/zadow-christiane-susanne-augusta-9224, https://sahistoryhub.history. sa.gov.au/people/augusta-zadw.

43 Philippa L. Fletcher, 'Agnes Milne', Australian Dictionary of Biography, adb. anu.edu.au/biography/milne-agnes-anderson-13100.

44 Kay Daniels, 'Annie Jane Duncan', Australian Dictionary of Biography, adb. anu.edu.au/biography/duncan-annie-jane-6043.

45 Beverly Kingston, 'Isabella Golding', Australian Dictionary of Biography, adb. anu.edu.au/biography/golding-isabella-theresa-belle-7040.

46 The Life and Times of Florence Kelley, https://florencekelley.northwestern.edu/ historical/timeline, pp. 1–2.

the co-editor of a newspaper pushing for industrial reform and the anti-sweatshop bill with Clarence Darrow Lloyd. Kelley's co-workers included both male and female deputies: Abraham Bisno, a union organiser, Mary Kenney O'Sullivan, previously a union organiser for the AFL, Fannie Jones of the Working Women's Council and the lawyers Alexander Bruce and John Ela, who assisted with prosecutions.[47]

Gender and remuneration

While in both French education and the Civil Service, males and females were remunerated differently, women often earning 30 per cent less than their male counterparts, the inspectorate had its own wage scales. Male and female inspectors were divided into five classes, each class having identical salaries for men and women. Between 1892 and 1920, the earnings in class five were 3000 francs and in class one 5000 francs. The differences in treatment on the basis of gender expressed itself in the scale of movement from one class to the next. While the turnover in the 1880s was of considerable magnitude and few women stayed long enough to achieve promotion, the situation changed in the 1890s and we find several examples of female inspectors staying until pension age at 67. Despite this, it is fairly easy to detect that, of a 20 per cent share of female inspectors, only 14 per cent of the inspectors reaching class 2 or 1 were women. These classes were, however, not out of reach and were attained by those with competence and a long career.[48]

It would also seem that the gender discrepancies in remuneration were more pronounced in Britain. In 1895, the salary of a female industrial inspector was £200 while her male counterpart earned £300. By 1908, both the male and the female inspectorate operated a hierarchical system, the Principal Lady Inspector had a salary of £500 that could rise to £600, but a male Deputy Chief Inspector earned £750–850. A senior lady inspector was paid £300–400, a senior male inspector the same, £300–400. A male superintending inspector earned £600–700 and this post was not available to women. The salary of a normal lady inspector was the same as that of an assistant male inspector, £100–300 per year (Table 6.2).[49]

47 Sklar, *Florence Kelley*, pp. 238–9.
48 Schweitzer, *Les inspectrices*, pp. 46–9.
49 McFeeley, *Lady Inspectors*, pp. 23–5, 114, 182.

Table 6.2   Salaries of industrial inspectors in Britain 1895 and 1908.

Male inspectors 1895	£300/year	Female inspectors 1895	£200/year
Assistant male inspector 1908	£100–300/year	Lady inspector 1908	£100–300/year
Senior male inspector	£300–400/year	Senior lady inspector	£300–400/year
Superintending inspector (male only) 1908	£600–700/year	Principal lady inspector	£500–600/year
Deputy chief inspector (male only) 1908	£750–800/year		

Sources: Royal Commission on Civil Service, Appendix to 2 Report, P.P. 1912–13 XV, 125; Dec. 1907 PRO LAB14/330035950; Mary Drake McFeeley, *Lady Inspectors: The Campaign for a Better Workplace* (Oxford, 1988), pp. 23, 25, 114, 182.

The job security varied considerably in Germany and it was fairly common that female inspectors had to undergo a 'test year' before gaining full appointment. In some areas, the posts were part time. In the early years of the twentieth century, a male inspector in northern Germany had a salary of 3000 marks while a female assistant inspector earned between 1500 and 2100 marks.[50] In the Netherlands, the posts tended to be full time, but the maximum salary of a female inspector was 2000 f while that of her male colleague was 3.500 f.[51] After a debate in the Norwegian parliament in 1909, a majority vote set the salary of the newly instituted female inspector at 2500 crowns with an increase of 250 after five years and another after 10 years in office. The starting salary of a male inspector was 4000 crowns and the age supplements 500, bringing the top salary to 5000 crowns against the 3000 of a woman.[52] Despite repeated efforts to achieve a higher degree of equality in salary levels, those of women inspectors in New Zealand remained persistently lower than the ones paid to men. The system remained in line with the general rules of the Civil Service.[53]

Denmark, however, became the exception to the rule of unequal pay. In 1901, a system with equal application rights and equal salaries was introduced for male and female industrial inspectors.[54]

[50] Schmitt, *Der Arbeiterinnenschutz*, p. 145.
[51] Bousardt, *Onder Vrouwelijke*, p. 36.
[52] Folkvord, *Betzy Kjelsberg*, pp. 96–7.
[53] Harrison and Nolan, 'Reflections', pp. 280–1.
[54] *Kvinden og samfundet* 37:17 (21.9 1901), p. 145.

We therefore find that, even though the educational level expected of the female inspectors was similar to that of the men, and sometimes higher, the gender difference in remuneration persisted. The two exceptions were France and Denmark. In the first case it was possible for women to reach male salary levels, in the second, actual equality was set as the norm.

The vestal virgins of the state and the mothers of the nation

As has previously been demonstrated, the marriage bar hit the Civil Service in different countries at different times, with Britain leading the way. These rules were also applied to the female inspectorate. From 1895, female factory inspectors in Britain could only be employed if unmarried. Likewise, the Public Service Commissioner of New Zealand introduced a marriage bar for the Civil Service in 1913. However, the early inspectors were not yet subject to such regulations. Grace Neill was married and the mother of a son; Margaret Scott Hawthorne was married and only divorced in 1915 after her retirement and then remarried.[55] In Australia, Augusta Zadow was married and a mother when appointed, while Agnes Anderson Milne was widowed and only remarried after her retirement.[56]

May Abraham, Tennant (inspector 1893–7), left her post a year after her marriage to a prominent politician. Lucy Deane married after retirement from the inspectorate, and the inspectors who remained in office also remained unmarried.[57]

When the inspection system was set up in Germany, it had not been clear that becoming an inspector was equal to a vow of chastity. In practice this was, however, the case, the first female inspector in Baden, Elisabeth von Richthofen, was dismissed upon marriage.[58]

The early steps towards a marriage bar in the Netherlands were taken already in 1910, with the demand that newly appointed female inspectors were to pledge to leave if they married. In 1923–4; however, the Civil Service was purged of married women, resulting in the sacking of not only the married but sometimes also the widowed. One of those sacked had worked in the department since the employment of the first women in 1899–1900.[59]

The different states in the USA have always had considerable autonomy and private employers have generally been able to set their own rules. The

[55] Harrison and Nolan, 'Reflections', pp. 271, 280.

[56] Helen Jones, 'Augusta Zadow', *Australian Dictionary of Biography*, adb.anu. edu.au/biography/zadow-christiane-susanne-augusta-9224, https://sahistoryhub.history. sa.gov.au/people/augusta-zadw; Fletcher, 'Agnes Milne'.

[57] McFeeley, *Lady Inspectors*, pp. 58–9; Martindale, *Women Servants*, pp. 146–9.

[58] Schmitt, *Der Arbeiterinnenschutz*, p. 145; Ayass, *Arbeiterschutz*, p. xxxii.

[59] Bousardt, *Onder Vrouwelijke*, pp. 54–7.

de facto marriage bar, affecting the educational sector, did not include factory inspectors. Florence Kelley was married, although separated, at her arrival in Chicago and later divorced, gaining custody of her children in 1893. While her marital issues became public property in connection with her divorce, her problems with working as an inspector were of a political nature and not directly related to her marital status.[60]

In France, virginity was not seen as a requisite for capacity to act as a factory inspector or civil servant. Two out of the seven female inspectors employed in France in 1892 were unmarried. In 1918, four out of eight were single, while in 1919 it was as many as five out of six and, in 1938, we find five single women out of 14 female inspectors. Widows were well represented among the inspectors as well as separated and divorced women. There are also several examples of marriage between female and male inspectors.[61]

Most of the Nordic countries did not see marriage as an obstacle to functioning in the employ of the state. The first female inspector in Norway, Betzy Kjelsberg, was not only married but a mother of six. Of the three inspectors in Denmark employed before WWI, Annette Vedel did not marry, but the second inspector, Julie Arenholt (appointed 1910), was married with one daughter and Ragna Schou had a husband and five children. Four years into her appointment, her husband died and she became the main provider for her family. In Finland, Vera Hjelt remained unmarried but her colleague Jenny Markelin-Svensson left spinsterhood behind three years after her appointment and became the mother of two during her career.[62]

The issue of the marriage bar does naturally reflect the general attitude to women and the belief that they were incapable of performing a job if they had a husband (serving two masters). Perhaps this is more revealing about the expectation of husbands than the capability of women? For men, the only profession where questions of the impossibility of divided loyalties arose and arises is that of the Catholic clergy.

While a large inspection district could be a problem for a woman with family commitments, the compulsory spinsterhood might also have unwanted consequences. In addition to the class difference between female inspectors and factory 'girls' being a reality that had to be contended with, one has to remember that all working women were not girls, some were also mothers, wives or widows. A Victorian middle-class upbringing was not perhaps the ideal vehicle for creating an understanding between these groups. Could a

---

[60] The Life and Times of Florence Kelley.

[61] Schweitzer, *Les inspectrices*, pp. 43–4.

[62] Folkvord, *Betzy Kjelsberg*, pp. 24, 36, 57; Ramm Reistad, 'Betzy Kjelsberg (1866–1950)', http://kvinnesak.no/info; Ravn, 'Julie Arenholt'; Ravn, 'Ragna Schou'; 'Fra utlandet', *Kvinden og samfundet* 18:24 (30.10 1908); Kuusanmäki, 'Markelin-Svensson, Jenny', pp. 556–7.

good girl from a wealthy background understand the issues of work, childbirth, drink, violent husbands and economic hardship, except from a philanthropic perspective? Those with personal experience, like Florence Kelley, might have been in a better position than some of the others. That said, personality and the capacity for empathy do not necessarily follow matrimonial lines. When the issue of childbirth and female work was the subject of discussion in 1903, Adelaide Anderson (a spinster) underlined the need not only to restrict the right of new mothers to work, but also to find them some economic support. On this point, she entered a collision course with her former colleague May Tennant, married into the Liberal administrative aristocracy. In vain, Anderson cited poverty and unsanitary conditions as the main causes of infant mortality and shied away from the prevailing 'blame the working mother' mantra. The British authorities and administration considered that stopping women from working was the priority; how they were going to sustain themselves was a secondary matter that could be left to charities.[63]

The views of Anderson were, on the other hand, shared by Betzy Kjelsberg, who did her utmost to mobilise women's organisations in Norway to support a proposition for the extension of social legislation to give female workers the right to economic support during the compulsory six weeks off work after delivery.[64] In this, she looked not only to Germany but also to Denmark, where the factory law of 1901 stipulated a month away from work at childbirth, and included economic support that was not channelled through the poor-relief system.[65]

Female factory inspection and patriarchy

At the time when organisations run by women were actively pushing for the extension of the female sphere, the power was still firmly lodged in the hands of men.

In many cases, appointing a female only became possible when political power was held by liberal or liberally minded groups: in Britain under a Liberal government, in Chicago under an enlightened governor from the Democrat party and in New Zealand with the assistance of men from the political left, who took an interest in the issue of social reform. In some parts of Europe the question of integrating women into efforts for improving the nation, even if it meant power sharing, were viewed more generally in a positive light.

---

63   Anderson, *Women in the Factory*, pp. 156–8; May Tennant, 'Infantile mortality', in Tuckwell et al., *Woman in Industry*, pp. 87–119, on pp. 88–9, 95–105.

64   Folkvord, *Betzy Kjelsberg*, pp. 146–51.

65   Astrid Elkjaer Sorensen, *Barsellogivningens udvikling i Danmark fra 1901*, http://danmarkhistorien.dk.

It is not, therefore, surprising that, when the political power shifted, newly introduced reforms and women appointed to office could suffer the consequences.

In Britain the unfortunate tie to the Liberal Party was felt particularly keenly by the female inspectors. In 1896, the Conservative Party came into government and a new chief inspector was appointed. May Abraham (Tennant), who had married a Liberal resigned, and the task of running the female department was dropped on Adelaide Anderson, who had been in office for two years. At the instigation of the male inspectors, the female department was stripped of a lot of its power, for example, the right to prosecute had to be applied for from the chief. By 1898, the new chief had found his footing and decided to reintroduce the right of the female inspectorate to instigate proceedings against law breakers.[66] The problems were, however, far from over. In the provinces many male inspectors viewed the work of the female inspectorate as encroaching upon their territory. Some of the retired military men, with little knowledge of hygiene or health, even though perhaps competent on machinery, reacted violently when factories that they had found perfectly adequate were classed as having substandard air and conditions by the female inspectors. The situation was not improved when the women gained support from the Chief Inspector of Factories.[67] Likewise, in Australia and New Zealand, issues related to the authority of the female inspectors and classification of the work led to conflict and even threats of dismissal. Agnes Anderson Milne was severely criticised for her attempts to act independently. The conflict escalated and, in 1907, she resigned and started working for the South Australian Co-Operative Clothing Factory. Harriet Morison, with her history of activity in the New Zealand Tailoresses' Union, was demoted from the factory inspectorate in 1908. While heading the Auckland Women's Employment Bureau she was asked to return on a part-time basis and de facto continued inspecting until her retirement in 1921.[68]

Power structures in the United States have often had ties to the political situation in the individual states. Hence, the work of the first female industrial inspector in Illinois, Florence Kelley, was also seriously affected by this phenomenon. She was appointed inspector by Governor John P Altgeld, a Democrat with great interest in social reform, who had very recently been elected to the governorship. In 1894, Levy Meyer and the Illinois Manufacturer's Association challenged the Factory Inspection Statute and the eight-hour provision for women as unconstitutional. The Supreme Court

---

66 McFeeley, *Lady Inspectors*, pp. 46–7, 60–1.

67 Livesley, 'The politics of work', p. 248; Report by the female factory inspectors for the year 1908, in Report of the Chief Inspector of Factories 1908 PP 1909 XXI Cd 4664, pp. 178–9; Anderson, *Women in the Factory*, pp. 33, 123.

68 Harrison and Nolan, 'Reflections', pp. 275–6; Fletcher, 'Agnes Milne'.

of Illinois ruled in their favour but upheld the prohibition of employment of children under 14 and the powers of factory inspectors. However, by 1896, there was a change of governor after the election was won by the Republicans and, in 1897, when her four years in office as Chief Factory Inspector was at an end, Florence Kelley was fired.[69]

The State of Baden had been one of the vanguards in employing female inspectors and the rules did not award female inspectors an inferior position as they did elsewhere in Germany. The system was by no means universally loved by the male inspectorate. Like in Britain, when a new head was appointed, the time seemed right for exercising pressure to weaken the position of the women. Also, like in Britain, the efforts were, at least for the moment, successful and Marie Braun, who saw her position radically undermined, left the inspectorate in 1907. The fear of competition from women also activated the male inspectors in Prussia, as late as 1913, to push for a weakening of the size and influence of the female share in the inspection activity.[70]

Sweden was the last Nordic country to appoint a female inspector. It is also interesting that the attacks against the first female inspector in Finland took place in the Swedish and not the Finnish press. In 1910, the debate about whether to employ a female inspector was pursued in Sweden. Fortuitously for the male inspectors in the south west, who were against the idea, the one Finnish colleague sharing their views was on a visit and happy to have his views published in the local press. He stated that female inspectors were useless and had no knowledge of machines and factories and gave faulty advice that had to be rectified by men. He also said that female factory workers preferred to approach male inspectors and that the sanitary and health aspects should not be part of factory inspection anyway. For such issues, female sanitary inspectors, not part of the factory system, could be employed. The statement was recited in the main Swedish newspapers and when the information reached Finland the reaction was swift. The next morning the following statement was published in the Finnish press, signed by all the other male inspectors:

The female factory inspection in Finland

Re a telegram from Gothenburg to Dagens Nyheter, published in our newspapers, where the correspondent states that the industrial inspector of the district of Lahti during his trip abroad has made negative comments about the female factory inspection in Finland we wish to point out that

We have never had any problems in working together with the female inspectors, on the contrary we have always with confidence worked together to improve conditions in factories

[69] The Life and Times of Florence Kelley.
[70] Schmitt, *Der Arbeiterinnenschutz*, pp. 143–5.

We have never been obliged to disagree with or make any changes to the technical advice provided by our female counterparts

There is no proof and completely a loose supposition that the female workers would rather talk to a male than a female inspector

We want to point out that inspector Kapy during his short, one year long, career as an inspector, has not been able to acquire knowledge about any other district than that of Lahtis, and that in this particular district the female inspector has a degree from the polytechnic institute in Helsinki, and has all the technical knowledge and competence that would be required from a District inspector. Disagreeing with inspector Artturi Kapy we, all the District inspectors in the country, hereby state as our opinion and experience, that the female inspectorate has well and truly shouldered its duties in Finland

Helsingfors the 24th of November 1910,

Oswald Bonsdorff, District inspector, Lahtis, Hugo Lindgren District inspector Viborg, Konstantin Jansson, District inspector Helsingfors, Karl G. Frietsch, District inspector Uleaborg.[71]

Some of the Danish female inspectors met with a negative attitude by owners of workplaces. Attacks in newspapers on female inspectors by men were also not restricted to Finland. In Norway, Betzy Kjelsberg was the subject of a severe newspaper attack as late as in 1914.[72]

Making it possible for women to gain a position of authority was in the minds of many also connected to direct physical attributes like female dress or the dress of a respectable lady. The danger of breaking down symbols of traditional gender barriers in the shape of garments was not absent in the issues raised in connection with the first generation of female inspectors. Representatives on the feminist Conference for Nordic Women in 1902 raised the question of whether it would be possible for women (ladies) to enter factories as their clothes would get entangled in the machinery. To this concern, Kjelsberg answered that if the clothes were a hindrance then the female inspectors could do their inspecting in trousers, which she herself incidentally donned when inspecting a mine some years later. Florence Kelley's reply to such questions was:

Female factory inspectors should wear the short, light and comfortable cyclist suit during work. Women who cannot part with corsets, high heels, white gloves and the many petticoats of our grandmothers, will of course

71 Hjelt-Cajanus, *Vera Hjelt*, pp. 196–8.
72 Folkvord, *Betzy Kjelsberg*, pp. 112–13.

not be able to keep up with those who wear the practical clothes of today's businesswoman.

Hjelt had much to say about the impractical and dangerous dress of the female workers and she suggested work clothes consisting of trousers and caps instead of dresses and shawls.[73]

Conclusion

Although the late nineteenth century saw a society with considerable class division, there was one thing working women and middle-class women could agree on: the need for female inspectors to inspect the working conditions of women. With increasing regulation relating not only to children but also women, somebody had to see that the rules were followed.

When these suggestions were being taken seriously, it had to be determined how the profession was to be defined and what kinds of qualifications were needed to fill the post of a female industrial inspector. While all countries did not demand a specific educational background, the profiles of the recruits display a certain level of similarity. Some had university degrees, others had worked in the educational sector or within hygiene inspection, however, experience of state or local authority administration was not unheard of. Unlike Europe, however, in Australia and New Zealand, even women with a history of engagement within the unions could be appointed.

In most cases, the female inspectors were paid less than their male counterparts and in Germany and the Netherlands they did not have the rights to intervene of a full inspector. In most cases the primary tasks were seen to be linked to making sure that existing legislation about women and children was followed. Some countries stated a desire for women with knowledge of technical matters while others specifically excluded this from the remit. Also, some countries included mediation in work conflicts in the work profile while others excluded such issues. As to personal characteristics, education often meant a middle-class background and the majority of the first generation female inspectors came from this part of society. The noteworthy difference between certain countries was that, while Britain, Germany and the Netherlands exercised the marriage bar, France and the Nordic countries did not do so.

---

[73] Folkvord, *Betzy Kjelsberg*, pp. 58, 125; Hjelt, *Berättelse 1905*, p. 96; Sklar, *Florence Kelley*, p. 298.

Selected biographies

Annette Vedel (1863–1943), Inspector 1901–21, Denmark

The father of Annette Vedel, the first female industrial inspector in Denmark, was a conservative, influential civil servant, who had little interest in the education of women. Her mother, on the other hand, was the daughter of a female author and came from a family of active feminists.[74] After passing her baccalaureate examination in 1887, Vedel pursued studies in mathematics under the guidance of her uncle C.G. Andrae. Andrae was an eminent mathematician but also engaged in politics and had connections to both sides of the family.[75] After several years of study, Vedel sought affiliation with an accredited university. It is possible that the Swedish origin of her mother made her look towards the newly founded University College in Stockholm. It is, however, more likely that she wanted to be connected with this institution due to its appointment policies regarding women. Professor Magnus, Mittag-Leffler, was an important figure in the department of mathematics. He was a firm believer in women's rights and the person instrumental to the professorship of Sofia Kovalevskaya in 1889 (the first female professor in Europe).[76] In addition to her studies in mathematics, Annette Vedel also came to hold the post of amanuensis at the department between 1894 and 1896, making it possible for her to study and earn a living simultaneously. Whether she could see the potential of statistics for a future career cannot be determined. It is, however, undisputable that her father, a Conservative, appointed Marcus Rubin, a well-known Liberal, to head the National Statistical Bureau in Copenhagen, an institution that did not have rules barring women from office. On her return to Denmark in 1896, Rubin did not hesitate to appoint Vedel to a post in the statistics office. To him, working with women was no problem, and she had acquired the right qualifications during her stay in Sweden. Rubin was an avid collector of economic and social statistics and during his time at the office numerous surveys were conducted. Vedel was engaged in the survey work and collected statistics on the standard of living of the working classes both independently and as part of the team. Some of the studies she published under her own name.[77]

74 *Dansk Biografisk Lexicon*/18, 'Vedel, Pet. Aug.', http://runeberg.org/dbl/18/0312.html.

75 379 *Dansk Biografisk Lexicon*/1, 'Andrae, Carl Christopher, Georg', http://runeberg.org.dbl/1/0276.html.

76 Lundin, *Nya Stockholm*, pp. 384, 391–2; *Kvinden og samfundet* 23.11 1901, p. 181.

77 Annette Vedel, 'Danske Arbejderfamiliers Forbrug', *Nationalokonomisk Tidsskrift 1902*, 3:10, pp. 321–69.

In 1901, the post of Female Inspector of Workplaces was created in Denmark. Annette Vedel was highly qualified and eminently suitable for such a post. It cannot be denied that her prospects were not diminished by the fact that her brother, at the time established in the Civil Service, was responsible for the appointment. One must not, however, automatically assume that such appointments were secured through nepotism only. Vedel had accumulated considerable knowledge and skill through her years in mathematics, statistics and working on social surveys that included the exploring of living and working conditions of the working classes. It is, however, relatively clear that the qualifications she had could not have been accumulated without her socioeconomic background.[78]

At the age of 60, Anette Vedel retired from the inspectorate and began to devote herself to organisational work. Her primary input was with organisations that promoted inter-Nordic cooperation in communication, research and culture. She sat on the board of Foreningen Norden (the Nordic Society) from 1925 to 1941 where she edited the journal Nordisk Tidskrift (the Nordic Journal for Science, Art and Industry). She also dedicated some of her time to Letterstedska Foreningen, an organisation promoting exchange and research between the Nordic countries through scholarships and other support. She was a long-term member of the women's organisation Kvindelig Laeseforening, and part of the board in the early years of the twentieth century. However, she withdrew from active participation in later life, due to personal disagreements with some other board members, and focused totally on her work linked to Nordic collaboration.[79]

Vera Hjelt (1857–1947), Inspector 1903–21, Finland

The first female inspector in Finland, Vera Hjelt, came from a less illustrious background than her Danish colleague, but with firm connections to education. Her father was the headmaster of a secondary school and Vera's grandmother and aunt were running a school for girls (where her mother had been teaching before her marriage). The school had also been responsible for the education of Vera and her sisters, therefore, none of them held any officially recognised diplomas.[80] At the age of 19, she lost her father and found herself in a position where her only income was a share of his pension. On the other hand, she was a free woman and part of the class close to education and the civil service. While Vera could hope for little economic support from her family, she was

[78] Thestrup, 'Kvinder i offentlige institutioner', pp. 175–96. 1991; Knudsen, 'Vedel, Fanny Annette'.

[79] Knudsen, 'Vedel, Fanny Annette'; 'Danmrks forste fabriksinspectrice', Kvinden og Samfundet (23.11 1901), p. 181.

[80] Hjelt-Cajanus, Vera Hjelt, pp. 32–3.

still part of the middle-class networks. A friend encouraged her to apply to the teachers training college and one of her aunts lent her the money. Those accepted to the course had to pass an entrance examination, which meant competing with young women who already had their baccalaureate.[81] Vera was, however, successful and even managed to secure a scholarship. At the college, she became acquainted with Uno Cygnaeus, the 'father of the Finnish primary school', who actively supervised the colleges in the early years.[82] The education sector experienced a period of considerable expansion at this time and those in the department of education were part of international networks exchanging information and visiting new institutions.[83]

Vera Hjelt had always taken more interest in science and technology and their practical application than in the arts. She had also found that there was a need to extend the concept of handicraft in the primary school curriculum. The teaching of woodwork or training for this was unknown in 1870s Finland. The situation in Sweden was, however, different. By the 1880s, the newly established handicrafts college in Sweden extended its activities and there was a need to employ female teachers for the girls' school. One of the recruitment drives also included the teachers training college in Finland and Hjelt saw a chance of combining training with teaching at the woodwork college.[84]

When returning to Finland in 1885, Hjelt applied for a state contribution to run courses in woodwork for teachers. In the meantime, she borrowed money, hired a hall and started a woodwork institute. Several of her projects were approached in a similar manner. She owned no property, had no important family connections, but made use of middle-class society and the fact that everybody knew one another. Because of being well known and having a reputation for paying what she owed, she always seemed to be able to get credit and support for her bank loans. In 1890, she set up a furniture factory where she, among other things, manufactured woodwork models for schools and a collapsible workbench that she had patented.[85] While her institute was open to everybody, she particularly encouraged young middle-class girls to consider becoming teachers, and particularly handicraft teachers, and was often successful in her endeavours.

The late nineteenth century was an active period for the women's movement in Finland. Vera Hjelt attended meetings, did some lecturing, famously

81 Gösta Cavonius, *Den svenska lararutbildningen i Finland 1871–1974* (Helsingfors, 1988), pp. 248–9.

82 Hjelt-Cajanus, *Vera Hjelt*, pp. 40–3; Cavonius, *Den svenska*, pp. 20–1.

83 Hietala, *Tietoa, taitoa*, pp. 210–11.

84 Ann-Charlotte Ericson, 'Slöjdlärares undervisning', thesis, Department of Education, University of Gothenburg (Gothenburg, 2007), pp. 7–8; Hjelt-Cajanus, *Vera Hjelt*, pp. 67–58.

85 Hjelt-Cajanus, *Vera Hjelt*, pp. 80–8, 91.

'Protective Legislation for Women' at the Union of Finnish Women in 1909. She also wrote the pamphlets 'Women in the Practical Field (1888)' and 'The Social and Political Co-operation between Men and Women in Finland (1911)'[86]. She herself was an example that technology, science and working with your hands were perfectly possible for a woman. Many of her activities attracted some attention in the small-town atmosphere of late nineteenth-century Helsinki. The Society of Finnish Women participated actively in lobbying for a female inspector and, when the post was created in 1903, the head of the organisation, Alexandra Gripenberg, encouraged Hjelt to apply. The Society was an organisation for middle-class women and Gripenberg was later seen to make unguarded statements about the wisdom of allowing working-class women into Parliament.[87] At this stage, however, the working women's unions and the bourgeois women's organisations were in agreement about the need for a female inspector.[88] Several of the male inspectors and the Industrial Board also saw the issue in a favourable light. To what extent pressure was being exerted in the background by female family members remains unclear. Female inspectors were at this point to be found in several countries and the international information network did not supply any negative information. The fact that Vera Hjelt had been successfully running a school and then a factory, overseeing economy, manufacture and the workplace, did affect her chances. As the remit of the female inspector included issues related to safety in the workplace, Hjelt had the kind of knowledge deemed suitable.[89] The backing of the influential gentlemen on the Industrial Board was useful, and in the early stages also necessary for the female inspectors. Although Hjelt had the support of her male colleagues at the early stages of her career, she felt the need to demonstrate competence and acumen through activity and reporting of her work. The increase in female industrial work created a considerable workload, particularly as Hjelt was also engaged in special surveys like one about the needle trades in 1908 and on living standards of the working classes some years later. This was acknowledged in 1908 through the creation of a post of Assistant Female Inspector; a post that was transformed into that of full Inspector from 1909 and, not by chance, was awarded to Jenny Markelin, the first female engineer matriculated from the Institute of Polytechnics.[90]

Vera Hjelt continued following the development of studies of working conditions and workplace inspection in the other Nordic countries and Germany, Austria, Sweden, Denmark and Switzerland in 1904 and 1906 and with a

---

86   Vera Hjelt, *Qvinnan på de praktiska arbetområdena* (Helsingfors, 1888).
87   Hjelt-Cajanus, *Vera Hjelt*, pp. 143–4; Hentilä, 'Maa jossa piiatkin', pp. 175, 183.
88   Ensimmäinen, *yleisen työläisnaisten*.
89   Hjelt-Cajanus, *Vera Hjelt*, pp. 143–5.
90   Hjelt-Cajanus, *Vera Hjelt*, p. 197; Vera Hjelt, *Undersökning af nalarbeterskornas yrkesforhallanden* (Helsingfors, 1908), pp. 117–18.

government grant in 1909. She also made trips to exhibitions of technological development and safety devices and visited factories where such devices were in use. Her reports contain frequent comparisons with factory legislation in other countries and descriptions of industrial innovations. Whenever there was an opportunity she was happy to collaborate. When a new female industrial inspector, Betzy Kjelsberg, was to be appointed in Norway, she accompanied Vera Hjelt on her inspections in 1908 to familiarise herself with the work.[91] In 1909, Hjelt was elected to the Finnish Parliament (together with 22 other women) but retired from parliamentary work in 1917 after going against her political party and voting for the eight-hour day together with the Socialists. During her career in Parliament, she participated in committee work and took the initiative on issues related to night work and maternity leave, industrial inspection, the setting up of separate institutions for young offenders, the creation of vocational education and apprenticeships, etc.[92]

In addition to her inspection work, she published a study of the working conditions of women in the textile trade and one about the economic conditions of labourer's families. Her continuing interest in technology and safety in the workplace, boosted by trips to Germany, inspired her to set up a safety exhibition, which circulated around the country. When the exhibition got state funding and could be developed into a safety museum, she retired from the inspectorate to devote herself full-time to work place safety. She held the post of curator from 1921, developed the museum, wrote pamphlets and books and lectured until the age of 74 when she finally retired. She died at the age of 90 in 1947.[93]

From the earliest reports until the latest pamphlets, Vera Hjelt was passionate about protecting people from hazards in the workplace; dust, dirt, dangerous machinery and chemicals and lack of fresh air. Her desire for decent working hours, equal treatment of women workers and legal protection and accident compensation was more important than party loyalty. Her single-minded attitude and desire for practical solutions made her fearless and earned her respect not only among social liberals but even among the Socialists.[94]

    91 Hjelt, *Undersökning af nalarbeterskornas*, pp. 132, 166–8; Hjelt-Cajanus, *Vera Hjelt*, p. 195.
    92 Hjelt-Cajanus, *Vera Hjelt*, pp. 161, 207–8, 224–30.
    93 Sinikka Forelius, 'Työväensuojelu ja huoltonayttelystä työsuojelunäyttelyyn 1909–1999', http://www.tyovaenperinne.fi/tyovaentutkimus/1999 (accessed 11 August 2007); Vera Hjelt, *Arbetsskydd mot olycksfall och ohälsa* (Helsingfors, 1939).
    94 Hjelt-Cajanus, *Vera Hjelt*, pp. 189, 227–31, 255–7, 265.

Adelaide Anderson (1863–1936), Inspector of Factories 1894–1921, Chief Woman Inspector 1897–1921, Britain

Adelaide Anderson was the daughter of A.G. Anderson, a wealthy Scottish ship-owner. Her grandfather was the principal of a gymnasium in Aberdeen. The family was mobile because of the father's occupation. Adelaide was born in Australia and educated in Germany and France. As a young woman she studied first at Queens College, Harley Street, and then entered Girton College, Cambridge at the age of 20. At Girton, she met Margaret Llewelyn Davies, who studied there 1881–3. Davies became general secretary of the Women's Co-operative Guild in 1889 and gave Anderson the opportunity to lecture at the Guild after her graduation.[95]

In 1892, the Royal Commission on Labour started its work. The commission was unique in the sense that it employed a number of lady assistant commissioners, who were recruited to collect information about women's work and working conditions. To function, the Commission also needed administrative staff. As economy was an issue the Commission, secretaries Geoffrey Drage and John Burnett appointed more female than male clerks.[96] By the 1890s, women with degrees were on the increase but posts were few. Of the clerks, 13 were female Oxbridge graduates and one of these was Adelaide Anderson. Later in life, when she commented on her progress to industrial inspector, she considered the appointment (1894) as linked to her work for the Commission. During her two years there she had learnt finalising reports and the Commission had also made use of her proficiency in languages, enabling her to study literature on labour conditions in French and German.[97]

After passing her administrative exam, Anderson joined May Abraham and Mary Paterson as an inspector of factories. Her early reports show preoccupation with the persistent breaking of rules regarding the working day, illegal and unpaid overtime and moving of women from one task to the other, for example from the workshop to the shop after a full working day. She bemoaned the fact that when achieving a successful prosecution the fines were generally so small that some employers paid, and then went on to break the law over and over again.[98]

Anderson had hardly worked as an industrial inspector for more than two years before the government changed to Conservative and the Chief inspector of Factories, Sprague Oram was replaced by Sir Arthur Whitelegge MD. May Abraham married and resigned. Some of the male inspectors had

---

[95] Girton College, *Girton College Register 1869–1946* (Cambridge, 1948), pp. 17, 24.

[96] Harrison, *Officials of Royal Commissions*, Introduction.

[97] Anderson, *Women in the Factory*, pp. 9–19; Martindale, *Women Servants*, p. 47.

[98] Report of the Chief Inspector of Factories for the year 1895, PP 1896 XIX c 8067, pp. 11–13.

been dissatisfied with the autonomy of the female inspectors, as they would have preferred the women as assistants and under their supervision. The new chief was a medical man, rather than one with technological experience and, still not sure of how to run his department, he was eager to avoid conflict. Therefore, he went along with a proposal of stripping the women of the right to conduct prosecutions, unless authorised by the chief. The head of the female department was renamed 'Principal Lady Inspector' and the right to operate as a separate section was at the same time recognised. In this situation, Anderson found herself promoted to head a department stripped of a lot of its power, but expected to do as much work as the male colleagues with less pay. The task was gigantic and no less so because of ambiguities in the legislation, fear of complaining among female workers and obstruction by male colleagues in the provinces.[99]

By 1898, however, a modus operandi with the new chief had been established. Anderson was anew given the right to authorise prosecutions to be conducted by the female inspectors. Over time, collaboration with Whitelegge functioned well, particularly in cases of occupational disease and dangerous substances.[100] Anderson took a special interest in laundries, and according to Hilda Martindale, who was recruited and trained by Anderson, keeping up with her was not always easy. She told the following anecdote: 'You and I will visit laundries tomorrow'. This was an honour much appreciated by the junior inspector but on the day after a long morning of most energetic inspection of laundries, in one of the least salubrious of suburbs, one o clock came. Miss Anderson said brightly; 'Now we can take the opportunity to pay some mealtime visits'. It was not until nearly three that she said: 'I think a cup of tea somewhere would be pleasant before we go on to the next place'. It would seem that the efforts were not fruitless, the laundries changed from 'unsanitary places with dangerous unfenced machinery' to 'some of the most healthy and safe places of employment in this country' due to the work of Anderson and her colleagues.[101]

The fact that the inspectors not only strived to uphold the law, but also to extend it into areas originally not included in the regulations, demonstrates the seriousness with which the inspectors approached their work. During the early decades, the minimum working age was changed and rules were brought in about sanitation and dangerous substances. Fencing of machinery became subject to stricter control. The one issue that continued to be a problem was monitoring legal working time. Still, in 1911, Anderson raised the question

---

[99] Tuckwell et al., *Woman in Industry*, pp. 178–9; Anderson, *Women in the Factory*, pp. 33, 123; McFeeley, *Lady Inspectors*, pp. 46–7, 60–1.

[100] McFeeley, *Lady Inspectors*, pp. 46–7, 60–1.

[101] Hilda Martindale, *Some Victorian Portraits and Others* (London, 1948), pp. 48–9.

of fines being out of proportion with the economic advantage of breaking the factory laws. This unfortunate circumstance was making the work of the inspectors very difficult indeed.[102]

Undoubtedly the origin of the first female inspectors affected their outlook. There were, however, some differences, possibly because of personality or other reasons. Martindale tried to explain Anderson's attitude to her work as dedication and empathy rather than doing a job, and cited a story by the trade union leader Julia Varley: 'When my father was caught round a shafting in the mill and was badly hurt I was going to see Miss Anderson that evening at her hotel, but I sent my young brother to explain why I could not come. Miss Anderson came straight round to see me although it was already midnight.'[103]

When contributing research on women's work to the Committee on Physical Deterioration in 1903, Adelaide Anderson underlined in her report the need not only to restrict the right of new mothers to work, but also to find them some economic support. She expressed scepticism towards the ability or willingness of charitable institutions to shoulder this responsibility (the solution advocated by the committee). She put forward evidence that these institutions turned out the mothers two weeks after delivery, when the law did not allow them to return to work until four weeks had passed. Her former colleague May Tennant, now married into the group of upper-class Civil Servants, had fewer problems in deploring the lack of mothering among the working classes. While Anderson pointed out that poverty and unsanitary conditions have direct links to infant mortality, Tennant went along with those considering the working mother to be the main culprit.[104]

Anderson was a pioneer, tireless and fearlessly making her mark. Her tendency to be legalistic was probably a legacy of her early years in the inspectorate, when power was given and then taken away. While her ability to inspire confidence was acknowledged by those around her, she also felt the need to document the successful activity of the female inspectorate in a history of this body, published in 1922. As a retirement gift she received a considerable sum of money that she decided to use for travel to South Africa, Australia, New Zealand and Burma. She was invited to study the labour conditions in China and became a member of the Commission on Child Labour of the Municipal Council of Shanghai in 1923. Her account of the labour conditions was published in 1928 under the title of Humanity and Labour in China. She worked on the mission of the International Labour Office to Nanking in 1931 regarding the factory inspectorate in China, and in 1932–3 she was a member of the Universities China Commission. She also travelled in Egypt and reported

[102] Report of the Chief Inspector of Factories 1911, PP 1912–13 XXV Cd 6239, p. 152.

[103] Martindale, *Some Victorian Portraits*, p. 48.

[104] Anderson, *Women in the Factory*, pp. 156–8; Tennant, 'Infantile mortality', pp. 88–9, 95–105.

on the conditions of child labour. Her last journey to Africa was undertaken at the age of 72, shortly before her death.[105]

Florence Kelley (1859–1932), Inspector 1893–97, Chicago, Illinois, USA

Florence Kelley was the daughter of congress man William Darrah 'Pig Iron' Kelley and Caroline Bartram (Bonsall). Her father grew up in a family of modest means because of the early death of his father, but managed not only to acquire a profession but also a law degree and a position as a judge. During Florence Kelley's childhood he was one of the richest men in Philadelphia. The family members and their close friends were abolitionists and supporters of female enfranchisement.[106]

Although Florence commenced her education at home she was sent to university as one of the first groups of women allowed into Cornell University in the so called co-ed study programs. She studied languages, history and politics and graduated from Cornell in 1882.[107] After some unsuccessful attempts to gain entrance to graduate study in Pennsylvania and Oxford she accompanied her brother on a tour to Europe. While there, an old friend made her aware of the fact that the University of Zurich, as the only university in Europe at the time to do so, accepted women for graduate courses. Hence she enrolled in 1883 with the purpose of studying Law and Government.[108] During her time in Zurich, she came into contact with radical groups and social reformers. She also made the acquaintance of Friedrich Engels and started a translation of his works. One of her new friends was the Russian medical student Lazare Wischnewetzky. The friendship developed into romance and the couple married in 1884. The following year, their first son, Nicolas, was born, followed by a daughter, Margaret, in 1886.

That year, Kelley also concluded her studies in Law and Government and the family moved to New York. Life in New York was far from easy. Wischnewetzky was not licensed to practice medicine and the family suffered from economic problems. Kelley published articles and pamphlets in Germany and the USA, particularly on the issue of children's work. In 1888, a third child, Bartram, was born but the relationship was by now problematic as Wischnewetzky tended to resort to physical abuse when intoxicated or in a bad mood. William Kelley died in 1890 after a long struggle with cancer and little help could be expected from the family. New York only accepted infidelity as a cause for divorce and, therefore, Kelley escaped from her husband and moved to Chicago with her three children. In Chicago she had friends who

---

[105] Martindale, *Women Servants*, pp. 48–50.
[106] Florencekelley.northwestern.edu/florence/father.
[107] Sklar, *Florence Kelley*, pp. 50–3, 56–60.
[108] Sklar, *Florence Kelley*, p. 82.

could arrange accommodation and work, and the divorce laws of Chicago also included violence and abuse as valid reasons for the termination of a marriage. Kelley settled in Hull House, a social settlement applying Christian Socialism, founded by social reformers Jane Addams and Ellen Gates. The settlement was placed in the slum part of Chicago and engaged in education, child care, etc. Soon after her arrival, Kelley began her work at Hull House studying living and working conditions in Chicago.[109] The family of Henry Demarest Lloyd of the Chicago Tribune took in her children and their nurse to live in the countryside outside the town. In 1892 Kelley was appointed Special Agent of the Illinois State Bureau of Labor Statistics, to fill in schedules on working conditions. This year she was also taken to court by her husband who demanded the return of the children to him. The case gained a lot of publicity, but the court decided not to grant the application. At this point Kelley was successful in gaining employment related to her interests. In 1892 she was hired by the Illinois Department of Labor and, in 1893, the Illinois General Assembly set up Joint Special Commissions to investigate sweatshops. Florence Kelley and Mary Kenney were appointed investigators.[110] In 1893 she also achieved her goal of being appointed Factory Inspector for a four year term with an annual budget of 12,000 dollars. In addition, she was awarded money for employing assistant inspectors, one of whom was Alzina Stevens, a union activist. She also enrolled at the Northwestern University School of Law where she completed her legal education in 1895.[111]

Through the period 1893–7 she devoted herself wholeheartedly to the work as Factory Inspector. The four reports she submitted are not only reports on the work of the inspectors but in depth studies of working and social conditions in Chicago. Many of the reports dedicated considerable sections to the plight of children in sweatshops, in candy factories and particularly in the glass works. She not only lists the infringements against the legislation, but also suggests improvements that would make it easier for inspectors to see to the welfare of women and children. She used her contacts and their influence to spread information about the conditions in which, for example, garments were produced in the slum tenements, and the dangers of textiles acting as vectors in the spread of disease during the smallpox epidemic in 1894.[112] She suffered a depressing defeat in 1895, when the Illinois Supreme court declared the shorter working day for women unconstitutional. It was, however, of some consolation that the court upheld the authority of the inspectorate and did not overthrow regulations brought in to protect children. The political climate in Chicago was, however, changing towards support for the Manufacturers

[109] Sklar, *Florence Kelley*, pp. 195–8.
[110] Sklar, *Florence Kelley*, pp. 206–8; florencekelley.northwestern.edu/florence/1892.
[111] Sklar, *Florence Kelley*, pp. 236–9; *Chicago Daily Tribune*, 14 July 1893, p. 3.
[112] Sklar, *Florence Kelley*, pp. 245–55, 280–1.

Association and more conservative policies. When the governor John Peter Altgeld was replaced by a Republican, John E. Tanner, in 1896, the future of Florence Kelley looked far from bright. When her four years as an inspector were up, she was fired, in August 1897.[113]

Her immediate concerns at this point were of an economic nature but she was fortunate enough to find work as a part-time librarian at the John Crerar Library in Chicago. She also intensified her writing activities and managed to negotiate a standing honorarium for a set of articles from Heinrich Braun's *Archiv für Soziale Gesetzgebung und Statistik* (Archive for social legislation and statistics). The articles were connected to her experiences as factory inspector and the problems of child labour, sweating, etc. At this period of time Kelley applied unsuccessfully for several posts, among others for one as Inspector in New York; she also intensified her contacts with women's organisations with social reform agendas. On a personal level, she finally managed to attain a divorce decree in June 1900.[114]

By 1899, the consumer movement had taken on new roles in many American cities. The women in the organisations raised the issues of consumption with a conscience. Aims were set up of refusing to buy products produced in sweat shops or inhuman conditions. 'White lists' were to be produced to make consumers aware of how and where goods were produced. At the same time efforts were made to set up an umbrella organisation for the various consumer groups. The society embraced aims to achieve a minimum wage and limit the working day for women and children. Kelley was eager to promote such ideas and, when the National Consumers League was established in 1899, she was asked to join as Secretary and Inspector. From 1899 to her death in 1932, Kelley functioned as Director of the League. During her time in office, the services of Lois Brandeis were engaged to fight the rulings of shorter working hours being unconstitutional. The efforts were successful in that the US Supreme Court ruled in their favour in 1907.[115]

During the first decade of the twentieth century, Kelley also engaged in political movements. In 1905 she joined Upton Sinclair and Jack London in forming the Intercollegiate Socialist Society, of which she was President 1913–1920 and, in 1909, she assisted in founding the Association for the Advancement of Colored People. Florence Kelley died in February 1932.[116]

---

[113] Sklar, *Florence Kelley*, p. 390; florencekelley.northwestern.edu/Florence/inspector.

[114] Sklar, *Florence Kelley*, pp. 297–9.

[115] Sklar, *Florence Kelley*, pp. 308–9.

[116] Sklar, *Florence Kelley*, pp. xvi, 311; https://florencekelley.northwestern.edu; Florence Kelley and Marguerite Marsh, 'Labor legislation for women and its effects on earnings and conditions of labor', *The Annals of the American Academy of Political and Social Studies* 143 (1929), pp. 286–300.

Betzy Kjelsberg (1866–1950), Inspector 1908–36, Norway

Betzy Borresen Kjelsberg was the daughter of the skipper Thor Borresen and his Scottish wife Jessie McGlashan. Betzy grew up bilingual, which later in life created several advantages. At the age of six, Betzy lost her father and her home, as the widow and little girl were left nothing but debts and all available property had to be auctioned. After a brief stay with relatives of her late father, mother and child moved to the town of Drammen where her mother started running a small boarding house. Some years later, one of the lodgers, a shopkeeper, offered his landlady marriage and gradually the family started growing. The stepfather paid for Betzy's education in the best girls' school in the area and she also had lessons in music and dance. The school curriculum combined social studies and law with cooking and sewing. Not long after her twelfth birthday, the family moved to the capital, Kristiania, and Betzy entered Miss Bauer's School for Girls, one of the first girls' schools that awarded the same exams as in those for boys. The headmistress was German by birth and used the language in part of her teaching. Betzy later praised this practical acquisition of yet another language.[117]

When finishing school, Betsy found a job as a cashier in a shop, but her inclination was towards more studies. The university would not accept women until 1882, but in 1883 a private educational establishment advertised a two-year course for women, culminating in a bachelors' degree in arts. The phenomenon attracted a lot of debate, but Betzy Kjelsberg and four others applied. Two of the women on the course later went on to take medical degrees. Betzy, however, never did succeed in taking an exam, as during her second year she met and fell in love with a young lawyer called Oluf Kjelsberg. She married at the end of August in 1885, only 18 years old, and five months later her first son Otto, was born. The family set up house in a building where her husband could run his law office and Betzy did the secretarial and administrative work. As the family expanded with a son Thor in 1892, a daughter Laura in 1893, Olaf in 1896, Bergljot in 1897 and Betzy the younger in 1901, the family had both a cook and a children's nurse. In addition to working as an administrator for her husband, Betzy engaged in the burgeoning women's movement, an interest that had started during her time as a student. She also made a sensation in the small town by being the first woman seen in a trouser-skirt on a bicycle in a public street.

In 1894 she was asked by a female shop assistant if she could not help with creating an organisation for shop assistants. The days were generally long and the wages low, often the day lasted from 8 o'clock in the morning to 9 o'clock in the evening, with a one-hour lunch break and no pay for extra overtime. A call was published addressing women working in shops and post

[117] Folkvord, *Betzy Kjelsberg*, pp. 11–16.

offices, and 60 ladies turned up for the first meeting. The organisation was a success, particularly the sickness benefit fund, and it also spawned activity among a group of workers that had seen unionisation only in the capital before this time.[118]

Kjelsberg was, since her early days, active in the women's movement; she was chair of the local women's organisation, Drammen Kvinnerad, she also participated in the work of the national organisation, Norsk Kvinnesaksforening. She particularly engaged herself in the issues of votes for women, female educational opportunities and questions of household economy. She stood as a candidate in local elections and was elected in 1901 and 1904. When on the local council, she voiced initiatives about free public libraries, free dentistry for poor primary school children, local hygiene, for example public toilets and the need for female police officers to handle questions related to children, youth and women. It would seem that between 1897 and 1909 her husband had serious problems with alcohol, starting because of some professional disappointments. By 1910, however, both Betzy and her husband were active in the teetotal movement and Oluf Kjelsberg was elected into the local council as a representative of the anti-alcohol party.[119]

When the opportunity to become Factory Inspector arose, Kjelsberg applied after consultation with her husband and her mother. With six children of school age and an occupation including travel, a promise by her mother to move into the house and help with childcare was a necessity. After her appointment as Female Inspector of Factories and Workplaces, she worked hard for health and hygiene, supervision of the work of children, the need to stop illegal overtime and the introduction of the eight-hour day.[120]

In the 1909 Parliamentary election, women had a restricted right to vote and Kjelsberg was nominated as a candidate, although not elected. She did not lower her profile though, but became the first woman on the board of the leftist party Venstre. By 1919, she was the first woman to speak at the ILO conference in Washington. In 1921, all women in Norway had the vote and she was again nominated as candidate for Venstre; she stood also in 1924 and for the last time in 1930. The list voting system, however, putting men at the top of the list and women further down, was a way of assuring that female candidates, although nominated, were not elected.[121]

In 1935 she celebrated her 25 years as Factory Inspector and in 1936 she retired at the age of 70, after demands from the pension office about not allowing her to work after reaching pension age. As a high-profile woman who did not fear public speaking, she suffered ridicule from political opponents

---

[118] Folkvord, *Betzy Kjelsberg*, pp. 26–32.
[119] Folkvord, *Betzy Kjelsberg*, pp. 70–5.
[120] Folkvord, *Betzy Kjelsberg*, pp. 91–2, 99–102, 105–12, 198–9.
[121] Folkvord, *Betzy Kjelsberg*, pp. 140, 210–12, 260, 265–9.

Figure 4   The social democratic Venstre Party in Norway tended to
prefer male candidates. However, the women's section in Kristiania (Oslo)
unanimously backed Betzy Kjelsberg and managed to place her first on
the candidate list instead of second in 1921. *Vikingen*, no. 40 1921.

and was sometimes caricatured in the press. She did, however, gain public
recognition and support both from those she inspected and those to which
she reported.[122]

Aline Valette (née Alphonsine-Eulalie Goudeman (1850–99), Inspector 1884–93, France

Aline Valette, one of the most famous French feminists, was the daughter
of a railway worker. She trained as a teacher and ran an educational establishment in Lille before her marriage and move to Paris. In 1880 she married
the lawyer M. Valette, but separated in 1885 with the responsibility for two
young children. The separation was not of an amicable nature and, in 1891,
the court stated that the ex-husband had left the country and not contributed
to the upkeep of his children for several years.

Valette continued working in female education and published the book
'*La journée de la petite ménagère*', which was used widely in girl's schools
for decades. She was engaged in the leftist union movement in the 1870s and
1880s, and by the 1890s in the Workers Party. She was recruited as Assistant
Industrial Inspector in the administrative area of the Seine in 1884. In 1891,
she was elected President of the Federation of Feminist Organisations in

---

[122] Folkvord, *Betzy Kjelsberg*, pp. 316–17.

France, counting 35,000 members and, in 1892, she founded the weekly '*L'Harmonie sociale*', a publication promoting the rights and interests of women. The journal published both articles on the advances in the position of women nationally and internationally, and also on the judicial position of women. She raised questions that were considered controversial, like the position of feminists in the Workers Party in '*Cahier des doleances feminines*' in 1893. She wrote about the issue of equal pay and equal legal rights, but also about the access of women to all occupations, both in the public and the private sector. She demanded the abolishment of the laws placing women in an inferior position in relation to men. However, *L'Harmonie* also praised motherhood as the most noble and necessary of all functions, in line with the views presented in the maternalist discussion. Her level of activity made inroads into her ability to fulfil her duties as Inspector and in 1893 she left her post and became a full-time journalist working for the feminist journal *La Fronde*, founded by Marguerite Durand. Despite her overt connection to the feminists she navigated her relations to the socialist movement and became the first female secretary of the Workers Party. Even after her departure from the Inspectorate, she continued taking an interest in the working conditions of women, female wages and the evils of home work and publishing about these issues.[123] For example, in 1897 she wrote an article about matchstick work, lead and necrosis. In 1898, under the heading of 'female work' she published a series of articles about working time in textile work, factories and shops, putting forward the case of workers and underlining the fact that continuous disregard of existing legislation was normal.[124]

Aldona Sochaczewska-Juillerat (1860–1945), Inspector 1893–1911, France

Aldona Sochaczewska-Juillerat was the daughter of an officer in the Polish army and a French mother. Her father died when she was a year old, leaving a widow with seven children. Three of Aldona's sisters entered the professions and, after passing the exam, Aldona was appointed Industrial Inspector in 1893. She commenced her work in Rouen and Dieppe with surrounding areas and advanced well in her career. In 1902 she was transferred to Paris with her area of activity concentrated on the left bank.

---

123 Schweitzer, *Les inspectrices*, pp. 34–5; Seine (France) Conseil général (1891) *Mémoires de M. Le préfet de la Seine & de police et procès-verbaux des délibérations*, https://books.google.com/books?id=pHMAAAAAYAAJ&pg=PA259.

124 Aline Valette, 'Les empoisonnées de travail', *La Fronde* 24.12 1897, p. 1; Aline Valette, 'Dans l'atelier de couture', *La Fronde* 1.1 1898, p. 2; Aline Valette, 'Salaires de famine', *La Fronde* 3.2 1898, p. 2; Aline Valette, 'Dans la filature lyonnaise', *La Fronde* 24.2 1898, p. 2; Aline Valette, 'Dans les magasins', La Fronde 6.3 1898, p. 2; Aline Valette, 'Abus patronaux', *La Fronde* 15.5 1898, p. 1.

In 1903, she married the head of the Hygiene Commission and of the Commission of Unhealthy Habitations, anti-tuberculosis activist, Paul Juillerat.

The couple were active in the Ligue Social des Acheteurs and Association Nationale pour la Protection Légale des Travailleurs. Some of the aims were to actively oppose the abuses of home work. The members of the organisation published articles in la *Revue économique international*. In 1907, Aldona Juillerat, the first and only woman to publish in the journal, wrote the article '*L'inspection du travail*', a critical overview of the economic role of the inspection activity, its effects, its problems and its shortcomings, stating that the inspection should be less focused on details and the desire to seem to achieve something; the concentration should be on the important issues. She also criticised the insufficient number of inspectors and the difference in position between men and women. Four years later she published '*L'activité feminine en France au xx siècle*', where she underlined the need for female education of the same standard as that awarded males. She also commented on the need for a female vote. However, she concluded by stating the view that men and women have complimentary roles and that women are in some respects inferior. She retired from the inspectorate at the age of 50 and died in 1945 after 10 years of widowhood. Aldona Juillerat was part of the early generation of French Inspectors who did not represent socialist views, but were active supporters of social reform, improvement of working conditions, health and hygiene.[125]

Marguerite Bourat, Inspector 1907–37, France

Marguerite Bourat grew up as an orphan under the care of her uncle, a locksmith. She was given access to education and took the administrative exam in 1907. While waiting for information about her appointment to Inspector she travelled to London. There she attended lectures by the Fabians at the London School of Economics. After making the acquaintance of Sidney Webb, the contact resulted in her contribution, 'The skin and fur trades' (on home work) to the volume 'Seasonal trades' published in 1912. Some years later she published '*Le salaire feminine en France et en Angleterre*', which was translated for the American journal Proceedings of the Academy of Political Science in New York.

During her activity as inspector, she communicated actively with the trade union activist and feminist Jeanne Bouvier, who also functioned in '*l'office francais du travail a domicile*'. The collaboration inspired Bouvier to make an effort to push for the establishment of tariffs for home workers, placing them on an equal footing with factory workers. In 1923, Marguerite Bourat and Jeanne Bouvier were engaged in the government enquiry on the conditions

---

[125] Schweitzer, *Les inspectrices*, pp. 37–8; 'Aldona Juillerat', http://aehit.fr.

of work in the domestic sector. The two women became friends and not only worked but also spent holidays together. Bourat also collaborated with her co-inspector Alice de la Ruelle-Geubel who stood close to the labour unions.[126]

Marie Baum (1874–1964) inspector 1902–07, Germany

Maria Johanna Baum was the third of six children in a doctor's family in Danzig. Her mother was active in the women's movement. Between 1891 and 1893, Maria attended courses preparing her for the baccalaureate (*abitur*). As women at this point were unable to gain access to university studies in Germany she enrolled at the University of Zurich for the purpose of studying chemistry. After her doctoral degree in 1897, she worked for a time as assistant at the University, despite the fact that the authorities would have preferred a man and Swiss national. Later she returned to Germany and took up a position at the chemical industry firm Agfa in Berlin. In 1902, she was appointed Factory Inspector in Baden at the recommendation of the departing Inspector, Else von Richthofen. During her time as inspector she particularly highlighted the plight of children and young workers. She also published a study of female workers in 1906, '*Drei Klassen von Lohnarbeiterinnen in Industrie und Handel in der Stadt Karlsruhe*'. The study was based both on observation and a survey of female factory workers, female garment makers and shop workers. It included information about the origin of the women, their educational level and their living and working conditions. Baum was particularly concerned about problems related to health, family duties and infant mortality. Her suggestions for improvement of conditions, however, had little impact. In the end she found her work as Inspector too problematic, as she was subject to ultimate decisions by the male inspectorate. She left her post in 1907 to become General Secretary of *Verein für Säuglingsfürsorge und Vohlfahrtspflege* (the Society for Infant Care and Welfare) in Düsseldorf. She was soon promoted to chairman of the organisation, which she ran until 1914. During WWI she was recruited as scientific adviser into the department for inspection of housing. She also worked closely with the women's organisation *Bund Deutscher Frauenvereine* until the 1930s. In the 1920s she was active as consultant for the Ministry of Work in Baden and promoted protection of people living in rented property and social security issues. She also supported the further educational estab-lishment for girls, *Soziale Frauenschule*, in Hamburg, where she gave courses on social welfare and social legislation. For a short time she was a member of the Deutsche Demokratische Partei, and participated in the work of the first parliament of the Weimar Republic on a new constitution. She left the party in 1921 because of disagreements about policy. In 1926, she also left

---

[126] Schweitzer, *Les inspectrices*, pp. 39–40; https://en.wikipedia.org/w/index. php?title=Jeanne_Bouvier.

the Ministry of Work because of its increasing bureaucracy and a negative attitude to women. After two years of travel, she obtained a teaching post at the Institute for Social and Political Studies at the University of Heidelberg in 1928. She also continued her work on women and social work and welfare at the *Deutsche Akademie für soziale un pädagogische Frauenarbeit*. While growing up in a protestant family, as great niece of the composer Felix Mendelssohn Bartholdy, Baum was classified as one quarter Semitic by the National Socialists; as a consequence, she lost her post at Heidelberg in 1933 and her right to publication was curtailed. Through the 1930s and until the end of the war Marie Baum stayed in close contact with clergymen and Christian organisations assisting the departure of persons subject to persecution. After 1945, she resumed her teaching at the University of Heidelberg and continued her research into her 80s. She died at the age of 90 in 1964.[127]

[127] Manfred Berger, 'Baum Marie', online Social Lexicon Bonn 2022, Das netz für die Sozialwirtschaft, https://www.socialnet.de/lexicon/Baum-Marie.

7

Factory Inspection Activity

Don't they want to be protected?

> THE MAN. Call in the inspector! What sort of fool are you? They dread the
> inspector more than I do. EPIFANIA. Why? Don't they want to be protected?
> THE WOMAN. The inspector wouldn't protect them, ma'am: he'd only
> shut up the place and take away their job from them. If they thought you'd
> be so cruel as to report them they'd go down on their knees to you to spare
> them. THE MAN. You that know such a lot ought to know that a business
> like this can't afford any luxuries. It's a cheap labour business. As long as I
> get women to work for their natural wage, I can get along; but no luxuries,
> mind you. No trade union wages. No sanitary arrangements as you call
> them. No lime washings every six months. No separate rooms to eat in. No
> fencing in of dangerous machinery or the like of that: not that I care; for I
> have nothing but the old gas engine that wouldn't hurt a fly, though it brings
> me under the blasted Workshop Act as you spotted all right. I have no big
> machinery; but I have to undersell those that have it. If I put up my prices
> by a farthing they'd set their machinery going and drop me. You might as
> well ask me to pay trade union wages as do all that the inspector wants: I
> should be out of business in a week. EPIFANIA. And what is a woman's
> natural wage? THE MAN. Tuppence hapeny an hour for twelve hours a day.
>
> (George Bernard Shaw, *The Millionairess*, Act III (London, 1934))

Factory and workshop owners, factory law and abidance

The intrusion of factory inspectors onto the premises of businesses in Britain
was often not welcomed. Even before the advent of women on the scene,
there are examples of local authorities forming a protective shield around a
businessman against representatives of the central administration.

On 1 May 1885, Thomas Clarke, miller of Earsham, physically attacked
inspector Hudson in the yard of his mill and on the road. The local magistrates
held that the assaults were justified and did not issue any fine for assault. The
excuse was that the inspector had not shown his credentials. As the miller
appeared after the inspection had commenced and immediately proceeded with
the attack, the producing of certificates had proved fairly difficult. The magistrates also refused to issue a fine for obstructing the inspector in performing
his duties, as the inspection had de facto taken place. The inspector attempted

to explain that part of his duties was to inform the owner of any remarks that needed to be made, but the justices could find no reason for a complaint. While the inspector in question did not suffer from the problem of being a woman, similar problems of obstruction of inspections and the closing of ranks locally were not unusual in the following decades. Particularly those breaking the rules did not view inspectors in a positive light.[1]

In France, the female inspectors were usually treated with politeness but there were some rare examples of verbal and even physical attacks, particularly when the same place had to be visited repeatedly to point out, that shortcomings had not been corrected.[2]

The work of Florence Kelley in Chicago was disrupted by the employers forming The Illinois Association of Manufacturers under the direction of Levi Mayer, as early as 1893. The association and Mayer challenged the Factory Law as unconstitutional in the Supreme Court of Illinois. In 1895, the Court ruled that the eight-hour provision for women in the factory inspection statute was unconstitutional. However, the powers of the inspectors to continue their work was upheld as was the rule of banning work for children under 14.[3]

In Germany, the restricted power of female inspectors made their work difficult. They lacked the right to impose fines and even when the male inspectorate took action breaking the factory laws was fairly cheap.[4]

While the power to impose direct sanctions was not within the remit of the female inspectors in Norway and Finland, they generally engaged in direct dialogue with employers. Vera Hjelt was a great believer in convincing employers of the advantages of changes rather than threatening with punishment. In factories and large enterprises, this approach often worked reasonably well. As these inspectors were also expected to mediate in conflicts, and if possible avoid strikes, their role became slightly different from that in other countries. Fairly often, a communication could be established, and the cases of argumentative proprietors was more often connected to small workshops, where costs tended to be presented as reasons for lack of protection. Equally, in Denmark, the proprietors of small businesses took less kindly to interference.[5]

[1] Report of the Chief Inspector of Factories and Workshops for the year 1885, PP 1886 XIV, pp. 30–82, on p. 80; Report of the Chief inspector of Factories 1901, PP 1902 XII, pp. 36–43, 54.

[2] Schweitzer, *Les inspectrices*, pp. 75–6.

[3] http://florencekelley.northwestern.edu/florence/

[4] Schmitt, *Der Arbeiterinnenschutz*, pp. 137, 150.

[5] Ravn, 'Julie Arenholt', p. 1; Hjelt, *Berättelse 1903*; Hjelt, *Berättelse 1905*; Folkvord, *Betzy Kjelsberg*, p. 122.

The female touch and the organisation of work

During the discussions about the desirability to employ women in the inspectorate, the nature of women had been brought forward as an argument both for
and against. In contemporary society there has been much talk about female
multi-tasking and organisational skills. Whether particular female skills came
into play, or the reasons were to be found in new people bringing in new views,
the female sections of the inspectorate introduced innovations into the work.

The British reports in the 1870s and 1880s were focused on accidents,
with detailed listing of prosecutions with results and overviews of regional
economic development. There was no information about the exact number of
visits paid to factories over the year, only miles travelled, because they were
necessary to get travel expenses paid. Very little information was included
about the exact number of factories that were subject to inspection rules. All
this became clear later when 10-year statistics and overviews started to be
supplied. After the new regulations were introduced in the 1890s and female
inspectors were employed new ways of recording the activity were brought in.
When Lucy Deane was employed, she set up a system of indexing workplaces
in west London that were to be inspected. She copied data on 300 establishments acquired from the District Inspector, and deleted hundreds, as they no
longer existed. She also surveyed the area by driving around and looking for
lighted windows, then went in and checked if commercial activity was going
on. In the first year, she registered altogether 6000 establishments on her
index cards. The female inspectorate also collected information on laundry
accidents, including time, place and how long the person had been working
that day. They gathered statistics on lead poisoning, recording the health, age
and sex of the person, the time of employment and what kind of work he/
she had been doing.[6]

Following the example from her colleague in Finland, the female inspector
in Norway decided to forego the lugging of massive ledgers around on her
inspection trips. Instead, information was transferred to a record card system,
easily indexed and cross referenced, complemented by files into which extra
pages could be added. The office of the female inspectorate also began using
typewriters, although the cost of the machine was seen as unnecessary to
start with by the Civil Service. The inspectors also made clear that they were
available in the office some evenings. The aim was to facilitate meetings with
workers who did not want to approach them in the presence of the employers.[7]

In general, we find that the collection of statistics came to be an integral
part of the work by many of the female inspectors. Some had been engaged in

---

6 McFeeley, *Lady Inspectors*, p. 112; Report of the Chief Inspector of Factories
1900, PP 1901 X Cd 668, p. 350.
7 Folkvord, *Betzy Kjelsberg*, pp. 104–5, 126.

such work before they embarked on their career as inspectors; others conducted surveys or collected statistics as part of their duties. This activity could be connected to the need for accumulating data to demonstrate a problem. On other occasions, the work was part of the process of illuminating the living conditions of men and women of the working classes.

Hygiene and sanitation

The issues that had been considered suitable for female inspectors were those related to hygiene and sanitation. For example, in Denmark, the second female inspector, Julie Arenholt, appointed in 1910, was to be exclusively engaged in inspecting health and hygiene in the bakeries and cake making and distributing outlets in the Copenhagen area. Even where the authority of the female inspector was circumscribed, hygiene was seen as a suitable remit. We also find that such issues were frequently and repeatedly discussed in the reports of the female inspectors in Australia. Annie Duncan highlighted dirty conditions, the heat in workplaces and the reluctance of employers to provide drinking water and hand washing facilities. The latter was seen to encourage workers to while away precious working time at wash basins. In this case, the persuasion by the inspectors was successful. In Norway, the provision of soap and towels remained an issue in some workplaces as late as 1920.[8]

Washrooms and toilets were also a problem in Britain and after years of struggle a recommendation by the Women Inspectors finally got the Secretary of State to issue and order (1901 and 1903) about sufficient and suitable sanitary accommodation. However, the report from 1903 still records for a textile mill:

> Dark unventilated conveniences, used indiscriminately by men and women, opened directly to spinning rooms … No attempt to secure privacy was made, the doors were without fastenings … the whole connected, not with a drain, but a huge cesspool.[9]

Even when huge improvements were achieved, the inspectors were faced with considerable backsliding; during WWI and in the 1920s it became once more necessary to insist on washrooms with soap and water and toilets provided with doors.[10]

---

[8]   Ravn, 'Julie Arenholt'; Joy Damousi, 'Female factory inspectors and leadership in early 20th century Australia', in Joy Damousi, Kim Rubenstein and Mary Tomsic (eds), *Diversity and Leadership: Australian Women Past and Present* (Canberra, 2014), pp. 169–88, on p. 181; Folkvord, *Betzy Kjelsberg*, p. 111; Bousardt, *Onder Vrouwelijke*, pp. 31–2.

[9]   Anderson, *Women in the Factory*, pp. 43–5; Report of the Chief Inspector of Factories 1903, PP 1904 X Cd 2139, p. 203.

[10]   McFeeley, *Lady Inspectors*, p. 151.

The question of adequate toilets was not solely a British problem. In her report from 1905, Vera Hjelt remarked with horror on the shortage of toilets in some factories in Finland, and that the employer had not always considered it necessary to provide the facilities with a lock. In other places there was tardiness in the provision of wash basins and drinking water. The cold winters in Scandinavia also created issues like the need for cloakrooms to store outdoor garments, and complaints about factories being freezing cold on a Monday morning were not unusual.[11]

While some workplaces in Britain did suffer from heat, the opposite was more often the case. Before the regulations of 1895 there were no rules about provision of a reasonable temperature in the workplace, and not until 1901 the need to provide a heating device that did not pollute the air. Still, in 1904, the report cites ample examples of inadequate heating and air polluted by gas jets. We even find examples of employers refusing to provide heating. In actual fact, Adelaide Anderson remarked that many workplaces did not comply until well into WWI. Equally, while the 1878 act stated that workrooms had to be cleaned, the provision of adequate ventilation to improve air quality was not mandatory until 1901, nor was keeping flooring dry (except for laundries, 1895).[12]

In her contribution to the report of 1897, Rose Squire laments the inability of inspectors to intervene in ventilation issues:

> One instance is that of a large room in a factory occupied by over a hundred women and girls, each having 250 cubic feet of space (obtained by measuring up into the angle of the high pitched roof, as in the absence of any height limit is of course permissible), seated elbow to elbow in double rows facing one another at tables 2 1/2 feet wide, all windows closed to exclude dust and dirt from the white garments being made. Entering the room at 12.30 pm the unpleasant sensation of air vitiated by human breath is experienced, but it is just dinner time and to be presumed that the workers will disperse into the outer air and the room be sweetened by open windows before the afternoon work commences. But there is no regulation prescribing that a workroom shall be cleared and aired during meals, and in this factory no one is allowed to leave the premises until work ceases for the day; so food is produced from parcels and baskets, warmed or cooked in the room if required and eaten by the employees as they sit each at her machine.

She continues by pointing out that in France the ventilation of work rooms had been mandatory since 1893 and that eating in working areas had been prohibited.[13]

---

11 Hjelt, *Berättelse 1905*, pp. 79–81; Hjelt, *Berättelse 1908*, pp. 128–30.
12 Anderson, *Women in the Factory*, pp. 39–40, 44; Report of the Chief Inspector of Factories 1904, PP 1905 X Cd 2569, pp. 246–7.
13 Report of the Chief Inspector of Factories 1897, PP 1898 XIV, c.9281, p. 100.

As France had regulations about crowding and lack of fresh air in factories and workshops, we can see infringements of the rules catching the attention of the inspectors. All workplaces did not comply and, as late as in the 1920s, workplaces were found in breach of the acts. The inspectors highlighted hygiene problems but also the lack of proper control over the presence of potentially dangerous gases in the workrooms.[14]

The late nineteenth century and the early twentieth century were times with the uncomfortable presence of tuberculosis in society. While factory and workshop owners generally had no objections to providing spittoons and 'no spitting' notices, the problems extended further than this.[15] In her report from 1893, Florence Kelley raised the sensitive issue of the spread of disease through contaminated fabrics and finished garments:

> It is not generally understood by purchasers of expensive tailor-made garments that even the most fashionable merchant tailors give out work to be finished in the home of the workman …

In 1893, the problem was not only tuberculosis but, in many homes of workmen, somebody was ill with smallpox and the disease could and was spread in textiles. The city authorities, including some of those engaged in healthcare, tried to minimize the problem and the inspectors were not even provided with accurate information about the cases. This was particularly evident after Kelley arranged a public burning of some expensive cloaks infected with smallpox.[16]

The concept of hygiene and the nature of the spread of disease was not necessarily common knowledge before WWI (as perhaps even today). In cotton fabric manufacture, it was usual for the weavers to make the weft moist, for the purpose of pulling escaping threads, by spitting water onto the fabric. As a sizeable portion of the fabric was sold as unbleached cotton, it underwent no further cleaning before it landed in the shops. Considering that tuberculosis was widespread and female factory workers were not immune, this practice created a health problem. Vera Hjelt consulted doctors to verify her suspicions and talked repeatedly with foremen and workers, but the practice persisted. In the end she saw no other solution than to recommend informing the general public of the risks and to urge people to wash unbleached cotton before use. She also conducted a losing battle in her endeavours to improve air quality

---

[14] Schweitzer, *Les inspectrices*, pp. 77–8.

[15] Hjelt, *Berättelse 1905*, pp. 77, 80–1; Hjelt, *Berättelse 1908*, p. 122.

[16] First Annual Report of the Factory Inspectors of Illinois for the year ending December 1893, pp. 9, 11–18, 20–1; Second Annual Report of the Factory Inspectors of Illinois for the year ending December 1894, pp. 43–57; florencekelley.northwestern. edu/Florence/1894.

in the factories and workshops. The problem was not exclusively created by working practices, but also by windows being closed by older workers to stop drafts. In many cases, the air conditioning vents and opening mechanisms of windows had to be placed away from the reach of workers or locking systems installed. To minimize the controversy, Hjelt sometimes managed to achieve agreement about thorough airing of the workrooms during the lunch hour.[17]

As mentioned above, the habit of eating by machines, on dirty work tables or even near toxic materials was far from unusual. While a relatively early ban existed in France, other countries proceeded more slowly. In the absence of a dedicated space for meals, sitting with sandwiches in the lap was far too common an occurrence. The creation of canteens, or at least separate dining areas, therefore, became central to the activity of several female inspectors.[18] In Denmark, the law of 1919 brought in new rules about sanitation and cleaning and banned eating in workrooms. Betty Kjelsberg did not only work for separate eating areas in the factories, she also joined forces with organisations to set up cheap eating places for workers in urban centres.[19]

Children, work, education and health

In a small bookbinders on Katajanokka they were not very particular and when I and Aino Johansson went and asked they promised to take us and we started on 11 of September(1906). There were only two shop rooms. The workers were the master himself, 4 men and 4 women and about 10 little girls and 2 boys. Later we realised that we had caused trouble between the union and master Siren as you were not allowed more than one apprentice girl per fully trained adult. The inspector came now and then but he did not find this out because whenever he came us little girls were sent down to 'tidy' in the paper store ... The advantage of working in a small place was that we were allowed to learn all aspects of bookbinding. In large shops the tasks were divided so minutely that even people who had been there for years only knew their own particular one ...[20]

When the earliest workplace regulations were introduced in 1840s Britain and France they specifically targeted the age at which children could be allowed into factory work and working hours of women and children. By the 1870s, the minimum working age was 10 in Britain and 12 in France and

[17] Hjelt, *Berättelse 1903*, pp. 212–13, 216–17; Hjelt-Cajanus, *Vera Hjelt*, pp. 152–3.

[18] Folkvord, *Betzy Kjelsberg*, pp. 108–11; Hjelt, *Berättelse afgifven af kvinnliga yrkesinspektören i Finland för år 1906* (Helsingfors, 1907), p. 80; Anderson, *Women in the Factory*, pp. 25–6.

[19] *Beretning om Arbejds og Fabrikstillsynets Virksomhed Aaren 1919 og 1920* (Copenhagen, 1922), pp. 15, 17; Folkvord, *Betzy Kjelsberg*, pp. 188–9.

[20] Salmela-Järvinen, *Alas lyötiin vanha maailma*, pp. 9–11.

an increasing amount of rules regarding women had been introduced. In addition, many other countries had joined the path of workplace regulation. The argument for employing women in the inspectorate was linked to the perceived ability of women to deal with the welfare of women and children. The story of the work of the female inspectors during their first decades in office does indeed reveal that trying to make sure the laws were followed was far from an easy task. The situation was not improved by the various caveats, making possible half-day work for young children, overtime in certain situations and in the early stages, workers who conspired with the employers to circumvent the regulations. Having people at work for part of the day inside, part of the day outside a factory and hiding young workers, sending work home with women to be finished at all hours, etc. were fairly widespread practices.[21]

While the factory regulations of the late nineteenth century were in many cases focused on restricting the work of underage children, a set of regulations were also brought in to ensure that those in work would not be prevented from attending school.

The British Factory and Workshop Act of 1878 had made education of children up to 10 years mandatory and ruled that 10–14 year olds could only be employed for half days in all trades. In addition, children and young teenagers also needed certificates of fitness. The 1891 act raised the working age in all sectors to 11 years. However, overseeing the working hours of children in Britain posed a number of problems. The teaching profession was very positive to the raising of employment age from 11 to 12 years. There were numerous statements by teachers that the children employed in textile work as half-timers were often tired, usually hungry and followed the teaching badly.[22]

In 1901, the new Factory Act set the minimum working age at 12 and underlined that working did not mean staying out of education. However, it became necessary to introduce a new regulation two years later (1903 Employment of Children Act) making it unlawful to employ a half-timer in two places, and preventing children of 12 and younger from working full time.

In relation to this, Miss Paterson stated:

> Amongst the changes in the law during my official service few were so completely satisfactory as those which have contributed to the passing of the half-timers. Each advance in a year in the age for entering on employment was accompanied by gloomy forebodings of the result to industry of preventing a child from acquiring facility while its fingers were still supple – as if a non wage

---

[21] Anderson, *Women in the Factory*, pp. 27–8, 30–1; McFeeley, *Lady Inspectors*, p. 151; Schweitzer, *Les inspectrices*, pp. 15, 59–61, 85; Schmitt, "'All these forms of women's work'", pp. 125–49, on pp. 126–7, 131–3, 136–8, 141–2.

[22] Report of the Chief Inspector of Factories for the year 1895, PP 1896 XIX c 8067. Report by the Lady Inspectors 1895, p. 13.

earning child sat with hands folded in inaction – and by some people of the effects on character of too much leisure in youth. A well-known sheriff added to his reluctant convictions of several firms for illegal employment of children an exhortation to me to consider carefully what I was doing before bringing more cases to this court. In his opinion I was doing much to fill the place with young criminals who would have me to thank to some extent for their ruin.[23]

Many children and young persons were examined and a certificate provided to allow them to work. The reports of the inspectors revealed that 300,000–400,000 children and teenagers were inspected every year and of these about one per cent were rejected before 1908 and after that slightly stricter criteria seem to have been applied (see Table 7.1).

Table 7.1   Persons examined and passed for fitness certificates in factories and workshops, Britain.

	Boys 14–16	Girls 14–16	Boys 13–14	Girls 13–14	Boys 11–13 half-time	Girls 11–13 half-time	All inspected	Rejected
1899	135,251	94,457	68,979	58,254	24,260	26,069	412,141	4241
1900	132,436	95,747	73,618	61,423	20,143	19,106	406,594	4121
1901	126,450	97,524	56,058	47,746	22,729	22,451	376,691	3733
1902	133,364	112,666	47,679	40,195	21,876	20,971	381,067	4316
1903	129,525	107,342	40,580	35,551	21,575	20,756	359,275	3946
1904	117,717	102,174	36,872	33,867	19,052	19,912	333,190	3596
1905	126,907	116,306	37,447	35,312	20,024	20,570	356,566	5012
1906	139,722	124,486	40,631	38,527	20,710	21,259	385,415	5454
1908	116,221	133,148	37, 287	37,462	18,336	18,156	370,809	10,199
1911	158,106	176,638	43,245	43,269	18,115	19,778	459,151	15,188

Sources: Report by the Chief Inspector of Factories for the year 1906 XV, p. 32; Report 1910, p. 256; Report 1912–13 XXV, p. 293.

The early decades of the twentieth century saw an intensification of the attention by the inspectors on young British workers. From 1905, visits were made to medical officers of health and conferences arranged with certifying surgeons as cooperation between authorities increased. By 1913, this included the education authorities and the juvenile labour exchange, with the result that, when a child with health problems left school to enter the factory, the certifying surgeon

---

[23] Miss Paterson on her views and experiences in the matter of young children and work, Anderson, *Women in the Factory*, p. 167.

was notified to alert him of the need for a thorough examination. In addition, bonus points could be collected by diligent school attendance for entry into the workplace at 13. The working age of 14 was not introduced until 1920.[24]

The situation of child workers in 1890s Chicago sorely tested the newly appointed factory inspector Florence Kelley:

> The enforcement of section four of the law brings to light a deplorable amount of illiteracy among working children. Thus, in the first case prosecuted, that against Gustav Ravitz for the employing of a girl under fourteen years of age in his tailor shop, it was shown in court that the child had been brought thirteen years before to Chicago from Poland, yet she could not read or write in any language, nor speak English. Neither she nor her mother knew the year of the child's birth and an interpreter was required to speak with them both.

> A little girl thirteen years of age, found at 120 West Taylor street (Baugartner's knee pants shop) sewing on buttons in the bedroom of the sweater's family was discharged. She is a Russian Jewess three years in this country and does not know her letters. She was taken bodily to the Jewish training school and entered as a pupil.

> Greek, Italian, Bohemian, Polish and Russian children are constantly encountered who cannot read or write any language. Children who cannot spell their name or the name of the street in which they live are found at work every day by the deputies.

> Where these children are under fourteen years of age they are turned over to the compulsory attendance officer of the Board of Education. For those over the age of fourteen the State prescribes no educational requirement and unless they look deformed, undersized or distressed the inspectors have no ground upon to withdraw them from their life of premature toil. And in no case can we insist on rudimentary education for them.

> In this respect Illinois law is far from abreast with the laws of Massachusetts and New York. In Massachusetts every child must attend some school throughout the period during which the public schools are in session until fourteen years of age. And in towns and cities in which there is manual training in the schools the children must attend school until the completion of the fifteenth year. New York goes even farther and empowers her inspectors to order peremptorily the discharge of any child under sixteen years of age who cannot read and write simple sentences in the English language. Such a clause as this last one would cause the transfer of many hundreds of Illinois children from the factory to the schoolroom.[25]

---

[24] Anderson, *Women in the Factory*, pp. 172–3; McFeeley, *Lady Inspectors*, p. 106.

[25] First Annual Report of the Factory Inspectors of Illinois for the year ending December 1893, pp. 13–14.

In her Third Annual Report (1895), Florence Kelley pointed out that children as young as eight were found in glass factories. The employers had struck an unholy pact with the orphanage and took these children into employment. No registers were kept of the numbers or at least they were not shown to the inspectors. Kelley described the situation as being as bad as the stories from the early days of industrialisation in Britain. Already the previous year Kelley had observed that the glass company had been allowed to appoint people for the local school board, and therefore, these made no effort to see that children went to school instead of working.[26]

During the early years of her inspectorate, Kjelsberg found children of 10–11 years in glassworks and tobacco manufacturing in Norway. The regulations had loopholes that allowed children over 12 to work for a limited time outside school hours. Although the intention had been to provide opportunities for training, and reserve lighter tasks for the young, this was not always the case in practice. Factory work was not supposed to be included and any work that endangered health was not allowed. As the rules were not followed, the inspectorate pushed for amendment of the legislation. From 1916, a ban was introduced on children under 14 working in glass factories and by the autumn the same year working in tobacco factories also became prohibited.[27]

Although all inspectors, for example in Denmark, were to be active in overseeing protective legislation as to danger in the workplace and legal working hours, the female inspector, Fanny Vedel, was responsible for examining the conditions of women and children, particularly in the textile sector. Children under 18 were, however, not only working in textiles but were to be found in baking, chocolate and sweets factories, the tobacco industry and dairies, garment manufacture, carpentry, shoemaking, machine industry and printing. In 1919, the working hours of young people who had finished school but were under the age of 18 became restricted to 10 hours, not to be performed after 8 in the evening. Young people studying at technical schools or other vocational education classes were to finish work by 6 pm to enable them to attend such classes. However, should it be necessary for their education, permission could be granted by the Ministry of the Interior for children over 15 to work after 8 pm.[28]

When Hjelt commenced as factory inspector in 1903, the issue of children, work and literacy was on her agenda. After probing the issue she was able to state that although she had reason to take a serious look into the working hours of teenagers, literacy was good. She had only found one young person, a 16 year old, who was unable to read and write. The industrial surveys conducted

26 Third Annual Report of the Factory Inspectors of Illinois for the year ending December 1895 pp. 15–17; Second Annual Report of the Factory Inspectors of Illinois for the year ending December 1894, pp. 13–14, 17–18.

27 Folkvord, *Betzy Kjelsberg*, pp. 153–6, 123–4.

28 *Beretning om Arbejds*, pp. 18, 45–53.

in the same time period also recorded good literacy rates, an issue probably connected to rules about literacy, first communion and the subsequent right to marry.[29] In 1907, she had reason to return to the issue of child work as she had found numerous 14 year olds doing 10 hour days in factories and workshops. The parents wanted the children to find work, as the families were poor. The owners were also willing to engage the children if they could produce a certificate that they had finished compulsory education. In many places, part-time work, the legal seven hours, was not available; the options were full-time or no work at all. The inspector suggested the setting up of paid apprenticeships and training programs for the children who had finished school but were not old enough for work (i.e. 15 years). Depending on the time of the year a child was born there could be a considerable gap before attaining legal working age and examples can be found from working-class biographies of parents asking employers to take on a child who had not turned 15 but had finished school:[30] In France, attending school became obligatory from the 1880s. The regulations also made it illegal for children under 13 to work outside the home. The wide spread practice of craft businesses in a domestic environment created problems for overseeing the work of minors. Family businesses were not regulated and subject to inspection. The inspectors were, on the other hand, aware that a domestic enterprise could be, and sometimes was, quite extensive, including numerous workers and engaging children on a full-time basis.[31]

Annie Duncan also highlighted the issue of child labour in Australia. Unlike the situation in Chicago where orphans were sent to factory work, the children under 14 Duncan discovered working in factories instead of attending school did so often with the approval of their parents. Both parties saw the entry into paid work as better than staying in education. One field where children had been allowed to work was fruit picking. When the sector became industrialised, children under 13 had been allowed into the factories. She identified the dangers of situations where lack of supervision saw these children operating machines that were unsuitable to their age and physical strength and put them in danger of serious accidents. She was, however, able to determine that new regulations and a change in wage levels had the effect of eliminating the youngest workers and replacing them with women of mature age by 1914.[32]

Also elsewhere, like in Helsinki, some employers tried to get around regulations related to the work of teenagers:

[29] G.R. Snellman, *Tutkimus Suomen kutomateollisuudesta* (Helsinki, 1904), p. 189; Pentti Lempiäinen, *Rippikäytäntö Suomen Kirkossa uskonpuhdistuksesta 1600-luvun loppuun* (Helsinki, 1963).

[30] Hjelt, *Berättelse 1903*, p. 228; Hjelt, *Berättelse 1908*, pp. 127, 136–8.

[31] Schweitzer, *Les inspectrices*, p. 58.

[32] Damousi, 'Female factory inspectors', pp. 169–88, on p. 183.

We worked a nine hour day but it was divided in a strange way. We started working at eight in the morning, in the afternoon there was a lunch break of two hours from one to three and then we continued working until seven. For us there was no curtailing of the time even though according to the law we were not allowed to work more than seven hours per day. Sometimes we had to do overtime, even until ten or eleven at night. That was not nice as most of us lived far away. For the same reason the two hour lunch was impractical, it was impossible to go all the way home so we bought milk and a bun from the shop. After lunch we played in the paper store in the cellar.[33]

Sweating and the textile trade

One of the arguments put forward about the need for female inspectors was related to the problems observed in the garment manufacturing sector. Although it was in line with Victorian ideology that if married women had to work they should preferably be doing it in their homes, by the second half of the nineteenth century it had become abundantly clear that garment work, both in workshops and particularly in the home, had developed into underpaid slavery.

The textile trade, particularly tailoring, often employed women and children. It was a well-known fact that the working hours were excessive and employers ignored regulations. In London, tailoring the work often continued until 10–11 pm, or even midnight, with sweating, overcrowded workrooms, no ventilation and lack of toilets. The employers were aware of the threat posed by inspectors and doors were locked when they approached. Female workers were hidden in lavatories, bedrooms or kitchens, areas into which the male inspectors could not penetrate.[34] Cooperation was needed with the medical officer and sanitary inspectors to deal with miscarriages both in the East End and the West End. Work was common on Sundays, late at night until midnight with no breaks and no overtime notices; work was also sent home with workers to be finished. The workers were ushered out into the street using back doors. When such ruses failed, the seamstresses claimed to be family members, the 'wives' and daughters of the proprietor, doing private work for a friend. Customers were often to blame: despite the fact that the highlights of the social calendar were not unexpected events, ladies appeared at the last minute and demanded whole wardrobes in an instant. The inspectors pointed out that if granting of overtime for the tailoring trade was stopped, a system collapse was unlikely, but better planning would be necessary. The women and girls were also not paid for the overtime, but it was actually forced out of them for free.[35] The assumptions

---

[33] Salmela-Järvinen, *Alas lyötiin vanha maailma*, pp. 9–10.

[34] Report of the Chief Inspector of Factories and Workshops for the year 1885, PP 1886 XIV, pp. 16–17.

[35] Report of the Chief Inspector of Factories for the year 1895, PP 1896 XIX c 8067, pp. 11–13, 46–8.

were correct: the female inspectors were more capable of entering different kinds of rooms, and were also able to visit female workers in their homes and probe issues. They also used friendly quarters in the press to illuminate issues that the Factory and Workshops Acts did not cover. They were given tips by friends and relations of women who worked inhuman hours and made raids on tailoring businesses.[36]

Although the garment trade was not of the same magnitude in Australia, the issue of 'sweating', i.e. home production of garments as piecework, for pitiful remuneration existed as a socioeconomic problem. Agnes Milne devoted a considerable part of her career to highlighting the evils of the sweating trade. As a trade unionist as well as an inspector, she actively lobbied for the concentration of textile work to factories that could be inspected for compliance with factory legislation. She not only discussed these issues in her reports but also published articles on the subject. The purpose of her engagement was to actively change existing regulations to outlaw practices that had a deleterious effect on workers. Her activity and that of her colleagues actually came to fruition and Australia became the first country in the world to introduce tariffs and a minimum wage for garment workers. The rules were gradually rolled out over the country and covered all Australia by 1908. Through these regulations, the payments for garment work in the home were put on an equal footing with that in factories. The outcome in the long run was a concentration of the work in factories and workshops, which could be more easily monitored.[37]

The problems related to garment manufacture were not unknown in Northern Europe. Already, in 1894, the Statistics Office had conducted a special survey in Copenhagen on the economic and social conditions of seamstresses. Following this example, a similar study charted the seamstresses in the Norwegian capital, Kristiania, in 1906.[38] Two years later, the Female Factory Inspector in Finland published a survey she had conducted on the working conditions of women working in the garment trade, particularly those in workshops. She also published an article in 1913 describing the working conditions and wages of women home workers in a comparative perspective. She demonstrated that in the Nordic countries home work was primarily restricted to the textile

[36] Anderson, *Women in the Factory*, pp. 31, 35–8; Report of the Chief inspector of Factories 1901, PP 1902 XII, p. 153; Report of the Chief Inspector of Factories 1903, PP 1904 X Cd 2139, p. 224; Report of the Chief Inspector of Factories 1911 PP 1912–13 XXV Cd 6239, p. 152.

[37] Damousi, 'Female factory inspectors', pp. 177–9; Vera Hjelt, *Det industriella hemarbetet* (Helsingfors, 1913).

[38] Poul Sveistrup, *Syersker, Et Bidrag til Belysning af de Københavnske Syerskers Livsvillkaar* (Copenhagen, 1894); *Arbeids og Lonningsforhold for Syersker i Kristiania* (Kristiania, 1906), Det statistiske Centralbureau; Hjelt, *Undersökning af nålarbeterskornas*.

sector, whereas box making, chain and nail making and packing of pins as practiced in Britain was virtually unknown. The article was commissioned by the society for the protection of workers and social insurance, where it had been presented and discussed.[39] While the working hours and sometimes cramped conditions of workshops could be far from ideal, neither Finland, Norway or Denmark suffered from the practices of factories handing out tasks to home workers to the extent of Britain and the cities on the European continent. The full time home workers were mostly seamstresses who worked for private customers in their own right, not in a putting out chain. However, both seamstresses in their own homes and those in tailoring workshops did suffer from seasonal overwork and, at other times, shortage of work. The needle trade was notoriously underpaid and women in workshops also saw the engaging of young unskilled workers as a problem. When demand increased, it was also not unknown for employers to send work to be finished in the home. Betzy Kjelsberg collaborated with social reformers and women's groups to collect evidence about actual earnings and to put pressure on legislators to achieve a system of minimum wage for home workers in the textile sector. The project was successful and, by 1918, the garment workers had been brought in under a regulated wage system.[40]

In the early years of female inspection in the Netherlands, a special survey was conducted on sweating in homes. This hidden underpaid work performed by women and children, not only in textile work, but also other parts of the economy, was the subject of a special exhibition in 1909. Thereby, the general public was given insights into a social evil that needed rectifying.[41]

Statistics of the extent of home work in France were collected by Jeanne Bouvier in 1896 and at that point there were indications that the number of registered home workers exceeded that of any other European country.[42] The economic problems of women in the needle trades were subject to a special study from 1900 highlighting the insecurity of employment and depressed wages.[43] The inspectors took it upon themselves to raise awareness about the negative sides of home work in the textile trade and the fact that it was outside the remit of inspections. Loopholes existed, as economic activity in the home had traditionally been seen as a family business employing all family members in various capacities. In the textile sector it had, however, often developed into an enterprise employing outside workers. Sleeping alcoves were also to be found where the girls spent the night. Extra-long days were common, as

---

[39] Vera Hjelt, *Det industriella hemarbetet* (Helsingfors, 1913).
[40] Vera Hjelt, *Undersökning af nalarbeterskornas*, pp. 54, 76–7, 92, 106–7; Folkvord, *Betzy Kjelsberg*, pp. 131–3.
[41] Bousardt, *Onder Vrouwelijke*, pp. 40–3.
[42] Schweitzer, *Les inspectrices*, pp. 63, 74.
[43] d'Haussonville, *Salaires et misères de femmes*.

was sending work home to be finished, and working days of 14 hours or more were detected. The sector suffered from seasonal unemployment on the one hand and excess work at other times. Particularly rich customers tended to demand garments being finished for the next day. Large enterprises used layers of subcontracting, which resulted in grotesque underpayment. It generally encouraged malpractices, like paying per piece instead of hour. Efforts were made to extend the Law of 1892 to make inspections possible.[44] One route was to define localities with machines as not part of the private sphere in 1909. When all efforts seemed futile, the inspectors decided to approach the issue through the regulations of 1904 regarding healthy and hygienic habitations. Finally, in 1915, a number of political factions from the right to the left united in pushing for rules covering work on domestic premises and stipulating unified tariffs based on time instead of piece. In some instances, the solution could only be found through actually timing the work in the presence of an inspector. While the practical introduction of the reform was far from easy, and took some time, the rules resulted in the unification of the pricing in the garment sector. As the issue also affected the price for the manufacture of uniforms for the army, the inspectors sometimes found themselves at logger-heads with local authorities. In addition, there were parties who objected to the introduction of a minimum wage. Because the new regulation extended the inspections into private homes and small units, the need for an increase in the number of inspectors became apparent.[45]

When Florence Kelley started her work as Inspector of Industries and Workplaces in Chicago in 1893, she immediately turned her attention to sweating and the garment trade. In her First Annual Report of the Inspectors of Illinois she recorded how the tailoring shops employed children and demonstrated examples of defects in the system of medical certificates. She found that some doctors issued certificates without even examining the child, never mind finding out the conditions of the workplace or the tasks the child was to perform.

> Another occupation conspicuously injurious to children is the running of buttonhole machines by foot-power. As a typical case: Joseph Poderowsky, aged fourteen years, was found by a deputy inspector running a heavy buttonholer at 204 West Taylor street, in the shop of Michael Freeman. The child was required to report for medical examination and pronounced by the examining physician rachitic and afflicted with a double lateral curvature of the spine. He was ordered discharged, and prohibited from working in any tailor shop. A few days later he was found at the same machine. A warrant was sworn out for the arrest of the employer, under Section Four of the law, but before it could be served the man left the State ...

---

44 Schweitzer, *Les inspectrices*, pp. 59–62.
45 Schweitzer, *Les inspectrices*, pp. 68–73.

From the point of view of the public health the contractor's shop is by no means rendered innocuous by the law as it stands, although much has been accomplished. Thus the requirement of the medical certificate for all minors found running the sewing machine by foot-power has greatly reduced the number of very young girls employed in this way, and the prosecution of contractors has much reduced the number of children in shops ... Although the overcrowding and the employment of children, which has hitherto prevailed in the sweater's shops are now under control of the inspectors, yet the excessive speed and intensity of the work, the use of foot-power and the grinding poverty of these workers, over which the inspectors have no control, these three forces combined still end in consumption as the characteristic disease of the sweater's victims ... It is true that the law pronounces these homes workshops and places them under the supervision of the city Board of Health and the Factory inspectors. But it is unfortunately true that no inspection can guard the children of these families from disease.'[46]

Laundries, hours, accidents, children, institutions

The British factory and workshop law was intended to cover all large places of employment. However, the laundries, with a predominantly female and child workforce, were problematic. The female inspectors gathered information to demonstrate the need for further legislation relating specifically to laundries. Abraham visited laundries in 1893 and provided information to Herbert Asquith, who was active in Parliament and wanted an amendment to the factory acts to include laundries under regulation.

Working hours were often 70–80 hrs/week at irregular times; the conditions were wet and hot. The hot irons, escaping steam and new, dangerous machinery caused a number of accidents. The owners claimed that accidents were due to the carelessness of workers. Deane and Squire had visited hand laundries in Kensington in 1893 as health inspectors, and found the conditions appalling. The English custom of laundry out Monday and back on Sunday affected the structure of the working week and the situation was not improved by the attitude of free enterprise of the owners. If the workers did not like it, they could find other work. When the Chief Inspector, Sprague Oram, set up a special inquiry on working conditions in laundries 1895, the laundry workers greeted the inspectors with pleasure.

As a result of the reports, January 1896 brought an amended factory act, laundries were brought under regulation, bringing in restriction of working hours but no specified time of day (impossible to supervise). However, the

---

[46] First Annual Report of the Factory Inspectors of Illinois for the year ending December 1893, pp. 9, 11–18, 20–1; Second Annual Report of the Factory Inspectors of Illinois for the year ending December 1894, pp. 43–57.

employers now had an obligation to keep records of accidents and to install guards on machinery (which was checked by male and female inspectors).[47] In 1899, a special district for the female inspectorate was instigated in west London. The district included 4000 female workplaces, many of which were laundries.

The female inspectors demanded systematic accident information; they prosecuted where they found no guards in place. As a result, there was a clear reduction in accidents. They also collected statistics correlating the frequency of accidents with long hours of work. In 1907, a new amendment was introduced to the Factory Act, limiting work to 60 hrs/week for women and 30 hrs/week for children.[48] The question of working age and physical fitness in laundry work was also a problem facing the inspectors when tackling the field in Ireland. Here, many laundries were operated by religious organisations using orphans, the mentally ill and unmarried mothers (Magdalene laundries) as workforce. These institutions were excluded from the Factory Acts at the urging of Irish MPs, only voluntary inspections and suggestions for improvement were allowed. The inspectors expressed concern about the health and safety of the inmates, as they encountered little girls of nine years working long hours on a poor diet. In 1907, these institutions were brought under the law and inspections; however, when Ireland became independent, the inspection ceased.[49]

A study of the situation in institutional environments revealed that charitable institutions were not always conspicuous for the welfare of women and girls under their care. In France, the Red Cross ran institutions where young girls were engaged in textile work. The inspectors found that these girls were housed in dormitories sleeping up to 16 people, supervised by nuns in a semi-prison-like environment still in the 1920s.[50]

When the laundries in France were subjected to a special enquiry in 1911–13, other issues were raised. The nature of the problem was, however, different in the sense that the sector was, if not dominated, at least populated to a considerable degree by small home laundries. As these often only employed one person, the owner herself, the hours were not so much in focus as were hygiene issues. The law of 1905 had clear specifications about the handling of dirty and clean linen and the separation of the two. The enquiry revealed that the home laundries were ill equipped for the task and regulations were

[47] Report of the Chief Inspector of Factories 1897, PP 1898 XIV, p. 107.

[48] Anderson, *Women in the Factory*, pp. 32–4.

[49] Hilda Martindale, *From One Generation to Another, 1839–1944: A Book of Memoirs by Hilda Martindale* (London, 1944), pp. 95–6; Report of the Chief inspector of Factories 1908 PP 1909 XXI Cd 4664, pp. 178–9; Anderson, *Women in the Factory*, pp. 33, 123, 141–3.

[50] Schweitzer, *Les inspectrices*, pp. 83–4.

generally not followed. Space was restricted and the laundresses were unable to create the necessary places for storage of laundry waiting to be processed. The spaces for washing also varied considerably.[51]

Shop work and hours

Even the service sector was not free from risks to health and wellbeing. Shop work was particularly plagued by extraordinarily long hours. When the Lady Inspectors in Britain highlighted the fact that rules about legal working hours were flaunted, they were challenged by the employers, who claimed that shop work was not subject to the Factory and Workshop legislation. The reason for seeing themselves as outside the law was that noting was manufactured in a shop, only sold. Rose Squire, who was not afraid of taking on a challenge and who had found women working in shops at midnight packing goods, faced the lawyer of the shopkeepers in court. There in front of the public she proceeded to pack and decorate a frilly hamper of the type expected to be produced in the West End chocolate shops after hours. She was indeed victorious in proving that what the shop assistants were engaged in was productive, time-consuming work.[52] Elsewhere, the inspectors noted that apart from low wages and long hours, the demand that shop workers should stand all day had a detrimental effect on their health. In Australia as well as France, the inspectors called for chairs to sit on. Hjelt even included a design for a flip chair for shops in her report from 1908.[53]

Jenny Markelin made a special survey of female work in the cafes and restaurants of Helsinki, and in 1913, urged increased inspection and control.[54]

Studies of working conditions in the past have tended to see the division line between workers and employers, proletarians and capitalists, not elsewhere. Historical reality is not always as clear cut and 'sisterhood' has not in every case been in evidence even between working women. Because of the early female vote in Finland, and the presence of women representing socialist parties, some conflicts were aired in the political arena with women's voices.

A survey commissioned by the Industrial Board in 1907 had revealed that not only was a 10-hour day normal in shop work, but sometimes it extended to 12 hours or more, and working on Sundays was normal. There were some

51 Schweitzer, *Les inspectrices*, p. 82.

52 Rose E. Squire, *Thirty Years in the Public Service: An Industrial Retrospect* (London, 1927), pp. 67–8, 72–3.

53 Damousi, 'Female factory inspectors', p. 182; Schweitzer, *Les inspectrices*, pp. 77–8; Hjelt, *Berättelse 1908*, p. 143.

54 Jenny Markelin-Svensson, 'Undersökning rörande arbetsförhållandena i restauranger och hotel, matserveringar samt kafeer i Helsingfors', *Arbetsstatistisk Tidskrift 1914*, pp. 275–302.

Figure 5   In the long-running discussion about not forcing shop assistants to stand
all day, the employers stated that fitting chairs behind a shop counter was not feasible.
To counter the argument Vera Hjelt designed a flip chair which would easily fit into
the space and be flipped up when not in use. Vera Hjelt, *Inspection Report* 1908.

differences between town and countryside, but in general, the hours were
bad, and not in line with existing regulations in other fields.[55] Therefore, a
committee was appointed to draw up suggestions for improvement of the
working conditions of shop assistants. In the committee proposal, shops were
to be subject to existing legislation as to working hours and, therefore, Sunday
work was to be abolished. This proposal was vehemently opposed by the
female Socialist delegate in Parliament, Hilja Parssinen. As a representative
of working women, she insisted on the need to be able to buy fresh bread and
milk on Sundays. The Union of Shop Workers had already, in 1901, asked for
a 12-hour day, and by 1905, the demand was set at 11 hours. Considering that
the labour unions were clamouring for an 8-hour day at this point in time, the

[55] G.R. Snellman, *Tutkimus Suomen Konttori-ja kauppa-apulaisten oloista*
(Helsinki, 1909).

situation was far from equal. Even in administrative circles, it was acknowledged that certain groups in society were lagging behind, which is why the survey had been conducted. The outcome of the debates in Parliament and the newspaper debate was that, although the working hours in shop work were streamlined with existing regulations, those working in food shops selling milk and bread had to work on Sunday mornings.[56]

Not only women and children

Female inspectors and occupational hazards, lead poisoning

When women appeared in the inspection arena, they were faced with a gigantic task. Factory legislation was often ambiguous, and workers, particularly female workers, lived in fear of the sack if they voiced complaints. In addition to this, there was obstruction by male colleagues in the provinces.[57] In Britain, some of these issues converged in the case of the fight against lead poisoning, an illness connected with work in pottery factories.

In china scouring, lead dust is released into the air and gets stuck on clothes, in hair on hands and, therefore, on uncovered food, drink, etc. The disease called 'potters rot' attacked the respiratory organs, causing chest pain and eventually ending life. In addition, the painters and dippers suffered from 'plumbism' (lead poisoning) through absorbing lead through the skin, causing paralysis, blindness, nausea, pain, miscarriages and eventually, death. Pottery workers rarely lived to an old age. No compensation was given to pottery workers for illness or death before 1906. Despite proof to the contrary, manufacturers considered it impossible to replace lead with other materials. They blamed the workers for being careless, for not washing themselves and having unhealthy habits and, thereby, endangering their own health. The local inspectors in Staffordshire, Bevan and Knyvett, supported the views of the factory owners in a report from 1892.[58]

A year after the female inspectorate was instituted, Lucy Deane set about inspecting the potteries in Stoke (1894) and in her report she highlighted a series of shortcomings. In addition, she pointed out that, in France, regulations had been imposed preventing the use of children and young people under the age of 18 in work involving lead. After a study of the report and information from

[56] Marjaliisa Hentilä, *Keikkavaaka ja kousikka, Kaupan työ ja tekijät 1800-luvulta itsepalveluaikaan* (Helsinki, 1999), pp. 134–5, 137–9.

[57] Report of the Chief inspector of Factories 1908 PP 1909 XXI Cd 4664, pp. 178–9; Anderson, *Women in the Factory*, pp. 33, 123; McFeeley, *Lady Inspectors*, pp. 46–7, 60–1.

[58] Anderson, *Women in the Factory*, pp. 103–5; Report by the Chief Inspector of Factories for the year 1893, PP 1894 XXI Report 1892, pp. 27–30.

the inspections, the Home Secretary issued special rules specifying ventilation and sanitary measures in potteries. The rules were not positively received and the manufacturers considered them undue interference in economic activity from the government. In 1897, the Chief Inspector of factories, Whitelegge, considered it of some importance to do a follow up and sent Paterson and Deane for an intensive investigation to the potteries in the spring. The aim was to produce a report on occupations and symptoms of illness by the end of year. The results were not encouraging, as no improvement in the health and hygiene situation could be seen. The view of the local inspector, J.H. Walmisley, was that the potters' grievances were 'all rot' and the new rules a dead letter.[59]

Armed with the new set of data, Lord Asquith and other Liberals put forward the need for an extension of the Employers Liability Bill, and the institution of a permanent position of Female Inspector in Stoke. The Conservative Home Secretary, White Ridley, resisted such an extension.[60] District Inspector J.H. Walmisley in Stoke on Trent, previously an engineer and works manger in the potteries, agreed with the manufacturers and considered that the grievances of workers in connection with lead poisoning 'was all rot'.

In 1898, the lead poisonings were aired in court in London. The aim was to prove that the death of a former pottery worker had been caused by lead poisoning. When called to participate in the court hearing in July, Walmisley made excuses for not coming down to London. When the case was postponed and he finally came, he did not bring the documents relating to the inspections of the factory where the deceased had worked. The Home office did not allow inspector Lucy Deane to participate until after pressure from the coroner. She testified about the conditions in the factory on her visits. Medical specialists and other witnesses demonstrated that the deceased, Mr. Mumford, was a sober man and, therefore, lead poisoning was the most likely explanation for his symptoms and death.[61]

Although scientific specialists, like Dr Thomas Oliver who had made extensive research on lead and health of workers, pointed out in a report that lead could be replaced for glazes, but the pottery owners refused to consider making changes to the manufacturing process. When a petition was sent from the potteries and a deputation of disabled pottery workers approached the Home Office, the petition was ridiculed and the deputation was not well received. However, the Chief Inspector, Whitelegge, was a medical man and despite

[59] Report of the Chief Inspector of Factories 1897, PP 1898 XIV, pp. 100–2; McFeeley, *Lady Inspectors*, pp. 65–6.

[60] British Parliamentary Papers, Parliamentary Debates, fourth series, volume 51 (1897), col. 1156–7.

[61] McFeeley, *Lady Inspectors*, pp. 70–1.

the unwillingness of the ruling Conservative Party to make improvements in the lead poisoning issue, the campaign persisted. The Female Inspectors, Anderson and Dean, were sent to the potteries by Whitelegge in early 1900 to make a detailed report. They found cases of poisoning, illness, carelessness and lack of cleanliness in the factories. These new efforts resulted in the introduction of new special rules for working with lead in the autumn of 1900. The factory owners protested and, as a counter move, prevented visits from the female inspectors and withheld work registers. In November 1901, a trial period for the new rules began and in 1904, Hilda Martindale was appointed Inspector to be stationed in Staffordshire. Both the local inspector and the local MP were furious, but unable to change the decision and, in 1906, the Employers Liability Bill was extended to include poisoning in the workplace. Although the efforts to demonstrate the connection between toxic substances and industrial disease were eventually successful in china manufacturing, the work was far from finished.[62]

The inspectors in other countries also began including questions of poisons like lead and phosphorous in their reporting on health and hygiene.[63] Questions were raised about the ability to prove the connection between work in unhealthy conditions and industrial disease. This was particularly problematic when employers got rid of workers who were ill and by the time the condition was medically established the worker already had another occupation.[64]

As there were concerns about the possible health implications of rag picking, a special survey was conducted in Finland in 1908, with emphasis on types of illness found in this occupational group. A high frequency of 'rag picker's fever' (nausea, fever, sense of discomfort) during the first year or months of working was documented. The illness was, however, neither recurring nor of particularly long duration (from one to seven days; in some cases, up to two weeks). It was suggested that some kind of immunity was formed. Other diseases, especially of the contagious kind, were rare. It was suggested that the origin of the rag material, in combination with it being stored for a year or more (often including winter) might have an effect on the survival of cholera bacteria and others that had been documented in other countries. The vast majority of workers, 68 per cent, claimed to be in good health, while 24 per cent stated themselves to be in fairly good health. The women were mainly adult and a sizeable proportion in their 50s or 60s. The work was badly paid and had low status but very flexible working hours. The inspector recommended improvements in ventilation and devices to extract

[62] Martindale, *From One Generation to Another*, p. 84; McFeeley, *Lady Inspectors*, pp. 72–3; Anderson, *Women in the Factory*, pp. 106–7.

[63] Bousardt, *Onder Vrouwelijke*, p. 44.

[64] Hjelt, *Berättelse 1906*, pp. 192–3.

all dust and textile particles. She also underlined the need for good washing facilities and a total ban on eating in the workrooms.[65]

Occupational hazards, accidents and prevention

The fight for the protection of the potters from poisons revealed the need not to restrict the activity of the female inspectors only to women and children. While these two groups remained the main focus, overstepping boundaries became common or even the norm in some countries.

When the second Female Inspector in Denmark, Julie Arenholt, was appointed and her remit was to be the bakeries in Copenhagen, a male-dominated sector, this was hailed as a victory by feminist organisations.[66] A closer look at the activity of some of the female inspectors reveals, however, that the welfare of all workers was not outside their agenda. Betzy Kjelsberg inspected work in mines, not just the sorting on the surface, when she visited mining communities. Likewise, she travelled to logging camps, not just to talk with the female cooks, but with all the workers. As a consequence, she was approached with problems not only by female but also by male workers.[67]

While anything related to technical issues was, in many countries, seen as the prerogative of male inspectors, the introduction of machinery into laundries, a female territory, created a dilemma. At the time, Adelaide Anderson pointed out that the mechanisation of the laundries brought in machines unfamiliar to the male inspectors as well as to their female counterparts and the fencing, to prevent occupational hazards, could as well be checked by a woman as by a man.[68]

Kjelsberg also took the initiative in raising awareness about the defective sums paid to women who had lost the use of, or perhaps altogether lost, a limb in an industrial accident. Equally, Hjelt pointed out in her reports how 60 per cent of normal earnings were hardly enough to keep a woman after an accident.[69]

Kjelsberg worked hard to make sure that the Great National Exhibition of Norway in 1914 would include a section about the dangers posed to workers in factories and workshops, and installations that could promote their health. During trips to Germany and Sweden, she had familiarized herself with information about dangers and protective devices. In Dresden, she had been particularly impressed by a demonstration of the dangers of dust particles and

[65] Vera Hjelt, *Yrkessjukdomsstatistik I, Lumparbeterskorna i Finland, Meddelanden fran industristyrelsen* (Helsingfors, 1909), pp. 184–9, 198–201.

[66] *Kvinden og samfundet* 26:21 (1910), pp. 239–40.

[67] Folkvord, *Betzy Kjelsberg*, pp. 118–22.

[68] Anderson, *Women in the Factory*, p. 141; *Kvinden og samfundet* 20:24 (1904), pp. 197–8.

[69] Folkvord, *Betzy Kjelsberg*, p. 129; Hjelt, Vera, *Berättelse 1903*, pp. 235–6.

the importance of fans to remove these. In addition to mechanical protection devices, she also managed to include the modern, self-threading textile weaving machine. This eliminated the need for workers to suck the cotton thread with their mouths, whereby they not only inhaled fibres but could also spread tuberculosis. This particular part of the exhibition attracted comments in the press and two years later a law was passed banning the use of machines necessitating the sucking of the thread by the worker.[70] The elimination of this practice by modernising the machinery had also been on the agenda in the reports by Hjelt in Finland. In addition she had a lot to say about the dangers posed to the health of female workers because of the fashion of shawls, aprons with bows at the back, headscarves and unpinned hair. She highlighted the connection between such modes of dress and terrible accidents, and promoted plain work clothes, including flat caps and trousers.[71]

Hjelt, just like Kjelsberg, studied avidly the industrial innovations that helped to minimize accidents by installing protective devices and emergency brakes. She often had a very direct and practical attitude to promoting health protection. When women in Finnish industry working with toxic substances and in areas filled with dust and textile fibres refused to wear protective mesh masks, because they looked like dog's muzzles, Hjelt designed one of muslin strips padded with cotton wool that looked less foul, and was cheap and easy to wash.[72] Her continuing interest in technology and the safety in the workplace, boosted by trips to the continent, particularly Germany, inspired her to set up a safety exhibition, which circulated around the country. When she retired from the Inspectorate and the exhibition was awarded state funding, it was developed into a safety museum. For the remainder of her life she dedicated herself to workplace safety and innovation. She held the post of Curator from 1921, developed the museum, wrote pamphlets and books and lectured until the age of 74.[73]

Work, skill and earnings

Vera Hjelt conducted several surveys on working and living conditions during her time as inspector. As part of these and on her inspection rounds she encountered a number of complaints related to the undercutting of wages through the employment of young, unskilled workers, a problem already raised by the

---

[70] Folkvord, *Betzy Kjelsberg*, pp. 169–72.
[71] Hjelt, *Berättelse 1905*, pp. 94–6.
[72] Hjelt, *Berättelse 1908*, pp. 142–3.
[73] Vera Hjelt, *Berättelse afgifven af kvinnliga yrkesinspektören i Helsingfors, Tammerfors och Uleaborgs distrikt för 1909 jamte reseberättelse*, pp. 8–9; Forelius, 'Tyovaensuojelu'; Hjelt, *Arbetsskydd*.

women's unions in 1900. In her report from 1911, she made an appeal to the Industrial Board to act and improve the opportunities for young women to improve their earning capacity and enhance the skill levels in female work:

> Contemporary economic development has created a situation making it necessary for women to participate in productive work. The industry which has relieved women of many domestic tasks, now provides work in many fields. A better education would however, give access to better earnings. The same education for girls as for boys would place them on equal footing when competing for better paid employment instead of less competent workers accepting lower pay replacing those with better education. Therefore the answer of society should be: the same vocational training for girls and boys with apprenticeships where these are necessary. This should be in the interest of everybody and would prevent workplaces being filled with incompetent people who depress wages. The correctness of this supposition is evidenced by the situation in printing where the same education and the same wages have been applied to males and females for a long time and there is no evidence of workplaces being flooded by women accepting lower pay. Naturally there will always be fields particularly suited to women or to men. At times of unemployment, which unfortunately are experienced also by our country, it is necessary to explore new fields and new opportunities. For example, in the countryside there is a shortage of women specialising in many types of crafts and the male craftsmen are often not attracted by rural areas ...'[74]

Conclusion

The field of activity for the first generations of female factory inspectors was wide and absorbing. They were also not allowed to forget that they, as women, represented an anomaly. When Grace Neill came to her office in the Government building in Wellington she had to make her entry either before or after the men who worked there, not at the same time.[75]

The thing that is fairly evident is that, even though they had to engage in fierce battles, they did represent something new and different. The old view had been that 'Factory inspecting requires activity and acumen and the stern authority of a man to enforce obedience to his interrogatories'. The stern authoritarian approach was in many cases replaced by diplomacy and efforts to convince rather than to give orders. As the fines that could be imposed were in many cases pitiful, in comparison with the money that could be made by breaking rules, discussion could be more fruitful. The work to introduce improvements and changes like the provision of soap and water might also

[74] Vera Hjelt, *Berättelse afgifven af kvinnliga yrkesinspektören i Finland för år 1911*, pp. 36–7; Ensimmaisen, *yleisen työläisnaisten.*

[75] Margaret Tennant, 'Neill, Elizabeth Grace', *Dictionary of New Zealand Biography*-Te Ara, https://teara.govt.nz/en/biographies/2n5/neill-elizabeth-grace.

be met more positively when the suggestion came from a woman. In some cases, however, the clashes were of considerable magnitude and could result in the loss not only of the battle but the war.

Table 7.2   Number of factory and workshop inspectors in France 1893.

Locality	Female	Male
Paris	10	15
Chateauroux	0	5
Dijon	0	5
Bar-le Duc	0	7
Lille	1	8
Rouen	0	6
Nantes	1	4
Bordeaux	1	4
Toulouse	0	5
Marseille	1	7
Lyon	1	8
Total	15	74

Source: Sylvie Schweitzer, *Les inspectrices du travail 1878–1974* (Rennes, 2016), p. 157.

Table 7.3   Prosecutions for breaching the factory and workshops acts, Britain 1901.

Faulty registers of children, overtime, accidents, poisoning	439	Children	
Notices not posted	158	No fitness, certificate	70
Obstruction of inspector	8	Employment at night, before or after legal hours	87
Dangerous machinery not fenced	198	In prohibited industry, cleaning machinery	12
Blocked fire escape or doors	3	Young person	
Cleanliness, ventilation, crowding	62	Working before or after hours, at night, on Sunday, at mealtime	1015
Failure to supply information	72	Without certificate	465

Women working at illegal times	1058	Cleaning machinery in motion, in prohibited industry	12
Breaking of dangerous trades rules	44	Parental obligations, school, certificates	16
Truck	29	Other	15

Source: Report of the Chief Inspector of Factories 1901, PP 1902 XII, pp. 36–43.

Table 7.4   Number of male and female inspectors and prosecutions, Britain, selected years 1895–1911.

Year	Total inspectors	Female inspectors	Prosecutions male inspectors	Prosecutions female inspectors
1895	100	4	3188	128
1896	110	5	3341	74
1899	134	7	3574	230
1900	137	7	3287	208
1901	138	8	3770	265
1906	163	12	4155	229
1910	200	18	3644	410
1911	200	18	4449	455

Sources: Report of the Chief Inspector of Factories 1904, PP 1905 X Cd 2569, pp. 885–9; Report of the Chief inspector of Factories 1906 XV, p. 916; Report of the Chief Inspector of Factories 1911 PP 1912–13 XXV Cd 6239, pp. 288, 342–5.

8

Class, Gender and Communication

Nondescript combatant against, drink, poverty, factory owners and the medical profession[1]

Trust and mistrust

Complaints received, complaints resolved

Although there had been activity among working women and female unions to achieve the employment of female inspectors, there was not an immediate coming together when the female inspectors commenced their work. There were even instances when the women sided with employers, regarding the inspectors as their enemies. During the early years, in 1896, there was even an example of a woman in Leeds (Annie Michell) taking Adelaide Anderson to court for physical assault, claiming that the Inspector had grabbed and shaken her when she did not answer questions. The outcome was in favour of the Inspector, as the court could clearly see that the small and timid Inspector was unlikely to form a physical threat to a woman the size of her accuser. The case brought bad publicity, however.[2] Adelaide Anderson assessed the situation in the early years as one where the women had become so used to being ignored and misused that they had slid into lethargy, expecting no improvement. Her view was that only through activity and publicising that activity could the inspectors convince the female workers that the situation could change.[3]

As conversations regarding problems were unlikely in the presence of the employer or the foreman, confidential visits in women's homes would create better chances of communication.[4]

It would seem that Anderson was right. When the newspapers reported on prosecutions, as the appearance of the 'Lady Inspectors' in court was a novelty, the notion that change was possible did penetrate the awareness of at least some women. There was an increase in the number of complaints by female workers, or their families, received by the female inspectors, doubling in 1896

---

1 Margaret Tennant, Grace Neill's description of herself.
2 McFeeley, *Lady Inspectors*, pp. 53–4.
3 Anderson, *Women in the Factory*, pp. 37, 41–2.
4 Anderson, *Women in the Factory*, pp. 24, 35, 45–7.

(to 381) in comparison with the previous year. With an increasing number of complaints also came an increasing number of prosecutions.[5]

The creation of posts fixed to a specific locality cut down on time used for travel and increased the opportunities of contact with the women in the workplaces and outside. In 1913, the women's branch of the inspectorate visited nearly 7000 factories and 4000 workshops, investigated 700 accidents, conducted 373 prosecutions and received 2014 complaints. As a consequence, by 1913, there was no time anymore for special investigations, because all the time of the female inspectors was taken up by investigating complaints brought to them, primarily by the workers themselves. By this time, the right to independent work had been reinstated for more than 10 years thanks to the diligence and perseverance of Anderson.[6]

Table 8.1   Female inspections, prosecutions and complaints, Britain 1895–1914.

Year	Female inspector prosecutions	Convictions	Sanitary defects	Complaints	Female visits
1895	128	125	425	198	
1896	74	76	669	381	
1897	92	86	286	426	3687
1898	207	203	291	477	5261
1899	230	218	273	494	5427
1900	208	195	525	644	5956
1901	265	255	529	726	6833
1904	206	182	781	955	8395
1905	280	262	771		8796
1906	229	218	816		10,335
1908			999	1250	7941
1910	410	385		2093	11,658
1911	455	444		2025	11,291
1913	373			2014	11,000
1914				1812	

Sources: Report of the Chief Inspector of Factories 1904, PP 1905 X Cd 2569, pp. 885–9; Report of the Chief inspector of Factories 1906 XV, p. 916; Report of the Chief Inspector of Factories 1911 PP 1912–13 XXV Cd 6239, pp. 288, 342–5; Annual Report of the Chief inspector of Factories 1914–16 XXI Cd 8051.

---

[5]   McFeeley, *Lady Inspectors*, pp. 17, 51–2.
[6]   McFeeley, *Lady Inspectors*, pp. 113–14; Anderson, *Women in the Factory*, p. 216.

In Germany, the contacts did not always function very well between the female inspectors and the female workers. In Leipzig, Miss Sedelmeyer received only a handful of complaints in her early years and from 1902 she devoted herself to inspecting small laundries and workshops and promoting urban child care. In Berlin, Miss Reichert was hampered by rules making it impossible for her to communicate her findings outside the bureaucracy. Many of the 15 complaints communicated to her in 1900 and the 24 in 1901 were about issues not subject to the factory legislation and, therefore, outside her mandate. The problem was, in many cases, that in fear of losing their jobs, the women preferred to be silent or in some cases lie about the situation in the workplace. Certain inspectors saw the problem in the fact that many female workers were unaware of what protection the law might actually have for them. While the female inspectors themselves, in Germany, suffered from employment insecurity and felt that the restricted power of female inspectors made their work difficult, working women were also hesitant to voice complaints in fear of the sack.[7]

Communication was not always easy elsewhere. Although Florence Kelley made popular speeches at union meetings, she was never successful in gathering the support of the unions for the women who lost income when the eight-hour day was introduced in Chicago. She believed that, ultimately, the eight-hour day would bring more employment opportunities and even if this did mean a cut in earnings in the short term, things would improve. Those who lived on a limited income did not view things in the same light. Some women reacted negatively to their cut in wages because of the shorter working day and joined the employers in criticism of Kelley. She also needed the help of Jane Addams from Hull House in communicating with immigrant families who were unable to understand why she barred their children from workplaces.[8]

Trouble in the north

Not much more than 6 months after Vera Hjelt had commenced her time as an inspector she was faced with troubling times, where her ability to shoulder her task and her solidarity with working women was questioned. She was called to a factory to mediate in a strike. During her first visit the women complained about a forewoman that they said maintained unfair and too strict discipline, set fines and dismissed people. They also complained that a foreman had engaged in untoward physical contact with the workers. When Hjelt asked about the physical contact the replies were evasive. When the foreman was queried, he admitted to having smacked the bottom of one of the women. He was reprimanded and steps were taken to remove the unpopular forewoman. After some time, a new strike had erupted in the factory, and this time the

---

7 Schmitt, *Der Arbeiterinnenschutz*, pp. 137, 148–50.
8 Sklar, *Florence Kelley*, pp. 240, 245–6, 263–4.

local union had become involved. Men in other factories were about to embark on strikes as well, as the foreman was still in employment. The factory stated that they were looking for a replacement and had not yet found one. Some men from the local socialist organisation appeared in the factory with the intention of removing the foreman physically, as he had interfered with the women. By now, the community was on strike and it was spreading to other factories owned by the company. In addition, two women had now signed a document produced by the local socialist organisation stating that they had been raped by the foreman. The strike was spreading and the socialist papers discussed the issue and accused the female inspector of having no interest in the welfare and virtue of the working woman. The foreman had already left – not only the factory but the country – and the company ordered people back to work unless they wanted the sack. Some workers had given their notice in the general confusion and had been replaced. The discussion rolled on in the newspapers for some considerable time. There were multiple attacks on the female inspector, declaring her unsuitable for her job and unsympathetic to working-class women. Her efforts at finding jobs or economic support for the families who were in dire straits, as a consequence of the sackings and notice giving, was never commented on.[9]

The story illuminates some things fairly clearly. Although the female unions had wanted a female inspector, by 1904, when she had been in office but a short time, the female inspector was seen as an outsider, to whom one was unwilling to divulge details of an intimate nature. In the end, it was easier to tell male colleagues who appointed themselves as champions of their class and went to actively remove the transgressor and enticed the union to go on strike in sympathy. Another thing is how avidly the issue was embraced considering that the male unions did little for female wage levels, and only through forming their own organisations were the women usually able to get their voice heard. A still more interesting thing is that the male inspectors present at several stages of the saga never received any criticism or attacks on their competence or character. Hjelt wrote one newspaper reply, explaining her position, and then went on with her work. It would seem that she, like Anderson, realised that only through actions would it be possible to gain the trust of the women she had been appointed to protect

Judging by incidences the following year, she might have been correct. When she engaged in mediating strikes, the communication with the workers had improved considerably.

A strike at the Kushakoff candy factory in Viborg started on 24 April because of a reduction in wages. The factory gave their reason as the rising price of sugar. The women could not fathom why they should be the ones to

9 Hjelt-Cajanus, *Vera Hjelt*, pp. 158–63, 166–71, 188–9.

carry the consequences of the price rise. The new wages had already been in use for 24 days without the workers having been informed.

When I visited the factory on the 1st of May the owner had returned from abroad which had caused delays in negotiations with the workers. Mr Kushakoff was perfectly willing to listen to me. He stated that his intention was not to retain the reduction that had been introduced during his absence. He also promised that the workers would be compensated for the period when they had been subject to the reduction in wages. The other complaints proved to be less relevant and Kushakoff also promised to follow all regulations about termination of employment etc. The conflict could thereby be resolved ...

While in the town I received an application to mediate in a strike, that was about to erupt in the bottle washing plant of a brewery. When meeting with the women I was told that the brewery had employed a person who was to control the quality of their work. The salary cost for this person was to be reclaimed from the workers. They could not see why they should be sponsoring a foreman/woman through their earnings. When making enquiries at the brewery it was stated that the reason for employing an overseer was that when rinsing equipment had been installed the rinsers had been allowed to keep their old salaries in spite of their work being eased by the machines on the condition that the work was to be immaculate. As badly rinsed bottles had been discovered, it was considered justified to employ a person to check the work and deduct the cost from the wage packets of the workers. While admitting that although the brewery might be justified from a superficial point of view I pointed out that somebody employed by the company in whatever capacity could not have their salary paid by the workers. For something on that line to be possible it would have to be included in the work contracts originally signed. As no such contract existed the company agreed to the workers keeping their full remuneration. On the other hand it was underlined that those who after being warned would demonstrate sub-standard work would lose their jobs. Through my intervention the 4 workers who had been dismissed were awarded 14 days wages.'[10]

Both Hjelt and Kjelsberg found it a problem that, when visiting factories, they were taken around by the bosses and foremen and found it difficult to communicate with the workers. To eliminate the problem, Hjelt visited canteens of factories during lunch breaks and also walked workers home to have undisturbed conversations and find out problems. Kjelsberg let it be known that she could be contacted in the evening at her hotel, rather than talk when the women would be overheard. The success of Kjelsberg in convincing the owner to connect their workrooms to the electric grid, where the women

[10] Vera Hjelt, *Berättelse 1905*, pp. 104–6.

had been struggling with oil lamps for years, in one case, and achieving improvement in the living conditions of cooks in mining communities, even though this was not part of her remit, earned Kjelsberg a reputation of being engaged in the problems of workers. As a result, she earned their trust and was repeatedly invited by unions to give talks and advice about improvements of the working environment.[11]

Over the years, Hjelt found that, not only working women, but also their friends and labour organisation representatives started to contact her about their problems. While she engaged herself in disputes and successfully managed to achieve some wage increase, she also took on problems of individuals. The fact that she acquired a chair for a woman with bad legs and moving of old women to lighter duties demonstrates that she did listen and act. As a campaigner for a safer workplace, her engagement in securing accident compensation for victims when there were delays in payment is perhaps not surprising. However, the installation of longer levers suitable for a woman and the installation of separate female WCs bear witness of the discussions between the women on the factory floor and Hjelt.[12]

Maternity leave and support

The question of the working mother and the welfare of infants was one of the contentious issues of the late nineteenth century; an issue that even today remains to some extent unresolved. While some countries have taken a pragmatic view, with crèches and paid maternity leave, others persist with the view that if a woman does not want to choose between work and motherhood she has to solve the problems herself. On the other hand, society insists on the bringing forth and bringing up of healthy generations, and blame and stick is always available for women stepping out of 'their place'.

In the late nineteenth century, the concern about welfare of infants was widespread and, in the view of many, the solution was getting women out of the factory and into the home. This ideology was particularly widespread among the parts of society who knew little about economic hardship. Despite the views of conservative and religious circles in Germany, the social insurance system also included support for women around the time of confinement. Since the 1880s, health insurance paid economic support for the four weeks women were obliged to be out of work. From 1891, maternity leave was extended to six weeks after childbirth and by 1911 the economic support was also extended. However, even in Germany, the economic support was in many cases insufficient and work during the maternity pause did occur. In some factories

---

11 Folkvord, *Betzy Kjelsberg*, pp. 118–23, 126–8; Hjelt, *Berättelse 1908*, pp. 130–1.
12 Vera Hjelt, *Berättelse afgifven af kvinnliga yrkesinspektören i Finland för år 1907* (Helsingfors, 1908), pp. 159–61, 168–9; Hjelt, *Berättelse 1909*, pp. 11–12.

systems were set up by which the factory health insurance paid women an additional sum to make them economically secure during the six weeks of maternity leave. There were even factories that started paying additional support in the early years of the twentieth century to women who pledged not to work for three months after confinement and engage in breast-feeding their babies.[13] Similar support systems were introduced in Austria-Hungary, in Italy and in Norway and Finland. Britain, the Netherlands, Belgium, Spain, Portugal, Switzerland and Sweden had, however, by 1912 made no provisions for economic support of women while preventing them from working for four weeks.[14]

When Anderson acted as an expert consultant in the Inter-Departmental Committee on Physical Deterioration 1903, the issue of childbirth and female work was for obvious reasons the subject of discussion. Anderson, with the help of other female inspectors, made extensive studies of industrial centres, mothers' work and infant mortality. They were able to demonstrate that the reasons for high infant mortality levels were not to be found in work of the mother, but the sanitary and economic conditions. Mining areas were as plagued by child mortality as industrial centres, and these were regions famous for low female employment. Anderson underlined the need not only to restrict the right of new mothers to work, but also to find them some economic support. The committee memorandum underlined prohibition on employment in factories and workshops within four weeks of delivery for women. The committee also only recommended charitable efforts for sustaining the mother economically. Anderson expressed scepticism towards the ability or willingness of charitable institutions to shoulder this responsibility as she had evidence that these institutions turned out the mothers two weeks after delivery, two weeks before they were allowed back into work.[15] In vain, she cited the figures for the reduction of infant mortality after the Mulhouse Alsace maternity fund became operational. This initiative functioned successfully with contributions of employer and employee. From 1904 on, the female inspectors collected evidence on the subject of the economic and social situation of working women after delivery and the welfare of infants. It took seven years before any economic provision was issued (the National Insurance Act 1911).[16] Her former colleague, May Tennant, now married into the group of upper-class civil servants, had no problems in deploring the lack of mothering among the

---

13 Schmitt, *Der Arbeiterinnenschutz*, pp. 210, 215.

14 Jenny Markelin-Svensson, 'Kvinnoskyddslagstiftning och moderskapsforsäkring', *Modern socialpolitik*, Föreningen för arbetarskydd och socialförsäkring I Finland, Band II (Helsingfors, 1912), pp. 13–16.

15 Anderson, *Women in the Factory*, pp. 154–6.

16 Martindale, *Some Victorian Portraits*, pp. 48–50; Anderson, *Women in the Factory*, pp. 157–8.

working classes. She ignored the studies of her former colleagues and went with the popular view that a mother's place is in the home.[17]

The views of Anderson were shared by Betzy Kjelsberg in Norway who did her utmost to mobilise women's organisations to support a proposition for the extension of social legislation to give female workers the right to economic support during the compulsory six weeks off work after delivery.[18]

Likewise, during her career in parliament, Vera Hjelt participated in committee work and worked for the introduction of maternity support:

> Maternity support should be part of health insurance and should be applied in all fields of work. The mandatory pause at the time of confinement is not to be extended beyond the time that is covered by the health and maternity insurance.[19]

Night work

One of the issues that divided the feminists and the socialists was the night work question. The feminists insisted on equal rights and restrictions for all. The Labour movement and the International Socialist Conferences specifically wanted protection for women in restricting hours and a ban on night work. In this question, they were on equal lines with conservative and religious political powers and organisations. As mothers and potential mothers, women were to be protected.

The early labour laws focused on the protection of women and children and the existence of these rules were part of the process that created the female inspectorate. Interestingly enough this issue came to be one that drew a dividing line between female inspectors in different countries and also was the cause of conflicts and division.

While the restrictions on female hours were seen as a positive and necessary improvement in Britain and the USA, the definition of night work and its consequences were subject to criticism in some other countries, particularly those with a shorter history of industrial work. Florence Kelley was one of the very vocal spokeswomen for shorter hours for women and a ban on night work. Still, in 1929, she devoted a long section to the matter in her article in 'Labor legislation for women and its effects on earnings and conditions of labor', and categorically denied that restrictions had any effect on the employment opportunities of women.[20]

---

[17] Anderson, *Women in the Factory*, pp. 156–8; Tennant, 'Infantile mortality', pp. 87–119, on pp. 88–9, 95–105.

[18] Folkvord, *Betzy Kjelsberg*, pp. 146–51.

[19] Statement by Hjelt in Parliament 1909; Hjelt-Cajanus, *Vera Hjelt*, pp. 229–30; *Kvinden og samfundet*, 24:18 (1908), p. 232.

[20] Florence Kelley and Marguerite Marsh, 'Labor Legislation for Women and Its

However, in Germany, it would seem that women in some sectors were affected, particularly in printing and industries with seasonal intensity like sugar beet factories. The ban on female night work from the 1890s in Germany resulted in women losing their jobs in the sugar industry and in printing. Women who were legislated out of the workforce wrote letters to the authorities pleading for easing of the rules because of the effect they had on their personal circumstances. Some employers in the printing sector attempted to argue that replacing women with men and boys affected the quality of the work. They also underlined that the workforce was well supervised and that any man who would interfere with the women would lose his position. The arguments had little effect.[21] The curtailing of the working week had in many cases the effect that while men finished their working day early on Saturday, women then went to work, as they were engaged in cleaning jobs after they had lost their normal employment. Therefore, their ability to perform motherly duties and provide the cosy home, envisaged by some, deteriorated rather than improved.[22]

In her report from 1905, Hjelt highlighted the resistance among women, particularly in the textile sector, against any proposal to 'curtail the female freedom to work'. She underlined the need to consult working women before making radial changes to legislation. She also spoke out against the proposal in parliament:

> The legislation about night work in industry should not be related to the sex of the employees, but geared to the type of industry and job description. It should be the same for all grown up workers whether male or female. Particular rules should be introduced about work around machines and continuing work processes. The legislation about protection of workers should not be an issue related to emotions but judged in relation to industrial knowledge. We should scrutinise the possible boundaries for improvement of working life within different fields and this should apply equally to adult men and women. We could take example from the law of 1908 about bakeries whereby the ban on night work is the same for men and women working in Finnish bakeries.[23]

At the initiative of Hjelt, a grant was acquired to make a special enquiry about working women, night work, their socioeconomic conditions and attitude towards a potential ban on night work for women. Employers were

---

Effects on Earnings and Conditions of Labor, *The Annals of the American Academy of Political and Social Science* vol. 143 (1929), pp. 286–300.

21 Schmitt, *Der Arbeiterinnenschutz*, pp. 152, 161–2, 170, 173.

22 Schmitt, *Der Arbeiterinnenschutz*, p. 203.

23 Hjelt, *Berättelse 1905*, pp. 83–4; Hjelt-Cajanus, *Vera Hjelt*, p. 229; Jenny Markelin-Svensson, 'Kvinnoskyddslagstiftning', pp. 11–13.

also approached to find out what their reactions would be as far as female employment was concerned if such a ban was implemented. The results showed that 69 per cent of the female workers were against a ban and the employers stated that the result of such a ban would be a shrinkage of the female part of the labour force. The proposal was overturned and the ban was not implemented. As the socialist organisations wanted the ban, Hjelt was subject to abuse in the labour press. However, when the rule was brought in, many women who were able to continue working expressed their gratitude.[24]

At more or less the same time, a proposal was put forward in Norway for the introduction of a ban on female work at night. When Kjelsberg visited the mining districts where women worked in the sorting sector, they approached her to make clear their resistance to the curtailing of the female working day. In general, the level of female night work in Norway was not very high but particularly women who worked in cleaning resisted as they were able to work when the husband was at home. Rather night work than starvation was their slogan. Kjelsberg took it upon herself to be the spokesperson for the women she had met and talked with. The proposal for a ban on female night work was defeated in parliament in 1909.[25]

In Denmark, the Female Inspectorate was divided on the night work issue. On the one hand, Julie Arenholt and the Female Printing Workers Union were against it, while Ragna Schou sided with the International Labour Unions in wanting to introduce a ban. The women's organisations announced with joy the successful news from Finland that the ban had been avoided under the heading 'The freedom of women to work'.

The women of the Printer's Union arranged a large protest meeting in Copenhagen to make their views clear. They were unwilling to experience the fate of their German sisters in becoming cleaners instead of trained professionals in the printing sector. Although the debate continued for some time and again highlighted a clash with the views of the International Labour Unions, in Denmark, as in Finland and Norway, the proposal was never accepted. It would seem that the fears were well founded. In Sweden, where the ban was implemented in 1911, nearly a thousand women had lost their jobs in printing and food processing within 12 months and the printing sector closed its training to women.[26]

---

[24] Hultin, *Yötyöntekijättäret*; *Kvinden og samfundet* 26:6, pp. 59–60.

[25] Folkvord, *Betzy Kjelsberg*, pp. 117–18.

[26] Ravn, 'Julie Arenholt'; Ravn, '"Lagging far behind"', pp. 210–33, on pp. 220–1; Schmitz, *Kvinnor, Kamrater*, pp. 68–9; Neergaard, Louise, 'Fabrikslovens Revision', *Kvinden of Samfundet* 3:27 (15.2 1911), pp. 24–5.

External and internal activity

The female inspectors did not only work to uphold the law but some of them actively worked to change existing regulations. Where it was possible, they used formal, where not sometimes informal, channels.

In 1903, Anderson sat in the Physical Deterioration Committee and voiced the need for economic support for new mothers. She and her colleagues also worked within political circles outside the Inspectorate to improve and extend the labour laws. After her retirement she was connected to international organisations trying to highlight the issue of child labour in China and in Egypt.[27]

In Australia and New Zealand, the female inspectors used lobbying and writing articles in the press to improve the conditions of female workers and achieve legislative changes. They also collaborated with suffrage organisations and unions.[28] Margaret Cuthbertson was also President of the Victorian Women's Public Service Association and engaged in the work of the Free Kindergarten Union. After her retirement she devoted her time to educational organisations and served on the board of several hospitals.[29]

When Florence Kelley lost her job as Factory Inspector of Illinois, she continued her activity in other organisations. While in between employment, she contributed with commissioned articles for the *Archiv für Soziale Gesetzgebung und Statistik* (Archive for Social Legislation and Statistics), a journal founded by Heinrich Braun (the husband of the famous feminist Lily Braun). The journal had its ideological home in social democratic thinking, that state-led social reform was the road towards social justice. Kelley provided articles on female factory inspection, the Supreme Court and the working day, child labour, the sweating system, free public libraries, homework in the USA, the Italians in Chicago and factory inspection in New York. She was a founder member of the National Consumers League and acted as Director from 1899 to 1932. The League pursued a campaign for the welfare of working women. The organisation aimed at the introduction of a minimum wage and a limit on working hours for women and children. As the efforts had been thwarted through the courts in Chicago and later in New York, they engaged one of the best lawyers, Lois Brandeis, to conduct their case in the US Supreme Court in 1907.[30] The ongoing efforts to improve the conditions of working women and children and the continuous battle in the courts were also discussed by

[27] Martindale, *Some Victorian Portraits*, pp. 48–50; Anderson, *Women in the Factory*, p. 155.

[28] Nolan and Harper, 'Morison, Harriet'; Melanie Nolan, 'Hawthorne, Margaret', *Dictionary of New Zealand Biography* Te Ara, https://teara.govt.nz/en/biographies; Daniels, 'Annie Jane Duncan'; Damousi, 'Female factory inspectors', p. 173.

[29] Hyslop, 'Cuthbertson Margaret Gardiner'; Damousi, 'Female factory inspectors', p. 170.

[30] https://florencekelley.northwestern.edu.

Kelley in an article published three years before her death, 'Labor legislation for women and its effects on earnings and conditions of labor'.[31]

In France, the inspectors inventively used new interpretations of existing legislation as well as promoting changes and extensions of existing law. Aline Valette was instrumental in the formation of a union for teachers and later joined the Union of Journalists. She was also one of the first women to be accepted onto the board of the Socialist Worker's Party where she was active in the 1890s. She did not, however, turn her back on the conditions of workers, but believed that the issues should be tackled outside the inspection system.[32]

Equally, Aldona Sochacrewska-Juillerat (1860–1945) poured her energy into the *Ligue social des acheteurs,* an organisation with aims not unlike those of the National Consumers League spearheaded by Florence Kelley. Although Aldona Juillerat functioned as an inspector until the age of 50 she was not oblivious to the shortcomings of the inspection system. She, like to some extent Agnes Milne in Australia, wanted to bring the problems to the attention of a wider public by publishing her misgivings in the article '*L'inspection du travail*' (1907), where she questioned the effectiveness of the system, among other things because of the small number of inspectors in a massive field.[33]

During her years in parliament, Hjelt directly tried to influence political decisions, for example the working day, youth and maternity issues. She raised the questions of work time and breaks, and the need for a proper annual holiday. She moved for the setting up of separate institutions for young offenders, the creation of vocational education and apprenticeships and mandatory female health inspectors in urban areas. She also crossed party lines and collaborated with women from other parties.[34]

Her colleague Jenny Markelin (Industrial Inspector 1908) gave talks and published in the journal of the Organisation for the Protection of Workers and Social Insurance, among other things about the protection of women and maternity insurance (1912) and social problems in certain female occupations (1915). In 1913, Markelin transferred to the municipality of Helsinki to inspect and train inspectors. When the department for social work was founded in 1918 she was appointed the first female Chief Inspector and later she attained an Assistant Chief Inspector-ship at the Ministry of Social Work where she remained active until her death in 1929.[35]

[31] Kelley and Marsh, 'Labor legislation for women', pp. 286–300.

[32] Justinien Raymond, 'Valette Aline (née Goudeman Alphonsine, Eulalie)', https://maitron.fr/spip.php?article86187; Schweitzer, *Les inspectrices*, pp. 34–5.

[33] Schweitzer, *Les inspectrices*, pp. 37–8; http://aehit.fr.

[34] Hjelt-Cajanus, *Vera Hjelt*, pp. 224–30; Hjelt, *Berättelse 1908*.

[35] Kuusanmäki, 'Markelin-Svensson, Jenny', pp. 556–8; Jenny, Markelin-Svensson, 'Om communal yrkesinspektion', Föreningen för arbetarskydd och socialförsäkring i Finland, Band IV, häft 4 (Helsingfors, 1916); Jenny, Markelin-Svensson, 'Sociala

Betzy Kjelsberg devoted her activity in local government and party politics to the welfare of women, the protection of children, nutrition, hygiene and education. She worked hard to get the backing of feminist organisations for maternity leave and strived to find common ground between working women and the middle classes. In her campaigning for sobriety she connected with both groups.

The first three female inspectors in Denmark were active in political and feminist organisations. Ragna Schou stood close to the National and International Labour Union movement. Julie Arenholt was the Chair of the women's organisation *Dansk Kvindesamfund* from 1918 to 1921; she also sat on the board of the organisation for female suffrage and was the editor of its journal. When women in Denmark were allowed to stand for local councils in 1909, Arenholt was elected as a representative of the leftist party (*Det Radicale Venstre*). She acted as a local councillor from 1909 to 1912 and again from 1913 to 1917. The fact that she had a degree in engineering resulted in her being consulted continuously on technological issues. During the years of WWI she was called to work in a government commission on economic and household questions.[36]

Conclusion

One of the main reasons for employing female factory inspectors was that they would be better suited to communicate with women. Several of the female inspectors found that a contact with working women could not be immediately established. However, over time, the opinion of Neill and Hawthorne in New Zealand, Duncan in Australia, Anderson in Britain, Kjelsberg in Norway and Hjelt in Finland was that communication had been established and complaints were communicated. They believed that, as women, their ability to understand the problems were better.

Kelley, on the other hand, while acknowledging that female inspectors were well suited to communicate problems to women's organisations, considered that their skills in talking to working women were no better than those of a man. The key issue in her opinion was whether the person had a union background. Her own deputies were both men and women but many of them had union ties.[37] To what extent she was correct is difficult to say. The working-class and union background of some of the inspectors in NZ made

---

missförhållanden inom särskilda kvinnoyrken', Föredrag och diskussioner Föreningen för arbetarskydd och socialförsäkring I Finland, Band IV (Helsingfors, 1915).

36 Ravn, 'Julie Arenholt', pp. 1–2; *Kvinden og samfundet* 21:26 (1910), pp. 239–40; *Kvinden og samfundet* 12:8 (15.12 1915), pp. 2–3.

37 Sklar, *Florence Kelley*, pp. 298–9.

communication with working women easy but on the other hand created problems with factory owners and administrative bureaucrats.[38]

Taking upon themselves the task of inspector also involved these women in discussions with members of their own class, less obvious to a present day audience. When the idea of the female inspector was introduced, many among the feminist movement held the opinion that a Lady Inspector had to behave like a lady and dress like a lady to raise moral tone and to gain the respect of factory owners.[39] At the same time, female dress was used as a reason for women being unsuitable as inspectors and working as foremen in other fields. Even among feminists, the question was raised whether the garments of a lady would make her unfit to fulfil her duties in a factory. During the decades of female entry into the inspectorate, female dress underwent a trans-formation. The tightly laced corsets, figure-hugging jackets and bows on the backside of dresses were replaced by more relaxed long lines and cycling and sportswear for ladies. Betzy Kjelsberg readily adopted these novelties although her suggestion of trousers for inspecting purposes was not accepted with good humour by the delegates of the feminist conference in 1902.[40] Florence Kelley also viewed the new mode of dress as suitable for inspection work.[41]

Vera Hjelt was less interested in her own garments than in those of the women in the factory. She promoted new types of working clothes because of the connection between headscarves and dresses and accidents.[42] Being a woman also made Hjelt highlight the fact that there were occasions of unwanted attentions towards female workers by male foremen, which made the employment of female foremen more urgent; an issue also raised by other inspectors. She demanded changes in the practice of body searches at sugar and candy factories. Should the searches continue, they were no longer to be conducted by men.[43] Likewise, Kjelsberg took it upon herself to achieve changes in the sleeping quarters of female cooks in mining communities and lumber camps. Designated separate quarters or buildings were to be supplied for the women to preserve privacy and decency.[44]

There is no doubt that the female inspectors worked hard to improve working conditions. Those with access to political decision-making also made efforts to promote issues like working hours, social legislation, protection of children, etc. They did not accept the boundaries of the bourgeois parties but

---

[38] Harrison and Nolan, 'Reflections', pp. 273, 275.

[39] *Dagny 1903: 2*, 'Kvinnliga yrkesinspektorer', p. 42.

[40] Folkvord, *Betzy Kjelsberg*, pp. 58, 125; Katrine Pedersen, 'Kvinder som Meijeribestyrere', *Melkeri tidende* 1892, p. 130.

[41] Sklar, *Florence Kelley*, p. 298.

[42] Hjelt, *Berättelse 1906*, pp. 94–5.

[43] Hjelt, *Berättelse 1903*, pp. 232–4.

[44] Folkvord, *Betzy Kjelsberg*, pp. 118, 120–1.

insisted on retaining the right to cooperate with women of other parties in issues of social legislation.[45]

The social divide was not absolute even though it manifested itself in many cases. However, the meetings after hours and the efforts to find a forum where working women could voice complaints without being spotted by employers is an indication of the desire by the inspectors to listen. The fact that more and more women did contact the inspectors and that these took action is, if anything, a sign of dedication to the task. The impression one gets is that particularly Hjelt and Kjelsberg and Anderson, but also some of the others, had a pragmatic attitude to their work. While this did not necessarily include identifying with the women on the factory floor, it meant that they did their best to achieve what these women wanted. From the point of view of a female factory worker it was probably more important to get a raise, accident compensation, a chair to sit on and a toilet separate from that of the men, than a hug from the inspector telling them how sorry she was for their predicament.

The position of inspector was new and navigating it far from easy. It is possible that some unusual personal qualities were necessary when facing restrictions about when to enter a building to avoid encountering male colleagues, like Grace Neill. Despite such rules, she persisted in her task as a 'Nondescript combatant against, drink, poverty, factory owners and the medical profession.'[46]

---

[45] Hjelt-Cajanus, *Vera Hjelt*, p. 224.
[46] Margaret Tennant, Grace Neill's description of herself.

Table 8.2 Complaints addressed by the female inspector, Finland 1908.

Type of complaint	Nr	Investigated	Action taken	Pending	Submitted to other authority	Outcome
Fear of contagion from workmate with TB	1	1	1			Removal to other room of instigator, spittoon installed
Request for unified lunch break to enable airing of workroom	3	3		3	3	
Cleaning of rooms during work	3	3	3	2	2	One cleaner to clean ex hours
Large fines for late arrival	4	4	4			Adjusted to smaller fines
Factory cold on Monday	4	4	4			Heater fixed and Sunday heating arranged
Pipes frozen in WC	1	1	1			Fixed
Broken WC	2					Fixed
Broken heater	2					Fixed
Substandard workrooms	2	2	2			Move to other premises
Repairs of workroom	1	1	1			Fire before repairs happened
No spittoons	2	2	2			Installed instantly
No rubbish bin	1	1	1			Installed
No cleaner	1	1	1			Employed
Young person in night work	1	1	1			Sorted
Young persons too long day	13	13	13			Sorted

Complaint					
Complaint about foreman and illegal firing	1	1	1		Re-engagement, acceptance of complaints, no strike
Fired without rightful wages	7	7	7		14 days' wages paid
Instant dismissal	2	2		2	Court proceedings
Instant dismissal	1	1	1	1	Court proceedings, hired lawyer
Incorrect dismissal	1	1	1		Women three days' wages plus damages
Mediation in dispute about wages	2	2	2		Acceptance of the demands of the workers
Low starting wages	1	1	1		Minimum wage raised from 1.25 to 1.50 per day
Overtime payment	1	1	1		Accepted
Accident compensation demand	4	4	4		Increase in one case, three according to regulations
Accident compensation	1	1			Not accepted, misinformation provided
Wage deductions because of goods from factory shop	1	1	1		System removed
Use of minors for dangerous work	2	2	2		Stopped
Food poisoning at canteen	1	1	1		Police called to investigate, called in health authority
Altogether	64	64	5	8	

Source: Vera Hjelt, *Berättelse afgifven af kvinnliga yrkesinspektören i Finland för år 1908* (Helsingfors, 1909), pp. 120–4.

Conclusion

Contemporary scholarship still has a tendency to view female work in industry not as a sizable contribution to economic history but as a social problem. The female worker has not been considered an independent economically active person, but a victim of a defective system. By recreating women of the past into victims, whether of the capitalist system or patriarchal society, we take away their agency. We refuse to allow them to be thinking persons who made rational choices. In doing so, historians play into the hands of the male view of the past. If working women were just victims, they can be relegated to a corner of social history.

Once upon a time, before manufacturing in Europe became history, the author of this book had the opportunity to visit a veneer factory. We were taken through various rooms, ending up in one with only female workers. The noise was incredible. The women cleaned out branches and replaced them with plugs. Two women opposite one another banged away with mallets at sheets of veneer spat out by a machine. We were told that only women could do such work fast enough and without hitting each-others' hands.

The Finnish factory inspector tells us in her report form 1904 how skill and specialisation was not outside the female scope, when an effort was made to replace women in the factories dealing with small items of wood, the male workers were found to be far less effective. On the other hand, the inspector acknowledges the problem of female mobility in certain industries, resulting in lower earnings, because of employment history. In this connection, she points out that the reason for women leaving was the option of earning more in the summer loading and unloading ships.[1] The key piece of information here is that women looked for opportunities to earn and if staying in the factory did not provide chances of advancement, you could just as well look for employment where more money was offered. As female earnings were low, short-term solutions became more likely. Slim chances of advancement also promoted less interest in unionisation. On the other hand, we have evidence that women were not lethargically hanging on to any job but actively looking for opportunities and better pay.

In the nineteenth century, large parts of Europe and the Western world saw increasing urbanisation and an orientation of the economy towards industrial production. This trend was particularly noticeable after 1860. Although industrial work expanded in many sectors, many, albeit not all, of those viewed as part of the female domain in preindustrial society also employed

---

[1] Hjelt, *Berättelse 1903*, pp. 229–31.

large proportions of women in factory work. Because of regional differences in industrialisation, the female factory worker was a normal sight in some regions while virtually invisible in others. Unlike the image often presented of female work, the age and demographic division was variable. Women of all ages, single, married, widowed and divorced walked through factory gates in the late nineteenth and early twentieth centuries.

Unlike heavy industry, the textile industry and garment production were fields with a majority of female employees. As these sectors also had considerable numbers of young workers, the groups in society engaging in social reform actively strived for introduction of regulations and inspection of the working environment. The early activity to remove young children from factories was fairly successful, at least in theory. However, once the idea of regulation and inspection was accepted, extending the rules was seen as necessary. The presence of women in the factory was, according to the middle classes, a social problem. It was diametrically opposite to the idea of the homemaker and the angel in the home.

One of the problems for working women in the past was low rates of unionisation and, therefore, low earnings. When we examine the situation of women we find that the unions did not want them. We also find that they were not always wanted in the political parties either. In some countries, females did not have the right to join parties and organisations; women were de facto second-class citizens. The political left was not particularly eager to espouse the issue of female voting rights; the working man was a man not a woman. At the same time the movement continuously underlined the class divide and when signs of female collaboration over class lines in the vote issue could be detected, such activity was stamped out.

The presence of women in the factory was a problem for male unions because they represented competition and also a threat to the patriarchal ideology embraced by working-class, as well as middle-class, men. A male breadwinner system gives power to men and takes it away from women. The segregated work tasks with different pay was nothing new, on the contrary, it was part of the old gender division of labour in rural society. The fact that women could and sometimes did replace men in factory work was perceived as a real danger. The low level of unionisation by women created, however, a protective barrier and fixing of task segregation made women second-class workers.

It is a well-known fact that the earnings of women were a fraction of those of men. But when one scrutinises the options available to women it is not difficult to understand that the factory for many provided earning opportunities superior to those in farm work or domestic employment. By the early twentieth century, domestic work was also by many seen as socially degrading and the tangible control of the employer over all aspects of life as intrusive. Despite the discrepancy in wages between men and women, a long career in factory work could mean a decent income. However, even a small income could mean the difference between solvency and insolvency in a working-class family. In addition, female workers generated links with female family members, like mothers, daughters and sisters, or with female workmates, for the purpose of increasing rent-paying capacity or living standard.

By the second half of the nineteenth century, a universal unease about the state of factories had resulted in the development of compulsory compensation for workplace accidents in many countries. In addition, the question of poisonous substances and their links to illness and death among workers became an issue. The employment of children operating machinery and working hours unsuitable to their age had set in motion a series of regulations to ameliorate the situation and to minimise the risk of accidents. As rules might not be followed, a system of inspection was created.

In conjunction with the regulations, another set, specific to women, saw the light of day. As the welfare of females, particularly in relation to health and sanitation, was seen as a female matter, several quarters made the suggestion of employing female inspectors. On this point, we see a united effort by feminists and working women. Their motives might have been different but their goal was the same.

The nineteenth century had been a time of increasing interest in female education. Despite the suspicions among some men about the advantages of an educated wife, movements saw the light advocating not only female literacy but access to all kinds of knowledge. In some countries, this was viewed as a step in the nation building process while others depicted the role of the mother as the educator of her children as crucial for family life. By the late nineteenth century, the health and hygiene movement identified female education as vital for scientific child care and homemaking. Whatever the reasons, female educational establishments proliferated, in some countries within the state sector, in others, privately run. Once females had attained grades and diplomas they sought employment and new innovations in the clerical sector were seen as amply suitable for women. When the Civil Service opened its doors, the step to the employment of female workplace inspectors was not long.

When protective workplace legislation was developed, politicians of the right and the left came together declaring their desire to protect women in industrial work. In actual fact, the position of women as workers was eroded with the introduction of different working hours and special rules. A study of accident statistics clearly reveals that women were less prone to workplace accidents than men. Despite this, the regulations before 1890 and many after this time were specific to women and children, few or none protected all categories of workers. Although men were more often in danger from accidents threatening their physical health, women were viewed as being in moral danger when young, in physical danger as mothers or mothers to be and generally in danger as providers of home comforts for their families.

Therefore, special rules were introduced for women. Nobody ever asked the working women their opinion or made it possible for them to asses and explain their problems until the event of workplace surveys and the employment of female factory inspectors.

The situation of, on the one hand, having female factory workers and, on the other hand, educated women wanting to enter the Civil Service created the ideal situation for employing women as factory inspectors. Their task was viewed differently in different countries. While all agreed that an important task was to stop the employment of underage workers and see that teenagers worked legal hours, the definition of the other tasks varied. Health and hygiene matters figured prominently; these were issues suitable for a woman. However, the raising of the moral tone in the workplace and guiding young women in the right direction was also on the agenda. The feminist organisations who vigorously supported the idea of the female inspector were the same middle classes who wanted to teach working-class women social responsibility, hygiene, good mothering and healthy cookery and household economy, even though they themselves employed cooks, washerwomen and nannies and had never been short of money.

The debate about the female inspector was originally fierce, particularly in Britain. Women were not viewed as having the authority necessary for inspection work. The authority issue came to be debated in several countries and not only in the context of female inspectors but any position where a woman might be higher up in the hierarchy than a man (see Appendix 6). In Britain, the problem was solved by creating a special department for women under the control of the Chief Inspector, a man, and separated from that of the male inspectors. In some countries the female inspectors were appointed to assist their male colleagues and were subject to their authority. Where such hierarchies did not exist, and even where they did, the female inspectorate could envisage a rocky start. In most places, however, some type of modus operandi was established and the work could commence.

The fact that the women often wanted to make changes to how inspection was conducted and how much involvement was expected caused some friction in the early years. On the one hand, when the female inspectors overstepped what was considered their remit, there were rumblings. Old diehards who had cosily collaborated with factory owners and denied the existence of industrial disease did their utmost to sabotage the work of the women. Misogynists attacked the female inspectors in newspaper articles. The female workers were often frightened of repercussions if they communicated their problems to the inspectors. The class divide was not always easy to cross if one had little experience of doing so. Where some of the inspectors had a background in the female union movement they suffered from complaints that they overstepped their boundaries and showed too much enthusiasm for their task. After a series of initial problems, many of the inspectors found their footing. New ways of running registers and introduction of innovations like typewriters speeded up the work. The approach to problems was also often slightly different from their male colleagues. Factory owners did not necessarily respond negatively to negotiations and diplomacy, particularly when dealing with a woman. In large factories, the owners might not even be aware of sanitary deficiencies, while in other cases a friendly approach could be the key to achieve an improvement, sometimes even one that was not subject to existing regulations.[2]

After the inspectors had demonstrated that they were willing to take complaints by female workers seriously, the complaints started multiplying. More and more effort was put into investigating issues that had been brought to the notice of the inspectors by the workers. While there were examples of continuous problems with performing satisfactory inspections, there were also many examples of inspector and worker pushing for the same improvements.

It has been argued that the appointment of female factory inspectors was not so much an action that had a positive effect on the situation of working-class women; it was more a means of creating employment opportunities within the Civil Service for educated middle-class women. The new 'Lady Inspectors', were distanced from the women they inspected and particularly engaged in retaining and advancing the position of the female inspectorate. The post of Female Factory Inspector was, in many cases, the sign of recognition of (middle-class) women as skilled, competent Civil Servants. The issue of competence is, however, important. When a woman needed skills and training or diplomas to attain a post, it was no longer an issue of operating in the sphere of womanly sympathy and charity with the refinement of a lady. The professionalisation was of considerable importance, but just as the ladylike image excluded working-class girls as possible candidates, so did the obligatory presence of higher education. There is no doubt that these representatives of the early phase in female entry into the Civil Service operated within their given networks. One of these was the network of female inspectors in different countries.[3] They also made use of connections to improve working conditions. Both the old male professional elite and the middle-class women's organisations were mobilised in the pursuance of the strategies. Possibly because of their educational background, the inspectors cultivated an open approach through literature of working and living conditions elsewhere and through trips to factories and exhibitions in other European countries. Innovations in technology and machinery of a higher safety standard in Germany caught the interest in England and Scandinavia, as did factories with schools and crèches,

---

    2   Elna Dalberg, 'Om kvindelig Fabriksinspection', pp. 197–9; Hjelt, *Berättelse 1905*, pp. 90–1, 106; Hjelt, *Berättelse 1908*, pp. 127, 131; Hjelt-Cajanus, *Vera Hjelt*, p. 191; Folkvord, *Betzy Kjelsberg*, pp. 104–5, 114, 122.

    3   Hjelt, *Berättelse 1909*; *Kvinden og samfundet* 26:6, pp. 59–60; Folkvord, *Betzy Kjelsberg*; Daniels, 'Annie Jane Duncan'.

well equipped canteens and modern housing. The fact that economic support at confinement was available within the state social security system in some countries was also highlighted.[4]

The story of the activity of the early generations of female inspectors has many positive features. It also gives us a chance to gain some insights in how and under what conditions women had to operate around 1900. In some cases, the work was surrounded by so many restrictions that the inspector left the post and continued her work in the social welfare sector or in journalism and politics. These women did not give up on the cause, the welfare of the working woman, but envisaged it being better served from another podium. Some were discarded by the wayside because of rules that prevented them from marriage and a career in inspection. There were also examples, like in the case of Florence Kelley, where local political conditions prevented continuation within the inspectorate. Even in this case, we can detect efforts to stay true to ideals by engaging in other organisations. Some remained, however. Betzy Kjelsberg stayed on the job until the bureaucrats declared her too old to continue, she also stayed true to the political party that stood for the rights of the ordinary worker. Adelaide Anderson soldiered on until retirement and then took on assignments abroad related to the conditions of child workers. Vera Hjelt extended her career in inspection with the running of the Workplace Safety Exhibition until shortly before her death.

While Tennant turned her back on the working woman after being firmly incorporated through marriage in the administrative upper class, this must not be seen as typical behaviour of the inspectors. In her quiet way, Anderson stayed in the other camp. Kelley's political radicalism and belief in the unions was evident. Kjelsberg stood as a candidate for the Labour Party repeatedly in local and national elections. In Denmark, both Arenholt and Schou were active in party politics on the left. Hjelt left parliamentary politics after voting against her own party and with the Socialists for the eight-hour day. In France, several of the early female inspectors had links either to the unions or left-wing politics. The activity and the rising power of the Liberals and Labour in Australia and New Zealand were in several cases instrumental to the appointment of female inspectors.

The inspectors originated in a different environment from the working women but when they got to grips with their task their problem was more their lack of power to achieve what they wanted than lack of desire to act. The situation was truly remarkable in the sense that it made possible the meeting of two groups that would otherwise have been distanced from each other. There is no doubt that the work of the first female inspectors with all its problems gave an opportunity to act and to make a difference. When we

---

[4] Folkvord, *Betzy Kjelsberg*, pp. 97–8, 152–3; Anderson, *Women in the Factory*, pp. 46–7, 157–8.

study their activity and strategies to not only supervise regulations but improve and change within their remit and outside it we find that female interaction not only made communication of problems possible, but it actually improved the chances of creating a better workplace.

One of the things we find is that they defended the working women against the slurs on their morals and behaviour. They underlined that it was the men and the foremen that exercised brutish behaviour to which they subjected the women. In Britain, Norway and Finland as well as in Australia and New Zealand they asked for the introduction of female foremen and workers' representatives, health workers, police women, etc. to deal with women and see to female problems.

APPENDIX 1 – THE RIGHT FOR WOMEN TO VOTE IN NATIONAL ELECTIONS

Appendix Table 1.1   The right for women to vote in national elections.

New Zealand	1893*	The right to vote but not the right to stand as a candidate
Australia	1902	
Finland	1906	
Norway	1913	
Denmark	1915	
Germany	1918	
Britain	1918**	While all men over 21 had the vote, women had to be over 30 years old, single or widowed or with a husband paying more than £5 in tax
Sweden	1921	
France	1940	

Sources: Ross Evans Paulson, *Women's Suffrage and Prohibition: A Comparative Study of Equality and Social Control* (Glenview, Illinois, 1973); Jad Adams, *Women and the Vote, A World History* (Oxford, 2014), pp. 176–94, 437.

APPENDIX 2 – WOMEN IN THE WORKFORCE

Appendix Table 2.1   Female industrial activity in Italy.

Italy 1911			
Women all ages	29.0%	Men all ages	66.2%
15–20 year olds	52.6%	15–20 year olds	89.9%
10–14 year olds	31.5%	10–14 year olds	53.0%
Female activity rate 1901	37.5%		
Female activity rate 1911	35.1%		

Note: Female activity rate 1901 37.5%, 1911 35.1%, decrease over time because of fewer child workers and also work among the elderly (p. 51). 1905 in textile industry 10,927 girls less than 10 years old, 59,543 12–15 years, 119,738 15–21 years 130 815 women older than 21.
Source: Francessca Beltio, *The Sexual Division of Labour: The Italian Case* (Oxford, 1988), pp. 50–1, 58.

Appendix Table 2.2   Industrial employment in the USA.

	Males	Females	% women
1870	1,615,598	323,770	16.6
1880	2,019,035	531,639	20.8
1890	3,745,123	846,619	18.4

Source: Annie MacLean, 'Factory legislation for women in the United States', The *American Journal of Sociology* (1897–8), pp. 183–205, on p. 186.

Appendix Table 2.3   Male and female industrial workers in selected states of the USA.

1895	Males	Females	Females %
New York	492,679	137,190	22
Massachusetts	272,246	98,019	24
Pennsylvania	451,417	76,860	14

Ohio	410,362	31,932	13
New Jersey	131,647	28,914	18
Delaware	177,471	28,099	14
Connecticut	89,192	26,899	23

Source: Annie MacLean, 'Factory legislation for women in the United States', The *American Journal of Sociology* (1897–8), p. 187.

Appendix Table 2.4   Registered female occupational activity in Spanish urban areas.

Location	Year: 1900	Percentage of females	Sector percentage		
			Primary	Secondary	Tertiary
Spain	1,382,600	14.5			
Barcelona	103,438	19	0.1	65.2	34.6
Granada	10,714	4	0.3	11.5	88.1
Madrid	60,364	15	2.5	15.9	81.6

Note: Of all registered active, 18.8 per cent female, decrease over time to less than 10 per cent by 1930.
Sources: Rosa Maria Capel Martinez, 'Mujer y trabajo en España de Alfonso XIII', in R.M. Capel Martinez (ed.), *Mujer y Sociedad en España 1700–1775* (Madrid, 1982); Ministerio de Cultura, pp. 207–40, on pp. 213, 216.

Appendix Table 2.5   Marital status of female industrial workers in Finland 1910–12, Sweden 1909.

	Finland Single	Sweden Single	Finland Married	Sweden Married	Finland Widow	Sweden Widow	Women over 15 in employment
Tobacco factory	71%	72%	22%	20%	7%	7%	Finland 1890 41%
Textile factory	85%	84%	10%	11%	5%	4.2%	Sweden 1890 28%
Bakery	82%		14%		4%	1%	
Printing works	89%	93%	9%	5%	2%	1.3%	Finland 1910 48%
Mechanical industry	64%	87%	19%	8%	17%	4.6%	Sweden 1910 30%
Paper-mills	69%	94%	19%	2.7%	12%	2.7%	
Night-shift 1911	68%		17%		15%		

Sources: G.R. Snellman, *Tutkimus Suomen konepajoista* (Helsinki, 1911), pp. 62–3; G.R. Snellman, *Undersökning angående pappersindustrin* (Helsingfors, 1912), p. 20; Tekla Hultin, *Yötyöntekijättäret Suomen teollisuudessa* (Helsinki, 1911), pp. 44–7; Lynn Karlsson, *Mothers as Breadwinners, Myth or Reality in Early Swedish Industry?* (Uppsala, 1995), pp. 20–5.

Appendix Table 2.6   Occupational activity of married working-class women in Vienna 1912–14.

	Work outside home	Work in the home
Full-time work	20	20
Part-time work	12	12
Occasional work		10
Not working		18

Source: Survey of working class households in Vienna, Josef Ehmer, 'Frauenarbeit und Arbeiterfamilie in Wien', in Hans Ulrich Wehler (ed.), *Frauen in der Geschichte des 19. und 20. Jahrhunderts* (Gottingen, 1981), pp. 438–73, on p. 471.

Appendix Table 2.7   Work by husband and wife, Dundee 1901.

	Wife Employed	Total Wives	No Wife	Total Men
West Dundee	1040	2010	186	2196
	51%			
East Dundee	524	1267	97	1364
	41%			

Note: In Dundee, employment available for women included both factory and other work outside the home, as well as 'putting-out'-type work (p. 25).
Source: Dundee Social Union, *Report on Housing and Industrial Conditions in Dundee* (Dundee, 1905), p. 45.

APPENDIX 3 – WOMEN, WORK, EARNINGS AND FAMILY

Work as a servant, Britain

I was the only servant. I had to be up at six in the morning, and there were so many jobs lined up for me that I worked until eleven o'clock at night. The mistress explained that she was very particular; the house had to be spotless always. After all, they were professional people and used to very high standards. I had to clean all the house, starting at the top and working down, sweeping and scrubbing right through. Heartstoning the steps from the front door to the pavement took me an hour alone. I was most conscientious. The meals I remember well. For breakfast I had bread and dripping. There were often mice dirts on the dripping to be scraped off first. Dinner was herring, every day; tea was bread and marge. I didn't have a bath during the month I was there, I wasn't given the opportunity; in fact there was no time to comb my hair properly, which was long – down to my waist; it grew so matted my mother had to cut off a lot of it when I finally came home again.

My room was in the attic. There was a little bed in the corner, a wooden chair and a washstand. It was a cold, bare utterly cheerless room.

(Lilian Westall, house maid in John Burnett (ed.), Useful Toil, Autobiographies of Working People from the 1820s to the 1920s (London, 1974), p. 216)

Factory work contra domestic work USA

When they (parents) went back (1914) I was thirteen and working here, so I begged my mother to leave me … My sister was eighteen and my brother sixteen. The woman who kept the boarding house said to my mother, 'As long as they mind me, you don't have to worry. If they don't mind me I'll write you and let you know.' So my mother went back to Canada and we stayed here, but I'm the only one in my family who has always lived in Manchester.

If I wanted to go back on the farm, I'd have to go work in private houses in Montreal and Quebec, take care of the house, wash the clothes, help with the food and whatever there is to be done. Housemaid. My mother didn't want that because we were brought up in the States, and she knew that if her girls were going to go wrong, they were going to do it away from home also. So she said, 'At least if they work in the mills, they work a certain hour, they get paid, they do what they want.' But she wanted us to stay with a woman that she could depend on. And it was a family life for us in the boarding house. The woman I boarded with had six children.

(Tamara Hareven and Randolph Langenbach, *Amoskeag: Life and Work in an American Factory City in New England* (London, 1979), pp. 202–3)

Appendix Table 3.1   Domestic service in Britain 1871–1911.

Domestic servants	England and Wales	Of total female population	Scotland	Of total female population
1871	1,508,888	12.8%	155,307	8.9%
1891	1,759,555	11.6%	190,051	9.1%
1911	1,662,511	11.1%	159,658	6.5%

Source: Nigel Goose, 'Working women in industrial England', in Goose, Women's Work, pp. 1–28, on p. 9, Elizabeth Roberts, *Women's Work 1840–1940* (1988), p. 31.

Female work, family and factory, Finland

My mother was weaving at home when we were young. She carried 150 foot of fabric on her back to town. She got 10 penny per foot and that is what we lived on before she started work at the sawmill. At the the mill, she loaded wood on a cart. Then my grandmother moved to live with us and mum found work at the factory. In 1908 she was still loading, she worked from 7 in the morning to 6 in the evening. At the factory she worked from 6 in the morning to 6 in the evening. Sometimes she had to do a long weekend shift from 6 on Sunday morning to 6 on Monday morning.

In my childhood we ate potatoes and salted herring, bread and milk. We did not always have butter and often we cooked porridge using whole oats. You would boil the oats soft, add rye flour and pour milk on top. That was water gruel and I cried when I had to eat it. We made pea soup, other soups, potato porridge and porridge of rye flour. There was little difference between Sunday and weekday food. When we were baking we made oven pancake. We usually baked sourdough rye bread and mixed grain yeast bread, hardy ever buns. I have never had to go short of rye bread, except in the summer 1918. We picked lingon berries and preserved them for the winter. In the autumn we picked mushrooms that were cooked and fried. 'Be careful to pick edible mushrooms' the children used to be told.

(Bo Lönnqvist, Ivar Nordlund, Maria Stahls and Katia Bask (eds), *Industrisamhalle och Arbetarkultur* (Helsingfors, 1997), p. 57)

The women would not have be able to work without the Kindergarten. They went into the factory at eight, at twelve home and at one back and then work until five. When the day was longer or the husband was on late shift we would pay the lady at the Kindergarten a couple of shillings and she would keep the children for longer.

(Regina Kopl and Leopold Redl, *Das Totale Ensemble, Ein Führer duch die Industriekultur In südlicher Wiener Becken* (Wien, 1989), p. 66)

I started working in 1912 when I was eleven ... I started my first job in the spinning room, and my last job was weaving at the Chicopee mill. My last job in the Amoskeag was in 1935; that's when it closed down. I was one of the last ones to come out. My father and two brothers worked in the mills. My father used to help in the dress room, setting the beam up for the drawing-in girls. We were thirteen in our family, eleven children and my mother and father. My mother had sixteen children but five died as babies.

When I was eleven my father had a birth certificate made for me in the name of my sister Cora who died as a baby, because you couldn't work unless you were fourteen. I worked in the old Amoskeag as Cora but I was naturalized in 1936 as Valeda. Now I stick to Valeda because of Social Security.

(Tamara Hareven and Randolph Langenbach, *Amoskeag: Life and Work in an American Factory City in New England* (London, 1979), p. 202)

After the introduction of the first factory law in Norway in 1892 the work of children was to be controlled. In Roros, 144 fathers wrote to parliament to express their dis-satisfaction:

The work is easy and outside in the fresh air, although under cover and we have had a good contribution to our income when boys of 8 and 10 have been able to earn from 20 to 40 crowns per month during the summer. The education has either not been disrupted as the working time is during the summer holidays.

The fathers added that many would have to apply for poor relief if they were deprived of the earnings of their children (Edvard Bull, 'Barn I industriarbeid', in Bjarne Hodne and Solvi Sogner (eds), *Barn av sin tid* (Oslo, 1984), pp. 77–88, on p. 80).

Children and work, Denmark

In 1898 a survey was conducted in Copenhagen about the work of primary school children outside school hours. Depending on part of town, the percentage working children varied from 10 to 30 per cent, with the lowest percentages in fee-paying schools. Information was collected about the work of altogether

5054 boys and 7761 girls under the age of 14. At this point in time the work in factories was regulated and the survey documented 852 boys and 222 girls in factory work. Although the dairies employed many boys (339) only 2 girls had found this kind of employment. Working as an errand boy or errand girl was the largest singular group, 3356 boys and 1091 girls managed to acquire some income this way (Kjobenhavns Borgarrepresentatnters Forhandlingar fra den 6 April till den 20 Marts 1899, 59 Aargang II bind (Kjobenhavn, 1899), pp. 1651–5; Skoledirektors betretning om skolelevers arbejde udenfor skoletiden 1898, Kobenhavns Borgerrepresentanters Forhandlinger fra den 6te April til den 20de Marts 1899, Aargang II (Kobenhavn, 1899)).

In the Danish tobacco industry women replaced the children after 1900, particularly after 1913 when child work was drastically reduced through legislation. The women did seldom get skilled tasks but were mostly operating in the less skilled, less well paid jobs (Marianne Rostgaard and Inger Bladt, *Tobakken og byen, C.W. Obels Toaksfabrik 1787–1995* (Aalborg, 2004), pp. 86–7).

Appendix Table 3.2   Wages of men and women in industry, Denmark.

Year	Wages in Crowns		
	Skilled males	Male workers	Female workers
1882	3.04	2.37	1.37
1892	3.35	2.56	1.43
1898	3.84	3.05	1.67
1904	4.11	3.43	1.90
1909	4.56	3.96	2.17

Source: Knut Knudsen, Anne Caspersen, *Kampen for en bedre lillvaerelse* (Copenhagen, 1991), p. 94.

Appendix Table 3.3   Female yearly earnings in early twentieth-century Finland.

Budget study 1908	Marks		Industrial statistics	Average female wages – marks
	Minimum	Maximum		
Textile factory	446	1456	Textile industry 1904	514
Paper mill	509		Paper industry 1912	599
Tobacco factory	596	1770	Tobacco industry 1903	598
Cork factory	453	995	Printing 1907	668
Shoe factory	883		Glassworks 1913	505
Factory knitter	510	1296	Bakery 1905	559
Seamstress	240	826		
Washerwoman	159	614		
Ironing	467	1106		
Manual labourer	562	839		
Market trader	184	865		
Factory worker unspecified	727	789		

Sources: Vera Hjelt, *Undersökning av yrkesarbetarnes lefnadsvillkor I Finland 1908–1909* (Helsingfors, 1911), pp. 29–30, 138, 153–5 (female household heads only); G.R. Snellman, *Undersökning angående tobaksindustrin* (Helsingfors, 1903); G.R. Snellman, *Undersökning angående textilindustrin* (Helsingfors, 1904); G.R. Snellman, *Undersökning angående pappersindustrin* (Helsingfors, 1912); Kaarina Vattula, 'Kvinnors forvarvsarbete i Norden under 100 ar (1870–1970)', *Studia Historica Jyvaskylaensia 27* (Jyvaskyla, 1983).

To find an answer to the issue of whether women could not demonstrate the same skills as men a study of wages by task was undertaken. This revealed that, for example, female foremen in cigarette making were only paid 62.5 per cent of male foremen's wages. No men worked in cigarette making (by hand), however female cigarette machine handlers were only paid 50.4 per cent of their male counterparts. While sorting and packing was clearly female dominated as was drying and stripping, the few male dryers and strippers were paid twice as much as the women. However, the female packers and sorters were paid 85.5 per cent of male sorters. So while tasks were often segregated, if there was an overlap women were paid less.

Of the women who had been in employment 2 years or less 50 per cent were in the lowest income bracket (under 300 marks per year) while no males were paid such wages. The other half of new female arrivals earned between 500 and 750 marks. Of the males employed 2 years or less 60 per cent earned 300–500 marks, 20 per cent 750–100 and 20 per cent +1000 marks. If we analyse the situation of person who had been working between 10 and 20 years we find that 47 per cent of the males had reached the highest income bracket (+1000) and 50 per cent the next highest while only 1.85 of the women with similar employment history had reached an income over 1000 marks and 14.4 per cent earned 750–1000 marks. Among those working for more than 20 years we find similar discrepancies in male and female wages (G.R. Snellman, *Undersökning av tobaksindustrin* (Helsingfors, 1903), pp. 86–7).

Appendix Table 3.4   Gender and earnings in relation to time at work, percentages, Finnish tobacco industry.

	M	F	M	F	M	F	M	F	M	F
Marks	>300		300–500		500–750		750–1000		1000+	
2 y or less		50	60			50	20.0		20.0	
2–10 y	2.3	2.2	11.6	24.1	18.6	61.2	45.4	10.3	22.1	2.2
10–20 y		1.8		22.4	2.8	60.1	50.0	14.2	47.2	1.8
20 + y	1.8	2.2		25.4	17.8	58.3	22.3	10.9	57.8	3.6

Source: G.R. Snellman, *Undersökning av tobaksindustrin* (Helsingfors, 1903), p. 204.

APPENDIX 4 – ACCIDENTS, WORKPLACE ACTS AND REGULATIONS

Accidents Austria

It was quite common for people to catch their finger in the paper machine. When you looked carefully you could find that many people were one finger short, Hermann had lost one, Norbert, Franzi and Edi the whole hand. If you were not able to perform your duties you would be placed somewhere else … Usually you would not get fired and it would go to the factory board. That is what we had the unions for, to protect people.

(Kopl, Regina and Leopold Redl, *Das Totale Ensemble, Ein Führer duch die Industriekultur In südlicher Wiener Becken* (Wien, 1989), p. 72)

Appendix Table 4.1   Britain: Type of accidents reported to certifying surgeons 1906 and, in brackets, 1892.

	Males over 18	Females over 18	Boys 13–18	Girls 13–18	Boys 11–14	Girls 11–14	All
Fatal	999 (331)	12 (17)	98 (68)	6 (6)	1 (4)	- (-)	1116 (426)
Loss of r arm/hand	55 (34)	6 (4)	13 (4)	2 (4)	- (1)	- (-)	76 (68)
Loss of l arm/hand	56 (30)	5 (1)	16 (10)	5 (1)	1 (2)	- (-)	83 (44)
Part of r hand	1075 (271)	155 (66)	368 (185)	119 (56)	7 (15)	5 (9)	1729 (602)
Part of l hand	1104 (257)	130 (47)	302 (152)	111 (58)	4 (13)	3 (3)	1654 (530)
Part of leg/foot	93 (20)	2 (-)	15 (13)	1 (1)	1 (2)	- (-)	112 (36)
Fracture	774 (373)	53 (73)	177 (194)	18 (50)	6 (23)	2 (9)	1030 (722)

Loss of sight	46 (13)	11 (9)	8 (2)	4 (3)			69 (27)
Eye injury	1206	41	156	11	1		1415
Head/face	2164 (422)	247 (114)	244 (112)	89 (52)	5 (6)	- (11)	2749 (717)
Burn	3127	73	408	51	4	2	3665
Wounds/ bruises	14,426 (2740)	1836 (503)	3752 (1595)	1077 (440)	78 (145)	26 (48)	21,195 (5471)
Total	25,688	2636	5679	1541	112	40	35,696 (8643)

Source: Report of the Chief inspector of Factories 1906, PP 1907 X, p. 363.

Factory regulations in selected countries[1]

Britain

- 1844: The Factory Act applied to textile factories. Women and young persons (13–18 years old) were allowed to work a maximum of 12 hrs/day, children under 13 a maximum of 6.5 hrs/day, no children under 8 could be employed.
- 1847: Women and children (13–18 years old) were allowed to work a maximum of 10 hrs/day or 58 hrs/week (the shift system remained).
- 1850: Women and children (13–18) were only allowed to work between 6 am and 6 pm or 7 am and 7 am in textile factories, working time was increased to 10.5 hrs/day.

---

[1]   Anderson and Wright, 'Labour legislation'; Anderson, *Women in the Factory*, pp. 27–8; Martindale, *Women Servants*, pp. 46–7; Tuckwell et al., *Woman in Industry*, pp. 146–52; McFeeley, *Lady Inspectors*, pp. 7–8; Schweitzer, *Les inspectrices*, pp. 15, 59–61, 85; Wecker, 'Equality for men?', pp. 63–90, on pp. 65–73; Schmitt, '"All these forms of women's work"', pp. 125–49, on pp. 126–7, 131–8, 140–2; Jansz, 'Women workers?', pp. 188–209, on pp. 195–9; Grandner, 'Special labor protection', pp. 157–62; Hageman, 'Protection or equality?', pp. 267–90, on pp. 269–75; Ravn, '"Lagging far behind"', p. 222; *Lov om Borns og unge Menneskers Arbeide I Fabrikker 23 maj 1893 (law about the work of children and young persons 23 of May 1893): Lov om Arbejde I Fabrikker og dermen legestillede Virksomheder samt det offentliges tillsyn hermed 11 april 1901 (law about work in factories and similar activities and the public inspection of such places 11 of April 1901)*; Law about Preventing Accidents When Using Machines etc. of 12 April 1889, by royal declaration Christian IX of Denmark; Neergaard, 'Fabrikloven vedtaget', pp. 114–15; Kettunen, *Suojelu, Suoritus, Subjekti*, pp. 44–5.

- 1866: Municipal authorities were required to appoint sanitary inspectors.
- 1871: The Civil Service reforms stipulated that positions were to be open to those who passed public examinations, from this point, a person was not to acquire a post through privilege and connections.
- 1874: Factory Act stipulated a minimum age of 10 years for employment in textile factories.
- 1878: Factory and Workshops Act specified the following:

    All factories and workshops employing more than 50 people to be inspected regularly by government inspectors, not local authorities.

    The working day was fixed, including provisions for pauses and holidays.

    Children up to 10 years were to attend compulsory education.

    Children 10–14 years old could only be employed for half days in all trades.

    Certificates of fitness for children and young persons had to be provided.

    Women were not to work more than 56 hrs per week.

    Some domestic workshops were brought under the regulations.

    Women and children were not allowed to work with lead.
- 1883: Lead Poisoning Act required provision of ventilation, lavatories and separate eating areas for persons working with lead.
- 1891: Factory Act specified the following:

    Requirements for fencing machinery.

    Women were prohibited from working for four weeks after giving birth.

    Working age in all sectors was raised to 11 years.

    The Home Secretary could declare a trade dangerous and prohibit or limit the time of employment of any class of person (i.e. including adult males).

    The administration of sanitary measures was to be handled by the local Sanitary Authority, with increased manpower.
- 1895: Factory Act specified the following:

    Temperature in workrooms was to be regulated.

Lavatories had to be provided in premises where poisonous substances were handled.

All cases of industrial poisoning had to be reported.

Penalties were stipulated for allowing clothes to be made in localities with infectious disease present.

The sanitary conditions of outworkers were regulated.

All workplace accidents had to be reported and investigated.

Standards were set for overcrowding in workrooms.

The inspectors were given the power to order fans.

Regulations about fencing machinery were defined.

Young persons were prohibited from cleaning machinery.

Safeguards against fire were stipulated.

Overtime for young persons was prohibited, including circumventing regulations by employing the same person inside and outside a factory during the same day.

- 1901: Factory and Workshop Act specified the following:

Minimum working age was raised to 12 and young children had to participate in education.

Set meal times were introduced.

Fire escapes became compulsory.

Overtime of adults was subject to regulation.

Dangerous processes were regulated.

Provisions were made for reporting accidents.

Outwork was to be controlled.

Laundries became subject to regulation and inspection.

Wages of piece workers were regulated.

Rules were brought in about ventilation, drainage of floors and examination of steam boilers.

Children were prohibited from cleaning machinery in motion.

A Justice engaged in or officer of the same trade as a person charged with an offence could not act at the hearing and determine the charge.

- 1903: Employment of Children Act stated that no half timer could be employed in two places.

- 1906: The Notices of Accidents Act stipulated obligatory reporting of accidents in mines, quarries, factories and workshops.
- 1907: Factory and Workshop Act brought all laundries, including trade and charitable, into institutions that should be inspected.
- 1916: Regulations were passed about provisions regarding separate rooms for eating, access to drinking water, seats, cloak rooms and washing conveniences.
- 1921: The situation of workrooms and the provision of light were brought under regulation.

France

- 1841: A regulation was brought in that the working day of 8–12 year olds could not be more than 8 hours, 12–16 year olds could do a 12-hour day, and neither group was allowed to work during the night.
- 1848: The working day for adults was fixed at 12 hours.
- 1851: Exceptions could be made by local authorities in, for example, printing, engineering works, work at furnaces, manufacture of projectiles for war and government work related to defence or national security.
- 1874: The minimum age to embark on work in factories was set at 12 years, boys aged 12–16 and girls 12–21 years could work a 12-hour day, and 16 Divisional Industrial Inspectors were appointed by the state to control the legality of working hours.
- 1885: Workplaces under regulation were industrial establishments using engines or continual furnaces, or workshops with more than 20 workers.
- 1892: Ban on night work by women, compulsory one day of rest per week for women and adolescents; men included in 1906. No work underground in mines for women, only surface work. The working day for adults was set at 12 hrs.
- 1900: The working day for women and young workers was reduced to 11 hours. No employment of children under 13 except for 12 year olds who could produce an educational and medical certificate.
- 1902: The working day in mixed workplaces, including women and young people, reduced to 10.5 hrs.
- 1904: The working hours for young people set at 10 out of every 24 hours, one-hour meal break.
- 1905: All miners were to work a nine-hour day.

- 1907: An eight-hour day for all was introduced.
- 1906: The ministry of work was created.
- 1910: An orientation of inspection towards hygiene, accident prevention and amelioration of conflicts.
- 1936: the working week was adjusted from 48 to 40 hours for all workers.

Germany

- 1839: The first regulations of children's work.
- 1878: Prohibition of women working for three weeks after childbirth. Ban on the work of women underground in mines and in dangerous industries at night.
- 1887: Proposal of a total ban on night work by women. Maternity leave extended to four weeks. Female work to cease at 6 pm on Saturdays and Sundays. Married women were to work only 10 hours per day.
- 1891: Workers Protection Act stipulated the following:

    Strict regulations to ensure workplace safety.

    Ban on Sunday work for all.

    Women to work 11 hours per day.

    Children under 16 to work 10 hours per day.

    No night work for women and children (8.30 pm to 5.30 am).

    No industrial work for children under 13.

    Maternity leave extended to six weeks.
- 1903: Stricter rules on child labour. Children's Protection Act.
- 1918: An eight-hour day was brought in for all workers.

Switzerland

- 1815: In Zurich, children under 9 were prohibited from working in factories, 9–16 year olds to have a working day of a maximum of 12–14 hours.
- 1824: No work for all after 9 pm in spinning factories.
- 1843: A 13-hour day was introduced in cotton spinning.
- 1864: A 12-hour day was introduced in all factories.
- 1868–73 all cantons introduce a six-week break in work for women after childbirth.
- 1877: No night work for men and women, but some exceptions for men possible. Women were not allowed to clean machinery in motion. Married women banned from doing overtime. Unpaid maternity leave two weeks before and six weeks after giving

birth. Children under 14 banned from factory work. 11-hour day
for all.

- 1884: 11-hour day also applied to millinery production and other
  trades in Basel.
- 1888: Rules extended to all enterprises employing three women or
  more, except retail.
- 1904: Inclusion of retailing shops, only domestic workers
  excluded.

The Netherlands

- 1880s and 1890s: The marriage bar was introduced and female
  post office workers and teachers were dismissed on marriage.
- 1888: An 11-hour day was introduced for young people between
  12–16 and women. No Sunday work, no work between 7 pm and
  5 am, 1-hour meal break for women. No work for four weeks
  after childbirth for women. The law applied to factories and large
  workshops; agricultural work and domestic work was not included.
- 1913: Compulsory sickness insurance was introduced for all
  workers.

Italy

- 1886: Ban on work in industry for children under 9 and for
  children under 10 in underground mining.
- 1890: Law for the prevention of accidents. Fencing of machinery
  became compulsory. Sanitary conditions were to be improved in
  industrial workplaces and mines.
- 1899: Night work for children under 12 prohibited. Children aged
  12–15 were only allowed to work 6 hours at night.
- 1902: Night work for women and for boys under 15 was banned.
  The six-day week was introduced. The age of employment of
  children in factories, laboratories, quarries and mines was raised
  to 12. Underground work was only allowed after the age of 14. No
  employment of women within a month after childbirth.

Spain

- 1900: No work for women within three weeks after childbirth.
  Eleven-hour day in industry. Children under 14 in industrial work
  only to work a six-hour day, in other commercial activities, eight
  hours. No work for children under 10. No night work between 6
  pm and 5 am for children under 14.
- 1904: Sunday a day of rest in industrial work.

Austria

- 1881: 11-hour day. Ban on women working within four weeks after childbirth. 60-hour week for 16–18 year olds and for young women between 16 and 21. No night work for boys under 18 and for women.
- 1883: The factory inspectorate was introduced.
- 1888: Unpaid maternity leave ameliorated through moderate benefits under the Workers Sickness Insurance Act. Small workshops not subject to the rules. Eleven-hour day with breaks; the actual time between starting and finishing could be 12½ hours. The Austrian Social Democrats demanded an 8-hour day for men and women. No Sunday work. No night work for anybody and no special categories.
- 1896: Demands for equal pay, also seen as a way of solving the problem of unfair competition.

Norway

- 1892: The Factory Protection Act of Norway banned women working in mines and cleaning and oiling machines in motion. No work for six weeks after childbirth. Factory work prohibited for children under 10. Limited working hours for children under 18.
- 1890: The Labour Party proposed an eight-hour day. Workers under 18 and married women should have a six-hour day and no night work.
- 1901: The Liberal Party introduced a proposal for national labour insurance, the eight-hour day, as well as improvements to the factory legislation.
- 1909: Factory Law specified the following:

  Ban on work by children under the age of 10.

  A six-hour day for children between 10 and 14.

  A 10-hour day for children between 14 and 18.
- 1909: The ban on night work for women was rejected and parliament refused to ratify the Bern Convention of 1906, against the wishes of the Liberals.

Denmark

- 1873: Law about children and young people working in factories stated the following:

  No children under 10 years.

  Children between 10 and 14, 6.5 hours maximum and only between 6 am and 8 pm.

14–18 year olds no more than 12 hours and only between 5 am and 9 pm.

2 hours lunch break and rest between 8 am and 6 pm.

Meals to be taken outside the workroom.

No work for children on Sundays and holidays.

Children and young people subject to medical inspection before starting factory work.

- 1889: Law about preventing accidents when using machines stated the following:

  Working machines had to be constructed and placed, and connecting moving parts be fenced or covered, so that the workers engaged with them could only in cases of extreme carelessness come into connection with moving parts when pursuing their normal duties.

  No child under the age of 10 was allowed to work with machines powered by steam, electricity, etc. in factories, apart from agricultural machinery if supervised by their parents.

  Children under the age of 16 were not to supervise or independently work any machinery that could be described as dangerous or clean or oil parts of such machines when in motion.

  All machines connected to a central power engine are to be supplied with an independent switch-off mechanism or have a signal system between the individual machine and the central power source.

- 1901: Law about work in factories and similar workplaces and public inspection of these stated the following:

  No children under 12 allowed to work in factories.

  Until children had finished school, they could only work for six hours per day including a half-hour rest after four and a half hours' work.

  No work before 6 am the morning and 8 pm.

  No Sunday work for children.

  When attending school, no work in the one and a half hours before school starts.

  Maximum working day of 10 hours for 14–18 year olds.

  Heated room for all workers to take their meals.

Workrooms to be adequately lighted for the purpose of working and all parts of machines to be clearly visible, if flammable materials are handled in the room, the artificial light is to be at a safe distance and quality.

- 1913: Factory Acts stated the following:

Ban on the work of children under 14 in factories until they have finished education.

Children under 12 can only work with agricultural machines if supervised by their parents, the ban did not include work with horses.

Home workers were to be registered and set prices used for the work.

Four weeks of maternity leave.

Any workplace with 25 women or more is to provide a warm room in winter where mothers could breast-feed their infants.

No night work restrictions for women.

The Ministry of the Interior empowered to restrict working hours for men and women in activities that could be deemed dangerous to the health.

Finland

- 1889: Children under 12 were not allowed to be employed in industry; 12–15-year-olds worked a 7-hour day; 15–18-year-olds worked 14 hours, including 2 hours rest. Children and young women were not allowed to work underground in mines or breaking stones. Women and children could not be asked to clean or grease machinery in motion.

Appendix Table 4.2   Working time for men and women in Denmark.

Year	Men – Copenhagen	Year	Women – Copenhagen
1870	10.9 hrs	1872	10.5 hrs
1900	9.6 hrs	1898	9.6 hrs
1914	9.2 hrs	1914	9.4 hrs

Source: Svend Aage Hansen, *Okonomisk vekst I Danmark 1720–1914* (Copenhagen, 1972), p. 257.

Appendix Table 4.3   Working hours in the USA 1895.

	Hours per day	Hours per week	Comments
Connecticut	10	60	Hours/week absolute
Florida	10		
Georgia	11	66	Women under 21 in textiles
Illinois	8	48	Repealed 1895
Indiana	10		Under 19 in textile mills
Louisiana	10	60	Meal hour included
Maine	10	60	More for repairs
Maryland	10	60	Under 21-year-olds in textile
Massachusetts	10	58	
Michigan	10	60	1 hour for dinner included
Minnesota	10	60	Women
Missouri	8	48	Longer possible
North Dakota	10	60	
New Hampshire	10	60	May exceed
New jersey	10	60	Females and men under 18
New York	10	60	Women under 21
Ohio	10	60	Minors
Pennsylvania	12	60	
Oklahoma	10		More cannot be demanded
Rhode Island	10	60	
Wisconsin	8	48	More cannot be demanded

Source: Annie MacLean, 'Factory legislation for women in the United States', The *American Journal of Sociology* (1897–8), pp. 183–205, on p. 201.

Appendix Table 4.4   Night work, Denmark.

	Industrial workers	Women	Women	Female factory night workers
1897	177,000	31,000	21%	
1906	207,000	48,000	23%	c. 300 (in printing)

Sources: Danmarks Haandverk og Industri ifolge Taellingen den 12 Juni 1906, *Danmarks Statistik*, Statistisk Tabelverk 5 Rekke (Copenhagen, 1908), Statens Statistiske Bureau, pp. 111–37; Anna-Birte Ravn, '"Lagging far behind all civilized nations": the debate over protective labor legislation for women in Denmark 1899–1913', in Wikander, Kessler-Harris and Jane Lewis (eds), *Protecting Women: Labour Legislation in Europe, the United States and Australia 1880–1920* (Urbana, 1995), pp. 210–33, on p. 211.

The night work survey in Finland 1911

In Finland, 1911, the percentage of married and widowed women out of all women in night work was not dissimilar to those in daytime work in some industrial sectors. However, the total proportion of female workers was higher. In a 1920s study, a larger proportion of widows could be found among the women engaging in such work than among those doing day shifts. In the paper mills surveyed, no less than 30 per cent of women on the night shifts were widows. While the saw mills engaged only 15 per cent of widows for night work, it was still more than in daytime. In both surveys, the women were vocal in their condemnation of plans to restrict their right to work nights unless similar restrictions would be introduced for the men. They were aware of operating in a niche which offered employment opportunities and a slightly better wage, and they argued that their options were night work or unemployment. Despite suffering exhaustion from lack of sleep (because of problems resting in crowded flats), these widows expressed particular concerns about possible restrictions to night work; they did not believe that work during the day would be available. Their stated reason for working nights was that income from other family members was insufficient and that night shift work could be combined with family duties. Sixty per cent of these widows were supplying the needs of young children, while the rest had at least one child with some earnings (Tekla Hultin, *Yötyöntekijättäret Suomen teollisuudessa* (Helsinki, 1911), pp. 44–7; Jenny Markelin-Svensson, 'Kvinnoskyddslagstiftning och moderskapsförsäkring', *Modern socialpolitik*, Föreningen för arbetarskydd och socialförsäkring I Finland, Band II (Helsingfors, 1912, pp. 12–13).

APPENDIX 5 – EDUCATION

90 per cent of the 300 female students in the 'high school for young ladies' came from lower middle-class families. The fathers were craftsmen or kept small shops. They did not want their children to participate in state-run education. Their idea was that attending 'a higher school' was better. The question of what occupation their daughter should aim for did not arise. Generally the children of workers did neither attend the higher school for ladies nor the secondary schools preparing for the Gymnasium (and the baccalaureate). Our school was the exception ... I used to read in the morning before school about the debates in parliament and the regional assembly on issues related to women's education. My mother thought I was mad.

(Karin Roi Frey, *Wenn alle Stricke reissen, dann wird sie noch einmal Lehrerin, Lehrerinnen in biographischen Zeugnissen* (Bochum, 2001), p. 115)

We understood that we lived in a time of change, that we as female students were creating a new type of woman with independence and freedom but that we still were stuck in the old family structures. When we came home it was necessary to take on the role of 'daughter of the house'. Instead of spending time with our books and seminar papers in the holidays we had to help with the housework from morning to night, we were there to serve other family members. When I once tried to get out of these duties my brother said with friendly superiority, 'Learning to serve makes a good wife', and gave me his clothes for ironing.

(Karin Roi Frey, *Wenn alle Stricke reissen, dann wird sie noch einmal Lehrerin, Lehrerinnen in biographischen Zeugnissen* (Bochum, 2001), p. 122)

When you look back did you always want to be a teacher or would you have liked to do something else?

I would have liked to study law.

Why did you not ask your father if that would be possible?

He would never have paid for that. He went to his brother who was the one who made decisions in the family and said 'Can you imagine, she wants to go into higher education and university!' My uncle was rich and had married a woman with money, his own daughter studied law and so did the other one. He said: 'No, that cannot be, that is for us, not for you'. So I went into secondary education and became a teacher.

(Roi Frey, Karin, *Wenn alle Stricke reissen, dann wird sie noch einmal Lehrerin, Lehrerinnen in biographischen Zeugnissen* (Bochum, 2001), p. 121)

Appendix Table 5.1   Regulations affecting the education of women and their access to public service in the Nordic countries.

Denmark	
1739	Primary school
1859	Teacher training college
1875	Women's right to university studies and degrees
1901	First female industrial inspector
1915	Women allowed to vote in parliamentary elections
1921	Access to the whole Civil Service except defence and the clergy
Finland	
1863	Teacher training college
1866	Primary school
1897	Right to practice as medical doctor – private sector
1898	Right to teach in secondary school
1901	Access to university studies and degrees without the need for dispensation
1903	First female industrial inspector
1906	Women allowed to vote in parliamentary elections
1914	Right to practice as medical doctor – state and council sector
1916	Right to teach at university and higher education institutions
1926	Access to the Civil Service except the diplomatic corps, defence, the police force and the clergy
Sweden	
1842	Primary school
1861	Teacher training college in Stockholm financed by the state

1870	Entrance of women to the baccalaureate
1873	Access to university education and degrees
1909	Partial access to the Civil Service
1911	Access to some professorships but not head over men
1912	First female industrial inspector appointed
1919	First female industrial inspector took office and began work
1921	Women allowed to vote in parliamentary elections
1923	Equal access to employment except as court judge
1939	Removal of the marriage bar

Norway

1739	Primary school first introduction – applied, depending on region, 1828 or 1848
1860	Teacher training college
1884	Access to university studies and degrees
1889	Primary school universally available
1909	First female industrial inspector
1912	Access to the Civil Service except the diplomatic corps, defence, the government and the clergy
1913	Women gained the right to vote in parliamentary elections
1956	Access to the clergy

APPENDIX 6 – FEMALE INSPECTORS

Debates about women and the position of authority

When the question of appointing female inspectors arose it raised a number of objections.

The chief inspector of factories said (1879) 'I doubt very much whether the office of factory inspector is suitable for women ...' The problem was not only 'the general and multifarious duties of an inspector of factories would really be incompatible with the gentle and home-loving character of a woman' but the fact that 'Factory inspecting requires activity and acumen and the stern authority of a man to enforce obedience to his interrogatories ... and a female inspector having to submit herself in the witness-box to the cross-examination of an astute attorney ...'[1] The profession was visualized as giving orders in the factory and disputing with lawyers in court with a good portion of confrontation, therefore, a male prerogative.

The problem was seen to be part of differences in approach to problems by men and women. For example, the 1833 Factory Inquiry in Britain revealed that, while male mule spinners regularly hit their adolescent and child assistants with a strap to keep them working, the female mule spinners gave them food, or pennies to promote results. The strong arm wielding the strap was one of the reasons for male preference by manufacturers. Similarly this was viewed as a reason why female foremen should not be appointed.[2]

The strong-arm tactics still flourished in the 1890s. Adelaide Anderson gave an example of the deplorable level male foremen could sink to when exercising discipline: In 1895, a textile factory foreman turned a fire hose on a group of girls as a measure of discipline, chasing them into a vestibule, after which they had to walk home (in March) dripping with cold dirty water. Forty girls were subjected to this treatment. After examining the girls, the inspector made a complaint, but had no power to demand punishment of the foreman, apart from getting an apology, nothing could be done. She saw this as an example of the restricted powers awarded inspectors in the early days and the structural problems of female workplaces employing male foremen, who could resort to

---

[1] Martindale, *Women Servants*, pp. 51–2.
[2] Minoletti, 'The importance of ideology', pp. 121–46, on pp. 133–5.

abusive methods and violence to preserve their authority. Not until 1916 was welfare supervision brought under control of the inspectorate in Britain.[3]

The objections to women at work in general and women in positions of authority often came into one of the categories: a) Women have less physical strength so they cannot or should not work; b) Women wear the wrong kind of clothes; c) Men do not have respect for women, and subjecting them to coarse language and bad behaviour is bad for their morals.

Women and the dairy industry

In 1892, a discussion was conducted in the Danish Journal of the Dairy Industry about the possibility of employing female foremen.

Karl Fred Jensen claimed that female dress was unsuitable for work with machinery. The heavy lifting of milk churns was impossible for a woman. Communication with men transporting the milk would be on an unsuitable, coarse level, as men have no respect for women. The competition was already too fierce among men for the posts as dairy foremen. Women should engage in suitable fields, like shop work, hairdressing, clothes manufacturing, school teaching and hygiene.

Katrine Pedersen, who herself was a dairy foreman, replied that she was doubtful about the need to have physical strength to gain respect, or did Mr Jensen tend to engage in physical encounters to retain his position of authority? If this was the case, such respect was not worth very much. For a woman to retain authority she had to prove herself by showing her competence and taking on responsibility. Why a dairy should be particularly difficult for a woman, where she often had to deal with apprentices and young people, was difficult to understand. As to physical strength, women have had to handle heavy butter churns as dairy maids and dealing with such things is a matter of training and skill. Actually when in the position of foreman, heavy lifting it is no longer part of the duties. As to the problem with female dress, although there were no records of accidents caused by it, the attire could be modified and made more practical.

The reply to this by L.P. Larsen was a request for all male dairy workers to prevent women from gaining the position of foreman:

> This must be seen as one of the bad things of contemporary society where women want to become lawyers and doctors and all kinds of things. Soon they might even want entry into parliament – that would be great to have them helping there – and to argue ... let them stay as dairy maids doing their good work and keeping the standards of hygiene that only women can.[4]

---

[3] Report of the Chief Inspector of Factories for the year 1895, pp. 1896 XIX c 8067; Factory Inspectors Report 1895, p. 119; Anderson, *Women in the Factory*, pp. 26–7.

[4] Katrine Pedersen, 'Kvinder som Meijeribestyrende', *Maelkeritidende*, Dansk Meijeristforening, 1892, pp. 130–4; K.P. Larsen, 'Kvinder som meijeribestyrende', Maelkeritidende 1892, p. 130.

Appendix Table 6.1   Appointment of female inspectors before 1910.

1892	France	1901	Denmark
1893	Britain	1903	Finland
1893	Illinois USA	1906	Austria
1894	New Zealand	1906	Netherlands
1895	Australia	1909	Norway
1898	Hessen		
1899	Württemberg		
1899/1900	Preussen (Prussia)		
1902	Sachsen		

Sources: Beatrice Moring, 'Bourgeois and international networks as strategies for female civil servants in the late 19th and the early 20th century Europe', in M. Arrizabalaga, D. Burgos-Vigna and M. Yusta (eds), *Femmes sans Frontières* (Berne, 2011), pp. 271–90; Annika Akerblom, *Arbetarskydd for kvinnor: kvinnlig yrkesinspektion i Sverige 1913–1948* (Uppsala, 1998), pp. 23–5; Karl, Michael, *Fabriksinspektoren in Preussen: Das Personal de Geverbeaufsicht 1845–1945* (Opladen, 1993); Harrison, Barbara and Melanie Nolan, 'Reflections in colonial glass? Women factory inspectors in Britain and New Zealand 1893–1921', *Women's History Review* 13:2 (2004).

Appendix Table 6.2   Number of male and female inspectors in selected states of the USA.

	Inspection introduced in state	1895 Male inspectors	1895 Female inspectors
Massachusetts	1877	30	2
New Jersey	1882	7	
New York	1886	25	7
Connecticut	1889	4	
Pennsylvania	1889	16	5
Illinois	1893	4	7
Minnesota	1893	5	
Maine	1893	2	
Rhode Island	1894	1	1
Michigan	1895	8	1

Source: Annie MacLean, 'Factory legislation for women in the United States', The *American Journal of Sociology* (1897–8), pp. 183–205, on pp. 190–6, 201.

Appendix Table 6.3   Female inspectors in Germany 1905.

Preussen (Prussia)	4	Sachsen Coburg	1
Bayern	3	Sachsen Altenburg	1
Sachsen	5	Sachsen Anhalt	1
Württemberg	2	Hamburg	1
Hessen	2	Bremen	1
Baden	1		

Source: Michael Karl, *Fabriksinspektoren in Preussen* (Opladen, 1993), pp. 345–6.

Appendix Table 6.4   The first female inspectors in selected countries.

Britain	
1893	May Abraham (Tennant), Mary Paterson
1894	Adelaide Anderson, Lucy Deane
1895	Rose Squire
1897	Anna Tracey
New Zealand	
1894	Grace Neill
1895	Margaret Scott (Hawthorne)
1906	Harriet Morison
Australia	
1894	Margaret Gardiner Cuthbertson
1895	Augusta Zadov
1896	Agnes Milne
1897	Annie Duncan
Denmark	
1901	Annette Vedel
1910	Julie Arenholt
1914	Ragna Schou
Finland	
1903	Vera Hjelt
1908	Jenny Markelin-Svensson
Norway	
1909	Betzy Kjelsberg

APPENDIX 7 – INSPECTORS, ACTIVITY

I never cared for school I'd rather work than go to school. They used to take us during school vacation if we were fourteen or fifteen. Then at sixteen you'd start steady work. We all expected to work in the mill … My parents did not believe in education.

(Tamara Hareven and Randolph Langenbach, *Amoskeag: Life and Work in an American Factory City in New England* (London, 1979), p. 181)

My mother was hostile to 'modern regulations' of which compulsory education was one. She thought it unreasonable that other people should have the right to tell parents what to do with their children. On this point my father agreed … three years of school was enough according to my parents and what you had not learnt by the age of ten, you would never learn they repeated … I was not always able to go to school, I had to earn and every school day I missed was a workday with income. In the end my mother was sentenced to 24 days of incarceration because of my absences from school. One day two policemen came and took her to serve her sentence as she had not come of her own accord. This my mother never forgot, how a hardworking woman and good mother could be treated like that. I was so ashamed that I did not dare go out in the street.

(Adelheid Popp in Karin Roi Frey, *Wenn alle Stricke reissen, dann wird sie noch einmal Lehrerin, Lehrerinnen in biographischen Zeugnissen* (Bochum, 2001), pp. 111–12)

Appendix Table 7.1 Persons registered as employed in British inspected factories and workshops 1896–1901, gender and age.

	Men	Women	Boys 13–18	Girls 13–18	Boys 11–14 half-time	Girls 11–14 half-time	All females
1896	2,424,174	1,074,467	444,212	388,517	30,938	32,675	1,495,659
1897	2,484,370	1,077,115	463,088	401,054	27,936	30,237	1,508,406
1898–9	2,324,665	841,221	377,687	277,471	25,039	26,551	1,172,783
1901	2,467,553	909,699	398,849	323,902	20,579	20,965	1,254,566

Source: Report of the Chief Inspector of Factories 1904, PP 1905 X Cd 25691, p. 883; Report of the Chief inspector of Factories 1906, PP 1907 XV, pp. 918–21.

In 1896, more than 60,000 children between the ages of 11 and 14 worked in factories; in 1901 there were still more than 40,000 in this age group, including so-called half-timers. Source: p.p. 1902 XII, pp. 36–43.

Appendix Table 7.2   Workplaces in Britain visited by female inspectors.

Year	Female inspectors	Factories	Workshops	Total inspection visits
1895	4	2358	4599	11,457
1897	5	1496	2191	3687
1898	5	1272	1889	5261
1899	7	1258	2369	5427
1900	7	1342	2381	5956
1901	7	1352	3569	6833
1902	8	1870	2703	6619
1903	8	1911	3459	7642
1904	10	2100	3776	8395
1905	10	2673	3607	8796
1906	12	3245	4393	10,335
1907	12	3549	4666	8215
1908	15	4123	3818	7941
1910	17	6383	4482	11,658
1911	18	6613	4149	11,291
1912	18	5204	4149	11,273
1913	18	7000	4000	11,000

Sources: Report of the Chief inspector of Factories, P.P. 1902 XII, p. 54; Report of the Chief Inspector of Factories 1904, PP 1905 X Cd 25691, pp. 885–9; Report of the Chief inspector of Factories 1906, PP 1907 XV, p. 916; Report of the Chief inspector of Factories 1912–13 XXV, pp. 288, 342–5.

APPENDIX 8 – THE FEMALE INSPECTORS
AND SOCIETY

Report in the local newspaper *Silkeborg Dagblad*, 6 June 1910:

At the meeting of the women's organisation Dansk Kvindesamfund in Silkeborg 1910.

The factory inspector Ragna Schou tabled a resolution to back the proposal by the social democratic party about support for widows and orphans. The resolution found wide support. When the law about pensions for widows and orphans, constituting a civic right not part of the poor relief system, was passed in parliament in 1913, it was hailed with joy together with the new factory law, in the journal *Kvinden og samfundet*.

Silkeborg Dagblad Arkiv Silkeborg Arkiv Dansk Kvindesamfund
(/soeg?searchString=Dansk%20Kvindesamfund&ValgteArkiverIds=328)
(Elisa Petersen, 'Enkeloven og Fabrikloven vedtaget!, *Kvinden og samfundet* 15.5 1913, pp. 130–1)

Betzy Kjelsberg and contact with workers

Betzy Kjelsberg often gave talks at unions and worker's clubs. This was a way of establishing contacts with those best aware of existing problems. After the intervention to incorporate advice from workers in connection with the installation of new paper machines, her reputation as genuinely interested increased. After having approached the health authorities and local inspectors with no result, the workers association representing loggers turned to Kjelsberg. While she was aware that this was not part of the remit of a factory inspector, she still decided to make a visit.

Together with representatives of the workers I was rowing the flat boat along the river, watched the floating of the logs, the sorting etc. On land we went to numerous places to see the huts for eating and resting ... It is unbelievable that the officers have watched the dirt and mess year in and year out and done nothing.

She personally turned to one of the company directors and wrote to the overseer and begged them to remedy the worst problems instantly and later deal with the others. She was soon told by the workers that many of the problems had been rectified and received a heartfelt thank you for her visit (Magnhild Folkvord, *Betzy Kjelsberg: feminist og brubyggjar* (Oslo, 2016), pp. 126–7).

Florence Kelley and female inspectors

During her time in Europe, Florence Kelley came into contact with a large group of leading German-speaking intellectual Marxists. Her contacts gave her an outlet for publications that might not otherwise have found a receptive audience. Heinrich Braun was also able to pay her for publications, giving her an income after she lost her position as Inspector in Chicago. One of the articles in *Archiv für Soziale Gesetzgebung und Statistik* was on female inspectors and their role in the emerging activist state. In the article she underlined her conviction that the occupation should be open to all those interested. She also believed that working-class women would prove to be the best female inspectors, 'particularly those suggested by the unions', because they had good knowledge of the conditions and an interest in 'protecting fellow workers'. Her advice as to practical clothing sounded more like speaking to a middle-class audience, as neither 'the comfortable cycling suit' nor the unsuitable 'corsets, petticoats and white gloves of our grandmothers' sounded like the attire of factory women and union members. She also saw female factory inspectors as suitable for communication and giving talks that aroused sympathy 'in hundreds of women's clubs and scholarly institutions'. One of the most compelling reasons for appointing women was that they could stimulate the interest of women of 'the higher classes' in topics like 'child labour, the sweating system and working hours for women and children'. This description seems to fit Kelley herself rather than a female factory worker. In the same article, she proposes that the inspector does not have to be a woman but can as well be a man as there is no reason for women and children not communicating with a good inspector of either sex (Kathryn Kish Sklar, *Florence Kelley and the Nations Work: The Rise of Women's Political Culture 1830–1900* (Yale, 1995), pp. 298–9).

The National Consumers' League

The League launched a consumer's label by which it would be possible to identify goods manufactured under fair conditions. The New York branch wanted to create a 'white list' of department stores that met the standards on fair wages, hours, physical conditions, management–employee relations and child labour. To create the list, information had to be collected and for this the League wanted Florence Kelley. Kelley also wanted to achieve an overlap between the consumers label and that created by the unions to signify fair working conditions in manufacture. In 1899, she was employed as Inspector and Organizer and soon to be Secretary. The consumers' label fused the marketplace power of middle-class women's organisations with the interests of the union movement in ethical spending. Thereby Kelley could unite the two groups in society she saw as important for reform and progress in society (Sklar, *Florence Kelley*, pp. 310–11).

Her suggestions for responsible consumerism was among other things expressed in the following way:

> ... What are the sources of knowledge for the consumer today?
>
> Some lie ready at hand. Everyone can see how small is the newsboy in the street. If, in buying papers, we give the preference to big boys, we use the obvious means to encourage big boys and discourage little ones in the newspaper business in the streets. And nothing could be more clearly our duty than this. If the public refused outright to buy papers from little newsboys as it long ago ceased to buy hair shirts and horsehair furniture no little newsboys would be undergoing a daily process of ruin and demoralization upon our city streets ...

> (Florence Kelley, 'The responsibility of the consumer', *Annals of the American Academy of Political and Social Sciences* 32 (July 1908), pp. 108–12, on p. 108)

Appendix Table 8.1   Complaints addressed by the female inspector, Finland 1909.

Action taken	With employer
Insisted on accident insurance for workers	3
Achieved repair of workrooms in accordance with bakery law	43
Achieve repairs to floors, painting of walls, renewal of drinks pitchers	34
Suitable work clothes provided in bakeries	6
Providing workspace with flooring, double glazing, spittoons, wash basins, drinking water, cabinets for clothes and food	59
Washrooms, changing rooms, separate dining areas for women, separate WC for women, storage space, etc.	14
Achieved purchase of clogs for female workers	2

Chair for female worker with bad legs	1
Eye protectors for female workers	4
Achieved transfer of older women to lighter tasks	2
Achieved regulated lunch break	1
Payment for 2 weeks in case of dismissal	3
Cleaner employed	2
Installation of longer handle in paper press	1
Medical examination of workers who seemed ill	2
Required installation of ventilation	44
Installation of Emergency exit	1
Installation of light in WC	1
Installation of banisters	6
Installation of drain	1

Source: Vera Hjelt, *Berättelse afgifven af kvinnliga yrkesinspektören i Helsingfors, Tammerfors och Uleaborgs distrikt för 1909 jamte reseberättelse* (Helsingfors, 1910), pp. 11–12.

In 1911 a new set of complaints were received from the workers during the inspection trips. The issues were often on similar lines with previous years, lack of drinking water, bad air quality and dust in work rooms, cold or hot workrooms. These issues were relatively easily rectified by the inspector. More action was needed in questions relating to illegal overtime, unlawful dismissal and delays in payments in cases of dismissal, non-payment of accident compensation. Even in these cases, however, a positive outcome was achieved. When women expressed fear of going home after night work accommodation close to the factory was found (Hjelt, *Berättelse 1911*, pp. 3–4).

Complaints and dining areas

As I have been alerted to the fact that women have been subjected to disrespectful treatment by male co-workers in the communal dining areas I have suggested that these areas should be separated. Respectable women have come to me with oral and written complaints and asked me to take some action. I would hereby like to present an example proving the need for women to get their own dining rooms. When on one of my inspection trips I found two women with food baskets and soup in metal canisters having their dinner in the WC. When asked why frequenting such an unsuitable locality for the purpose of eating I was told of the inconsiderate disrespectful treatment in the dining area by male co-workers. The women had for three years in silence had their dinner in the WC as this was the only location in which they were free from abuse as they could lock themselves in. The

Owners of the factory had no idea about the situation and that the women were too afraid of the men to complain. In this case the situation could be helped by providing the women immediately with their own dining area but unfortunately all employers do not have the same attitude, particularly as situations like this tend to be kept hidden.

As many employers have not been willing to listen to my suggestions I considered that the situation could not stay as it is. Therefore at a meeting of the workplace inspectors the 23 of February 1906 I tabled the motion that we should unite and petition the industrial board for an amendment of the 1889 regulation that separate dining areas of men and women are to mandatory, particularly in factories that operate in night-time.

(Vera Hjelt, *Berättelse afgiven af kvinnliga yrkesinspetören i landet för år 1906* (Helsingfors, 1907), pp. 178–9)

Accidents and prevention

The arguments presented by Hjelt for the need to install emergency brakes provides understanding of the situation in factories and her description tallies uncomfortably well with the description of an accident by a girl in a textile factory in New England:

The number of accidents is still higher than it should be. In most cases it is unfair to blame the worker for being careless. It is not carelessness if there are momentary lapses of concentration. I am convinced that the reason for the too many accidents is to be found in the machines that are not provided with adequate protective systems and the existing ones are not properly positioned or maintained. Primarily I want to underline the need for integrated automatic protective devices. Another factor that increases the number of accidents is the lack of stopping mechanisms on the machine itself. Often the stopping device is not within the reach of the worker. When clothes or a hand has been entangled in the machinery it is important that the worker does not need to call for help, particularly as the noise in the factory often prevents him from being heard by the co-workers. In addition he cannot release himself to reach the stopping mechanism which often is located on the outside of the machinery. It is necessary that even a large machine can be stopped with the foot or using only one hand immediately from where the worker is standing.

(Vera Hjelt, *Berättelse afgifven af kvinnliga yrkesinspektören i Finland för år 1911* (Helsingfors, 1912), p. 9)

We weren't supposed to open the windows because they wanted the steam to stay in but the one who had worked on my frame the previous night had left the window open. I went close to it. I had already started my frame; and when I came back I stopped near the frame to put my lunch bag there. My dress was flared and the bottom got caught between the gears and started to roll around. I tried to pull it but I couldn't. The frame was still going. I tried to reach the handle and I couldn't. Bella and I were working back to back. I said 'Bella help me!' My dress kept going in and the reel was getting me in the back. When she saw that she came over and grabbed me in her arms to pull me. I said, 'Bella don't pull me! You're choking me! Try to stop the frame'. And she started to cry. 'Oh my God, what am I going to do?' One of the inspectors looked over and told another girl, 'This is the first time I've seen Bella and Ora fighting. What are they fighting about?' Then they looked closer and saw she was trying to help me. They stopped the machine and went over to get the boss.

Nobody could get me out of it. I was twisted all around the gears. Those gears should have been covered, but they weren't. The boss took his knife and cut my dress off. I was shaking like a leaf. I sat down on a box. Boy, was I shaking! ... He told the shipper to take me home. I said 'I can't go home like this! I've got no coat, no sweater, nothing! All the back of my dress is gone!' One of the night girls had forgotten her raincoat in there so they brought me the coat. And shaking like I was I went home, changed and went back to work the same day.

(Tamara Hareven and Randolph Langenbach, *Amoskeag: Life and Work in an American Factory City in New England* (London, 1979), pp. 189–91)

BIBLIOGRAPHY

Primary sources

Census of Helsinki, 1900, National Archive, Helsinki, Finland.
Emily Davies correspondence, Girton College library and archive, Cambridge, UK.
Memories of a Servant (1919–48), Girton College library and archive, Cambridge, UK.

Printed sources – official publications

UK

British Parliamentary Papers (1836) No 353, Factory Inspectors report.
Report of the Chief Inspector of Factories and Workshops for the year 1885, PP 1886 XIV.
Report of the Chief Inspector of Factories for the year 1893, PP 1894 XXI.
Report of the Chief Inspector of Factories for the year 1895, PP 1896 XIX c 8067.
Report of the Chief Inspector of Factories for the year 1896, PP 1897 XVII c 8561.
Report of the Chief Inspector of Factories 1897, PP 1898 XIV.
Report of the Chief Inspector of Factories 1898–9, PP 1900 XI.
Report of the Chief Inspector of Factories 1900, PP 1901 X Cd 668.
Report of the Chief inspector of Factories 1901, PP 1902 XII.
Report of the Chief Inspector of Factories 1903, PP 1904 X Cd 2139.
Report of the Chief Inspector of Factories 1904, PP 1905 X Cd 2569.
Report of the Chief Inspector of Factories 1906, PP 1907 X.
Report of the Chief Inspector of Factories 1906, PP 1907 LXXVI Cd 3333. PP 1908 XII.
Report of the Chief Inspector of Factories 1908 PP 1909 XXI Cd 4664.
Report of the Chief Inspector of Factories 1910, PP 1911 XXII Cd 5693.
Report of the Chief Inspector of Factories 1911 PP 1912–13 XXV Cd 6239.
Annual Report of the Chief Inspector of Factories 1913, PP 1914 Cd XXIX.
Annual Report of the Chief Inspector of Factories 1914–16 XXI Cd 8051.
Annual Report of the Chief Inspector of Factories 1915, PP 1916 IX Cd 8276.
Reports, commissions 3, Factories and Workshops, Appendix 7, Zz 2.

Medical Officers Report to the Committee of the Privy Council, Conditions of Nourishment, Smith 1864, PP XXVII.

The Annual Report for 1910 of the Chief Medical Officer of the Board of Education, Cd. 5925.

Royal Commission on Labour, the Employment of Women, PP 1892–4, XXIII c 6894.

Royal Commission on Civil Service, Appendix to Second Report, PP 1912–13, XV.

Royal Commission on Civil Service, First Appendix to Fourth Report, PP 1914, XVI, 353.

Select Committee on Post Office Servants PP 1906, XII, 775.

Board of Trade, Labour Department, *Accounts and Expenditure of Wage Earning Women and Girls* (1911), LXXXIX. PP. Cd 5963.

United States

First Annual Report of the Factory Inspectors of Illinois for the year ending December 1893.

Second Annual Report of the Factory Inspectors of Illinois for the year ending December 1894.

Third Annual Report of the Factory Inspectors of Illinois for the year ending December 1895.

The 6th and 7th Annual Reports of the US Commissioner of Labor 1890 and 1891.

Denmark

Beretning om Arbejds og Fabrikstillsynets Virksomhed Aaren 1919 og 1920 (Copenhagen, 1922).

Danmarks Haandverk og Industri ifolge Taellingen den 12 Juni 1906, *Danmarks Statistik*, Statistisk Tabelverk 5 Rekke (Copenhagen, 1908), Statens Statistiske Bureau.

Skoledirektørs betretning om skolelevers arbejde uden for skoletiden 1898, *Københavns Borgerrepresentanters Forhandlinger fra den 6te April til den 20de Marts* 1899, Aargang II (Copenhagen, 1899).

Law about Preventing Accidents When Using Machines etc. of 12 April 1889, by royal declaration, Christian IX of Denmark.

Norway

Arbeids og Lonningsforhold for Syersker i Kristiania (Kristiania, 1906), Det statistiske Centralbureau.

Census of Norway, the town of Moss, 1801, 1901.

Germany

Statistisches Jahrbuch für das Deutsche Reich (Berlin, 1895), Statistisches Amt.

Statistisches Jahrbuch für das Deutsche Reich (Berlin, 1899), Statistisches Amt.

Statistisches Jahrbuch für das Deutsche Reich (Berlin, 1907), Statistisches Amt.

France

Bulletin de l'inspection du travail 1905, Paris.
Seine (France) Conseil général (1891) *Mémoires de M. Le préfet de la Seine & de police et procès-verbaux des délibérations*, https://books.google.com/books?id=pHMAAAAAYAAJ&pg=PA259.

Italy

Camera Dei Deputati, *Relazioni della Commissione Parlamentare di Inchiesa sulle Condizioni dei Lavoratori in Italia* (Rome, 1963).
Roland Dubini, *L'unita d'Italia e la tutela da infortuni*, https://www.puntosicuro.it/sicurezza-sul-lavoro-C-1 (accessed 24 July 2018).

Austria

Die Arbeits und Lebensverhaltnisse der Wiener Lohnarbeiterinnen. Ergebnisse und stenographishes Protokoll der Enquete uber Frauenarbeit abgehalten in Wien vom 1 Martz bis 21 April 1896.

Finland

Official Statistics of Finland (OSF/FOS), The Industrial Board, reports and surveys:
Hjelt, Vera, *Berättelse afgifven af kvinnliga yrkesinspektören i Finland för år 1903* (Helsingfors, 1904).
Hjelt, Vera, *Berättelse afgifven af kvinnliga yrkesinspektören i Finland för år 1905* (Helsingfors, 1906).
Hjelt, Vera, *Berättelse afgifven af kvinnliga yrkesinspektören i Finland för år 1906* (Helsingfors, 1907).
Hjelt, Vera, *Berättelse afgifven af kvinnliga yrkesinspektören i Finland för år 1907* (Helsingfors, 1908).
Hjelt, Vera, *Berättelse afgifven af kvinnliga yrkesinspektören i Finland för år 1908* (Helsingfors, 1909).
Hjelt, Vera, *Berättelse afgifven af kvinnliga yrkesinspektören i Helsingfors, Tammerfors och Uleaborgs distrikt för 1909 jamte reseberättelse* (Helsingfors, 1910).
Hjelt, Vera, *Berättelse afgifven af kvinnliga yrkesinspektören i Finland för år 1911* (Helsingfors, 1912).
Hjelt, Vera, *Det industriella hemarbetet* (Helsingfors, 1913).
Hjelt, Vera, *Undersökning af nålarbeterskornas yrkesförhållanden i Finland* (Helsingfors, 1908).
Hjelt, Vera, *Yrkessjukdomsstatistik I, Lumparbeterskorna i Finland, Meddelanden fran industristyrelsen* (Helsingfors, 1909).
Hjelt, Vera, *Undersökning af yrkesarbetarnes lefnadsvillkor i Finland 1908–1909* (Helsingfors, 1911).
Hultin, Tekla, *Yötyöntekijättäret Suomen teollisuudessa* (Helsinki, 1911).
Snellman, G.R., *Undersökning av tobaksindustrin* (Helsingfors, 1903).
Snellman, G.R., *Undersökning av textilindustrin* (Helsingfors, 1904).

Snellman, G.R., *Tutkimus Helsingin, Turun, Tampereen ja Viipurin kansakoulu-laisten tyoskenteysta koulun ulkopuolella* (Helsinki, 1908).
Snellman, G.R., *Tutkimus Suomen Konttori-ja kauppa-apulaisten oloista* (Helsinki, 1909).
Snellman, G.R., *Tutkimus Suomen konepajoista* (Helsinki, 1911).
Snellman, G.R., *Undersökning angående pappersindustrin* (Helsingfors, 1912).
OSF XXVI Työtilastoa. A. Työssä kohdanneet tapaturmat 1890–1914 (Helsinki, 1915).
OSF, *Finlands Officiella Statistik, Arbetsstatistik XXVI A. Olycksfallen i arbetet* (Helsingfors, 1908).
OSF XXXII, 1, Sosiaalisia Erkoistutkimuksia 12 (Special social studies), Yötyöntekijättäret (Helsinki, 1935).

Printed sources – books and articles

Anderson, Adelaide, *Women in the Factory: An Administrative Adventure, 1893 to 1921* (London, 1922).
Black, Clementina, *Married Women's Work* (London, 1915).
Braun, Lily, *Die Frauenfrage: ihre geschichtliche Entwicklung und wirtschaftliche Seite* (Berlin, 1901).
Dalberg, Elna, 'Om kvindelig Fabriksinspection', *Kvinden og samfundet* 24:20 (1.12 1904), pp. 197–9.
Dundee Social Union, *Report on Housing and Industrial Conditions in Dundee* (Dundee, 1905).
Ensimmäinen, *yleisen työläisnaisten edustajain kokouksen pöytakirja 4, 5 ja 6 heinäkuuta 1900* (Helsinki, 1900).
Erismann, F., 'Die Ernährungsverhältnisse der Arbeiterbevölkerung in Central-russland', *Archiv für Hygiene* (1889), 9, pp. 23–47.
Gauffin, A., *Bostadsbehof och barnantal med afseende sarskildt a inneboendesys-temet i arbetarfamiljerna i Helsingfors* (Helsingfors, 1915).
Geijerstam, Gustaf, *Fabriksarbetarnes ställning i Marks härad* (Stockholm, 1894).
Geijerstam, Gustaf, *Anteckningar om arbetarförhållanden i Stockholm* (Stockholm, 1894).
Gonnard, R., *La femme dans l'industrie* (Paris, 1906).
Gripenberg, Alexandra, 'Dödeligheden mellem spaede Born og om gifte Kvinders Erhvervsarbejde', *Kvinden og samfundet* 38:17 (28.9 1901), pp. 150–1.
Groundstroem, Oscar, *Helsingin työväen taloudellisista oloista* (Porvoo, 1897).
d'Haussonville, Gabriel Paul Othenin de Cleron, *Salaires et misères de femmes* (Paris, 1900).
Kelley, Florence, 'The responsibility of the consumer', *Annals of the American Academy of Political and Social Sciences* 32 (July 1908), pp. 108–12.
Kelley, Florence and Marguerite Marsh, 'Labor legislation for women and its effects on earnings and conditions of labor', *The Annals of the American Academy of Political and Social Studies* 143 (1929), pp. 286–300.
Kempf, Rosa, *Das Leben der jungen Fabrikmädchen* (Leipzig, 1911).
Key-Åberg, K., *Inom textilindustrin i Norrköping sysselsatta arbetares lönevillkor och bostadsförhallanden* (Stockholm, 1896).

Kramers, Martina, 'Fra Holland', *Kvinden og samfundet* 35 (1919), p. 56.
Larsen, L.P., 'Kvinder som Mejeribestyrere', *Melkeritidende* 1892, p. 130.
Leffler, Johan, *Zur Kenntniss von den Lebens und Lohnverhältnissen Industrieller Arbeiterinnen in Stockholm* (Stockholm, 1897).
Lichtenfelt, H., 'Ueber die Ernahrung der Italiener', *Archiv für die Physiologie* 99 (1903), pp. 1–29.
Markelin, Jenny, *Nutid* (1909).
Markelin-Svensson, Jenny, 'Kvinnoskyddslagstiftning och moderskapsförsäkring', *Modern socialpolitik*, Föreningen för arbetarskydd och socialförsäkring I Finland, Band II (Helsingfors, 1912).
Markelin-Svensson, Jenny, 'Undersökning rörande arbetsförhållandena i restauranger och hotel, matserveringar samt kafeer i Helsingfors, *Arbetsstatistisk Tidskrift 1914*, pp. 275–302.
Markelin-Svensson Jenny, 'Om kommunal yrkesinspektion', Föreningen för arbetarskydd och socialförsäkring i Finland, Band IV, häft 4 (Helsingfors, 1916).
Markelin-Svensson Jenny, 'Sociala missförhållanden inom särskilda kvinnoyrken', Föredrag och diskussioner Föreningen för arbetarskydd och socialförsäkring I Finland, Band IV (Helsingfors, 1915).
Neergaard, Louise, 'Arbejdskaar for Kvinder i Samarbejde med Maend, Kvinner i Jernbane, Telegraf og Post Etaterne', *Kvinden og samfundet* 23 (15.4, 1907), pp. 51–2.
Neergaard, Louise, 'Fabrikslovens Revision', *Kvinden og samfundet* 3:27 (15.2 1911), pp. 24–5.
Neergaard, Louise, 'Fabrikloven vedtaget i Folketinget', *Kvinden og samfundet* 8:29 (30.4 1913), pp. 114–15.
Oliver; Thomas, 'The diet of toil', *The Lancet*, June (1895), pp. 1630, 1634–5.
Paludan-Muller, Astrid, 'Arbejdskaar for Kvinder I Samarbejde med Maend II, Kvinderne i Ministerierne og Magtsaten', *Kvinden og samfundet* 23 (30.6, 1907), pp. 91–2.
Paludan-Muller, Astrid and Louise Neeregaard, 'Arbejdskaar for Kvinder i Samarbejde med Maend III, Stats og Kommune Skoler', *Kvinden og samfundet* 23 (30.9, 1907), pp. 127–8.
Paton, D. Noël, J. Crauford Dunlop and Elsie Maud Inglis, *Study of the Diet of the Labouring Class in Edinburgh* (Edinburgh, 1902).
Pedersen, Katrine, 'Kvinder som Mejeribestyrere', *Melkeritidende* 1892, p. 130.
Petersen, 'Elsa, Enkeloven og fabriksloven vedtaget', *Kvinden og samfundet* 9:29 (15.5 1913), pp. 130–1.
Schou, Ragna, 'Arbejderbeskyttelse – Kvindebeskyttelse', *Kvinden og samfundet* 7:24 (15.3 1908), pp. 81–2.
von Richthofen, Elisabeth, *Uber die historische Wandlungen in der Stellung der autoritaren Parteien zur Arbeiterschutzgesetzgebung und die Motive dieser Wandlungen*, thesis Heidelberg 1901.
Schwimmer, Rosita, 'Berichte der ungarischen Gewerbeinspektion', *Arbeiterinnenzeitung* 22 (1902), pp. 5–6.
Valette, Aline, 'Les empoisonnées de travail', *La Fronde* 24.12 1897, p. 1.
Valette, Aline, 'Dans l'atelier de couture', *La Fronde* 1.1 1898, p. 2.
Valette, Aline, 'Salaires de famine', *La Fronde* 3.2 1898, p. 2.

Valette, Aline, 'Dans la filature lyonnaise', *La Fronde* 24.2 1898, p. 2.
Valette, Aline, 'Dans les magasins', *La Fronde* 6.3 1898, p. 2.
Valette, Aline, 'Abus patronaux', *La Fronde* 15.5 1898, p. 1.
Vedel, Annette, 'Danske Arbejderfamiliers Forbrug', *Nationalokonomisk Tidsskrift 1902*, 3:10, pp. 321–69.
Arbeiterinnezeitung 22 (1902).
Chicago Daily Tribune, 14 July 1893, p. 3.
Dagny 1903: 2, 'Kvinnliga yrkesinspektorer', pp. 39–44.
Kvinden og samfundet 26:21 (1910), pp. 239–40.
Zeitschrift für Frauenstimmrecht (Berlin, 1907–18).

Secondary Literature

Abrams, Lynn, *The Making of Modern Woman* (London, 2002).
Accampo, Elinor, *Industrialization, Family Life and Class Relations: Saint Chamond, 1815–1914* (Berkeley, 1989).
Adams, Jad, *Women and the Vote: A World History* (Oxford, 2014).
Agger, Gunhild and Hans Nielsen, *Hverdagsliv og klasserfaring i Danmark 1870–1920* (Aalborg, 1980).
Akerblom, Annika, *Arbetarskydd for kvinnor: kvinnlig yrkesinspektion i Sverige 1913–1948* (Uppsala, 1998).
Albisetti, James, 'Female education in German speaking Austria, Germany and Switzerland 1866–1914', in D. F. Good, M. Grandner and M. Maynes (eds), *Austrian Women in the 19th and 20th Centuries* (Providence, 1996).
Aldona, Sochaczewska-Juillerat, http://aehit.fr (accessed 13 June 2021).
Alexander, Sally, Anna Davin and Eve Hostetler, 'Labouring women: a reply to Eric Hobsbawm', *History Workshop Journal* 8:1 (1979), pp. 174–82.
Anderson, Adelaide and Carroll D. Wright, 'Labour legislation', *Encyclopaedia Britannica* (11th ed.) (Cambridge, 1911).
Anderson, Michael, *Family Structure in Nineteenth Century Lancashire* (Cambridge, 1971).
Anderson, Michael, 'The social position of spinsters in mid-Victorian Britain', *Journal of Family History* 9:4 (1984), pp. 377–93.
Angeles, Gloria and Franco Rubio, 'La contribución de la mujer española a la política contemporánea: de la restauración a la guerra civil (1876–1939)', in Rosa Capel Martinez (ed.), *Mujer y Sociedad en España 1700–1775* (Madrid, 1982), pp. 241–66.
Armstrong, Hazel, 'Workplace safety and accident compensation', *Te Ara The Encyclopedia of New Zealand*, http://TeAra.govt.nz/workplace-safety-and-accident-compensation.
Astrom, Anna Maria and Maud Sundman (eds), *Hemma bäst: Minnen fran barndomshem i Helsingfors* (Helsingfors, 1990).
Astrom, Margit, *Emma Irene Astrom* (Helsingfors, 1967).
Ayass, Wolfgang, *Arbeiterschutz*, 3 Band (Stuttgart-Jena, 1996).
Bairoch, Paul, 'Villes et développement économique dans une perspective historique', in Anne-Lise Head-König, Luigi Lorenzetti and Beatrice Veyrassat (eds), *Famille, parenté et réseaux en Occident* (Genève, 2001).

Bang, Gustav, *Arbejderrisiko*, Arbejdernes livsforhold under kapitalismen (1904) http://perbenny.dk/1912.html (accessed 22 May 2018).

Beddoe, Deirdre, *Discovering Women's History* (London, 1998).

Bell, Lady, *At the Works* (London, 1907).

Bennett, Judith, 'History that stands still: women's work in the European past', *Feminist Studies* 14 (1988), pp. 269–83.

Berg, Maxine, 'Women's work, mechanisation and the early phases of industrialisation in England', in P. Joyce (ed.), *Historical Meanings of Work* (Cambridge, 1987), pp. 64–98.

Berend, Ivan, *An Economic History of Nineteenth Century Europe – Diversity and Industrialization* (Cambridge, 2013).

Berger, Manfred, 'Baum Marie', online Social Lexicon Bonn 2022, Das netz für die Sozialwirtschaft, https://www.socialnet.de/lexicon/Baum-Marie (accessed 14 February 2022).

Beltio, Francesca, *The Sexual Division of Labour: The Italian Case* (Oxford, 1988).

Blom, Ida, 'Veien til juridisk likestellning', *Historica IV, Foredrag vid det XVIII nordiska historikermotet 1981* (Jyvaskyla, 1983), pp. 57–71.

Boak, Helen, 'The state as an employer of women in the Weimar Republic', in W.R. Lee and Eve Rosenhaft (eds), *State, Social Policy and Social Change in Germany 1880–1994* (Oxford, 1997), pp. 64–97.

Boot, H. and J.H. Maindonald, 'New estimates of age and sex specific earnings and the male-female earnings gap in the British cotton industry 1833–1906', *Economic History Review* 61:2 (2008), pp. 380–408.

Borderias, Christina, *Entre líneas, trabajo e identidad femenina en la España contemporánea la Compañia Telefónica, 1924–1980* (Barcelona, 1993).

Borderias, Christina, 'La transición femenina en la Barcelona de mediados del siglo XIX. Teoria social y realidad historica en la sistema estadistico moderno', in Carmen Sarasua and Lina Galvez (eds), *Privilegios o eficiencia? Mujeres y Hombres en los mercados de trabajo* (Alicante, 2003), pp. 241–77.

Borderias, Christina, 'Women's work and household economic strategies in industrializing Catalonia', *Social History* 29:3 (August 2004), pp. 373–83.

Borderias, Christina and Pilar Lopez, 'A gendered view of family budgets in mid-nineteenth century Barcelona', *Histoire et Mesure* XVIII:1–2 (2003), pp. 113–46.

Borderias Mondejar, Christina, Roser Gonzalez-Bagaria and Conchi Villar Garruta, 'El trabajo femenino en la Cataluña industriál (1919–1930): una propuesta de reconstrucción', *Revista de Demografia Historica* XXIX:1 (2011), pp. 55–88.

Bordin, Ruth, *Women and Temperance: The Quest for Power and Liberty 1873–1900* (Philadelphia, 1981).

Bourke, Joanna, *Husbandry to Housewifery* (Oxford, 1993).

Bourke, Joanna, 'Housewifery in working-class England 1860–1914', in Pamela Sharpe (ed.), *Women's Work: The English Experience 1650–1914* (London, 1998), pp. 332–50.

Bousardt, Marianne, *Onder Vrouwelijke Hoede, Vrouwen bij de Arbeidsinspectie* (s-Gravenhage, 1990).

Bowley, A.L. and A. Burnett-Hurst, *Livelihood and Poverty: A Study of Economic*

Conditions of Working Class Households in Northampton, Warrington, Stanley and Reading (London, 1915).

Bradbrook, M.C., *That Infidel Place: A Short History of Girton College 1869–1969* (Cambridge, 1969).

Bradley, Harriet, *Men's Work, Women's Work* (Cambridge, 1989).

Branca, Patricia, *Women in Europe since 1750* (London, 1978).

Braybon, Gail, and Penny Summerfield, *Out of the Cage: Women's Experiences in Two World Wars* (London, 1987).

Briggs, Lynelle, 'Celebration of the 40th anniversary of the lifting of the Marriage Bar', http://www.apsc.gov.au/media/briggs201106.htm (accessed 9 March 2020).

Broadberry, Stephen and Kevin O'Rourke (eds), *The Cambridge Economic History of Modern Europe 2, 1870 to the Present* (Cambridge, 2010).

Bull, Edvard, 'Barn i industriarbeid', in Bjarne Hodne and Solvi Sogner (eds), *Barn av sin tid* (Oslo, 1984), pp. 77–88.

Burnett, John (ed.), *Useful Toil, Autobiographies of Working People from the 1820s to the 1920s* (London, 1974).

Burnette, Joyce, *Gender, Work and Wages in Industrial Revolution Britain* (Cambridge, 2008).

Busby, Nicole and Rebecca Zahn, *A Dangerous Combination?*, https://dangerouswomenproject.org/2016/06/20/womens-trade-unionism (accessed 30 June 2022).

Camps, Enriqueta, *La Formación del Mercado de Trabajo Industrial en la Cataluña del Siglo XIX* (Madrid, 1995).

Camps, Enriqueta, 'Transitions in women's and children's work patterns and implications for the study of family income and household structure: a case study from the Catalan textile sector (1850–1925)', *The History of the Family* III:2 (1998), pp. 137–53.

Camps, Enriqueta, 'Mercados de trabajo modernos sin estado del bienestar: el sector textil catalan durante la dictatura de Primo de Rivera', in A. Carreras et al. (eds), *Homaje al Doctor Jordi Nadal: La industrialización y el desarollo económico de España* (Barcelona, 2002), pp. 1206–18.

Capel Martinez, Rosa Maria, 'Mujer y trabajo en España de Alfonso XIII', in R.M. Capel Martinez (ed.), *Mujer y Sociedad en España 1700–1775* (Madrid, 1982), pp. 207–40.

Capel Martinez, Rosa, 'La apertura del horizonte cultural', in Rosa Capel Martinez (ed.), *Mujer y Sociedad en España 1700–1775* (Madrid, 1982), pp. 109–46.

Carlsson, Sten and Jerker Rosen, *Svensk Historia 2* (Stockholm, 1970).

Cavonius, Gösta, *Den svenska lararutbildningen i Finland 1871–1974* (Helsingfors, 1988).

Chamberlain, Mary, *Fenwomen: A Portrait of Women in an English Village, History Workshop Series* (Oxford, 1975).

Chinn, Carl, *They Worked All Their Lives: Women of the Urban Poor 1880–1939* (Manchester, 2006).

Chvojka, Erhard, *Grossmutter, Enkelkindern erinnern sich* (Wien, 1992).

Cipolla, Carlo (ed.), *The Fontana Economic History of Europe*, The Emergence of Industrial Societies 1–2, The Twentieth Century 1–2 (Glasgow, 1979–82).

Clark, Anna, *Women's Silence, Men's Violence: Sexual Assault in England 1770–1845* (London, 1987).

Clark, Anna, '*The Struggle for the Breeches. Gender and the Making of the British Working Class* (Berkeley, 1995).

Cohen, Marilyn, 'Survival strategies in female-headed households: linen workers in Tullyish, County Down 1901', *Journal of Family History* XVII (1992), pp. 303–18.

Cook, Megan, 'Women's movement', Te Ara – The Encyclopedia of New Zealand, http:// www.TeAra.gov.nz/en/womens-movement/print (accessed 18 November 2021) (published May 2011).

Corfield, Penelope, *Power and the Professions in Britain 1700–1850* (London, 1995).

Costa, Dora L., 'From mill town to board room: the rise of women's paid labor', *Journal of Economic Perspectives* 14:4 (2000), pp. 101–22.

Coze, Werner and Jurgen Kocka, *Bildungsbürgetum in 19. Jahrhundert, I. Bildungssystem und Professionalisierung im Internationalen Vergleich* (Stuttgart, 1988).

Craig, Beatrice, *Women and Business since 1500* (London, 2016).

Craig, Beatrice, *Female Enterprise behind the Discursive Veil in Nineteenth Century Northern France* (London, 2016).

Dalzell, Robert F., *The Good Rich and What They Cost Us* (New Haven, 2013).

Dalziel, Raewyn, 'An experiment in the social laboratory', in Ian Fletcher, Philippa Levine and Laura Mayhall (eds), *Women's Suffrage in the British Empire: Citizenship, Nation and Race* (London, 2012), pp. 87–102.

Damousi, Joy, 'Female factory inspectors and leadership in early 20th century Australia', in Joy Damousi, Kim Rubenstein and Mary Tomsic (eds), *Diversity and Leadership: Australian Women Past and Present* (Canberra, 2014), pp. 169–88.

Daniels, Kay, 'Annie Jane Duncan', *Australian Dictionary of Biography*, adb. anu.edu.au/biography/duncan-annie-jane-6043 (accessed 9 November 2020).

Dansk Biografisk Lexicon/1, 'Andrae, Carl Christopher, Georg', http://runeberg. org.dbl/1/0276.html (accessed 21 January 2009).

Dansk Biografisk Lexicon/18, 'Vedel, Pet. Aug.', http://runeberg.org/dbl/18/0312. html (accessed 21 January 2009).

Dasey, Robyn, 'Women's work and the family: women garment workers in Berlin and Hamburg before the First World War', in R. Evans and W.R. Lee, *The German Family: Essays on the Social History of the Family in 19th and 20th Century Germany* (London, 1981), pp. 221–55.

Davidoff, Leonore and Catherine Hall, *Family Fortunes: Men and Women of the English Middle Class 1780–1850* (London, 1987).

Davies, Celia, 'The health visitor as mother's friend: a woman's place in public health 1900–14', *Social History of Medicine* 1:1 (April 1988), pp. 39–60.

Davies, Emily, 'Some account of a proposed new college for women', in *Thoughts on Some Questions Relating to Women 1860–1908* (London, 1910).

Davies, Margaret Llewelyn (ed.), *Maternity: Letters from Working Women* (London, 1915).

de Groot, Gertjen, 'Foreign technology and the gender division of labour in a

Dutch cotton spinning mill', in G. de Groot and M. Schrover (eds), *Women Workers and Technological Change in Europe in the 19th and the 20th Century* (London, 1995), pp. 52–66.

DeValt, Ileen, '"Everybody works but father": why the census misdirected historians of women's employment', *Social Science History* 40:3 (2016), pp. 369–83.

Dingle, A.E., 'Drink and working-class living standards in Britain 1870–1914', *Economic History Review* 4 (1972), pp. 608–22.

Dyhouse, Carol, *Feminism and the Family in England 1880–1939* (Oxford, 1989).

Earle, Peter, *A City Full of People* (London, 1994).

Ehmer, Josef, 'Frauenarbeit und Arbeiterfamilie in Wien', in Hans-Ulrich Wehler (ed.), *Frauen in der Geschichte des 19. und 20. Jahrhunderts* (Göttingen, 1981), pp. 438–73.

Ehmer, Josef, 'The making of the "modern family" in Vienna 1780–1930', *History and Society in Central Europe* 1:1 (1991), pp. 7–28.

Ehmer, Josef, *Familienstruktur und Arbeitsorganisation im frühindustriellen Wien* (Wien, 1980), pp. 150–61.

Elkjaer Sorensen, Astrid, *Barsellogivningens udvikling i Danmark fra 1901*, http://danmarkhistorien.dk (accessed 5.11.2020).

Epstein, Barbara, *The Politics of Domesticity: Women, Evangelism and Temperance in Nineteenth Century America* (Middletown, CT, 1981).

Eriksen, Sidsel, Per Ingesman, Mogens Melchiorsen and John Pedersen (eds), *Socialhistorie og samfundsforandring* (Arhus, 1984).

Ericson, Amy, 'Married women's occupations in 18th century London', *Continuity and Change* 23:2 (2008), pp. 267–308.

Ericson, Ann-Charlotte, 'Slöjdlärares undervisning', thesis, Department of Education, University of Gothenburg (Gothenburg, 2007).

Espuny Tomás, Maria Jesús, 'Los accidentes de trabajo: perspectiva histórica', *IUS Labor* 3 (2005), pp. 1–10.

Evans, Richard, 'Politics and the family: social democracy and the working class family in theory and practice', in R. Evans and W.R. Lee (eds), *The German Family: Essays on the Social History of the Family in Nineteenth and Twentieth Century Germany* (London, 2015), pp. 256–88.

Evans Paulson, Ross, *Women's Suffrage and Prohibition: A Comparative Study of Equality and Social Control* (Glenview, Illinois, 1973).

Feurer, Rosemary, 'The meaning of "sisterhood": the British women's movement and protective labour legislation 1870–1914', *Victorian Studies* 31 (1988), pp. 233–60.

Fletcher, Philippa, L., 'Agnes Milne', *Australian Dictionary of Biography*, adb.anu.edu.au/biography/milne-agnes-anderson-13100 (accessed 9 November 2020).

Folkvord, Magnhild, *Betzy Kjelsberg: feminist og brubyggjar* (Oslo, 2016).

Forelius, Sinikka, 'Työväensuojelu ja huoltonayttelystä työsuojelunäyttelyyn 1909–1999', http://www.tyovaenperinne.fi/tyovaentutkimus/1999 (accessed 11 August 2007).

Fout, John, 'The Viennese Enquête of 1896 on working women', in Ruth Ellen

Joeres and Mary Jo Maynes (eds), *German Women in the 18th and 19th Centuries* (Bloomington, 1986), pp. 42–60.

Fowler, Alan and Lesley Fowler, *The History of the Nelson Weavers Association* (Manchester, 1983).

Freismuth, Elisabeth, 'Die Frau im öffentlichen Recht', in Reingard Witzmann (ed.), *Die Frau im Korsett, Wiener Frauenalltag zwischen Klischee und Wirklichkeit 1848–1920* (Wien, 1985), pp. 30–40.

Froide, Amy, 'Disciplinary differences: a historian's take on why wages differed by gender in eighteenth and nineteenth century Britain', *Social Science History* 33:4 (2009), pp. 465–72.

Fuchs, Rachel and Victoria Thompson, *Women in 19th Century Europe* (London/ New York, 2005).

Galvez, Lina, 'Breadwinning patterns and family exogenous factors', in A. Janssens (ed.), *The Rise and Decline of the Male Breadwinner Family? International Review of Social History, Supplements* 5 (1998), pp. 87–128.

Garrett, Eilidh, 'The dawning of a new era? Women's work in England and Wales at the turn of the twentieth century', in Nigel Goose (ed.), *Women's Work in Industrial England* (Hertfordshire, 2007), pp. 314–62.

German History in Documents and Images, Forging an Empire: Bismarckian Germany 1866–1890, Table: Gainfully employed persons and their dependents by economic sector, https://germanhistorydocs.ghi-dc.org (accessed 22 May 2018).

German History in Documents and Images, Volume 4, Forging an Empire: Bismarckian Germany 1866–1890, Nominal wages, https://germanhistorydocs. ghi-dc.org (accessed 22 May 2018).

Girton College, *Girton College Register 1869–1946* (Cambridge, 1948)

Gittins, Diana, *Fair Sex: Family Size and Structure 1900–39* (London, 1982).

Glickman, Rose, *Russian Factory Women: Workplace and Society 1880–1914* (Berkeley, 1984).

Goldin, Claudia, *Marriage Bars: Discrimination against Women Workers 1920s to 1950s* (Cambridge, MA, 1988), Working Paper 2747.

Goodman, Jordan and Katrina Honeyman, *Gainful Pursuits: The Making of Industrial Europe 1600–1914* (London, 1988).

Goose, Nigel, 'Working women in industrial England', in Nigel Goose (ed.), *Women's Work in Industrial England* (Hertfordshire, 2007), pp. 1–28.

Goransson, Anita, *Fran familj till fabrik* (Lund, 1988).

Grandner, Margarete, 'Special labor protection for women in Austria 1860–1918', in Ulla Wikander, Alice Kessler-Harris and Jane Lewis (eds), *Protecting Women: Labour Legislation in Europe, the United States and Australia 1880–1920* (Urbana, 1995), pp. 150–81.

Guilbert, Madeleine, *Les femmes et l'organisation syndicale avant 1914* (Paris, 1966).

Guilbert, Madeleine, 'Femmes et syndicats en France', *Sociologie et Sociétés* 6:1 (1974), pp. 157–69.

Gunnlaugsson, Gisli, *Family and Household in Iceland 1801–1930* (Uppsala, 1988).

Guttormsson, Loftur, 'The development of popular religious literacy in the seventeenth and eighteenth centuries', *Scandinavian Journal of History* 15:1 (1990), pp. 7–33.

Haapala, Pertti, *Tehtaan valossa* (Tampere, 1986).

Hageman, Gro, 'Protection or equality? Debates on protective legislation in Norway', in Ulla Wikander, Alice Kessler-Harris and Jane Lewis (eds), *Protecting Women: Labour Legislation in Europe, the United States and Australia 1880–1920* (Urbana, 1995), pp. 267–90.

Häggman, Kai, 'Fran åldring till glad pensioner, pensionssystem och pensionstagare i Finland på 1900-talet', *Historisk Tidskrift för Finland* 2 (1998), pp. 337–55.

Hahn, Sylvia and Karl Flanner (eds), *Die Wienerische Neustadt* (Wien, 1994).

Hahn, Sylvia, 'Women in older ages', *The History of the Family* 7:1 (2002), pp. 33–58.

Hakim, Catherine, *Key Issues in Women's Work* (London, 2004).

Hammerton, James, *Cruelty and Companionship: Conflict in Nineteenth Century Married Life* (London, 1992).

Hansen, Svend Aage, *Okonomisk vekst i Danmark 1720–1914* (Copenhagen, 1972).

Hareven, Tamara, *Family Time and Industrial Time* (Cambridge/New York, 1982).

Hareven, Tamara and Randolph Langenbach, *Amoskeag: Life and Work in an American Factory City in New England* (London, 1979).

Harrison, Barbara, 'Suffer the working day: women in the "dangerous trades", 1880–1914', *Women's Studies International Forum* 13:1/2 (1990), pp. 79–90.

Harrison, Barbara and Melanie Nolan, 'Reflections in colonial glass? Women factory inspectors in Britain and New Zealand 1893–1921', *Women's History Review* 13:2 (2004), pp. 263–88.

Harrison, Elaine, *Officials of Royal Commissions of Inquiry 1870–1939* (London, 1995).

Heikkinen, Sakari, *Labour and the Market* (Helsinki, 1997).

Helperstorfer, Irmgard, 'Die Frauenrechtsbewegung und ihre Ziele', in Reingard Witzmann (ed.), *Die Frau im Korsett, Wiener Frauenalltag zwischen Klischee und Wirklichkeit 1848–1920* (Wien, 1985), pp. 21–9.

Hennock, E.P., *British Social Reform and German Precedents, The Case of Social Insurance 1880–1914* (Oxford, 1987).

Henriques, Ursula, *Before the Welfare State: Social Administration in Early Industrial Britain* (London, 1979).

Hentilä, Marjaliisa, 'Maa jossa piiatkin saa äänestää', in Leena Laine and Pirjo Markkola (eds), *Tuntematon työläisnainen* (Tampere, 1989), pp. 162–85.

Hentilä, Marjaliisa, *Keikkavaaka ja Kousikka, Kaupan työ ja tekijät 1800-luvulta itsepalveluaikaan* (Helsinki, 1999).

Hesselgren, Kerstin, 'Den kvinnliga yrkes och sundhetsinspektionen i England', *Dagny* 15 (1904), pp. 331–8.

Hietala, Marjatta, *Tietoa, taitoa, asiantuntemusta: Helsinki Eurooppalaisessa kehityksessä 1875–1917* (Helsinki, 1992).

Higgs, Edward, 'Women's occupations and work in the nineteenth century censuses', *History Workshop Journal* 23 (1987), pp. 59–82.

Hill, Bridget, *Women, Work and Sexual Policy in Eighteenth Century England* (London, 1994).

Hirdman, Yvonne, *Magfrågan: Stockholm 1870–1920* (Stockholm, 1983).

Hjelt, Vera, Slöjdens berättigade vid den s.k. lärda skolan (Helsingfors, 1886).

Hjelt, Vera, *Qvinnan på de praktiska arbetsområdena* (Helsingfors, 1888).

Hjelt, Vera, *Arbetsskydd mot olycksfall och ohälsa* (Helsingfors, 1939).

Hjelt-Cajanus, Ester, *Vera Hjelt, en banbryterska* (Helsingfors, 1946).

Hjerppe, Riitta and Per Schybergson, *Kvinnoarbetare i industrins genom-brottsskede 1850–1913*, Institute of Economic and Social History, University of Helsinki (Helsinki, 1977).

Hobsbawm, E.J., *Industry and Empire* (Harmondsworth, 1979).

Holborn, Hajo, *A History of Modern Germany – 1840–1945* (Princeton, 1969).

Holcombe, Lee, *Victorian Ladies at Work: Middle Class Working Women in England and Wales 1850–1914* (Hamden, CT, 1973).

Honeyman, Katrina, *Women, Gender and Industrialization in England, 1700–1870* (Basingstoke, 2000).

Howe, Renate, 'A paradise for working men but not working women: women's wagework and protective legislation in Australia 1890–1914', in Ulla Wikander, Alice Kessler-Harris and Jane Lewis (eds), *Protecting Women: Labour Legislation in Europe, the United States and Australia 1880–1920* (Urbana, 1995), pp. 318–35.

Hubbard, William, *Familiengeschichte, materialen zur deutschen Familie seit dem Ende des 18. Jahrhunderts* (München, 1983).

Hudson, Pat, 'Proto-industrialisation: the case of West Riding', *History Workshop Journal* 12 (1981), pp. 34–61.

Hufton, Olwen, *The Prospect Before Her* (New York, 1996).

Humphries, Jane, *Childhood and Child Labour in the British Industrial Revolution* (Cambridge, 2010).

Humphries, Jane and Benjamin Schneider, 'Spinning the Industrial Revolution', *Discussion Paper in Economic and Social History* 145 (University of Oxford, June 2016).

Humphries, Jane and Jacob Weisdorf, 'The Wages of Women in England 1260–1850', *Oxford Economic and Social History Working Papers* 33 (Oxford, 2014).

Hunt, Margaret, *The Middling Sort: Commerce, Gender and the Family in England 1680–1780* (Berkeley, 1996).

Hunter, Donald, *Health in Industry* (Harmondsworth, 1959).

Hyslop, Anthea, 'Cuthbertson, Margaret Gardiner (1864–1944)', *Australian Dictionary of Biography*, adb.anu.edu.au/biography/cuthbertson-margaret-gardiner-5858 (accessed 9 November 2020).

Jaakkola, Jouko, 'Sosiaalisen kysymyksen yhteiskunta', in Jouko Jaakkola, Panu Pulma, Mirja Satka and Kyösti Urponen (eds), *Armeliaisuus, yhtesöapu, sosiaaliturva* (Helsinki, 1994), pp. 71–162.

Jacobs, Anna and Larry Isaac, 'Gender composition in contentious collective action: "girl strikers" in gilded age America – harmful, helpful or both?', *Social Science History* 43:4 (2019), pp. 733–64.

Jansz, Ulla, 'Women workers? The labour law and the debate on protective legislation in the Netherlands', in Ulla Wikander, Alice Kessler-Harris and Jane

Lewis (eds), *Protecting Women: Labour Legislation in Europe, the United States and Australia 1880–1920* (Urbana, 1995), pp. 188–209.

Jaworski, Rudolf, 'Galicia: initiatives for the emancipation of Polish women', in Rudolf Jaworski and Bianca Pietrow-Ennker, *Women in Polish Society* (Boulder, 1992).

John, Angela, *By the Sweat of Their Brow: Women Workers in Victorian Coal Mines* (London, 1980).

John, Angela (ed.), *Unequal Opportunities: Women's Employment in England 1800–1914* (Oxford, 1986).

Johnson, Paul, 'Age, gender and the wage in Britain 1830–1930', in Peter Scholliers and Leonard Schwartz (eds), *Experiencing Wages: Social and Cultural Aspects of Wage Forms in Europe since 1500* (New York, 2003), pp. 229–50.

Johnson, Robert E., 'Family relations and the urban-rural nexus', in David Ransel (ed.), *The Family in Imperial Russia* (Urbana, 1978), pp. 263–79.

Jones, Helen, 'Women health workers: the case of the first women factory inspectors in Britain', *Social History of Medicine* 1:2 (August 1988), pp. 165–82.

Jones, Helen, 'Augusta Zadow', *Australian Dictionary of Biography*, adb.anu. edu.au/biography/zadow-christiane-susanne-augusta-9224, https://sahistoryhub. history.sa.gov.au/people/augusta-zadw (accessed 9 November 2020).

Jordan, Ellen, 'The exclusion of women from industry in 19th century Britain', *Comparative Studies in Society and History* 31 (1989), pp. 273–96.

Kaarninen, Mervi, *Nykyajan tytöt* (Helsinki, 1995).

Karivalo, Toini, *Widbom- suku* (Jyvaskyla, 1980).

Karl, Michael, *Fabriksinspektoren in Preussen: Das Personal der Gewerbeaufsicht 1845–1945* (Opladen, 1993).

Karlsson, Lynn, *Mothers as Breadwinners: Myth or Reality in Early Swedish Industry?* (Uppsala, 1995).

Kessler-Harris, Alice, 'The paradox of motherhood: night work restrictions in the United States', in Ulla Wikander, Alice Kessler-Harris and Jane Lewis (eds), *Protecting Women: Labour Legislation in Europe, the United States and Australia 1880–1920* (Urbana, 1995), pp. 337–56.

Kessler-Harris, Alice, *Women Have Always Worked: A Concise History* (Chicago, 2018).

Kettunen, Pauli, *Suojelu, suoritus, subjekti* (Helsinki, 1994).

Kingston, Beverly, 'Isabella Golding', *Australian Dictionary of Biography*, adb.anu.edu.au/biography/golding-isabella-theresa-belle-7040 (accessed 9 November 2020).

Kirby, Peter, *Child Labour in Britain, 1750–1870* (London, 2003).

Kleinberg, S.J., 'Children's and mothers' wage labor in three US cities 1880–1920', *Social Science History* 29:1 (2005), pp. 45–76.

Knudsen, Knut and Anne Caspersen, *Kampen for en bedre tillvaerelse* (Copenhagen, 1991).

Knudsen, Tim, 'Vedel, Fanny Annette', *Dansk Kvindebiografisk Leksikon*, http://www.kvinfo.dk/side/597/bio/1389 (accessed 5 September 2008).

Kopl, Regina and Leopold Redl, *Das Totale Ensemble, Ein Führer duch die Industriekultur In südlicher Wiener Becken* (Wien, 1989).

Kovacs, Maria, 'The politics of emancipation in Hungary', History Department Working Paper, Series 1, Central European University (Budapest, 1994).

Kuusanmäki, Jussi, 'Markelin-Svensson, Jenny (1882–1929)', *Suomen kansallisbibliografia* (Helsinki, 2005), pp. 556–8.

Kuusanmäki, Jussi, *Sosiaalipolitiikkaa ja kaupunkisuunnittelua, Tietoa, taitoa asiantuntemusta Helsinki eurooppalaisessa kehityksessä 1875–1917* (Helsinki, 1992).

Lähteenmäki, Maria, *Mahdollisuuksien aika, Työläisnaiset ja yhteiskunnan muutos 1910–30 luvun Suomessa* (Helsinki, 1995).

Lähteenmäki, Maria, 'Ansioäidit arvossaan', in Raimo Parikka (ed.), *Työ ja Työttömyys* (Helsinki, 1994), pp. 66–83.

Lande, Dora, Arbeitsverhältnisse in der Berliner Maschinenindustrie zu Beginn des 20. Jahrhunderts (Leipzig, 1910).

Leichter, Kathe, 'Arbeitsinspektion', http://www.arbeitsinspektion.gvat/AI/Arbeitsinspektion/Geschichte (accessed 6 July 2007).

Lempiäinen, Pentti, *Rippikäytantö Suomen Kirkossa uskonpuhdistuksesta 1600-luvun loppuun* (Helsinki, 1963).

Levine, Philippa, *Feminist Lives in Victorian England: Private Roles and Public Commitment* (Oxford, 1990).

Livesley, Ruth, 'The politics of work: feminism, professionalisation and women inspectors of factories and workshops', *Women's History Review* 13:2 (June 2004), pp. 233–61.

Llonch Casanovas, Montserrat, 'Insercion laboral de la immigracion y sistema de reclutamiento de la fabrica textile: Vilassar de Dalt, 1910–1945', *Boletin de la Asociación de Demografia Histórica* XII:2–3 (1994), pp. 149–61.

Llonch Casanovas, Montserrat, *Tejiendo en red. La industria del género de punto en Cataluña 1891–1936* (Barcelona, 2007).

Llorenç Ferrer, Alós, 'Notas sobre la familia y el trabajo de la mujer en la Catalunya Central (siglos XVIII–XX)', *Boletin de la Asociación de Demografia Histórica* XII:2–3 (1994), pp. 199–232.

Lönnqvist, Bo, Ivar Nordlund, Monica Ståhls and Katia Båsk (eds), *Industrisamhalle och Arbetarkultur* (Helsingfors, 1997).

Lundin, Carl, *Nya Stockholm* (Stockholm, 1890).

Malcolm, Tessa K., 'Sheppard, Katherine Wilson', Dictionary of New Zealand Biography, Te Ara – the Encyclopedia of New Zealand, https://teara.govt.nz/en/biographies/2s20/sheppard-katherine-wilson.

Manchini, Giulia, *Women's Labour Force Participation in Italy 1861–2016* (Rome, 2017), HB Working Paper Series, n. 8.

Mantl, Elisabeth, *Heirat als Privileg* (Wien, 1997).

Margadant, Jo Burr, *Madame le Professeur: Women Educators in the Third Republic* (Princeton, 1990).

Mark-Lawson, Jane and Anne Witz, 'From family labour to "family wage"? The case of women's labour in 19th century coalmining', *Social History* 13 (1988), pp. 151–74.

Markkola, Pirjo, *Työläiskodin synty* (Helsinki, 1994).

Markussen, Ingrid, 'The development of writing ability in the Nordic countries in the eighteenth and nineteenth centuries', *Scandinavian Journal of History* 15:1 (1990), pp. 37–63.

Martindale, Hilda, *From One Generation to Another, 1839–1944: A Book of Memoirs by Hilda Martindale* (London, 1944).

Martindale, Hilda, *Women Servants of the State 1870–1938* (London, 1938).

Martindale, Hilda, *Some Victorian Portraits and Others* (London, 1948).

Matovic, Margareta, 'The Stockholm marriage: extra legal family formation in Stockholm 1860–1890', *Continuity and Change* 1:3 (1986), pp. 385–414.

Maynes, Mary Jo, *Taking the Hard Road: Life Course in French and German Workers' Autobiographies in the Era of Industrialization* (Chapel Hill, 1995).

McDermid, Jane and Anna Hillyar, *Women and Work in Russia 1880–1930* (London, 1998).

McFeeley, Mary Drake, *Lady Inspectors: The Campaign for a Better Workplace* (Oxford, 1988).

McLean, Annie, 'Factory legislation for women in the United States', *The American Journal of Sociology* 3 (1897–8), pp. 183–205.

McMillan, James F., *France and Women 1789–1914: Gender, Society and Politics* (London, 2000).

Metz, Annie, 'Marguerite Durand et l'Office du travail féminin', *Archives du Féminisme*, 13 December 2007, http://www.archivesdufeminisme.fr/ressources-en-ligne/articles-et-comptes-rendus/articles-historiques/metz-marguerite-durand-loffice-du-travail-feminin (accessed 15 November 2022).

Meyerowitz, Joanne, *Women Adrift: Independent Wage Earners in Chicago 1880–1930* (Chicago, 1988).

Minoletti, Paul, 'The importance of ideology: the shift to factory production and its effect on women's employment opportunities in the English textile industries 1760–1850', *Continuity and Change* 28:1 (2013), pp. 121–46.

Modell, John, 'Patterns of consumption, acculturation and family income strategies in late nineteen-century America', in Tamara Hareven and Maris Vinovskis (eds), *Family and Population in Nineteenth Century America* (Princeton, 1978), pp. 206–40.

Moehling, Carolyn M., 'Women's work and men's unemployment', *Journal of Economic History* 61:4 (2001), pp. 926–49.

Mooser, Josef, *Arbeiterleben in Deutschland* (Frankfurt, 1984).

Moriceau, Caroline, 'Les perceptions des risques au travail dans la seconde moitié du XIX siècle', *Revue d'histoire moderne et contemporaine* 56:1 (2009), pp. 11–27.

Moring, Beatrice, 'Widows, children and assistance from society in urban Northern Europe 1890–1910', *The History of the Family* 13:1 (2008), pp. 105–17.

Moring, Beatrice, 'Bourgeois and international networks as strategies for female civil servants in the late 19th and the early 20th century Europe', in Marie-Pierre Arrizabalaga, Diana Burgos-Vigna and Mercedes Yusta (eds), *Femmes sans Frontières* (Berne, 2011), pp. 271–90.

Moring, Beatrice, 'Strategies and networks: family earnings and institutional contributions to women's households in urban Sweden and Finland 1890–1910', in Tindara Addabo, Marie-Pierre Arrizabalaga, Christina Borderias and Alastair Owens (eds), *Gender Inequalities, Households and the Production of Well-Being in Modern Europe* (London, 2010), pp. 77–94.

Moring, Beatrice, 'Women, work and survival strategies in urban Northern Europe before the First World War', in Beatrice Moring (ed.), *Female Economic Strategies in the Modern World* (London, 2012), pp. 45–72.

Moring, Beatrice, 'Women, family, work and welfare in Europe in the long 19th century. Budget studies, the nuclear family and the male breadwinner', *Revista de Demografia Historica* XXXIII:II (2015), pp. 119–52.

Moring, Beatrice, 'Production without labour market participation', *Historicka demografie* 43/2 (2019), pp. 233–56.

Moring, Beatrice, 'Female migrants, partner choice and socio-economic destiny – Finnish women in Stockholm in the 17th and 18th century', *Revista de Demografia Historica* XXXIX:1 (2021), pp. 53–75.

Moring, Beatrice and Richard Wall, *Widows in European Economy and Society 1600–1920* (Woodbridge, 2017).

Morley, Edith, *Women Workers in Seven Professions: A Survey of their Economic Conditions and Prospects* (edited for the studies committee of the Fabian Women's group) (London, 2017).

Munsterhjelm, Jacobina Charlotta, *Dagböcker 1799–1801* (Helsingfors, 1970).

Napias, Henri, 'Inspection hygienique des fabriques et ateliers', *Annales d'hygiène publique et de médecine légale* 10 (1883), pp. 412–25.

Nicolás Marín, María Encarna and Basilisa López García, 'La situación de la mujer a través de los movimientos de apostolado seglar: la contribución a la legitimación del franquismo (1939–1956)', in Rosa Capel Martinez (ed.), *Mujer y Sociedad en España 1700–1775* (Madrid, 1982), pp. 367–92.

Niggemann, Heintz, *Emanzipation zwischen Sozialismus und Feminismus* (Wuppertal, 1981).

Nolan, Melanie and Penelope Harper, 'Morison, Harriet', *Dictionary of New Zealand Biography* Te Ara, https://teara.govt.nz/en/biographies (accessed 10 November 2020).

Nolan, Melanie, 'Hawthorne, Margaret', *Dictionary of New Zealand Biography* Te Ara, https://teara.govt.nz/en/biographies (accessed 10 November 2020).

Nordström, Alf, *Om arbetarbostäder i Stockholm under 1800-talets senare del* (Stockholm, 1948).

Nørregaard, Georg, *Arbejdsforhold indenfor dansk Haandværk og Industri 1857–1899* (Copenhagen, 1943).

O'Day, Rosemary, *Education and Society 1500–1800* (London, 1982).

Ollila, Anne, *Jalo velvollisuus, virkanaisena 1800-luvun lopun Suomessa* (Tampere, 2000).

O'Neill, Gilda, *Lost Voices: Memories of a Vanished Way of Life* (London, 2006).

Page, Dorothy, 'Dalrymple, Learmoth White', *Dictionary of New Zealand*, http://www.TeAra.govt.nz/en/biographies/1d2/dalrymple-learmoth-white (accessed 10 November 2020).

Parejo, Antonio, 'De la región a la ciudad. Un nuevo enfoque de la historia industrial Española contemporànea', *Historia Industrial* 30:1 (2006), pp. 52–102.

Patterson, Rachel, 'Women of Ireland: change toward social and political equality in the 21st century Irish Republic', https://martindale.cc.lehigh.edu/sites/martindale.cc.lehigh.edu/files/Patterson.pdf (accessed 19 October 2023).

Peemans, Francoise, 'Fourcaut A., Femmes a l'usine en France dans l'entre-deux guerres', *Revue belge de Philologie et d'Histoire* 64:2 (1986), pp. 441–3.

Pember Reeves, Margaret, *Round About a Pound a Week* (London, 1913).

Perrin, Faustine, *On the Construction of a Historical Gender Gap Index*, Working Papers 5 (2014), Association Francaise de Cliometrie.

Pinchbeck, Ivy, *Women Workers and the Industrial Revolution 1750–1850* (London, 1930).

Poincaré, Emile Leon, *Traité d'hygiène industriel à l'usage des médecins et des membres de conseils d'hygiène* (Paris, 1886).

Plymoth, Birgitta, *Fattigvård och filantropi i Norrköping 1872–1914* (Stockholm, 1999).

Primander, Ingrid, *Elise Ottesen-Jensen-Arbetarrorelsen-Mannens eller Mansklighetens Rorelse?* (Stockholm, 1980).

Proust, Adrien, 'Nouvelle maladie professionelle chez les polisseuses de camées', *Annales d'hygiène publique et de médecine légale* 50 (1878), pp. 193–206.

Purvis, June, *Hard Lessons: The Lives and Education of Working Class Women in Nineteenth-Century England* (Minneapolis, 1989).

Pushkareva, Natalia, *Women in Russian History* (Abingdon, 1997).

Quataert, Jean, 'Survival strategies in a Saxon textile district during the early phases of industrialization', in Daryl M. Hafter (ed.), *European Women and Pre-Industrial Craft* (Bloomington, 1995), pp. 153–78.

Quiggin, Pat, *No Rising Generation: Women and Fertility in Late Nineteenth Century Australia* (Canberra, 1988).

Ramm Reistad, Gunhild, 'Betzy Kjelsberg (1866–1950)', http://kvinnesak.no/info (accessed 5 September 2008).

Rathbone, Eleanor, *How the Casual Labourer Lives* (Liverpool, 1909).

Ravn, Anna-Birte, 'Julie Arenholt', *Dansk Kvindebiografisk Leksikon*, http://www.kvinfo.dk/side/597/bio/1062 (accessed 5 September 2008).

Ravn, Anna-Birte, 'Ragna Schou', *Dansk Kvindebiografisk Leksikon*, http://kvinfo.dk/side/597/bio1211/origin/170 (accessed 5 September 2008).

Ravn, Anna-Birte, '"Lagging far behind all civilized nations": the debate over protective labor legislation for women in Denmark 1899–1913', in Ulla Wikander, Alice Kessler-Harris and Jane Lewis (eds), *Protecting Women: Labour Legislation in Europe, the United States and Australia 1880–1920* (Urbana, 1995), pp. 210–33.

Raymond, Justinien, *Valette Aline (nee Goudeman Alphonsine Eulalie)*, https://maitron.fr/spip.php?article86187 (accessed 27 January 2021).

Richards, Eric, 'Women in the English economy since 1700', *History* 59 (1974), pp. 337–57.

Riemer, Eleanor and John Fout (eds), *European Women: A Documentary History, 1789–1945* (Brighton, 1980).

Riesenfeld, Stefan A., 'Contemporary trends in compensation for industrial accidents here and abroad', *California Law Review* 42:4 (October 1954), pp. 531–78.

Roberts, Elizabeth, *Women's Work 1840–1940* (London, 1992).

Rodrigues, Javier Silvestre, *Workplace Accidents and Early Safety Policies: Spain 1900–1934*, Working Paper, Department of Economics – TARGET, University of British Columbia (Vancouver, 2005).

Roi-Frey, Karin de la, 'Wenn alle Stricke reissen, dann wird sie noch einmal eine Lehrerin', *Lehrerinnen in biographischen Zeugnissen* (Bochum, 2001).

Rose, Sonya, 'Proto-industry, women's work and the household economy in the transition to capitalism', *Journal of Family History* 13:2 (1988), pp. 181–94.

Rose, Sonya O., *Limited Livelihoods: Gender and Class in Nineteenth-Century England* (Berkeley, 1992).

Roser, Nicolau, *Trabajo asalariado, formación y constitución de la familia. La demanda de trabajo en la colonia textil Sedó y los comportamientos demográficos de la población, 1850–1930*, dissertation, Autonomous University of Barcelona (Barcelona, 1983).

Ross, Ellen, 'Rediscovering London's working class mothers, 1870–1918', in Jane Lewis (ed.), *Labour and Love: Women's Experience of Home and the Family* (London, 1986), pp. 73–98.

Ross, Ellen, 'Fierce questions and taunts: married life in working class London 1870–1914', *Feminist Studies* 8 (1982), pp. 575–602.

Rostgaard, Marianne og Inger Bladt, *Tobakken og byen, C.W. Obels Tobaksfabrik 1787–1995* (Aalborg, 2004).

Rowntree, Seebohm, *Poverty: A Study of Town Life* (London, 1903).

Rowntree, J. and A. Sherwell, *The Temperance Problem and Social Reform* (London, 1900).

Salmela-Järvinen, Martta, *Alas lyötiin vanha maailma* (Helsinki, 1966).

Salmela-Järvinen, Martta, *Kun se parasta on ollut* (Helsinki, 1965).

Sarasua, Carmen, *Criados, nodrizas y amos, el servicio doméstico en la formación del mercado de trabajo madrilèno 1758–1868* (Madrid, 1994).

Sawer, Marian, 'Women and government in Australia', Women_and_government_in_Australia_-_Dr_Marian_Sawer.pdf (welvic.org.au) https://www.womenaustralia.info/leaders/biogs/WLE0518b.htm#: accessed 19 October 2023.

Sayers, Dorothy, L., *Gaudy Night* (London, 1935).

Schmitt, Sabine, *Der Arbeiterinnenschutz im deutschen Kaiserreich* (Stuttgart, 1995).

Schmitt, Sabine, '"All these forms of women's work which endanger public health and public welfare": protective labour legislation for women in Germany 1878–1914', in Ulla Wikander, Alice Kessler-Harris and Jane Lewis (eds), *Protecting Women: Labour Legislation in Europe, the United States and Australia 1880–1920* (Urbana, 1995), pp. 125–49.

Schmitz, Eva, *Kvinnor, Kamrater ... Kvinnans roll i arbetarrörelsen* (Stockholm, 1982).

Schomerus, Heilwig, 'The family life-cycle: a study of factory workers in 19th century Württenberg', in R. Evans and W.R. Lee (eds), *The German Family: Essays on the Social History of the Family in 19th and 20th Century Germany* (London, 1981), pp. 175–93.

Schrover, Marlou, 'Cooling up women's work: women workers in the Dutch food industries 1889–1960', in G. de Groot and M. Schrover (eds), *Women Workers and Technological Change in Europe in the 19th and the 20th Century* (London, 1995).

Schweitzer, Sylvie, *Les inspectrices du travail 1878–1974* (Rennes, 2016).

Sharpe, Pamela (ed.), *Women's Work: The English Experience 1650–1914* (London, 1998).

Sharpe, Pamela, *Adapting to Capitalism: Working Women in the English Economy 1700–1850* (New York, 1996).

Sharpe, Pamela, 'The female labour market in English agriculture during the industrial revolution: expansion or contraction?', in Nigel Goose (ed.), *Women's Work in Industrial England* (Hertfordshire, 2007), pp. 51–75.

Shaw, George, Bernard, *The Millionairess* (London, 1934).

Shoemaker, Robert B., *Gender in English Society 1650–1850* (Harlow, 1998).

Simonton, Deborah, *A History of European Women's Work: 1700 to the Present* (London, 1998).

Sione, Patrizia, 'From home to factory: women in the nineteenth-century Italian silk industry', in Daryl M. Hafter (ed.), *European Women and Pre-Industrial Craft* (Bloomington, 1995), pp. 137–52.

Sklar, Kathryn Kish, *Florence Kelley and the Nation's Work: The Rise of Women's Political Culture 1830–1900* (Yale, 1995).

Smart, Judith, 'Modernity and mother-heartedness – spirituality and religious meaning in Australian women's suffrage and citizenship movements 1890s–1920s', in Ian Fletcher, Philippa Levine and Laura Mayhall (eds), *Women's Suffrage in the British Empire: Citizenship, Nation and Race* (London, 2012), pp. 51–67.

Smith, Jewel, *Transforming Women's Education: Liberal Arts and Music in Female Seminaries* (Urbana, 2019).

Spring Rice, Margery, *Working-Class Wives: Their Health and Conditions* (London, 1939).

Squire, Rose E., *Thirty Years in the Public Service: An Industrial Retrospect* (London, 1927).

Stanfors, Maria, Tim Leunig, Bjorn Eriksson and Tobias Karlsson, 'Gender productivity and the nature of work and pay: evidence from the late 19th century tobacco industry', *Economic History Review* 67:1 (2014), pp. 48–65.

Stanley, Liz (ed.), *The Diaries of Hannah Culwick, Victorian Maidservant* (London, 1985).

Stanley, Martin, *Women in the Civil Service*, https://civilservant.org.uk/women-history.html (accessed 9 March 2020).

Statistisk årsbok for Helsingfors 1908 (Helsingfors, 1910).

Statistiska centralbyrån, *Historisk Statistik för Sverige* (Stockholm, 1960).

Steinbach, Susie, *Women in England 1760–1914* (London, 2004).

Sulkunen, Irma, *Raittius kansalais uskontona* (Helsinki, 1986).

Sulkunen, Irma, 'The General Strike and women's suffrage', http://www. helsinki. fi/sukupuolentutkimus/aanioikeus/en/articles/strike.htm.

Sulkunen, Irma, 'Paradoksien ääanioikeus', in R. Knapas, K. Smeds and J. Stromberg (eds), *Boken on vårt land 1996* (Helsinki, 1996), pp. 331–9.

Sveinsdottir, Sinja, 'Agnes Nielsen', *Nationaltidende* (25.1 1937).

Sveistrup, Poul, 'Københavnske syerskers og smaakaarsfamiliers kostudgifter', *Nationaløkonomisk Tidsskrift* 3:7 (1899), pp. 578–629.

Sveistrup, Poul, *Syersker, Et Bidrag til Belysning af de Kobenhavnske Syerskers Livsvillkaar* (Copenhagen, 1894);

Swarbrick, Nancy, 'Primary and secondary education – education from 1840 to 1918', Te Ara – the *Encyclopedia of New Zealand*, http://www.TeAra.govt.nz/en/primary-and-secondary-education (accessed 18 November 2021).

Sweets, John F., 'The lacemakers of Le Puy in the nineteenth century', in Daryl M.
    Hafter (ed.), *European Women and Pre-Industrial Craft* (Bloomington, 1995).
Tannahill, Reay, *Sex in History* (London, 1981).
Tennant, Margaret, 'Neill, Elizabeth Grace', *Dictionary of New Zealand Biography-*
    Te Ara, https://teara.govt.nz/en/biographies/2n5/neill-elizabeth-grace (accessed
    10 November 2020).
Tennant, May, 'Infantile mortality', in Gertrude Tuckwell, Constance Smith, May
    Tennant, Nellie Adler and Adelaide Anderson, *Woman in Industry from Seven
    Points of View* (London, 1908), pp. 87–119.
The Life and Times of Florence Kelley, https://florencekelley.northwestern.edu/
    historical/timeline (accessed 11 September 2020).
Florencekelley.northwestern.edu/florence/father, florencekelley.northwestern.
    edu/florence/1892, florencekelley.northwestern.edu/Florence/inspector,
    https://florencekelley.northwestern.edu, florencekelley.northwestern.edu/
    Florence/1894(accessed 11 September 2020).
Thestrup, Anna, 'Kvinder i offentlige institutioner', *Fortid og Nutid* 3 (1991), pp.
    175–96.
Thomas, Christine, 'Women and the early Labour Party: Review of Nan Sloane,
    "Women in the room: Labour's forgotten history"', *Socialism Today*, 19 March
    2020.
Thompson, E.P., *The Making of the English Working Class* (Harmondsworth,
    1968).
Tilly, Louise, 'Gender, women's history and social history', *Social Science History*
    13:4 (Winter 1989), pp. 439–62.
Tilly, Louise A. and Joan W. Scott, *Women, Work and the Family* (New York, 1978).
Tuckwell, Gertrude, Constance Smith, May Tennant, Nellie Adler and Adelaide
    Anderson, *Woman in Industry from Seven Points of View* (London, 1908).
Turbin, Carole, 'Beyond conventional wisdom: women, wage work, household
    economic contribution, and Labour activism in a mid-nineteenth century
    working class community', in Carol Groneman and Mary Beth Norton (eds),
    'To Toil the Livelong Day': America's Women at Work, 1780–1980 (Ithaca,
    1987), pp. 47–67.
U.S. Department of Labor: Office of the Assistant Secretary for Administration
    and Management, *Factory Inspection Legislation*, http://www.dol.gov/oasam/
    programs/history (accessed 20 January 2021).
U.S. Department of Labor, *Progressive Era Investigations*, http://www.dol.gov/
    programs/history (accessed 20 January 2021).
U.S. Department of Labor, *Inspection, Enforcement, Compliance*, http://www.dol.
    gov/programs/history (accessed 20 January 2021),
Valenze, Deborah, *The First Industrial Woman* (New York, 1995).
Valetov, Timur, 'Migration and the household: urban living arrangements in late
    19th and early 20th century Russia', *The History of the Family* 13:2 (2008),
    pp. 163–77.
Valverde Lamfus, Lola, 'Survival strategies of poor women in two localities in
    Guipuzcoa in the nineteenth and twentieth centuries', in Beatrice Moring (ed.),
    Female Strategies in the Modern World (London, 2012), pp. 33–44.

Vattula, Kaarina, 'Kvinnors förvärvsarbete i Norden under 100 år (1870–1970)', *Studia Historica Jyväskyläensia 27* (Jyvaskyla, 1983).

Vattula, Kaarina, 'Lähtöviivallako? Naisten ammatissatoimivuudesta, tilastoista ja kotitaloudesta', in Leena Laine and Pirjo Markkola (eds), *Tuntematon työläis-nainen* (Tampere, 1989).

Verdon, Nicola, *Rural Women Workers in 19th Century England* (London, 2002).

Verdon, Nicola, 'Hay, hops and harvest: women's work in agriculture in nineteenth century Sussex', in Nigel Goose (ed.), *Women's Work in Industrial England* (Hertfordshire, 2007), pp. 76–96.

Volodin, Andrei, *Russian Factory Inspection (1882–1918): Cui Bono?* (Paris, 2008).

Wall, Richard, 'Work, welfare and the family: an illustration of the adaptive family economy', in Lloyd Bonfield, Richard Smith and Keith Wrightson (eds), *The World We Have Gained* (Oxford, 1986), pp. 261–94.

Wall, Richard, 'Some implications of the earnings and expenditure patterns of married women in populations of the past', in John Henderson and Richard Wall (eds), *Poor Women and Children in the European Past* (London, 1994), pp. 312–35.

Wandersee, Winifred, *Women's Work and Family Values 1920–1940* (Cambridge, MA, 1981).

Waris, Heikki, *Työläisyhteiskunnan syntyminen Helsingin Pitkänsillan pohjoispuolelle II* (Helsinki, 1934).

Weber Kellerman, Ingeborg, *Die Deutsche Familie* (Frankfurt am Main, 1974).

Wecker, Regina, 'Equality for men? Factory laws, protective legislation for women in Switzerland and the Swiss effort for international protection', in Ulla Wikander, Alice Kessler-Harris and Jane Lewis (eds), *Protecting Women: Labour Legislation in Europe, the United States and Australia 1880–1920* (Urbana, 1995), pp. 63–90.

Weiner, Lynn Y., *From Working Girl to Working Mother: The Female Labor Force in the United States 1820–1980* (Chapel Hill, 1985).

Wheen, Francis, *Karl Marx* (London, 1999).

Wikander, Ulla, Alice Kessler-Harris and Jane Lewis (eds), *Protecting Women: Labour Legislation in Europe, the United States and Australia 1880–1920* (Urbana, 1995).

Witzmann, Reingard, 'Zwischen anpassung und Fortschritt – Der Berufsalltag der Frau', in Reingard Witzmann (ed.), *Die Frau im Korsett, Wiener Frauenalltag zwischen Klischee und Wirklichkeit 1848–1920* (Wien, 1985), pp. 11–20.

Woollard, Matthew, 'The employment and retirement of older men 1851–1881', *Continuity and Change* 17:3 (2002), pp. 437–64.

Zarnovska, Anna, 'Women in working class families', in Rudolf Jaworski and Bianka Pietrow-Ennker (eds), *Women in Polish Society* (New York, 1992).

Zarnowska, Anna and Elzbeieta Kaczynska, 'Market related work and household work: proletarian women in Poland in the 19th century', in Erik Aerts, Paul Klep, Jurgen Kocka and Marina Thornborg (eds), *Women in the Labour Force* (Leuven, 1990), pp. 80–9.

INDEX

||||||||||||||||||||

Printed and bound by CPI Group (UK) Ltd, Croydon, CR0 4YY

19/03/2024

14472981-0001